Client or Patient?

Power and Related Concepts in Health Care

Nanci Willis Rinehart

R.N., M.S.N., R.T.C.

Ishiyaku EuroAmerica, Inc.

St. Louis • Tokyo

Book Editor: Gregory Hacke, D.C.

Ishiyaku EuroAmerica, Inc.
716 Hanley Industrial Court, St. Louis, Missouri 63144

Library of Congress Catalogue Number 90-56476

Nanci Willis Rinehart
    Client or Patient: Power and Related Concepts in Health Care

ISBN 0-912791-70-5

Ishiyaku EuroAmerica, Inc.
St. Louis • Tokyo

Composition by HiTec Typeset, Columbia, Missouri
Printed by Rose Printing, Tallahassee, Florida

CONTRIBUTORS

Antonio Arguello, R.N. is a staff nurse on an adult psychiatric unit at the Colorado Psychiatric Hospital in Denver, Colorado and a meditation instructor.

Donna Ault, R.N.C., M.S.N. is an assistant professor at Huson College in Bangor, Maine.

Judith Cavanah Turner, R.N., M.S. is Director of the Program in Nursing and Chair of the Health Arts Division at Casper College, Casper, Wyoming.

Virginia Doucet, R.N., M.A. is the Program Director of Bowling Green of Colorado.

Stephan Garman, R.N., M.A. is the head nurse on the eating disorder unit at Mercy Medical Center in Denver, Colorado and a past critical care nurse.

Velvia Garner, R.N., M.S. is Vice-Chair of The Colorado State Parole Board and a past assistant professor in nursing at the University of Colorado. She is currently on leave from her position as Director of Medical and Psychological Services for Juvenile Corrections of Colorado.

Joanne Glover, R.N., C.C.R.N. is the director of Porter Home Hospice in Denver, Colorado.

Carol Hannon, R.N., M.S., G.N.P.C. is a geriatric nurse practitioner at the Veterans' Administration Medical Center in Denver, Colorado.

Patti Kepple, R.N., B.S.N. is a staff nurse on an adolescent psychiatric unit at The Children's Hospital in Denver, Colorado.

Barbara Long, R.P.T. has a private physical therapy practice in Denver, Colorado, specializing in cranio-mandibular dysfunction.

Rosa Montemayor, D.P.M. is a podiatrist with a private practice in Lakewood, Colorado.

Nanci Willis Rinehart, R.N., M.S.N., R.T.C. is a part-time nursing instructor for the Program of Nursing at Regis College in Denver, Colorado, a part-time staff nurse on the psychiatric units of The Children's Hospital, the Colorado Psychiatric Hospital and Mercy Medical Center in Denver and a self-employed Reality Therapist.

Lisa Samenfeld, R.N., M.S. is a staff nurse on a pediatric psychiatric unit at The Children's Hospital in Denver, Colorado.

Gerri Willis Scarbrough, O.D. is an optometrist in Seattle, Washington. She is a consultant to the Veteran's Administration Medical Center in American Lake, WA.

Mary Ann Stallings, R.N., M.S. is a Clinical Supervisor on the adult psychiatric unit at the Colorado Psychiatric Hospital in Denver, Colorado.

Holly Williams, D.C. is a chiropractor with a private practice in Arvada, Colorado.

Cheryl Wrasper, R.N., M.S.N. is freshman level coordinator in the Program of Nursing at Casper Colleg, Casper, Wyoming.

Denise VandeWalle, D.D.S. is a dentist with a private practice in Lakewood, Colorado.

Acknowledgements

Thanks to our:

- families and significant others who have encouraged and supported us as we developed our own personal power.
- clients who have assisted the authors in the search for a more cooperative healthcare partnership.
- fellow health care professionals who have lent support, critiques and ideas to the authors in this search.
- students who have listened, questioned, and struggled with the power/control concept in client care.
- health care professionals who have gone before, mapping the paths to follow and avoid.

Nanci Willis Rinehart, R.N., M.S.N., R.T.C.

NOTICE

Medicine is an ever-changing science. As new research and clincal experience broaden our knowledge, changes in treatment are required. The editors and the publisher of this work have made every effort to ensure that the procedures herein are accurate and in accord with the standards accepted at the time of publication, but the final authority in all cases is the professional judgement of the attending physician.

Preface

"Patient" indicates a person patiently waiting to have something done to him, or the passive recipient of care. Conversely, as suggested by Carl Rogers and others in the past, "client" indicates a partnership. The persistent reference to the recipient of health care as "patient" serves to keep the "patient" in a "one-down" or powerless stance.

It is of vital importance to assist the client in the acquisition of more personal power and expression of it as he develops a responsible healthcare partnership within the health care community. As the concept of developing and maintaining personal power is the focus of this book, healthcare recipients are referred to as clients.

For the sake of simplicity, health care providers are usually referred to as "she" and clients as "he." This was chosen as a less cumbersome mode than the "he/she" format.

The client care chapters were written by a variety of health care professionals from divergent backgrounds. Experts in their fields, they chose the divisions of clients to be discussed and the style for the plan of care. This expression of individual professional philosophies, approaches and implementation methods enhances the client's options and respects the health care professional's uniqueness in client care planning.

This book is appropriate as a supplemental resource for practicing health care professionals or a text for advanced students. It demonstrates the application of a few concepts in a myriad of care settings and discusses the importance of identifying the biopsychosocial needs of individual clients, including power.

Nanci Willis Rinehart, R.N., M.S.N., R.T.C.

Contents

Acknowledgement
Contributors
Preface

1

Concept of Power

N. Rinehart

Introduction

The need to be in control is a basic goal for the thinking man. Power incorporates the ability and the freedom to make choices. The self-perception of being in control determines life events more then any other factor; only through feeling empowered with the authority to choose can one experience a sense of control (Cuming, 1981). Kanter (1983) stated, "the paths of power to self-confidence, to self-realization may be many, but they all have one starting point; awareness" (p. 18). Health care professionals are aware that this sense of power is vital to the well being of clients, the lack of which can lead to despair ultimately culminating in death (Seligman, 1975; Miller, 1983).

As promoted in nursing, self-care is a major factor in client education. It is based on the assumption that the client desires wellness and autonomy as much and as soon as possible. This premise is based on an almost primal need to control, for power, to focus energy in a more positive direction. Negative power can be equated with illness, as seen in the client who manipulates others through his extreme dependence or total helplessness. In other words, the perceived inability to focus energy in a positively directed path can be viewed as the antithesis of power and self-control.

Unfortunately, health care professionals are often subtly taught to exercise their control at the expense of their clients. Upon admission, the client is asked few questions about his personal preferences and often is left feeling that he is on an assembly line. Rarely does the client feel that his preferences are important, and he is expected to conform to the routine circumscribed by the care providers. It is customarily seen as an inconvenience to provide baths in the evening or peach jello instead of the hospital standard aged red. The health care system appears then to be the greatest source of promoting powerlessness in people when in their most susceptible state (Lerner, 1986). As Robinson (1972) stated, "once in bed, the individual is placed physically in the attitude of an infant on his back surrounded by care-taking people" (p.14). There are still too many Big Nurses in starched white, casting withering looks upon clients daring to ask assistance at 3 AM. Yet health care professionals are taught the importance of instilling a sense of power or self-control in their clients. "It is to note the discrepancies between what we know and what we do in the hospital environment" (Petrillo and Sanger, 1980, p. 1). To treat an adult as helpless is demeaning and encourages dependence rather than individual growth and recovery. The care-giver may have good intentions by overcompensating for the individual who is ill, but this further reinforces the perception of powerlessness and decreases self-esteem. "Overfunctioning works to hold a person in a helpless position" (McNeil, 1985).

Each client is an individual and must be assessed and cared for as such. Not all individuals admitted for an appendectomy will require the same plan of care, yet they are often treated like any other person with the same surgery. In reaction, the client exercises his sense of power in a variety of ways: he may be the 'model patient', never asking for anything assuming the nurses will automatically know his needs, or he may be afraid to cause the nurses any extra work, fearing their irritation. How many people sit in a dental chair, at the mercy of the dentist and the assistant, feeling sure that if the dentist became irritated, the dental procedure might be a more excruciating event? On the other hand, the client may well be one who makes frequent demands, afraid the health care providers ignore him unless he makes sure they spend time with him. That situation may indicate a client's need for more control. The fulcrum is the point or locus of control and how it is perceived as enabling the client to exercise his choices in a way that promotes his perception of increased power. That the client acts as a collaborator with the health care professional, and is an active and responsible participant in his care, was a concept promoted by Miller in 1975 (See Figure 1-1).

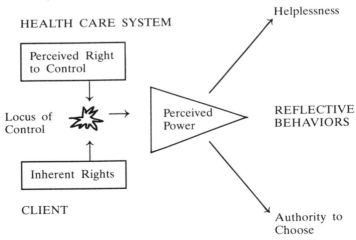

Fig. 1-1. Power Conflict in Health Care

Definition of Power

Power is the inherent ability to control behaviors surrounding life events, the freedom to make informed choices with the authority to act on them, and the conviction to realize those choices. Power is a "means of protecting ourselves against the cruelty, indifference or ruthlessness of other [people]" (Korda, 1975, p. 16). May (1972) stated "for the living person, power is not a theory but an ever-present reality which must be confronted, used, enjoyed, and struggled with a hundred times a day" (p. 57).

The three basic elements of power, according to Claus and Bailey (1977), are strength, energy and action, very little of which the ill client has in reserve, or is even allowed. There are many synonyms for the word "power." Among these are: authority, control, independence, hopefulness, acceptance, influence, serenity, satisfaction, self-assurance, potency, strength, and self-reliance.

Power can be a resource to draw on when illness occurs. The client who can maintain some sense of having control will heal more quickly or cope more efficiently than the client who feels powerless. This is evidenced by the increased rate of recovery in the client who has received preoperative teaching of techniques he can use to assist in his own recovery, versus the extended recovery time required by the client who has no knowledge base and expects the staff to "make him better." Increasing a client's knowledge base decreases his level of anxiety or stress associated with health care procedures. According to Holmes and Rahe (1967), a high number of negative stressors (Selye, 1974; Selye, 1979) leads to a higher incidence of illness or injury. Therefore, the opposite is also true: lowering the amount of negative stress in a given situation by increasing the client's knowledge base and his sense of personal power can result in more rapid healing, less post-operative complications, fewer accidents and increased resistance to infection.

For many people, power is a driving force, or a motivator of behavior. The motivation behind a person's striving for self- control is also helpful in the client's recovery. This can be seen in the small child who turns to the person feeding him, grabs the spoon out of their hand, spills his food yet declares "me do it" as opposed to the recovery of the child who passively allows his basic needs to be met without exerting any effort in self-care. Motivation is the stimulus of a desired behavior or effect, the energy or belief that leads to a given behavior.

Types of Power

Personal power is the power each individual needs "to feel powerful and to empower oneself" (Josefowitz, p. 3, 1980) and is the type of power being promoted in this book. As Cuming (1981, p. 5) stated, "to feel empowered is to have confidence in yourself, to trust your feelings and maintain a sense of personal worth regardless of the reactions of others." Robbins (1986, p. 5) defines power as "the ability to change your life, to shape your perceptions, to make things work for you and not against you."

Persons not seeing themselves as having power do not have a feeling of control in their life situations. This perceived lack of control, according to Fischman (1987), leads to more frequent illnesses than in those who report more feelings of power or control. These feelings of self-empowerment "determine life's events more than any other factor" (Cuming, 1981, p. 6). According to Kyes (1987, p.71), "if you think you have power, you do." One's own perception of power, or lack of it, influences their viewpoint for seeing the world. "One's sense of security may depend on the feeling that one lives in a rational world and can, through use of common sense and reasoning along with a degree of personal power, arrange one's life in a manner that is more or less satisfying" (Kelly, p. 205, 1985). That feeling of power can be gained "from many sources and in many forms. The wise person builds as large a stock pile as possible" (Kyes, p. 71, 1987). A person who has tapped these sources is less likely to become ill and will recover more quickly if illness should occur. This person may be said to have a hardy personality, and, according to Fischman (1987), shows "high levels of commitment, challenge and control."

May (1972) listed five types of power: exploitive, manipulative, competitive, nutrient, and integrative.

Exploitive power subjects a person to being used by those holding the power, with no choices or spontaneity. The client who has unusual numbers of seemingly needless tests performed is reflective of this type of power.

Manipulative power is the implicit control over another human. The client may have requested control by another at the beginning but then no longer desires it. When a client comes to a physician for an acute illness, he wants the doctor to help him get better, yet he quickly struggles to retrieve some portion of that control by having a chance to approve or veto plans for his care. The physician who pats his client on the shoulder and instructs him to just do as he is told and to trust the doctor to know what is best is exerting manipulative power.

Competitive power is that used against another human to add interest to relationships. Competition can be a positive or a negative type of power, depending on the intensity with which it is used, and the desired outcome. For instance, encouraging an adolescent to compete against a time set by an opposing team at the track meet may spur him on to better his own time. On the other hand, urging him to do as well, if not better, than an older sibling may have devastating consequences for his self-esteem.

Nutrient power is that authority which is imparted by caring for another person. It is the power found in the caring relationship of the nurse and her client, a mother and her child or a daughter caring for her ailing mother.

Integrative power is power obtained through working with or associating with another person. Answering questions by quoting the administrative policies would be a example of interacting with another person perceived as having power.

Wilkinson (1979) listed an additional seven types of power: informational, reward, referent, expert, legitimate, rational, and non-rational.

Informational power is that implicit strength which is gained through information being received. When a client is given information concerning his illness or the options available for treatment, the client develops a greater sense of power.

Reward power is gained through one person reinforcing another. Research has shown that giving positive feedback spurs clients on to greater attempts toward personal or therapeutic goals during hospitalization.

Referent power is gained through the affiliation by one person with an admired group or person, claiming familiarity. This is similar to May's integrative power, where role-modeling of another by the client can provide him with an enhanced sense of power.

Expert power results from a person having superior knowledge or skill in some area. This is the type of power utilized by physicians and nurses against the client, rather than for the benefit of the client. The health care professional feels that she can do her best for the client by exercising complete control because she is, after all, the "expert," (or for physicians, the "last word"). However, this type of care further retards the client's sense of self-esteem and potential for recovery.

Legitimate power is based on the public's universal agreement and acceptance of general norms or standards. An example of this type of power is found in the respect bestowed on the mayor, expressions reflecting society's acceptance of that individual's decisions as being superior, such as, "the doctor knows best." The police are paid by the taxpayers of a city to protect them and supervise the lawfulness of the citizenry.

Rational power is exhibited when a person can honestly and openly express his feelings and act accordingly, which results in the client perception of control and acceptance.

Non-rational power is demonstrated when hiding one's feelings and thoughts. The client who works hard at saying what he thinks the nurse or doctor wants to hear is acting on the power he derives from non-rational behaviors.

Perceptions of Power

Mistakenly, the very word "power" congers up the concept of exercising control over others or their environment. Often seen as a negative goal, power is not a need most people will admit to. In school, children are taught to "stand on your own," to be "self-sufficient." Conversely, society teaches that others' needs are more important than ours and that we actually have no control over events. These two principles are a catch-22, as manifested in the twelve year old who dresses as an adult but then is told not to do anything the parent might do.

However, as indicated by the definitions of power types identified by May and Wilkinson, there are some types of power which have positive effects for the persons exposed to or using them. Cuming (1981) stated "power becomes a dirty word only when it is used to disempower others and to create situations in which others must necessarily lose" (p. 2). In that sense, power is equated with intimidation.

To see power as a positive rather than a negative need requires a great deal of effort for some people, including nurses, as evidenced by the infrequency of using the nursing diagnosis of "powerlessness." This glaring omission is most obvious when examining concepts related to powerlessness. Clients are placed in a position of dependency while cared for by health professionals; their anxiety or poor self-esteem are readily assessed and interventions planned to help the client with these problems, while powerlessness goes unnoticed. Power, and its converse, powerlessness, can be misinterpreted by the health care professional.

Along with the concept of the term "powerlessness," this book will also explore some related concepts: anxiety, fear, grief, anger, noncompliance, self-care deficit, ineffective coping, and low self-esteem. These nursing diagnoses reflect negative behaviors by a client. The nursing process, however, should also be applied to finding and focusing on the client's strengths and encouraging the development of other assets. To this end, the strengths, or resources of personal power, will be identified in the appropriate sections of this book.

Clients and Power

There are many resources of power available to society. For instance, if a client is not as physically strong as he used to be, he still has other potential resources for obtaining power—physical, emotional, intellectual, spiritual and cultural. It is important to note that it is the physical aspect of the client that primarily presents itself to health care professionals. In a general care area of a hospital the client may not have his emotional status evaluated. In the psychiatric area the reverse is often true—the physical needs may not be addressed. Health professionals have been talking for the past several years about holistic medicine (Pelletier, 1977) or the biopsychosocial concept (Reiser, 1975). However, the continued emphasis of current clinical practice to ignore a large segment of the client's makeup invalidates these new philosophies, and ignores the interdependence of the body, mind and soul within a culture.

Clients historically perceive the doctor or nurse as a caring and giving person, extremely well prepared and responsible for their well-being. The painful truth is, however, that the health care system itself is not based on caring but on profit (Lerner, 1986). Bottom-line standards frequently conflict with holistic empathy and intervention, perpetrating such anachronisms in medicine. The disease model, which states that diseases happen to the client, encourages feelings of powerlessness and a perceived inability to control the outcome (Lerner, 1986). This is a much more palatable concept for the client to deal with than the previous belief that illness was a result of sin (although this is still practiced). On the other hand, holistic health attempts to encourage a client to take charge of his health and to care for his body. Some persons take this sense of responsibility to the extreme, flagellating themselves frequently for being poor caretakers of their own health. The result is a deeper sense of lack of control over the consequences.

As a client may view the health care provider as omniscient and omnipotent, the health care provider can greatly affect the outcome of the person's illness by her perception of the client. If the health care professional views the client as helpless, in need of protection from himself and unable to understand anything about his illness, she hinders the capacity of the client to feel confident enough to take as much control over his situation as possible. But if the nurse or doctor views the client as capable of making informed decisions and as having the ultimate say regarding events in the health care setting, the client will naturally assume a more assertive role and either recover more quickly or be more accepting of his health status.

In providing health care, the caregivers often ignore the client's rights. The "Patient's Bill of Rights" should be given to the client as he enters the health care system. Unfortunately, there are health care professionals who keep their clients ignorant of their rights, as it is easier and more expedient to not pause and explain things to the client, and seemingly more important to get through the necessary tasks in the minimal amount of time allotted. As an advocate for the client, the nurse needs to intervene when she observes the client's rights being violated. It is the nurse who must remind the medical students and residents that the client can be spoken to, rather than over as they all stand around his hospital bed. It is the nurse who must insist that the hands of all health professionals be washed between clients to decrease nosocomial infections. It is the nurse who must work with the client for a plan of action to reach his health care goals, and then assist the client in attaining them. Such advocacy, however, comes with a price. The assertive nurse in a structured environment often treads a thin line between assertive advocacy and "turf tramping."

All people who seek help from health professionals may experience a threat to their sense of power. Upon entering the health care system, most clients subconsciously register the first twinges of powerlessness. Having come to the health care professional because they can no longer think of any self care measures for their condition, they fall into the criteria of the sick role and quickly fall into the role of dependent care receiver. Depending on a person's perception of their locus of control, this experience can be satisfying or frustrating. The health care provider sets the tone for either self-care or dependent care. Powerlessness is a common thread among all clients, whether they have come for help with a minor complaint or for a complex problem like cancer or alcoholism. Either way they are often told in no uncertain terms that they are incapable of solving their problems.

The health care environment can also be depersonalizing, promoting a sense of powerlessness. Upon admission, the client becomes a number or a diagnosis. The shapeless gown, identification bracelet, and uniformity of the care area all strengthen depersonalization or feelings of insignificance in the client.

The Alcoholics Anonymous (A.A.) program claims a success rate of fifty percent because it recognizes the powerlessness of the alcoholic. The first step in A.A. discusses the fact that the person was powerless over his addictive behavior (A.A., 1976). However, the steps go on to encourage the person to seek a greater sense of control. In urging the alcoholic to turn loose of his problems and to let a Higher Power handle his difficulties, the A.A. program increases his self-perception of strength or power. This power is not the kind related to physical and emotional strength, but to that found in the spiritual realm, as well as the sociological power obtained through support groups (See Figure 1-2). Personal acceptance of problem areas that cannot be controlled by the individual is a goal found in a variety of self-help books and is a definition of maturity (Mandino, 1984; Glasser, 1984; Dyer, 1980, Friedman, 1985).

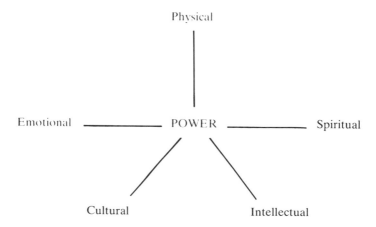

Fig. 1-2. Resources of Power

Concepts Related to Power

The concepts selected in this chapter are among those most commonly used by nurses in the United States. The negative side of each of these characteristics is the stem word for a nursing diagnosis. As Figures 1-3 and 1-4 illustrate, the connection between powerlessness and related concepts is bi-directional. As strength in each of these characteristics increases, so too do feelings of power and control of life events. The opposite of positive self-esteem is self-esteem deficit. Decreased anxiety's opposite is thus anxiety. Prolonged or abnormal grief is the negative side of acceptance, or grief resolution. Serenity is certainly opposite to anger. Self-care is obviously the converse of self-care deficit. Ineffective coping is the antonym of coping effectively.

Noncompliance is identified in clients more than health care professionals care to see. However, if a client is complying because he is intimidated, he is doing so from a powerless position rather than one based on informed consent or control. Fear directly relates to powerlessness in that decreasing fear increases the client's power sense. The more power or control the client experiences, the less he will express dissatisfaction with the health care system. By exercising control he helps in every step of his care. Less client dissatisfaction with the health care professionals and increased client participation in his own care will result in less risk of the health care provider facing a malpractice suit (Bernzweig, 1987). This fact alone should gain the attention of insurance companies and lead them to urge nurses and doctors to make allies out of their clients rather than to encourage minimal personal control (powerlessness) in the client.

Fig. 1-3. Nursing Diagnoses

The reactive characteristic, or nursing diagnoses most often connected to the loss of power are as follows (See Figure 1-3):

Anxiety. Anxiety is a tension with no specific focus. Stressful situations may result in a feeling of panic. With no certain knowledge of the future, humans are equipped with the fight or flight reaction in response to a potentially harmful situation, which may be physical, emotional, or spiritual. Anxiety is also the response to feeling out of control in a situation. Seeking health care (an area in which the client often has no control) is frequently perceived as a stressful event (Lerner, 1986). Thus, anxiety is the result of a loss of perceived power, which then feeds into a cycle of more anxiety, each response exacerbating the other.

Fear. Fear is tension with a specific focus. The person identifies a specific event as threatening to his comfort. When he thinks of a brain scan, for instance, and believes that the mechanizations will hurt him during the process, the client reacts in fear with its physiologic responses. Any client not familiar with diagnostic or therapeutic procedures may see the health system as threatening. Those health care providers who also find themselves as clients often fear the worst possible outcomes of the procedure or surgery. Illness and its treatment can be causes of fear. The fear of treatment is generally connected to the client's loss of power in the health care situation.

Grief. Grief is the feeling that occurs when a significant other is lost. This perceived loss is seen as being outside the realm of control of the person experiencing the grief. It is unalterable. Anticipatory grief is the sense of loss as a probability. The grief response can also be a direct result of powerlessness as experienced in the sick role, as the loss of control over disease pathology can be grievous. Therefore, the less in control the person, the greater the potential grief response.

Anger. Anger is not necessarily a negative event. It is the protective response of a person to a threat. Clients entering into the health care situation are often relieved of the responsibility for consent or making choices about what is done to them. This seeming abdication of authority is not always gladly welcomed. An angry response is easily observed when the child is physically restrained during a procedure. Most clients naturally fight back to gain some measure of control. Frustration over the loss of control results in the client expressing that powerlessness through obstinance and aggression in their reaction to the health care professionals around them. If the outburst of the client is particularly violent and more out of control, he may find himself under some form of restraint.

Noncompliance. Noncompliance is the behavior that countermands that prescribed or advised by the health care professional. Noncompliance confounds doctors and nurses on a daily basis: why won't the client do as he is told? The client may not value the directive given to him, or he may be exerting his sense of power by not following through with treatments suggested for his recovery or the maintenance of his health. He may comply grudgingly if he is intimidated or badgered into following the prescribed regimen. Having a choice in the events of one's life is important. Doing nothing is a choice that can be made, as well as that of doing something.

Noncompliance is a problem for all health care professionals, but particularly for those who do not understand or practice the principles of learning as well as allowing for the cultural implications of the instructions given to the client. Feelings of powerlessness in any domain interfere with the learning ability of the client; he is unable to filter out the negatives. These feelings can mushroom into the perception of total loss of control including a sense of powerlessness over his own self-care.

Self-Care Deficit. Self-care deficit is the lack of ability for, or knowledge of, the care for one's self (Orem, 1985). Perhaps the person does not know how, or is unable, to care for himself properly, or he may not value the self-care prescribed for him. Clients who no longer care for themselves have a lack of self-care ability, if not also the loss of self-respect.

If a person does not identify himself as having the ability to care for himself, he experiences a self-care deficit which leads to feelings of powerlessness. Self-care deficit also includes the clients who begin with feelings of powerlessness with a resulting inability for sufficient self-care for himself.

Ineffective Coping. Ineffective coping occurs when coping methods the person has used in previous situations are no longer effective. The client is using the best coping methods he knows, but these methods are ineffective in dealing with the current problem. This feeling of inadequacy to cope with his own situation results in feelings of powerlessness, which further decreases his functioning capability. Inability to cope with living can lead to despair, and subsequently death (Miller, 1983). This perceived powerlessness affects the potential of the client to cope with the stresses of illness. In believing himself to be unable to control his environment, the person is even less able to cope with the stresses of his illness—a vicious cycle.

Decreased Self-Esteem. Decreased self-esteem is the loss of respect for one's own abilities and worthiness. The client with poor self-esteem does not view himself as being capable of ever managing his life events. This sense of helplessness further decreases his self-esteem, and directly influences the client's sense of power.

Self-esteem is positively correlated to a belief in personal power. The person who is feeling a lack of power generally has a low self-esteem level; positive feelings about oneself are reflected in feelings of power and control.

Fig. 1-4. Expected Outcomes With Increased Power

Summary

Power has always been a basic human need. In ignoring the individual's need for power or control over his life events, the health care professionals inhibit the recuperative potential of the client. It is beneficial to the client as well as to the health care provider to strengthen the client's power base, by encouraging participation in his care.

There are many types of power, among which are positive uses of power, negative ones, and those that have the potential for both properties. Power is defined as the inherent ability to control behaviors surrounding life events—the freedom to make informed choices with the authority to act on them, and the conviction to realize them. Words interchangeable with "power" include authority, influence, and control.

Raw power is often perceived as being evil. Power, however, has many good uses, so it is not "power" per se, but how power is used and perceived that determines its identified definition in a given situation. The motivation behind control-seeking behavior is also situational. Motivation is the cause of behavior for a desired effect—energy or belief that leads to a given behavior.

Nursing diagnoses that relate to power, or powerlessness, include: anxiety, fear, grief, noncompliance, anger, and self-esteem deficit. These diagnoses carry the implication of dysfunction or undesirability. To take these negative connotations reflecting powerlessness and transform them in a more positive direction will help health care professionals focus on the client's strengths versus his pathology.

References

Alcoholics Anonymous (3rd ed.) New York: A. A. World Service, (1976).

Bernzweig, Eli. *The Nurse's Liability for Malpractice* (4th Ed.) New York: McGraw-Hill Book Company., (1987).

Claus, Karen, and Bailey, June. *Power and Influence in Health Care: A New Approach to Leadership*. St. Louis: C.V. Mosby, (1977).

Cuming, Pamela. *The Power Handbook: a strategic guide to organizational and personal effectiveness*. New York: Van Nostrand and Reinhold Company, (1981).

Dyer, Wayne. *The Sky's The Limit*. New York: Pocket Books, (1980).

Fischman, Joshua. Getting tough. *Psychology Today*. 21, 12, 26-28., (1987).

Friedman, Sonya. *Smart Cookies Don't Crumble*. New York: Pocket Books, (1985).

Glasser, William. *Take Effective Control of Your Life*. New York: Harper and Row, (1984).

Holmes, T., and Rahe, R. The social need adjustment rating scale. *Journal of Psychosomatic Research*, 11, 213, (1967).

Josefowitz, Natasha. *Paths to Power*. Reading, MA: Addison-Wesley Publishing Company, (1980).

Kanter, Rosabeth Moss. *The Change Masters*. New York: Simon and Shuster, (1983).

Kelly, Mary Ann. *Nursing Diagnosis Source Book*. Norwalk, CN: Appleton-Century-Crofts, (1985).

Korda, Michael. *Power: How To Get It, How To Use It*. New York: Random House, (1975).

Kyes, Joan J. *Ready, Set, Go: Developing Power Potential*. Marion Center, PA: J & J Associates, (1987).

Lerner, Michael. *Surplus Powerlessness*. Oakland, CA: The Institute for Labor and Mental Health, (1986).

Mandino, Og. *The Choice*. New York: Bantam Books, (1984).

May, Rollo. Power and Innocence. New York: W. W. Norton and Company, (1972).

McNeill, Deborah. Depression. In Jacobs, Margaret and Geels, Wilma (eds.) *Signs and Symptoms in Nursing*. Philadelphia: J.B. Lippincott Company, (1985).

Miller, Judith. *Coping With Chronic Illness: Overcoming Powerlessness*. Philadelphia: F. A. Davis, (1983).

Miller, S., Remen, N., and Barbour, A. *Dimensions of Humanistic Medicine*. San Francisco: The Study for Humanistic Medicine, (1975).

Orem, Dorothea E. *Nursing Concepts of Practice* (3rd Ed.). New York: McGraw-Hill, (1985).

Pelletier, Kenneth. *Mind as Healer Mind as Slayer*. New York: A Delta Book, (1977).

Petrillo, Madeline, and Sanger, Sirgay. *Emotional Care of Hospitalized Children: An Environmental Approach* (2nd ed.). Philadelphia: J. B. Lippincott, (1980).

Reiser, M. F. Organic disorders and psychosomatic medicine. In Arieti, S. (ed.) *American Handbook of Psychiatry* (2nd Ed.). New York: Basic Books, Inc., (1975).

Robinson, Lisa. *Psychological Aspects of the Care of Hospitalized Patients* (2nd ed.). Philadelphia: F. A. Davis, (1972).

Robbins, Anthony. *Unlimited Power*. New York: Fawcett Columbine, (1986).

Seligman, Martin P. *Helplessness*. San Francisco: W. H. Freeman and Company, (1975).

Selye, Hans. *Stress Without Distress*. New York: Dutton, (1974).

Selye, Hans. Self-Regulation: The Response to Stress. In Goldway, Elliott (ed.) *Inner Balance: The Power of Holistic Healing*. Englewood Cliffs, NJ: Prentice-Hall, Inc., (1979).

Wilkinson, M. B. Power and the identified patient. *Perspectives in Psychiatric Care*. 17, 6, 248-253, (1979).

2

Theories of Power

N. Rinehart

Introduction

Many theories and philosophies describe power as a basic human need. The following discussion conceptualizes the more common theories, most of which clearly promote an increased client power. In Figure 2-1, the theories discussed in this chapter are compared according to their emphasis on clients maintaining control of their own health care, the health care professional having control and the emphasis on an external locus of control.

Self-Care Theory

Self-care is the performance of certain behaviors toward oneself or the environment that have the common goal of promoting personal health and well-being (Orem, 1985). "Self-care agency" is the term Orem uses to indicate the client's ability to perform self-care. Since self-control over life events is seen as a basic need, the client must accept the prime assumption of self-care theory—the expectation to want wellness and autonomy.

Theory	Control		
	Client	Professional	External
Self-Care	X	X	
Control Theory	X		
Reality Therapy	X		
Locus of Control	X	X	
Health Belief	X	X	X
Systems Theory	X		X
Change Theory	X	X	X
Sick Role	X	X	
Values Clarification	X		

Fig. 2-1. Comparison of Theories

The universal self-care requisites to ensure each person's survival are: maintenance of sufficient intake of air, water, and food; provision for elimination; a balance between activity and rest, and between solitude and an active social interaction; prevention of hazards to human life; and promotion of human functioning (Orem, 1985).

Orem defines therapeutic self-care demand as "essentially a prescription for continuous self-care action through which identified self-care requisites can be met with stipulated degrees of effectiveness" (1985, pp.39-40). For Orem, the client comes to the nurse and enters into a verbal contract that stipulates the responsibilities allocated to the nurse and to the client. Nursing ideally is a partnership between the nurse and the client, and runs counter to the past perception of nursing which says: "I'm the nurse, so do what I say."

Orem (1985) defines nursing as the art and science designed to assist clients unable to provide care for themselves or others in an effort to meet their health care needs. The goal of nursing then is to assist clients in restoring self function and to teach improved health care techniques and coping strategies for dealing with losses that cannot be overcome. Depending on the amount of self-care deficit, the nurse may perform wholly compensatory, partly compensatory, or supportive-educative nursing care. Regardless of the level of nursing required, the emphasis of self-care is to restore or improve the client's capability to care for himself, thereby improving his self-esteem and personal power. For the three levels of care required, Figure 2-2 depicts the location of responsibility in each nurse-client relationship.

Example/ Illness	Required Care Level	Client Responsibility	Nurse Responsibility
Coma, Acute Mental Illness	Wholly Compensatory	None/Indicate Choices if Possible	Total
Diabetes, Appendectomy	Partly Compensatory	Shared	Shared
Healthy Antepartal Care, Immunizations	Supportive-Educative	Total	Support/ Teaching

Fig. 2-2. Responsibility in Self-Care Nursing

Sick Role

The sick role theory has been described as the stages an individual experiences in the acceptance of illness and the resulting self-expectations as he proceeds through the health care system to recovery. This particular theory was developed by Talcott Parsons in analyzing western industrialized society (Haber, Hoskins, Leach and Sideleu, 1987).

The sick role may, upon initial consideration, seem to require passivity of the client. It has, in fact, been used to explain the secondary gains some people achieve through claims of illness, as in the Munchhausen syndrome (Thomas, 1973). One of the secondary gains of the ill client is the exemption from routine work and social obligations. However, this exception is only tolerated by society if the client is willing to adhere to the other expectations of the sick role: the illness prevents willful recovery and is perceived as a failure to "get his act together." This assessment identifies the client's inability to recover via decision or by willpower, validating his claim to illness. Some laymen have difficulty understanding that clients with alcoholism, mental illness, or eating disorders cannot merely pull their inner resources together and get well without any help. Life for most of these clients is not so simple; "heal thyself" is not an option.

No matter what the illness, society only seems tolerant as long as the individual wants to recover—successfully! Malingering is unacceptable, so everyone offers help with their various home remedies. The stereotyped "sick" client then becomes encumbered with an implied expectation to follow those or some other imposition demonstrating their intent to recover. The goal of wellness is dumped on the ill client with the dictate to take control of his behavior, to mobilize any and all resources to improve his own health status. According to the sick role, the ill individual feels obligated to seek help from health care professionals. He is subconsciously expected to assess his illness and decide when to reach out for aid from persons knowledgeable in resolving his malady.

Beyond the seeking of medical assistance, the person is expected to cooperate in the treatment prescribed by the health care professional. His circle of support—family, friends, and co-workers—will be tolerant and concerned only as long as he complies with the regimen decided upon by his chosen medical expert in the health care system. The expectation of compliance with prescribed behavior is inherent in the health professional/client relationship. There is limited opportunity for personal feelings of power and self-control.

Control Theory

Glasser (1986) states that the perception of a situation is different with each individual. There is a marked difference in stress levels between the client who sees an event as impossible and another client who accepts the situation as a challenge. Both may be in the same situation, but the individual who sees the event as a challenge, portrays the ability to act, of self-control. That feeling of challenge rather than defeat from a situation reflects the range of anxiety, from mild to a level of anxiety that distorts perception of events, resulting in a negative stressor (Hays, 1961; Selye, 1956). The individual seeing the situation as impossible, gives up. The defeatist states once again, that fate has defeated him and there is no use in struggling to resolve the situation.

As well as the perception of things as controllable or not, the individual evaluates events as they relate to him. For example, an acquaintance who passes him on the street and doesn't say anything, triggers a conclusion that something is wrong, that they're mad at him. If, however, his wife passes him on the street and doesn't say a word, he will be much more concerned about the lack of recognition. The second situation is more personally significant to the individual than the other.

Glasser (1986) lists five basic needs for mankind, described as equal and universal: 1) survival, 2) belonging, 3) power, 4) freedom, and 5) fun. These needs can be met through effective or ineffective behavior choices. (See Figure 2-3).

1) **Survival** includes the need for all the biological essentials for human existence: water, food, air, and reproduction. These elementary needs are seen as originating in the "old brain," reflecting the union humans have with other animals. This can include curiosity—animals remain curious, whereas "within a few years of [formal schooling], most of that trait dies or [becomes] silent" (Holt, 1964, p. 196). In the "newbrain," however, are needs that animals either rarely experience or cannot verbalize.

2) **Belonging** includes love and cooperation. All people enjoy the camaraderie of being part of a group such as a club, church, business, or family; individuals need to belong to some group in order to feel secure in their sphere of influence.

Love is an aspect of the need to belong. Over the years with the changing structure of families, it has been found that in order to be fulfilled, people do not have to get married and/or have children. This is at variance with Erikson's developmental steps delineated in his book (1963). It was presumed that not participating in traditional marriage meant loneliness, if not emptiness. However, Erikson did in later years readjust his position concerning those who decided to remain single or not to have children (1980); it is normal to receive affection from friends and family members not living in the same house. Loneliness then becomes dependent on individual perception, and it may be very true that a person feels lonelier in the marriage relationship than outside of it. Recall Archie and Edith Bunker from television who best exemplify the myth of complimentary sex roles;

they do not have "the intimacy of a cooperative and efficient working relationship" (Steiner, 1974, p. 206).

Cooperation is included in the need to belong. The satisfaction achieved through cooperating with others can be an extension of the internal warmth perceived by belonging to a given group. A great deal of satisfaction can be derived from knowing that a person is able to help someone and that another is accepting enough of him to be his partner or assistant. However, these roles should be viewed as equal; otherwise there is only another power play. But "men and women need to work in a cooperative process of reclaiming their full power as human beings" (Steiner, 1974, p. 206). Matching love and cooperation helps eliminate the resentment by the wife who gives in and the husband who predominates. This script is replayed in the traditional doctor/nurse scenario—one on top, one down.

3) **Power** is a need that most people deny. (In this context the personal power of the individual is the type of power referred to.) Glasser (1986) identifies competing, achieving, and gaining importance as components of power. Power is also the ability to effect change, to the point of intimidating someone to do something (Steiner, 1974). Inevitably, there are abusers of power.

Successful competition is another aspect of power and can give a person the goal of besting himself or another person. Glasser does not say that winning is necessary, but having the knowledge that he has striven to attain a goal satisfies the need in and of itself. Winning becomes relative, as for the oncology client who loses the bout with cancer but in the process had a positive impact on others.

Achievements are important in bolstering a fragile self-esteem. Each succefful step in attaining goals can emphasize the worthiness of the individual—if that is of personal value. Whether the goal is self-feeding or obtaining a PhD, anyone can realize more personal power when that sought-after goal is achieved.

Gaining importance is another means of increasing personal power. Glasser does not advocate doing this at the expense of others; in fact, he defines responsible behavior as not being injurious to oneself or others. The Girl Scout who sells the most cookies, the businessman who gets a plaque for his service, or the nurse who achieves an administrative promotion to manager have all gained success in their own spheres and so further strengthen their image of self as worthy or positive. But just as power should not be at the expense of others, neither should it be at the expense oneself. All too often a person's inability to succeed stems from a learned fear of failure (Holt, 1964). The health professional often states conditions in a manner that implies that a lack of comprehension is the fault of the client. This power struggle is commonly re-enacted and serves only to empower the caregiver, promoting dependency by the client. For example, "Oh, the doctor knows what I take."

4) **Freedom** is another basic need that must be satisfied. Glasser includes the sub-needs of movement and choice under this need. Freedom of movement is the ability of a client to go where he wants whenever he wants. Loss of this freedom is exemplified by the jailed criminal—complete freedom to fail. The client who "loses it" and ends up in four-point restraints is classified as successful only when self-control is regained. The freedom to be is determined by the impact of behavior on society with the message: "you can be" whatever you want as long as you remain within the boundaries of acceptable behavior—a definition that varies with each job, each age group and each society.

Freedom of choice is important particularly to Western man. The ability to choose what to do in a situation—where to live, when to do something—is a factor of freedom. Perceiving that there are no choices is often a precursor of depression. The glazed emotionless countenance of people subsisting in a society with strictly limited choices is the same expression reflected by those with severe depression or shown in pictures of prisoners during the Holocaust.

5) **Fun** is needed by everyone during learning or playing. Initially, a client may offer negative feedback to learning as a fun activity. However, when reconsidered, he may realize that many recreational activities involve learning. For example, playing better tennis includes learning to do it with skill and strategy. Going on a vacation to Yellowstone Park inadvertently involves learning about geysers and mudpots. Most students do not perceive learning as a fun activity, but as a trial by fire (Holt, 1964), although it can be enjoyable if the teacher strives to make learning interesting and fun (Glasser, 1969). In teaching clients, the nurse needs to keep in mind this need for fun, and in doing so, try to eliminate the foreboding sense of imminent failure learned in school (Holt, 1964). The fun can be the success, however seemingly small, in day-to-day self-paced compliance that is relevant to the client—not the educator. "How can we foster a joyous, alert, wholehearted participation in life, if we build all our [education] around the holiness of getting the 'right answers'?" (Holt, 1964, p. 178).

Playing is an activity with a high enjoyment component. Most persons see playing as something children do and that adults do not have the time for. In reality, everyone needs to relax and do regularly what is fun for them. Fulfilling this need enables the person do his job better. Some adults have the ideal situation—they consider their work as fun and are relaxed in the environment of their work. When a person incorporates fun with the survival need for employment, he is indeed maintaining a positive sense of personal fulfillment.

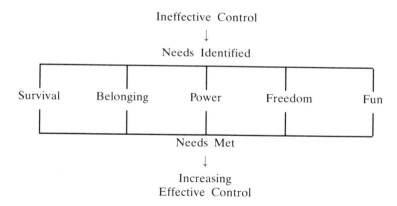

Fig. 2-3. Control Theory: Basic Needs

Glasser then discusses total behavior as having four components: acting, thinking, feeling, and physiology. He indicates that a relationship between the four components is necessary, for if one component is changed, the resulting behavior will be different.

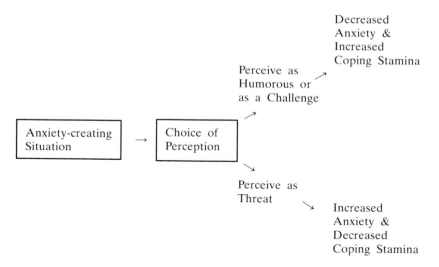

Fig. 2-4. Control Theory: Perceptual Choice

Since acting is the easiest to alter of the four components of behavior, Glasser advocates modifying the action to change the entire behavior. For instance, a person who is depressed cannot maintain that behavior or attitude if he is suddenly outside, walking briskly and singing. Therefore, by changing a person's actions, the feeling, thinking, and physiology will change. If a person is fearful of an upcoming interview with his employer, his stomach may reel with indigestion. If he stops focusing on the clock and concentrates instead on imaging or relaxation, his stomach will quiet and his performance during the interview will improve (Wubbolding, 1988). Imagining the source of anxiety as more human and childlike, diffuses some of the anxiety about speaking with someone in a power position (See Figure 2-4).

Reality Therapy

Reality Therapy is a collection of helping behaviors designed to aid the individual in making more effective choices in life and then taking responsibility for his demonstrated choices of behavior, with emphasis on the importance of assuming effective control.

Each client has a choice of behavior and perception. If a child must live in a specific environment, he may not particularly elect that situation but he can choose the perception he has of it. A client may require great amounts of work in learning to make decisions, with just the process itself sometimes being an impressive feat. For example, the adolescent may think that he can survive anything, waiting impatiently to be eighteen and old enough to leave home. With assistance, however, he may identify the fact that parents are rarely like Bill Cosby and that they are doing the best they can, just as his behavior is the best he can muster at any given time. His perceptions affect himself and, subsequently, those around him. The reality is that a person can only change himself. He has no control over other people or events. By changing his perception, though, other people in his environment may alter their behaviors. Of course, they may not change, but if the limitations of influence are acknowledged, he may choose to tolerate their lack of change (See Figure 2-5).

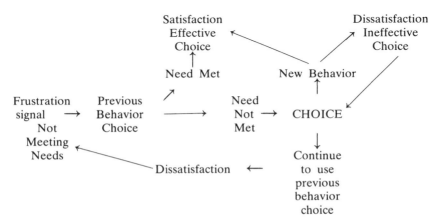

Fig. 2-5. Effective and Ineffective Choices

Glasser (1986) indicates that the perpetuation of an ineffective behavior is related to allowing the person to make excuses. Father John Doe (1952, p.17) defines excuses as "lies cleverly cloaked in a semblance of truth endeavoring to deceive another but usually only ending in self-deception." When a person begins to give an excuse for his behavior, Reality Therapists won't attend. They may interrupt with "the reality is that you did not get this done on time. Now, what can you do to ensure not repeating this behavior?" (Wubbolding, 1985). Care must be taken in this setting, however, to avoid one-up/one-down scripting, to avoid the tendency to lecture or use the omniscient "I told you this would happen if..." script. The reality is that "we are all taught to be one-up to certain people and one-down to others" (Steiner, 1974, p. 255).

Reality Therapy also suggests asking the client how he could sabotage the plan they have decided on. "What things or events might prohibit the completion of the plan?" After listing these interrupters, he is asked for methods he could use to be sure this would not prevent him from meeting his goal. In so doing, the client defeats all his usual excuses, plans to avoid new ones, and accomplishes his task in a responsible manner.

Another Reality Therapy technique involves asking "What do you want?" The client's needs and the manner in which they are being met are jointly reviewed. Then, the client is asked "Is what you're doing getting you what you want?" The client is encouraged to reflect on the behaviors he has used to meet his needs and how efficacious they are.

Glasser defines responsibility as not harming yourself or others; being destructive to oneself or to others is irresponsibility. Glasser does not use the diagnostic labels found in the **DSM III**, but rather labels any illness behavior as irresponsible. The individual is encouraged to evaluate his behavior as it relates to the rules of society, how effective his behavior is in achieving his wants, and then to choose responsible behavior in the future. The client—not the therapist or the nurse—makes these decisions and judgments. This self-choosing is self-empowerment. Glasser then encourages the client's use of more effective control to move toward becoming a successful or fulfilled person, rather than a failing or dissatisfied person. Glasser has designed a continuum with these extremes at either end. The individual does not stay in one position on the scale, but shows a tendency toward one end or the other. Glasser states that no one is in total effective control, or is consistently successful. Neither is there a person who is totally ineffective or failing. But again, success or failure is dependent on personal perceptions. Granted, the employee may see his position as preferable to the boss, which reflects a tendency to disregard the inequalities of power between people (Steiner, 1974). But the reality is that there is a difference, and the actual choices become less palatable when viewed realistically: "Do you want to work [for me] or not?" "Do you want to collect a paycheck?" "Do you want to stay married [at all costs]?" These choices inherently produce stress, because to be in control means to be in touch with oneself and environment, both physiologically and psychologically.

Locus of Control

The individual who sees life situations as controlled by himself is said to have an internal locus of control, or the image of being in control. This client wants to take control of his health care as much as possible. He identifies with the holistic image of health, feeling responsible for himself and his health.

The person who views the world in terms of luck and fate, does not acknowledge responsibility for his own health. This is the client who walks into the physician's office and says "fix me." He then will wait to have the health care professional do everything necessary to cure him. He will demonstrate unwillingness if the nurse requests that he participate in his care; he feels things just happen to his health with no influence from him. Therefore, today's health care professional must work to slowly introduce self-care practices, and gradually assist the client to view the world as at least falling partially under his influence (See Figure 2-6).

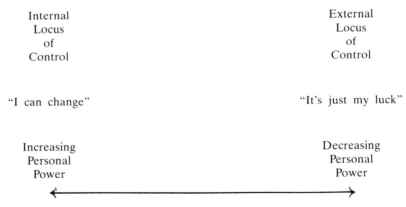

Internal Locus of Control	External Locus of Control
"I can change"	"It's just my luck"
Increasing Personal Power	Decreasing Personal Power

Fig. 2-6. Locus of Control

The public is increasingly aware of its responsibility for self health care; multiple television programs, commercials, and books give clients suggestions for self-treatment and myriad cures for problems previously believed to require a physician's attention. As this image of health care has evolved, the number of internally controlled clients should also have increased. But Dyer (1977) estimated that three-fourths of the American population is still externally controlled, although health care professionals are becoming aware of more internally controlled clients. These self-help clients are more reluctant to seek out health care when merely not feeling well; however, this avoidance of professional care can have negative results if the would-be client fails to identify an ailment that cannot be cured by diet, vitamins, exercise, and will-power. It's all well and good to be self-sufficient but, as with everything, a balance of power is preferable for current health care behaviors.

With that in mind, it becomes imperative that health care givers provide relevant health education to the public; they must go into the community and provide preventive health care teaching, rather than to wait in their professional cubbyholes for the ill to seek them out. It is easier—and much more cost effective—to help clients maintain their health than attempt to teach them prevention post facto (Ardell, 1981). Assisting the client in health maintenance will promote his feeling of and satisfy his need for self-control. That is primary care; that is a balance of power.

Health Belief Model

The Health Belief Model describes the relationship between decision-making behaviors and behaviors that relate to health beliefs (Stanhope, 1984). It is an attempt to define the reasons clients make the choices they do about seeking or refusing health care, and lists a variety of factors that contribute to their final decisions.

The first of these influences is the **belief system** of the individual. Several perceptions combine to form the belief system: the degree of perceived seriousness of the health problem, the amount of perceived susceptibility to the disease, the benefit expected in making a specific decision, and the barriers that discourage the client from making a certain decision.

Beyond his own perceptions of the situation, the client is swayed by **environmental cues**. Among these cues are messages from his favorite movie star, the headlines of the newspaper, messages in the music he likes, and the feedback he receives from his significant others.

Modifying factors, which also have potential for altering the individual's decision, include a pertinent identifiable data base which consists of age group, marital status, income level, sex, education level, personality style, societal expectations, and family position and responsibilities. Mothers often put the attainment of health care for their children ahead of their own health needs. Women may hesitate to make an appointment with their physician if they have gained weight and receive repeated negative feedback from the physician about their weight. Or the unemployed client asks why he should even bother going to the clinic as he cannot afford to buy any medication.

All of these factors are involved in the decision of the individual to participate or not, in behaviors to promote health and prevent disease. The client's authority to choose is emphasized in this model, thus reflecting personal power. It is never easy for the health care professional to accept the client's decision to forgo medical care for an illness, but that right must be respected. The health care provider can teach and demonstrate alternatives, but must always, in the end, honor the client's choices which are made in response to all the factors in the Health Belief Model (See Figure 2-7).

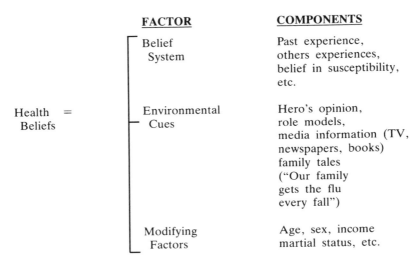

FACTOR	COMPONENTS
Belief System	Past experience, others experiences, belief in susceptibility, etc.
Environmental Cues	Hero's opinion, role models, media information (TV, newspapers, books) family tales ("Our family gets the flu every fall")
Modifying Factors	Age, sex, income martial status, etc.

Health = Beliefs

Fig. 2-7. Health Belief Model

Systems Theory

According to Systems Theory, each individual represents a system— a composite of many parts working together for the benefit of the whole person. The individual is a part of many larger systems, such as families, professions, clubs, and churches (Barry, 1984).

Maximum efficiency of the system relies on the high level functioning of each part; in other words, wholeness depends on wellness. The individual is responsible for maintaining the highest level possible of well-being; in so doing, the person fulfills his own needs, one of which is power.

Organization is an element of Systems Theory. The conglomerate (of parts or people) within a system are arranged in a specific manner so as to enhance the relationships among the various parts (Barry, 1984). The system cannot function optimally without the interaction of people in the system. In Systems Theory, the whole is greater than the sum of the parts (Durkheim, 1951).

Systems Theory incorporates the open or closed condition of a system. "Openness of a system refers to the extent to which it exchanges energy in any form with the environment" (Stanhope, p. 130, 1984). Most systems in the world are open, thereby influencing other systems. The degree to which a person meets his own need for power influences others in the work situation, at home, and in the same town or church (See Figure 2-8). For a system to be closed, there must be well defined boundaries and no exchange of any energy with any other system (Barry, 1984).

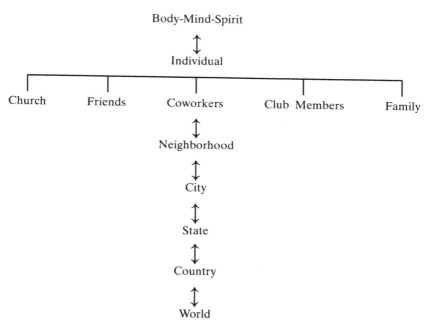

Fig. 2-8. The Human as a System

Change Theory

Change Theory explains the process whereby each person can accept and welcome change. The person who is rigid and unchanging is not, as some might suppose, a person with power but a person of weakness, frightened by change and paralyzed by the fear of being out of control. By his very rigidity, this person demonstrates a lack of internal control.

Bennis (1976) describes planned change as "a conscious, deliberate, and collaborative effort to improve operations of human systems... through the utilization of valid knowledge" (p. 4). Thorough planning for change entails the effort to make the choices as appealing or palatable as possible for each person affected.

Although the ultimate decision for acceptance of change must come from each person, the process described in Change Theory reduces resistance to change and makes acceptance more likely. Knowing the steps of Change Theory can be a source of power for the individual, as this knowledge aids him in understanding his own process for acceptance of change, and also assists him in introducing changes in the home or workplace. The steps are as follows;

1) **Unfreezing**. "Unfreezing begins with dissatisfaction with the present system or a feeling that there is a need for things to be different" (Stanhope, 1984, p.139). Individuals who are involved in the consequences of the change must come to the point of unfreezing. If they do not perceive a need for the change or that it is possible or worthwhile to attempt a change, the effort to effect that change will fail. This step in the change process is often ignored as in staff members concluding that the idea for change of their supervisor is not feasible.

2) **Moving** is the implementation of change, and is achieved by acting on the opinion that the situation can be improved. It requires an alteration in thoughts and personal values or the use of some type of power (Stanhope, 1984). The individual who admires another's manner of cooking hamburger and is interested enough to ask for an explanation of how it is done is at the unfreezing stage. However, when he tries to cook the meat in this new manner, the moving stage has been reached. When the moving stage is entered, through the use of personal power of choice, the individual will perceive his level of control. If, however, the administrator of a clinic does not achieve the stage of unfreezing with her employees to agree on possible behavior options, she may choose one of the alternatives and impose her choice on her employees, thereby commencing the trial process of using a different method for accomplishing a task. This exercise of positional power decreases the individual's sense of self-control necessitating a concerted effort by the administrator to acknowledge her heavy hand yet appeal to the employee to try each peer's suggestion until a general consensus can be reached concerning the optimal option.

3) **Refreezing**. Through the repetition of new behaviors selected during the moving phase, the actions become stabilized, habitual or accepted, as seen by the consistent use of one method for achieving a task by all members of the staff.

The alcoholic has developed an unhealthy habit, but the treatment process requires entry into the stages for change and the adoption of substitute behaviors for drinking, such as A.A. fellowship, sports or hobbies. If the new behavior satisfies the needs of the individual, especially if it is pleasurable, he will repeat its use until the behavior becomes a habit.

Through the use of the steps of Change Theory (Figure 2-9) the health care professional can assist the client in making changes that will improve or maintain his level of health. This enables the client to potentiate his self-esteem and power.

GOAL	UNFREEZING	MOVING	REFREEZING
Task to be accomplished	Possible options	Attempted options	Evaluation Behavior chosen
Arrive at work on time	Drive car (current behavior)		Too expensive, air pollution, no parking space
	Carpool	Tried for 3 weeks	Sometimes late to work
	Bus	Tried for 3 weeks	Less expensive, good time schedule, prompt
	Walk		Impractical, too far
	Ride bike		Weather interferes
	Train		Not scheduled at convenient time

Fig. 2-9. Change Theory

Values Clarification

Values clarification is a process used to identify those beliefs or opinions that a person feels are important enough in his life to act upon (Simon, 1974). By using this process to identify those ideas which are of importance to him, the individual reinforces his feeling of control in his life situations.

Values Clarification assists individuals in separating personal opinions and beliefs from those ideas that are significant to him. This process is easily seen in the adolescent who is rebelling against the constraints imposed on him. However, many adults have never gone through this process. The goal of helping an individual identify and act on his values may not be easily accomplished, but it may be satisfying for the psychiatric client and his therapist to make a decision.

In the three phases of values clarification—choosing, prizing, and acting—the following seven steps are necessary in changing a behavior from an opinion to a value:

1) The first step is *choosing freely*. This indicates that the client has made a decision without the undue influence of others. He is independent and in enough control of his own life to make his own decisions.

2) Secondly, he must have *chosen this belief from all the alternatives* he can think of. After considering all the options and then coming to a decision, the client reinforces his self-image of individually choosing a behavior.

3) The third step is *consideration of the consequences* of a given choice. After due reflection on possible consequences, the client can accurately be said to have met the criteria for choosing his own behaviors.

4) The fourth step, *cherishing one's decision.* enables the client to feel a sense of satisfaction and pride.

5) With *public affirmation*, the client confirms that this choice is one he is happy to have made. This does not necessitate evangelizing others, but does reinforce the concept of personal power through publicly admitting a value.

6) The sixth step involves *acting* on the individual's beliefs and then trusting in his choice. The client who has a Living Will filled out and, upon becoming ill, insists on its application is acting according to his voiced intentions.

7) The consistent *repetition of that action* is the last step in the values clarification process, and serves to cement the belief that "I can do this."

To qualify as a value, a decision or opinion must meet all seven of these steps, being acted on not only once but many times, becoming a pattern of behavior. This strengthens his self-image as that of being powerful.

Summary

There are many theories that relate to power or control in mankind. The theories discussed in this chapter include: Locus of Control, Sick Role, Control Theory, Change Theory, Reality Therapy, Values Clarification, Self-Care, and Systems Theory. All of these reflect the importance of power or control in a person's life. They encourage a positive self-esteem, decreased anxiety, decreased anger, self-care, effective coping, and compliance with health care. The theories discussed in this chapter are mentioned throughout the book in explanation of the power/powerlessness conflicts in a variety of client categories.

References

Ardell, Donald B. *High Level Wellness*. New York: Bantam Books, (1981).

Barry, Patricia D. *Psychosocial Nursing: Assessment and Intervention*. Philadelphia: J.B.Lippincott Company, (1984).

Doe, Father John. *The Golden Book of Excuses*. Indianapolis: The SMT Guild, Inc., (1952).

Durkheim, Emil. *Suicide*. Glencoe, IL: The Free Press, (1951).

Dyer, Wayne W. *Pulling Your Own Strings*. New York: Avon Books, (1978).

Erikson, Erik H. *Childhood and Society*. (2nd Ed.). New York: Norton, (1963).

Glasser, William. *Schools Without Failure*. New York: Harper & Row, Publishers, (1969).

Glasser, William. *Take Effective Control of Your Life*. New York: Harper & Row, Publishers, (1984).

Glasser, William. The Basic Concepts of Reality Therapy. Canoga Park, CA: Institute for Reality Therapy (1986).

Haber, Judith; Hoskins, Pamela; Leach, Anitai; Sideleau, Barbara. *Comprehensive Psychiatric Nursing* (3rd Ed.) New York: McGraw-Hill Book Company, (1987).

Hays, Dorothea R. Teaching a Concept of Anxiety to Patients. *Nursing Research*. 10. Spring. 108-113, (1961).

Holt, John. *How Children Fail*. NY: Pitman Pub. Corp., (1964).

Orem, Dorothea E. *Nursing: Concepts of Practice* (3rd Ed.). New York: McGraw-Hill Book Company, (1985).

Selye, Hans. *The Stress of Life*. New York: McGraw-Hill, (1956).

Simon, Sidney B. *Meeting Yourself Halfway*. Niles, IL: Argus Communications, (1974).

Stanhope, Marcia and Lancaster, Jeanette. *Community Health Nursing: Process and Practice for Promoting Health*. St. Louis: C.V. Mosby, (1984).

Steiner, Claude M. *Scripts People Live*. NY: Grove Press, (1974).

Thomas, Clayton L. *Taber's Cyclopedic Medical Dictionary* (l2th Ed.). Philadelphia: F.A.Davis, (1973).

Unknown. Erickson-Singles Are Reaching Maturity. *Casper Tribune*. Oct. 12. Casper, WY, (1980).

Wubbolding, Robert. Workbook for Reality Therapy. Presented in Canton, Ohio, August 18, 1985, (1985).

Wubbolding, Robert. *Using Reality Therapy*. New York: Harper & Row, (1988).

3

Personal Assets and Power Resources

N. Rinehart

Introduction

The five resources of power reflect the biopsychosocial concept of man: physical, intellectual, emotional, cultural, and spiritual. These resources encompass a large number of possibilities for assisting clients in the campaign to increase their sense of power or control in their life situations. Every client entering the health care system has strengths in some of these resource areas. If the client has a deficit in one area, the remaining resources of power can be fortified to compensate for that weakened area and help regain or maintain his feelings of control.

Among these five power resources are several common potential assets for clients. The assets must be identified and enhanced to assist the client in gaining the perception of (personal control. Each client has strengths, or assets, that must be identified, supported and encouraged. As the five resource areas blend into one another, so do the assets of the individual. The assets that occur in all five resource areas are: 1) strength, 2) motivation, 3) support system/networking, 4) coping, 5) knowledge, 6) perceptions, 7) self-esteem and 8) energy reserves or stamina (See Figure 3-1).

	Physical	Intellectual	Emotional	Cultural	Spiritual
Strength					
Motivation					
Support Systems					
Coping					
Knowledge					
Perceptions					
Self-Esteem					
Energy					

Fig. 3-1. Common Threads of Power Assets and Resources.

Strength

Strength is the amount of power necessary to meet a challenge. For many people, physical strength is a requirement for the perception of themselves as capable of changing their life situations. Increased strength in a paraplegic will enable him to care for himself with less demands placed on others for assistance. The elderly often worsen in health from malnutrition because asking for help with a can opener would be admitting they're helpless. Loss of physical strength results in feelings of powerlessness which turn into despair—and ultimately to death (Seligman, 1975).

Physical strength is a universal concern. Many individuals take for granted the ability of muscles and joints to perform correctly until some accident or illness robs them of that function. There are also those who push their bodies to higher performance—the marathoner or dancer, for example. Most people who enhance their own physical strength and condition report that doing so results in an improvement of their self-image, self-assurance, and confidence. It is not that these individuals are stronger than anyone else so much as that they feel in better condition and take pride in their efforts. It is desirable to be "adequately conditioned and feeling good and fully able to derive considerable satisfaction from the sensory joy of being in touch with your muscletone" (Ardell, 1977, p.157).

Dexterity and full range of motion are necessary for clients to meet the usual self-care demands. Maintaining flexibility to keep all joints and muscles in working condition is one rationale behind exercise, diet, and rest. Without the use of muscles and joint motion, either by the client himself or with the assistance of another person, the client will impair or lose his ability to perform his own self-care through contractures and atrophy (Flynn and Heffron, 1984).

As one of the resources of power listed, spirituality does not indicate that all clients must believe in a Supreme Being. However, those who do believe in a Higher Power find it a source of great comfort and report a feeling of strength that otherwise would be absent (Sehnert, 1985). Greer (1976, p.110) stated that "a Christian must continually work at achieving his maximum potential both spiritually and physically." Easwaran (1978) discussed the peace and strength gained through meditation on Hindu and Buddhist scriptures. The "Big Book" of Alcoholics Anonymous (1976) advocates creating one's own concept of God, and members acknowledge a great source of strength from depending on a Higher Power rather than on alcohol.

Having hope is a source of spiritual strength. Even within the most critical or terminal client, there flickers the hope that things will turn out for the benefit of all. The ability to project the mind into the future, to predict what the consequences of a behavior are probably going to be is the territory of humans alone (Glasser, 1986). That ability to identify the probabilities of the future offers each individual a ray of hope to believe there is always the possibility of beating the odds (Ferguson, 1980).

Intellectual strength is achieved through the continual gain of knowledge and understanding throughout life. Without periodic exercise of the mind and a challenge of its potential, the intellect of the individual becomes sluggish and passive, like a muscle grown flaccid through disuse (Steele and Maraviglia, 1981). Far too often, individuals reject their natural inclination to seek comprehension and decide that graduation from some level of schooling indicates that their days of learning have ended. The natural spontaneity of a child's curiosity is commonly stifled by society as the child is taught to not ask embarrassing questions. Rather than promoting the child's active participation in arriving at an answer to his question, the answer, or at least the one the adult wishes to express, is given to the child. By providing answers to children rather than encouraging their curiosity by assisting them in the search for answers to their own questions, society fosters the perception of needing others to cite solutions. This is seen in students who believe teachers must give them answers and the students' only responsibility is to memorize this data.

Tradition plays an important role in every society. If the individual behaves in culturally acceptable ways he is assured of cultural acceptance. This feeling of belonging is a source of cultural strength for the individual. The pride of the members of a cultural group in their traditions and standards promotes personal power. There is strength in numbers, the feeling of not being alone in daily struggles.

The strength of the individual's emotions relates to his feelings of powerfulness. If he does not feel that he has any control in his life, his emotional responses to life situations will be weak and easily swayed by the opinions of others. The belief that his feelings are unimportant or not acceptable further undermines the individual's base of personal power.

Motivation

Motivation is the cause of behavior for a desired effect, or the energy and belief that leads to behavior. There are many motivating factors involved in the behaviors of each individual. At times it is difficult to separate them as they are so firmly intertwined.

Emotional motivation is based on the individual's feelings. Is the person motivated to behave in a certain way because he is trying to avoid feeling afraid or lonely? Does that person behave in ways that are meant to promote a specific feeling, such as acceptance by, or guilt of another person? Does he behave out of the motivation of love or hate? Rather than behaving in response to, or in avoidance of an emotion, a client will have more sense of personal power if he can focus his emotions to promote behaviors that emphasize the feeling of personal control (Dyer, 1977).

Spiritual motivation leads to behavior focused on the avoidance of condemnation and the attainment of salvation; the Protestant work ethic, for example. However, if the spiritual motivation of a behavior is founded on faith and love for self as well as mankind, more personal power becomes available to the individual (Sehnert, 1985).

Sociocultural expectations serve as motivators in the client who has a strongly external locus of control. With a client who is more internally controlled, however, there is a reduced likelihood that he will be motivated by any influences of his sociocultural group (Dyer, 1977). The client's personal value system also serves as a motivating factor and is usually reflective of his upbringing, as noted in the Japanese culture, for example.

Physical motivation is demonstrated by behaviors resulting from pain or pleasure, or their avoidance. When pain is felt, the client physically retreats from that sensation (Pender, 1982). Pleasurable situations are sought after or arranged to ensure repetition of those sensations (Garland and Bush, 1982); examples are the Pleasure Principle or the Playboy Ethic.

If a client comprehends available information as worthwhile or helpful to his own situation, he is more disposed to be intellectually motivated (Pender, 1982). Curiosity is a strong intellectual motivator (Brown, 1983), and its results can be rewarded positively to the utmost—winning the Nobel Laureate.

Networking/Support Systems

Support systems are the group structures where the individual experiences acceptance and caring. Most individuals are secure in the knowledge that their families care for them, no matter what the rest of society thinks.

Networking is the reaching out by an individual to others who share a like interest or background, which leads to the construction of a network of acquaintances, which can be a tremendous individual source of power. A group that accepts a member and cheers him on, can be invaluable in the individual's risk-taking efforts as he strives to improve his life (Viscott, 1977).

Members of the spiritual community can offer strength, acceptance, reassurance, and hope to the ill client who feels powerless in his current situation. The need for contact with the spiritual support system is evidenced by the client who regularly attends a local religious group, one who finds himself alone or ill in a strange location, and for the client who feels the need to talk with someone about his spiritual needs (Reed, 1969). This communing ranges from sporadic church attendance to administration of Last Rites, providing closure and resolution of anomie.

Through learning coping strategies that are acceptable in the culture of origin or the culture one has adopted, each individual can have a sensation of being in control of his own life events. The individual's sociocultural environment can be a source of much support when taken into consideration by the health care provider. Only then can a plan of care for the individual by his health care provider be as effective as possible. This assessment and incorporation of the individual's cultural needs greatly improves the delivery of health care (Orque, 1983). If the individual behaves in a manner that conforms to the acceptable cultural standards he receives positive feedback from the members of that culture. If, however, he does not wish to participate in some of those behaviors and has become acculturated to another group, the reception he receives from his family and friends may be stressful (Brown, 1983; Lerner, 1986; Steinem, 1983).

Support networks are necessary for many persons to maintain emotional stability. Consider the multitude of self-help and support groups currently available. Access to a group that welcomes the individual with unconditional acceptance is emotionally supportive and empowering (Alcoholics Anonymous, 1976; Glasser, 1986; Wolberg, 1977). Success within these groups, however, is dependent on the client embracing their inherent values.

Intellectual support networks are basic to school education. A sense of belonging to an elite group is reward for the child who achieves placement on the honor roll when his friends are content to have passed the class. Many clubs and groups are organized around meeting some otherwise unmet academic need, as with Continuing Education offerings or national honorary fraternities.

Support groups in the physical realm include the groups of people who have common interests or goals and find inspiration for feelings of power in their numbers. This relates to street gangs as well as picketing health care professionals, aerobic dance class members to arthritis client groups learning new methods for doing self-care. There is a definite feeling of well-being when an individual feels he is a member of this group and draws strength from this belonging. It can be terrifying to not be a member and be surrounded by a group with different values, such as the parent at his adolescent son's favorite rock band concert.

Coping

Coping is the satisfactory meeting of a need. Coping mechanisms are those behaviors chosen as a protective device against the emotional pain of anxiety (Barry, 1984). The client may subconsciously choose from a wide array of defense mechanisms considered suitable to, or unnatural for, his specific developmental level. These strategies can be effective for long or short periods of time (Haber et al, 1987)—or not at all. The more effective the client's choice of coping style and the less he feels the need to resort to defense mechanisms, the more in control of his life he perceives himself to be (Glasser, 1986).

Emotional stability is a factor of affective power that correlates with the coping ability of an individual client. The more stable the client, the more capable he is to control his own life events, rather than resort to rationalization or the blame of others for their control over him (Glasser, 1986). As the client becomes more emotionally healthy, he relies increasingly on his own perceptions and judgments, and less on what others say (Viscott, 1976).

The physiology of man is structured so as to continuously shift with the imbalances of life in an attempt to maintain homeostasis (Pender, 1982); physical coping is the ability of the body to meet a biochemical need (Garland and Bush, 1982). Chronic stress results in a physiological and psychological drain on coping abilities, with the solution not infrequently being serious illness, injury or death (Kinzer, 1978).

Cultures serve the purpose of setting standards for coping with life's events during the individual's existence. The culture one belongs to dictates the acceptable mode for displaying happiness, approval, anger, and love. Mastering the coping style of one's cultural group underscores the control available to the individual. The severance of these cultural standards can promote feelings of power or powerlessness, depending on the individual's perception of the rebellion from the norm.

The ability of an individual to cope intellectually is often corroborated through earning certificates and degrees. The cognitive activity of the client contributes to his resultant behavior (Garland and Bush, 1982), determining the successful or failed completion of educational goals. The client who respects his intellectual ability is prone to exhibit interest in gaining control in the procedures related to his own health care (Lerner, 1986).

Spiritual coping is evidenced in the inner peace the individual gains through prayer or consultation with a representative of his faith. Dreaded clinical procedures may be met with courage after participation in a religious ritual, such as communion or meditation (Reed, 1969).

Knowledge

Knowledge is a collection of learned information. Knowledge about one's body, health, and options for treatment is necessary for a client to behold himself as having power or control over his own health care. The more an individual comprehends about the needs of his own body and the available avenues for meeting those needs, the more proficient he is in informed decision-making concerning his own well-being (Dyer, 1980; Sehnert, 1985).

If it is essential to have knowledge to feel in control of one's health care, then it is imperative that the client be able to learn. Health care professionals can assess the client's ability to learn, identify his abilities for tactile, visual or auditory learning (Flynn and Heffron, 1984), and then develop an expedient teaching plan. As Ferguson (1980) stated, "learning is not only like health, it is health" (p. 282). In order to maintain or recover his health or maximum health status, the individual must discover his own self-care needs and methods for meeting them. All individuals are capable of learning, but all individuals do not have the same capacity for instruction or the educational background from which mastery can easily occur. Therefore, health care professionals must pay close attention to the vocabulary used during teaching, so as to include words found in the literature and supplement those words with auditory and visual aids (Lerner, 1986). Clients who learn best when engaged in the manual aspects of the process, or those who must learn a manual task to carry out their self-care, such as a diabetic learning to give himself injections, must be assessed for their level of capability. For instance, a self-piercing stylette gun may be preferred for the client who must do his own Glucoscans, but who cannot bring himself to poke his finger.

The individual's perception of himself and of his intellectual ability also contribute to his cognizance of having power over his own health. Do I see myself as capable of learning the necessary information to perform self-care? Do I see myself as responsible for my own health? "The biggest factor accounting for insufficient self-responsibility in our society is probably the lack of effective health education to date" (Ardell, 1977, p. 105). If the health care professional can assure the client that he can learn the necessary information and that he not only has the right but the responsibility to be a partner in his own health care, the client realizes he has this control. That ownership of personal power increases with time and knowledge.

Knowledge of innovative techniques for meeting self-care needs enables the client to feel more physically independent (Flynn and Heffron, 1984; Sehnert, 1985). Sufficient knowledge of physiological limitations helps in the prevention of injuries to both the athlete and the arthritic (Ardell, 1977; Flynn and Heffron, 1984).

The expansion of an individual's repertoire of behavior choices for dealing with his environment serves to increase his sense of personal control. Knowledge helps the individual broaden his emotional choices and abets him in acquitting himself in a manner pleasing to and effective for him.

Knowledge of one's culture, its origin and traditions, promotes the feeling of control related to the choice of acting according to the cultural requirements or in choosing to behave contrary to the tenants of the past. Comprehension of the reasons behind behaviors that are blindly accepted by significant others can give one the awareness of increasing power. Families need to be engaged in the process of learning as well. The more information the family has, the more disposed they are to be supportive of the client's endeavors to follow his plan of care.

Knowledge of the expectations of comportment by the members and leaders of a faith group, as well as one's conception of a higher power, fosters personal power. Spiritual power is magnified in those who place importance in the belief in a higher power via participation in ceremonies or rituals established by leaders of that particular faith. Individuals draw on their beliefs to boost their feelings of control. Although some faiths cultivate fatalism and helplessness, the believers commonly express improved self-perceptions that intensify the feelings of power rather than the opposite.

Perceptions

Perception is the interpretation an individual assigns to an event as viewed through his senses and filtered through his values and past experience (Glasser, 1984). The client's feeling of being in control is potentiated by each of the five resources of power.

Perception can be altered by the emotional state of a client whose interpretation of a situation provide clues for helping him gain insight (Wolberg, 1977). Conversely, a client's perception of events as being unmanageable or threatening are going to impact negatively on his capacity to fully recover.

Just as personal values and past experiences affect a client's perception, so too does the intellectual resource of power. Perception of control is reflected in the amount of curiosity a client expresses about his plan of care. If he experiences himself as in control of his own health, he will seek out more information and assume the responsibility for his wellness (Pender, 1982). Robbins (1986) advocates the perception by clients of all situations as purposeful: with the encouragement of curiosity, acceptance, and openness about each life event.

The spiritual background of a client will influence his sense of control. If he has been surrounded by spiritual influences which encourage taking control of his life, he can more easily see himself as being powerful. If, however, he comes from a background of fatalistic beliefs, he will behave as more externally controlled, finding it uncomfortable to accept more responsibility for his health. Thorough assessment is needed to ascertain the potential for resistance by the client to staff attempts to place responsibility and control for his health care on his shoulders.

The physical aspects of perception add or subtract from the client's interpretation of events as being within his control. The relaxation and breathing practice of the expectant woman results in feelings of maintaining control when labor contractions begin. The young boy on a roller coaster feels out of control when a sudden and unexpected turn occurs; however, it may be just that lack of control and potential danger that leads to the thrill sought by getting on the roller coaster in the first place. It is standard practice to explain to the client sensations that may occur during a procedure, with the premise that if he knows what is coming, he can be better prepared and maintain the feeling of control (Flynn and Heffron, 1984). It is incongruent, but not uncommon, to find physicians who do not want nurses, or other staff members, to do any preoperative teaching for their clients.

The cultural influence in perception is evidenced by the societal values exhibited by the client (Orque and Bloch, 1983). The client raised in a German family may well be overtly inexpressive of strong emotions when a family member brings sad news. However, in relaying sad news to the Chicano client, an entire family will grieve vociferously against the insulting stressor (Henderson and Primeaux, 1981). In Western society it is impolite to suck on one's teeth and belch, whereas in other societies these are indicators of appreciation and are considered complimentary.

Self-Esteem

Self-esteem is the pride in worthwhile qualities that an individual identifies in himself, often reflective of the recognition received from others. An influential factor in the intellectual process of teaching or motivating the client (Pender, 1982), self-esteem can allow the client to see himself as a worthwhile person, interested in personal health education. If, however, the client sees himself as too dense to learn or as unworthy of positive attention, he will not respond well to any health care teaching (Pender, 1982).

The spiritual background of the client also influences his self-esteem. If the client feels positive about himself, he will see himself as important, capable of doing things for himself as much as possible, hopeful, deserving of divine intervention, and vital to society. If, however, the client feels he has sinned, that he cannot be forgiven, and does not deserve to recover from his illness, he will not recover effectively; nor will he feel that he has any personal power.

Cultural power has a strong influence on self-esteem. "When self-esteem is low, or when a situation is perceived as particularly threatening, the person is strongly in need of, and seeks out others from whom positive reflective appraisals of self-worth and ability to achieve can be obtained" (Aguilera and Messick, 1986, p.73). This need is met through a variety of sources: family, neighbors, self-help/support groups, clubs, professional groups, and friends.

Emotions are integral in the operation of self-esteem. Buscaglia (1972) reminds us of the necessity of learning to love self before being able to love others. In reference to the individual who has difficulty loving himself, Viscott (1971) states "it is very difficult for some people to become their own masters and to feel good about something merely because it pleases them" (p.38). Lowered self-esteem inhibits the sense of well-being. Thus, it is necessary for health care professionals to encourage an improved self-esteem in clients in order to enhance the clients' feeling of personal power.

Physical abilities and attributes greatly influence self-esteem (Sehnert, 1985; Wolberg, 1977). The self-esteem level of an individual and the esteem held for him by the community is reflected in the way he walks and talks (Pender, 1982). The hunchback of Notre Dame was not held in high esteem, as opposed to Olympic athletes, whose pride in their achievements is a mirror of their esteem.

Stamina

Stamina is the energy reserve to cope with unusual or sudden events and is essential for feelings of personal power or control. Maintenance of emotional stamina is required to enable a client to overcome any difficult situation that might arise. The amount of emotional stamina required in each situation is related to the severity of the stressor, the frequency of stressful events, the past experience of the individual, the effectiveness of previous attempts to cope with similar events, and the amount of strength available from the other four resources of power (Garland and Bush, 1982). If the client believes himself able to rise to the occasion, he will exhibit sufficient emotional stamina or the ability to maintain control and effectively manage his life events.

Reserves of physical capacity or those bursts of energy needed in a stressful situation or crisis, are important for each client. These physical stores can be banked dependent on the diet the client follows, the amount of rest he gets, the physical condition he is in, and the energy conservation methods used throughout the day. According to Dunn (1961), humans need a large store of "expendable energy" and the more wellness experienced by the client, the more energy reserve he has to spend. If a client feels in control, his tolerance for pain can increase dramatically, even though the pain stimulus is unchanged.

Intellectual stamina, or that ability to meet an unplanned intellectual challenge, is important in the study of creativity (Glasser, 1986). Glasser discusses the process of creativity, finding a new way for the individual to meet a need (1986). This ability to mobilize ideas into action reflects intellectual stamina. Without this ability to select more effective methods for meeting his needs, the client will experience an increase in anxiety and a decrease in his sense of personal power.

Cultural expectations of behavior provide stamina for the individual when he might otherwise not have it. Because it is expected of them, children of various cultures are subjected to, and tolerate, tortures and challenges never experienced by those in another culture, such as bound feet, stretched lips and necks, and circumcision for young girls. The energy to tolerate and accept these norms of behavior is derived from the individual's culture and denotes personal power that may be observed more easily by others than himself.

The spiritual energy or stamina of the individual is closely related to the expectations he has of himself, as well as those of others in his spiritual group. The history of the Jews is a fascinating story of spiritual stamina in the face of many trials and sorrows. Christian martyrs in Roman days were bolstered by their spiritual stamina, as are those individuals everywhere who hold to beliefs not accepted by the majority of the society in which they dwell.

Summary

The five resources for personal power: physical, emotional, intellectual, spiritual, and cultural, meld to increase the client's sense of power, each interdependent. As power is a basic need for all humans, each client meets that need in some manner, even if it may be ineffective or unhealthy. For the client who has an irreparable loss in one of these power resources, the other resources must be strengthened to compensate. The more centrally empowered a person perceives himself as being, the greater his sense of control. This is accomplished after a thorough assessment of the strengths, or assets, of the client in the five power resource areas.

Each client has assets that move him toward feeling personally powerful in self-health care. As power is a basic need to all humans, each client must meet that need in some manner, even if it is ineffective. The assets common to all five resources of power are: strength, motivation, support networks, coping, knowledge, perceptions, self-esteem, and stamina or energy reserves. By addressing each of these assets, the health care professional can assist the client in a program that will increase his sense of personal power and move him into a partnership with health care professionals instead of as recipient/victim of care.

References

Aguilera, Donna and Messick, Janice. *Crisis Intervention: Theory and Methodology* (5th Ed.). St. Louis: C.V.Mosby Company, (1986)

Alcoholics Anonymous. *Alcoholics Anonymous* (3rd Ed.). New York: World Service Office of Alcoholics Anonymous, (1976).

Ardell, Donald. *High Level Wellness*. New York: Bantam Books, (1977).

Barry, Patricia. *Psychosocial Nursing Assessment and Intervention*. Philadelphia: J.B. Lippincott Company, (1984).

Brown, William. *Welcome Stress! It Can Help You Be Your Best*. Minneapolis: CompCare Publications, (1983).

Buscaglia, Leo. *Love*. New York: Fawcett Crest, (1972).

Dunn, Halbert. *High Level Wellness*. Thorofare, NJ: Charles B. Slack, Inc., (1961).

Dyer, Wayne. *Pulling Your Own Strings*. New York: Avon Books, (1977).

Dyer, Wayne. *The Sky's The Limit*. New York: Pocket Books, (1980).

Easwaran, Eknath. *Meditation: An Eight-Point Program*. Petaluma, CA: Nilgari Press, (1978).

Ferguson, Marilyn. *The Aquarian Conspiracy: Personal and Social Transformation in the 80's*. New York: St. Martin's Press, (1980).

Flynn, Janet-Beth and Heffron, Phyllis. *Nursing: From Concept to Practice*. Bowie, MD: Robert J. Brady Company, (1984).

Friedman, Sonya. *Smart Cookies Don't Crumble: A Modern Woman's Guide to Living and Loving Her Own Life*. New York: Pocket Books, (1985).

Garland, LaRetta and Bush, Carol. *Coping Behavior and Nursing*. Reston, VA: Reston Publishing Company, Inc., (1982).

Glasser, William. *Positive Addiction*. New York: Harper & Row Publishers, (1976).

Glasser, William. *Control Theory*. New York: Harper & Row, (1986).

Greer, Eugene. *Toward Physical Excellence: For The Glory of God*. Fort Worth, TX: Harvest Press, (1976).

Haber, Judith; Hoskins, Pamela; Leach, Anita and Sideleau. *Comprehensive Psychiatric Nursing* (3rd Ed.). New York: McGraw-Hill Company, (1987).

Henderson, George and Primeaux, Martha. *Transcultural Health Care*. Menlo Park, CA: Addison-Wesley Publishing Company, (1981).

Lerner, Michael. *Surplus Powerlessness*. Oakland, CA: Institute for Labor and Mental Health, (1986).

Maltz, Maxwell. *Psycho-Cybernetics*. New York: Pocket Books, (1960).

Orque, Modesta and Bloch, Bobbie. *Ethnic Nursing Care: A Multicultural Approach*. St. Louis: C.V.Mosby Company, (1983).

Pender, Nola. *Health Promotion in Nursing*. Norwalk, CN: Appleton-Century-Crofts, (1982).

Reed, William. *Surgery of the Soul*. Old Tappan, NJ: Fleming H. Revell Company, (1969).

Robbins, Anthony. *Unlimited Power*. New York: Fawcett Columbine, (1986).

Sehnert, Keith. *Selfcare/Wellcare*. Minneapolis: Augsburg Publishing House, (1985).

Seligman, Martin. *Helplessness*. San Francisco: W. H. Freeman & Company, (1975).

Steinem, Gloria. *Outrageous Acts and Everyday Rebellions*. New York: Holt, Rinehart and Winston, (1983).

Viscott, David. *Feel Free*. New York: Pocket Books, (1971).
Viscott, David. *The Language of Feelings*. New York: Pocket Books, (1976).
Viscott, David. *Risking*. New York: Pocket Books, (1977).
Wolberg, Lewis. *The Techniques of Psychotherapy: Part One* (3rd Ed.). New York: Grune and Stratton, (1977).

4

Power Struggles at Different Life Stages

N. Rinehart

Introduction

Power is a basic human need no matter what age the individual. Power struggles can be covert or overt. Certain power struggles are considered inherent in the situation, such as that between employee and employer and the black client with his white health care providers. Development is a key factor in personal power and control. Some empowerment tactics are easily identified, whereas other behaviors designed to increase personal power are not as quickly observed. Throughout the life span, from the control the newborn achieves as a result of his cry, to the control of the elderly infirm over his immediate family members via the threat of his imminent demise, power struggles are normally present and creatively orchestrated to increase the perception of personal power.

Power During Growth and Development

Newborns. The newborn innately relies on his cry when he is hungry, lonely or uncomfortable. The response to his cry is reinforcing if it gets him what he desires. If, however, his cry does not lead to the desired outcome, the newborn may stop crying and seek another method of gratification, such as chewing on his blanket or sucking in his sleep. Rooting is a natural newborn behavior, aiding the newborn in finding nourishment. Without any sophisticated language, the newborn is quickly transferred to a source of food if he roots on his father's shoulder or his grandmother's chin. His needs are understood and his attempts at communication are rewarded.

Infants. Infants learn to trust the adults in their environment to meet their needs. "When an infant perceives a reliable response to his behavior, there is an increase in responding and emotional expression" (Dimond and Jones, 1983, p. 199). If trust is not established, distrust results. Either outcome of this growth and developmental stage can be seen as a power issue. The infant has the perception of personal power if he indicates a need and it is met. When his needs are not met, the infant will be creative in finding new and better ways to express himself. He knows, for instance, that Grandma will pick him up even though Mother will let him cry for a while before giving in to his loud demands for attention. Throwing toys, then crying, insures his becoming or continuing to be the center of attention. His personal power is the base from which he learns about his relation to his environment.

Toddlers. The world revolves around the toddler, or so he thinks. There is no world other than the one he perceives as centered on himself. References to objects and people are "mine" and "me," such as "my mommy" when confronting another child who gains attention from the toddler's mother. This focus on oneself serves the purpose of building a healthy self-esteem, though it does appear to be heavily weighted toward self-centeredness and conceit. Society gives the child the double message that you are important and should take care of yourself but be sure to let others' concerns go ahead of yours; it's not polite to be self-centered. The toddler learns self-control and willpower during this stage. He learns he can control his bodily functions, that satisfaction can be delayed for a brief period without any dire consequences and that he can persist until he achieves his goals. "No," copied from adults exerting their power over him, becomes a powerful word for the child in this age group.

Preschool. This child is learning purposeful behaviors to achieve goals. He is learning direction rather than random motion in his actions. He learns to take the initiative to work toward a specific goal and achieve it. The preschooler learns that he has the power to achieve things, that he can produce desired results with his efforts. He perceives himself as being more in control with each successful endeavor. "Me do it" becomes his battle cry in power struggles with the adults and older children in his environment.

School. Elementary school is a time of industry, learning more sophisticated methods for problem solving and evaluating self performance in meeting these challenges. It is the time of inferiority for the child who does not evaluate himself or perceive himself evaluated by others as successful in some area of learning (Ginott, 1965). He may see himself as powerless to change his life events and give up on himself, or he may perceive himself as capable of changing anything that is not meeting his needs, and he then goes on to achieve at a higher level of competence. The norm, however, is the child's perception that "every event must have a cause, and the power the child feels over the environment is supreme but unharnessed and undirected" (Dimond and Jones, 1983, p. 199).

Adolescent. Being neither adult nor child is the central conflict of adolescence. The identity crisis, or "Who am I?" syndrome, promotes poor self-esteem, and therefore feelings of powerlessness (Ginott, 1969). Personal power is the focus of the adolescent. His body is changing rapidly and leaves him feeling powerless. He strives to be independent, able to control his own destiny. The teenager who is sexually active is acting out the desire to be in control, to prove that he is an adult by sexually functioning as one. A struggle with his parents over the style of his hair is simply a power struggle, with the parents wanting to maintain control over their child and the adolescent trying to take control of his own life (Glasser, 1978). The adolescent is bewildered by his world and wants the reassurance of safety at home, though he consistently rebels against it. The adolescent attends to those things he believes he can control and ignores or postpones attention to those situations he feels he cannot control (Dimond and Jones, 1983). For example, choosing his classes and getting himself to a new classroom every hour aids the early adolescent in feeling in control, while he forgets that he is dependent on his parents for the clothes he wears to school.

As he progresses through adolescence, more and more decisions are expected of him. These decisions build a sense of being in control or, if the adolescent has trouble making decisions, he increasingly feels out of control, acted upon by external forces. The adolescent usually believes himself to be in personal control regardless of the ambiguity he experiences about his growing independence (Dimond and Jones, 1983).

Young adults. Although intimacy is the main achievement for this age group, there is a continuation of adolescent identity struggles in some cases. The young adult strives to be independent, to support himself in comfort and to gain more significant relationships with others. The maintenance of a household and self-support builds personal power. They experience power in creating new life or making the personal decision not to parent. They realize that the expectations of others include their acceptance of responsibility for their own behavior choices.

Middle adults. Middle adults often have more time to achieve the goals they set up for themselves when they joined the workforce. Their children are now grown and independent and they find themselves with more energy to devote to work and community efforts. They are the managers and directors in the workplace and/or the president of the community committee. They enjoy the productivity that they can see in themselves. Their self-image improves as far as their perception of personal power and productivity goes, but it starts to decrease in the area of physical attractiveness. Researchers have found that religious motivation, self-concept and occupation serve as the strongest indicators of personal power in this age group (Dimond and Jones, 1983).

Late adult. The elderly adult must come to terms with his past and accept the inevitable end to his existence. This does not imply that he should give up and allow the community to take over decisions concerning his life. He needs to remain in control of decisions that affect him and give to the community as a whole. "A major feature of aging in American society is the gradual but persistent loss of influence over one's life and community" (Dimond and Jones, 1983, p. 200). The elderly have much wisdom and many skills that can be passed on to the younger members of the community. When the elderly person is shut up in a community of the elderly, he does not have the opportunity to extend himself and pass on his knowledge and history to the young. His emphasis on not changing his environment or his ritual of daily activities is a way for him to express his personal power. Having things altered without his consent increases his feelings of powerlessness.

Birth Order

The birth order of each child in a family influences his feeling of personal power. Because of his position, he is expected to be the leader, the follower, the entertainer, the initiator of activities, the responsible example for the younger children or the compromiser (Leman, 19857. His perception of being in control, of personal power, is strongly affected by his interpretation of his family roles.

Oldest or Only. The older child may be able to intimidate the younger children and interpret this as having power over them. The eldest child is generally a pleaser of others, striving to live up to the expectations others have for him (Leman, 1985).

Many health care professionals were oldest children. Often older or only children spend a lifetime of codependent, caretaker behaviors (Beattie, 1987). He may be compliant or an overachiever. These behavioral characteristics are generally aimed at increasing a sense of personal power rather than promoting the unsatisfactory sense of power by right of birth order that they experience with younger siblings.

Middle. The middle child learns to fend for himself in many situations, as he is neither the oldest nor the youngest, the two siblings who receive the most family attention. Middle children can either learn to be responsibly independent or resentful of the attention that they feel they have been denied. They tend to become secretive and private. The middle child may avoid family contact and crave peer relationships more than one with any family member (Leman, 1985). They may resent pressure from older siblings, as they assert their ability to make up their own minds and do as they wish. The struggles for the middle child are with the older and younger sibling, between whom they are sandwiched, and the adults in their world who do not give them the attention they crave. With less attention paid them, and thus more freedom, the middle child is more likely to believe he has control in his life, making his own choices and steering his own course (Leman, 1985).

Youngest. The family's youngest child is often the princess or prince of the family. They demonstrate a strong urge to not do anything their older siblings have done—which may be difficult if they come from a very large family. The youngest child may have trouble learning responsibility as he grows older, as his older siblings have done things for him and he has been excused from chores that his elders performed well when they were his age. In a style of abusive power, the smaller child may quickly learn to scream whenever she thinks her big sister should get punished, because she knows her father always reprimands the older child when the younger screams. The youngest child is often the class clown and tends to be the family charmer (Leman, 1985). He is always the youngest, therefore the baby, and cannot easily break out of that role. Living under the shadow of the older children in the family, this child has the need to shore up his self-esteem and, therefore, his personal power.

Birth Sex

The sex of the child affects the child's perception of power. His feelings about himself are directly related to the significance his parents and others place on his sex. Society also places value on sex depending on its needs. In a family of few male children, the perpetuation of the family name gains importance. A community with few female children expresses joy at the birth of females who are necessary to continue the species.

Male. The male child often receives more approval, freedom, and acceptance than does his less-valued sister. The male child is seen as the one who will carry on the family history and name. He is expected to be tougher and, indeed, is handled much less gently. Male children are socialized to go out into the world and bring home a living for their less hardy mate. Caveman expectations are still being placed on men in many societies. He is supposed to be stronger than women and protective of them. Any failure to meet these expectations, or self-doubt about their ability to do so, places men in a position of diminished personal power. In some societies the expression of feelings by men is interpreted as a weakness, a less-than-manly trait (Gaylin, 1979). The willingness to accept women as equal is in conflict with the old messages passed to men in their youth and this leads to internal conflict that can be weakening.

Female. Female offspring are often socialized to be softer, cuter, frillier, gentler, and more emotional than their male siblings. Women are expected to be more domestic and to stay at home while the boys are out adventuring. Girls who like to roughhouse and play sports are labeled "tom-boys,"and their femininity questioned. Female children who are bright in mathematics and science will find themselves subjected to subtle hints that these areas are not suitable for girls and that men will not be interested in "brainy" women. Women with a strong sense of control in their life situations may find it extremely irksome to have individuals in their environment expect them to defer to men simply because it is feminine to do so.

The Balancing Act. With the influence of the women's liberation movement, this sexist socialization is slowly changing. However, even enlightened parents who make a strong effort to not socialize their children according to their sex may feel defeated when the child enters the preschool and school years, as their childrens' peers are going to dictate what is labeled "sissy work" or declare that "girls can't shoot a gun" (Thomas, 1974). The efforts being made to promote equal opportunities and freedoms for both sexes are beginning to have some effect, but it will be many years before their goal of improved personal power is completely realized.

In a discussion of the blurring of sex roles in the business place, Hart and Dalke (1983) list three choices of action for the conflicted individual: quit, assimilate, or renegotiate. The organization hiring the individual also has difficulties that result from the struggle between the sexes in redefining their roles: employee attitude change, employee selection and retention goals, and decreasing productivity (Hart and Dalke, 1983).

Power and Race

Members of the dominant race in a community experience a feeling of power as a result of being one of the majority. The need to belong is met in this situation, but it can lead to harassment of those in the minority. It is human nature to be uncomfortable with the unknown, or a situation that is divergent from the norm for the individual. However, it is a form of abusive power to inflict hardships on those who are unlike the majority or control group just because they are different. This is most clearly seen in the apartheid problem of South Africa.

Ethnic minorities are typically placed in positions of powerlessness by the majority group in society. Many ethnic minority women experience far more stressors than do the women of the majority race in a community (Parreno, 1983). Members of ethnic minorities have lower employment rates due to occupational segregation or the placement of those individuals in stereotypical work positions. In some situations, societal expectations of minority members are unrealistic, as in the common additional stress on black women executives of being viewed as having unlimited coping ability to handle any difficulty and to support the persecuted and worn-down (Parreno, 1983).

All individuals are more comfortable in a familiar environment and with fellow members of their cultural group. Any individual who has found himself in a strange location, surrounded by those who speak a different language and have different culturally acceptable behaviors, has experienced a brief version of the lifelong terror, helplessness and frustration felt by an ethnic minority member. Ideally, minority health care professionals would return to their own cultural groups to provide health care in a familiar environment for the client. However, jobs with higher paychecks tend to be those situated in facilities that provide care for members of the majority, or control, population. Also, there commonly is a lack of confidence in ethnic practitioners within their own community. Fear of going back to the same situation the individual left behind via his education is also a factor. It has been found that "improvement of the positions of women in the health care sector will occur only to the extent that women who are put in positions of power are representatives of and accountable to workers in the health sector as a whole" (Parreno, 1983, p. 313).

The individual who finds himself in the minority group may decide to take part in the society of the majority population only to find himself ignored when it is his turn in line, isolated when others speak a different language that he does not understand, or chided because he has a different color skin than the majority. In the frustration of these incidents, repeated many times a day, it is easy to become angry and, therefore, powerless.

Many health care professionals find it difficult to maintain therapeutic interactions with minority clients who are hostile (Thomas, 1981). Hostility is one result of adaptation to an unfriendly environment. It is common to find hostile members of the minority group in a society which is openly antagonistic to that group. Subtle, covert anger and resultant behaviors are often present in the society which hides the prejudicial limitations it places on minority members. Defensive behaviors on the part of health care professionals hinder the formation of therapeutic relationships with clients. As the hostility of the client is his method of adaptation to society, it is the health care provider who needs to adjust and choose appropriate coping measures in that situation. To expect the hostility of the client to diminish is unrealistic and puts undue stress on the client. Anger is not the problem in this situation, but the behavior chosen to express the anger may be.

The resulting behavior is the potential difficulty in the health care setting. Aimless or harmful anger increases powerlessness. Directed anger at life's unfairness and the resolution to change it are empowering behavioral choices. Individuals who unite in their anger about a racially unjust situation can accomplish change via their united efforts and rectify some of these conditions.

Henderson and Primeaux (1981) list observations that might assist the health care provider in realistically dealing with members of a different ethnic group:

1. Care providers cannot solve (clients') problems, but they may be able to help them solve their own problems.
2. The easiest, least creative response to transcultural conflict is to pretend that it does not exist.
3. (Client) knowledge of scientific medicine is alienating and every successful educational effort by practitioners tends to alienate clients from relatives and friends who do not have this knowledge.
4. Humor can help practitioners and clients over rough spots; we must be able to laugh at ourselves and with other people.
5. Previous transcultural experience is a valuable asset if it is used as a general guide. However, if viewed as offering the correct answer to every transcultural problem, experience will be a liability.
6. All care providers will make mistakes in transcultural interactions, but we should learn from our mistakes and not repeat them (p. xxiv).

The observable differences in individuals such as hair color, language, skin color, and eye shape will remain unchanged. However, the interpretation of those differences can be altered. The health care professional must work with her feelings regarding clients unlike herself. The client is, in some way, unhealthy and it is ludicrous to expect him to alter the coping styles that have served him well while he was healthy.

Understanding the general, rather than personal, nature of the minority client's coping style will lessen the stress for the health care provider. Building a trusting relationship, one in which the client can adapt self-care measures to his lifestyle, is difficult but not impossible, a challenge for each member in the power struggle. Every effort should be made to involve the client's significant others, make available foods he prefers and arrange for cultural acceptance of the client.

The provision of a translator is helpful in empowering the client; finding oneself sick in a strange environment and surrounded by professionals who speak in a strange language promotes powerlessness. There are still some members of the health care team that maintain that all clients coming to them should speak the majority population's language if they want health care, or suffer the consequences.

The expectation by some members of the majority population that their language should be spoken by everyone is grandiose indeed. When travelling in another country, this insistence that others arrange to speak the tourist's language is the result of overinflated self-importance. Part of the "ugly American" image is related to this expectation that others should inconvenience themselves for the American's comfort. Health care professionals who speak more than one language are appreciated by clients who cannot speak the language of the majority. (Perhaps, in the future, all health professionals will be required to speak one language other than their own and spend some time in a living situation where they are in the minority population.)

Learning about other cultures, their traditions and values, will aid the professional in planning effective care for the minority client. Cultural adaptations in the client's care will go far in building a trusting and accepting relationship between the client and his care providers.

Powerlessness of Waiting

Waiting is the postponement of a goal. This very delay of gratification creates power struggles for many individuals. The client waiting for the physician to see him is given a strong message concerning the power of the physician he must wait for, and in western society this delay is expected. This situation seems paradoxical when we realize that it is the client who employs the physician. However, if the client is viewed as powerful by the physician, the probability for an extended wait diminishes.

According to Levine (1987), there are ten rules for waiting:

1. Time has a monetary value.
2. Diminished supply increases the length of the wait and the willingness of individuals to do so.
3. Waiting for something increases its value.
4. Waiting decreases as status rises.
5. The position of the individual in the waiting line indicates his importance.
6. Society's privileged do not wait.
7. The control of time is powerful and the powerful control the time of others.
8. Waiting can be a positive experience, depending on the perception of the individual.
9. Waiting, or time, can be a gift of respect or affection to another individual.
10. The awaited goal must be delivered.

The behavior an individual chooses as he waits is a strong indicator of his sense of personal power. The individual's many options include:

1. Come prepared to wait and calmly do so.
2. Become angry and leave the waiting area, thus depriving himself of the awaited goal.
3. Become irritated and wait anyway.
4. Pay someone to wait in his place.
5. Send a bill to the individual he waited for.
6. Complain to the individual he had to wait for.
7. Acquire supplies that are less in demand.
8. Decide the wait is not worth it.

According to socialization, waiting is viewed differently. In Eastern Europe, citizens wait hours to purchase a pair of shoes. The Hispanic philosophy of mañana can be extremely frustrating to an impatient and punctual Anglos-Saxon individual. British queues are extremely orderly and polite. In contrast, Middle Eastern dignitaries can be as late as they wish for an appointment because they "cannot be late," reinforcing the idea that those who control the time of others have power, and those made to wait do not.

Normal Psychoses During The Lifespan

The commonality among the three easily identified stages of life, when it is normal to see psychotic behavior, is that in each stage the body is changing and hormones are increased or decreased. One effect of these raging hormones is to leave the individual with feelings of powerlessness over his bewildering behavior. These are the times when, more or less, society accepts it as normal to observe somewhat psychotic behavior. This behavior is an expression of a prolonged power struggle between the individual's mind and his bodily functions.

No matter what the cause of this feeling of helplessness over one's body, it is terrifying to the individual. There is a fear of never being in control again, further exacerbating the powerless feelings and panic associated with the situation. The individual knows his behavior is not always sensible and is often bewildered by his actions, wondering where such behavior came from, as it is not typical of his traditional style of behavior.

Adolescence. With the changes in their bodies and the surge of hormones, adolescents have a ready-made internal conflict. Additionally, they are wrestling through those years of non-child and non-adult that bewilder all individuals. They cannot find a clear-cut explanation of the expectations placed upon them because the world around them cannot decide what to expect from them. Peers become all powerful, and parents, the providers of food, clothing, and shelter, suddenly become the enemy. How does the adolescent justify taking food from his chief enemy? The confusion, the fanciful reality of their world and the struggle to learn coping mechanisms that work, all lead the adolescent to relatively psychotic behavior.

Pregnancy. The abdomen is stretching, the fetus kicks from within, bladder control is difficult, breasts enlarge, walking turns to waddling, and the mother-to-be feels like a beached whale. These changes happen without any choice by the mother, other than the choice to get pregnant, and leave the woman feeling powerless. The sudden mood swings of pregnancy might be diagnosed as manic-depressive in other individuals.

Mid-Life Crisis. Menopause, the cessation of ovulation, the drop in female hormones, the beginning of nightsweats, whiskers and susceptibility to coronary disease, all leave the woman feeling powerless. It used to be accepted that the psychotic-like behaviors of the menopausal woman were going to occur and were tolerated by society. However, with the advent of hormone augmentation, the psychotic symptoms are less tolerated. The women who cannot take these hormones must muddle through, often wondering if they are losing their minds.

Power Struggles With Authority

Teachers, parents, clergy, military, police, employers, administrators, higher ranking or higher educated peers, and God present images of authority. Although society set up these individuals as guardians, advisors, educators and leaders, the human urge is to rebel at the first sign of oppression. Mankind has a basic need for freedom (Glasser, 1984). This need is felt in the urge to make one's own choices, to go where one desires, and to not feel fettered by others' expectations. Young children demonstrate this urge clearly, but as the individual grows older he is socialized to accept some of these forms of higher authority. These individuals are given their positions of authority by society, yet they are often viewed with hostility by those who fear infringement of their freedom. The founding fathers of the United States identified these rights of freedom yet provided for authority to protect the freedom of the individual. This conflict places many individuals in a quandary: to obey, or to struggle with authority.

God. The power struggle mankind has with God is a common example of a love-hate relationship. Civilizations throughout history have established higher powers, or gods, to explain the world around them, gain acceptance from something or someone greater than themselves, and serve as justification for certain behaviors. If an individual agrees that this higher power is omnipotent he may perceive a struggle within himself to accept a degree of powerlessness when compared to the higher power. The degree of powerlessness varies with the individual's perception of his god.

Many individuals believe God to be a punishing and severe judge, waiting for them to make an incorrect move so that they will roast in Hell forever. Others believe that God is loving and concerned, only wanting the best for them. Whatever the viewpoint, the struggle is often apparent between the assigned power of the diety and the inferior power of the individual. How often does one hear "How could God allow this to happen?" or "What does God want from me?" Welcome or not, the struggles between mankind and higher powers are built-in. With the frailties of mankind, the unreliability and inconstancy, some form of god who is constant and omnipresent is important for the individual who is searching for an explanation of life.

Clergy. The power struggle with clergy is a result of the interpretation by individuals of their relationship with a higher power. The clergy are persons assigned to teach and remind their congregation of the relationship they have with their higher power. The clergy has had the position of go-between for individuals and their god. Being human, clergy exhibit the same range of responses to their mantle of authority as any other group of individuals, from kind and concerned, to stern and punitive. Conflicts with clergy are easily resolved if the parishioner can move to another parish or drive down the road to a different congregation. However, in some communities, there is no other choice of faith or congregation and the clergy hold ultimate power.

These struggles enhance feelings of powerlessness within the individual. For example, a woman in the Catholic faith who cannot afford another child, resorts to taking birth control pills. She may suffer guilt and powerless feelings as a result of her dilemma, hoping that the Pope will change his mind. The power that she attributes to the Pope places her in a state of powerlessness and in a power struggle.

Parents. Parents assume the task of raising and protecting their young. While the child is young this is fairly easily accomplished. However, adolescence hits the family like a lightning bolt, as the youth fights against the authority of his parents in an effort to establish his own mastery as he nears adulthood. This normal power struggle is painful and bewildering for both the child and his parents. It is a relief when one's child becomes an adult going through the struggles of parenthood and they return with the message that the parents were a lot more intelligent than they gave them credit for when they were rebelling against them.

Employers. Employers serve as parents-in-absentia for their employees sometimes. Depending on the self-esteem level of the employee and employer, the relationship can be nurturing or destructive. Is it necessary for the employee to fight his employer's every decision? Yet, those in authority are rarely loved and much too often feared for their perceived power over the employees. This difficulty relates to the feelings of powerlessness by the employee placed under another's rule. Additionally, the powerlessness of the employer is demonstrated by his inappropriate use of power to cover the conflict he feels inside that perhaps he won't be obeyed, the workers will revolt, or his decisions won't be correct ones.

As is true for the other power struggles that commonly occur, the conflict between the employer and employee can be diminished by an alteration of perception by one or both of the members in the struggle. For example, energetic young adults who work in a Fast Food restaurant may aspire to different careers when they finish college, but they choose the degree of happiness in their work situation by the interpretation they put on it, and the decision they have made to make the best of their present circumstances. Not only are these individuals happier at work, they please their employer more often and have loyal customers who return often to bask in their positive attitudes.

Military. In recent years, the military has learned about the need for individuals to express their freedom. The military has long been depicted as a force with total control over the individual and a tendency toward deliberate cruelty. However, the military has altered to express more human compassion and allowance for individuality, a change that leads older military members to question whether these newer and younger personnel will obey orders at all in an emergency. They feel that the military has lost some of its powerfulness by softening the approach to new recruits, In other words, the power of the military fed off the powerlessness it inflicted on its members, as is typical in any situation of abusive power.

Police. Police are employed to protect community citizens. However, frequent power struggles with police lead to the police being feared or despised. Members of society expect the police to answer their needs when they have trouble, but they are angered when they are given a speeding ticket. The individual may decide that the police are only there to harass him, as reflected in the complaint, "What do they mean there aren't enough of them to catch the dope dealers? There would be if they'd stop hiding on corners to catch middle-aged salesmen who are going five miles too fast in their cars."

Teachers. Teachers are expected to have superhuman traits. For instance, the first grade teacher must nurture each child's ego, cope with thirty wiggling six-year-olds, and, in the process, teach them all to read within nine months, a monumental task. The teacher finds herself challenged with the need to present learning as fun, need-fulfilling, empowering, freeing and, simultaneously, maintain control of a room full of restless children with short attention spans.

Add to this the constant power struggle expressed by every child to his teacher: "I don't have to do what you say, you're not my mother," and "Dad says you're a silly woman, so how can a silly person teach me anything?" This power struggle is present in all teacher-student relationships but varies in degree and expression as the student and teacher assess their perceptions of each other and the task before them.

The power struggle in education is changing with the attitudes of society. A college professor, used to being revered by students and asked for assistance, is accosted by an angry student waving a failing test paper and shouting, "Don't you feel ashamed that you couldn't teach me any better than this?" Add to this irresponsible attitude the pressure to decrease attrition rates in college and it becomes a wonder that any college faculty continue to teach.

Summary

Power struggles occur throughout the life span. Focusing on power resources and strengthening these resources yields positive perception of control/power and increased self-responsibility, which leads to improved or maintained health and smoother transitions to each new stage in growth and development.

Each of these power struggles is found in normal relationships in society. They occur regularly, but with a wide range of emotional interpretation. It is the individual's interpretation or perception of each situation that determines the degree of frustration, stress or anger that the occasion elicits.

References

Beattie, Melody. *Codependent No More: How To Stop Controlling Others and Start Caring for Yourself.* NY: Harper & Row, (1987).

Conway, Jim and Conway, Sally. *Women in Mid-Life Crisis.* Wheaton, IL: Tyndale House Publishers, Inc., (1985).

Dimond, Margaret and Jones, Susan Lynn. *Chronic Illness Across The Life Span.* Norwalk, CN; Appleton-Century-Crofts, (1983)

Gaylin, Willard. *Feelings: Our Vital Signs.* NY: Ballantine Books, (1979).

Ginott, Haim. *Between Parent and Child.* NY: Avon Books, (1965).

Ginott, Haim. *Between Parent and Teenager.* NY: Avon Books, (1969).

Glasser, William. *Reality Therapy For Parents.* Los Angeles, CA; Educator Training Center of the Institute for Reality Therapy, (1978).

Glasser, William. *Taking Effective Control of Your Life*. NY: Harper & Row, (1984).

Hart, Lois and Dalke, David. *The Sexes at Work: Improving Relationships Between Men & Women*. Englewood Cliffs, NJ: Prentice-Hall, Inc., (1983).

Henderson, George and Primeaux, Martha. *Transcultural Health Care*. Menlo Park, CA; Addison-Wesley Publishing Company, (1981).

Leman, Kevin. *The Birth Order Book: Why You Are The Way You Are*. NY: Dell Publishing, (1985).

Levine, Robert. Waiting is a power game. *Psychology Today*. April. 24-33, (1987).

Orque, Modesta Soberano; Bloch, Bobbie; and Monrroy, Lidia S. Ahumada. *Ethnic Nursing care: A Multicultural Approach*. St. Louis: C.V. Mosby Company, (1983).

Parreno, Sister Heide. Ethnic minority women and nurses in the health care setting. In Orque, Bloch and Monrroy (eds.). *Ethnic Nursing Care: A Multicultural Approach*. St. Louis: C. V. Mosby Company, (1983).

Thomas, Donna. Black American patient care. In Henderson, George and Primeaux, Martha (eds.) *Transcultural Health Care*. Menlo Park, CA: Addison-Wesley Publishing Company, (1981).

Thomas, Marlo. *Free To Be...You and Me*. NY: McGraw-Hill Book Company, (1974).

5

Power to the People: Health Promotion

N. Rinehart, P. Kepple, and A. Arguello

Introduction

Increasing numbers of individuals are gaining awareness of their responsibilities concerning their health status. They are joining health spas, starting walking programs, buying larger percentages of their food supplies from health food stores, exercising along with aerobics tapes, and attending stress management and journaling classes. Improved health, it seems, is being encouraged by everyone from ministers to starlets, reformed drug addicts to fitness experts. However, the main group of professionals most nearly connected with the human body and its correct functioning, health care professionals, are hardly represented in this army of health awareness advocates.

Promoting health is the objective toward which all health care professionals must move (Ardell, 1977). It is more positive to maintain or improve the client's health than to wait for them to come in to repair damage that could have been avoided with some health promotion teaching and recognition of the importance of prevention. In assigning responsibility for health to the client, the health care professional is helping the client increase his perception of personal control (Miller, 1983).

Encouragement of the client to be in control of his own health status is a relatively new stance for health care professionals. There is a dramatic lack of health care promotion and maintenance in the required classes of professional schools in the health care field. One can identify this lack by merely examining the number of hours spent in classes dealing with disease as opposed to those with a health promotion focus.

Implications of Health Promotion

Wherever the concept is accepted that disease is a symptom of an unhealthy lifestyle, a raging controversy exists. Society is becoming more aware of its health needs. An awareness revolution exists and is gaining converts daily. Knowledge and education are the revolutionaries' weapons. The quest for optimal health is the battleground.

The whole fabric of civilization is being torn asunder and rewoven before our very eyes. Toffler (1980) wrote one of the most informative books of the eighties, *The Third Wave*. It addresses the sweeping changes in family, marriage, the economy, work and play (Toffler, 1980).

The stress accompanying these changes has so affected mental health that stress management has become a national enterprise. It is interesting to note that stress management did not come to society's attention until quite recently. Biofeedback makes use of technology to counteract the effects of a technological society. Society has entered the space age, the age of information, the age of Aquarius.

Technology has erased borders, and shrunk the planet. The nuclear plant accident in Russia affected the health of thousands in many different countries. How does one keep up with not only one's personal health, but also the global community? It begins with the exercising of one's personal power to make informed choices. Stress management makes sense and is an active personal power exercise. It has been demonstrated and researched that the effects of unrelieved stress are ultimately death. Selye (1976) felt it to be of such great importance that he has spent a lifetime studying and researching stress. Selye's books, *The Stress of Life* (1976) and *Stress Without Distress* (1974), are monuments to that endeavor and a gift to all of humanity. There is an abundance of literature relating to stress management available.

In many instances, standard health care treats symptoms while the roots of the problem remain. What does this mean in terms of an effective treatment? When are clients asked about their lifestyle? Have they ever been asked? The usual health care routine is to ask about the symptoms of the problem and then order a treatment for the relief of those symptoms.

The physician and the nurse have differing viewpoints from which the client is assessed (Barry, 1984). The physician's primary focus is to cure disease; nursing education emphasizes the caring component of health care (Flynn and Heffron, 1984). Both have educations heavily loaded in the domain of illness care. Neither profession has viewed prevention as warranting a heavy emphasis in the course work required to sit for licensure boards.

Even so, both professions identify the importance of health promotion as opposed to waiting for illness to overcome the client. Why, then, are the educational systems of these professions so encumbered with studying disease? Where are the representatives of these professions in the health promotion field? The practice of medicine should actually be called illness care rather than health care as "it is built upon diagnosis of disease, the repair of the injury, and the treatment of symptoms" (Travis and Ryan, 1987, p.15). Some health care professionals are working in this area, but lack of funding and society's failure to see the issue as important have kept the number small relative to the population that needs to be reached (Stanhope and Lancaster, 1984).

In Japan, it is common to find health care emphasized on a daily basis in places of employment. It is more cost effective to prevent illness in the employee and save the company from paying for sick time.

It is a sad commentary on the state of Western society that insurance companies more readily cover expenses for illness than for health promotion. There is an obvious lack of understanding or initiative on the part of some insurance companies to promote health maintenance. A complete physical and appropriate health promotion teaching could save insurance companies a large amount of money.

The question that emerges is who benefits from this distortion? The fact that it took years before health insurance would cover a tubal ligation, but willingly paid for women to have multiple children, is an example of a lack of financial, moral and/or social enlightenment. Who made the most money from repeated pregnancies, rather than a simple operation? It was assuredly not the family that had to support these children. Was the health care system lining someone's pockets rather than providing health care that had its emphasis in health promotion.

Due to a lack of health promotion funding, those health care professionals who wish to help in prevention of illness and promotion of health are unable to pay for what is an obvious need in society. As long as "health" insurance rewards illness, it is more precise to call it "illness" insurance, for there is little correlation between the insurance companies and health promotion or maintenance.

Without the financial backing of the government or insurance companies, there is financial risk for the health care professional who teaches health maintenance and promotion. Without financial support, many health care professionals simply cannot afford to spend time outside of the traditional health care system, even if it makes more sense to them than waiting for illness to bring clients to them.

Dentists are realizing that the improvement of dental care has eliminated much dental illness, while adding the responsibility of health teaching and promotion to their practices. However, some dental insurance persists in not covering dental exams or prophylactic treatments.

Individuals with eating disorders often find it difficult to get insurance coverage for hospitalization in an eating disorder unit, but they have no problem getting coverage for the cholecystectomy, myocardial infarction or vein stripping which may be a direct result of the eating disorder.

Mental health care is also seen by many companies as not important enough to be paid for, but the physical manifestations that result are covered. The high number of hospital beds taken up by those whose emotional state caused the physical illness is steadily growing. It is more logical to provide preventive mental health care than to wait for the stomach lining to perforate, the heart to stop or the stroke to occur. Logic does not seem to be a major ingredient in the health care system at this time. Concerned individuals have begun to look elsewhere for assistance in health maintenance. The obvious individual to rely on most is oneself; who else knows the individual better than himself? Self-care has become a catch phrase for the self-help book market in recent years.

Self-Care

Self-care is the care one takes of one's own health needs. It includes health promotion, illness prevention, and caring for oneself when ill (Hill and Smith, 1985). Self-care does not mean forsaking access to health care professionals, but doing what is possible for oneself (Sehnert, 1985). The term "self-care" came into being when individuals became interested in their own health needs and promoting health (Riehl-Siska, 1985).

Not all individuals are interested in their own health needs. Regardless of the emphasis on health promotion and responsibility for one's own self-care, many clients persist in ignoring their self-care needs (Steiger and Lipson, 1985). Clients must be carefully assessed for their own values and encouraged to be responsible for themselves. The client who will not listen, learn, or be responsible should at least have the information written down for him and sign a waiver that indicates that he takes full responsibility for doing as he wishes with the information and suggestions given to him. The decision to do nothing is just as much a decision as one to act on the information presented.

Locus of Control

Health promotion can be achieved by both internal and external types of individuals. The person with an internal locus of control assumes the responsibility for his health and the person with the external locus of control will do whatever he is told to do by someone he sees as an authority figure. The externally controlled person will not learn to listen to his own body, nor will he continue his regimen of health promotion if his authority figure dies, moves or withdraws his support. Internal control is more conducive to consistent health promotion behaviors.

The client's locus of control may conflict with the health care professional's expectation of client behavior. Figure 5-1 demonstrates the relationship between internal and external loci of control and the anticipated role of the client in relation to the health care professional. The function of the client in the traditional care setting, where an external locus of control is expected, is that of dependence and interdependence with the care provider, indicating more control on the part of the health care professional.

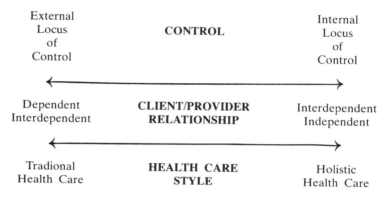

Fig. 5-1. Locus of Control-Care Provider Continuum

Conversely, the client with the internal locus of control will be more gratified with the prospect of a partnership with the health care professional, the provider supporting the idea that the client will work with the system via interdependence and independence. This more internally controlled role blends well with a holistic health care system. The rapid evolution of holistic health care centers and adjunctive health therapies such as acupressure and therapeutic touch indicates that Western populations are becoming more internal in their loci of control, more interested in building their personal power.

Reality Therapy

Reality Therapy encourages the adoption of more productive behaviors into an individual's lifestyle. It is more efficacious to maintain and promote health than to become ill and risk not regaining the prior status of health after recovery.

Glasser (1976) suggests replacing negative, harmful, addictive behaviors with positive and healthful addictive behaviors. The characteristics of a positive addiction are: 1) noncompetitive, 2) easy and doesn't require much mental effort, 3) does not depend on others participating, 4) has some value (spiritual, emotional, or physical), 5) with persistence, performance will improve, and 6) can be done without self-criticism (Glasser, 1976).

All behavior is purposeful in meeting a need (Glasser, 1984). As individuals have choices in the behaviors that will meet their needs, they may choose effective or ineffective behaviors. If a chosen behavior does not meet a need as well as the individual wishes, he can select another behavior aimed at meeting that need and appraise its effectiveness in being need-fulfilling (Glasser, 1984).

Values Clarification

Values contribute to health promotion by way of motivation for actions taken. Everyone values health. Some individuals expect another person to achieve health for them without the expectation of needing to do any work to achieve it. In going through the clarification process, the consequences of certain behavior choices can be identified and the client can then decide the level of his responsibility for his own health. Health care professionals employ a small portion of this decision-making process when they as if getting home and keeping the bill down for the hospital stay is important, and then advise the client that he will have pneumonia if he does not cough and deep breathe, resulting in a longer hospital stay and a larger bill. Clarifying one's values motivates the individual to look at the consequences, to consider his options carefully and to make the decision that is right for him, without pressure from the health care professional or his family.

CASE STUDY

Mona is a 43 year-old white female. She is a wife and mother of three children. Her children are 17, 14, and 2 years old. The youngest of the children has the long term disability of cerebral palsy which requires special schooling and physical therapy. Along with the immense needs of her family, Mona's mother is an elderly widow recovering from a cerebrovascular accident.

Mona's husband of 20 years is currently working long hours for a construction company but is facing a layoff when the jog is completed. Mona works, part-time during the summer season and full-time during the winter, as an LPN at the local nursing home. Mona works the night shift to accommodate the needs of her family during the daytime.

The family is active in school and community events. Both adolescents participate in football, basketball, and track. Both Mona and her husband enjoy involvement in the PTA, civic groups, sports and various social activities. The youngest member of the family has her own special needs, physical therapy three times a week and daily developmental interventions.

One morning, Mona stopped to visit a co-professional and friend, Val, between car pooling the children to school and taking the baby to speech class. Val is a registered nurse at the local health clinic. Their conversation began with how busy the children were this time of the year and about Mona starting back to work full-time this week.

"You look a little overspent this week, already," Val commented.

Mona replied with a sigh, "I feel exhausted and it's only Tuesday. I don't know how I'm going to make it through the rest of the winter at this rate."

"Is there something new going on?"

"Not really, I just feel so tired and run down. Maybe it's just getting used to the night shift again."

Val suggested to Mona that she stop at the clinic and have a physical, possibly some bloodwork.

Mona replied, "I have so much to do, with the kids, work, the house, my mom's house and groceries, and my poor husband. I don't even have time for me. Besides, our insurance won't cover a physical. I don't have any spare pennies this month."

Mona rose slowly from her chair and began to leave, chatting superficially with Val about car pooling for the next day. After Mona's departure, Val began to wonder what she could do as a community health nurse. She realized that many of her friends as well as other women in the community were dealing with the same issues. Why was personal health and well-being last on the list of priorities for these women?

Assessment

How can this community health nurse reach Mona without her first having to suffer from a major illness and needing to come to the clinic? In that case, when Mona reaches the clinic the focus will be one of illness rather than wellness. In illness, choices are limited by the requirements for regaining health, limiting personal power.

Mona has many factors already limiting her perception of personal power. These factors include: family, special needs of a child, financial responsibilities, household care and many others. She is stressed by these limitations every day. The likelihood of this client demonstrating a positive response to another limitation is close to nil.

As it currently stands, the health care system brings health care to the client as a limitation. This is largely due to the fact that interventions primarily occur after the illness has become too difficult for the client to manage on her own. If this community health nurse follows the traditional view of health, she promotes feelings of powerlessness over illness in both her clients and herself. Once in treatment, the health care professional usually observes the requisite course of illness care instead of creatively meeting the needs of the individual.

Nursing, as all other health care professions, falls into the dilemma of negativity. The basis of nursing care is developed from the philosophy of "taking care of" or "fixing" what is wrong with the client. Interventions in nursing come from the negative stance that illness is already in existence. Most, if not all, of the currently accepted nursing diagnoses come out of following the illness path itself. If the client is on a medication that would blur vision, for instance, the nursing diagnosis becomes "Potential for injury related to vision impairment," instead of "Potential for mood and functioning alteration related to medication."

Nursing care validates the sickness or illness role. Nursing care meets a variety of needs, many of these are dependent needs of the client. Support systems usually remain docile until extreme circumstances kick them into gear, thereby validating the unhealthy behavior of getting support "when ill." Personal efforts then become focused on meeting needs, not on moving forward in growth and achievement.

Looking at nursing care from this viewpoint, two choices are apparent: 1) allow the client to continue to develop dysfunctional coping patterns, eventually leading to illness (the standard time to approach health care providers) or 2) become positively aggressive in providing the client with healthy support systems and information. Developing a new focus of health care is the current challenge. Beginning with "potential strengths," healthy options for the client can be developed.

Using this focus, Mona is seen in a new way. With the amount of responsibility she has and the time frame in which she accomplishes it, she appears to be a very successful organizer. Given more avenues to choose from, she may have more time to herself, time to meet her own needs. A new health-oriented nursing diagnosis of "Potential to meet own stress reduction needs," identifies client power and places the health care provider in a monitoring role rather than a "need-meeting" one.

The traditional health care focus is on limitation, what clients can't do, and the actions they must take to return to health. In this system, the health care professional identifies problems and helps Mona turn them into motivational activities. One "problem area" for Mona is obesity. The current nursing diagnosis would be "Alteration in nutrition—more than body requirements." It would appear that the choices are limited to reducing the amount of requirements taken in, increasing exercise and weight management.

However, approaching this problem from a "health" perspective the health care professional might use a nursing diagnosis such as "Potential for increased physical well being" or "Potential for increased socialization." The client now has a much wider range of choices, thus, more personal power that she may place greater value on. These choices are focused on already healthy clients, with encouragement toward a more optimal functioning instead of only "back to normal." The focus moves from negative to positive motivation. Interventions for Mona could then revolve around such things as dinner clubs with a nutritional focus and an increase in the number of her recreational activities. This positiveness increases the value the client may place on the intervention.

The nurse in this setting needs basic assessment information. Looking at Mona and her current level of functioning, both the nurse and client identify the following stressors:

Family

1. Child care/special needs care
2. Caring for an elderly parent
3. Adolescents at home
4. Working/night shift
5. Husbands layoff

Personal

1. Overweight
2. 43 years old
3. Caretaker
4. Support system
5. Female
6. Main financial support six months out of year

Un the conventional health care system, stress is seen as a negative influence, increasing the risk for illness. Health care continues to be focused on illness. The question health care providers need to ask is "is stress negative?" Stress can be a positive influence in the growth and development of the individual. Seen in this light, the client's power is greatly increased and directly related to the choices they make.

The health care professional needs to look at the basic perceptions of the individual: her value of self, body image, and relationship to the world around her. An accurate assessment of these attitudes in the client is a way to initiate client responsibility for her own health care. If a particular difficulty or identified problem is not seen as stressful by the client, inducement toward healthier patterns of behavior will not succeed.

Self esteem is directly affected by the amount of personal power one has. The assessment of Mona and the demands being put on her by her environment indicated that her personal power was limited. Mona has three children, a husband, job, and parent requiring her attention in a day's time. Her investment in herself is related to how much time she has left after meeting the needs of her immediate external environment, and the value she places on herself. Health care professionals must change the focus of assessing clients from a negative disease orientation to a positive strength identification and facilitate the promotion of increased self esteem and personal power. It would appear that the objectives of health care revolve around

assessing and maintaining the illness state. With the focus on finding
problems or seeing clients in a negative light, why would clients wish
to spend time looking at what they're not doing?

Through the use of the nursing diagnosis and medical diagnosis
systems, loss of personal power is promoted, inflicting a major blow
to the self esteem. Prior to the ill client entering the health care
system, the client's positive self esteem and personal power is already
threatened. The health care system validates the client's negative value
of himself by using diagnostic processes that focus on the problems
the client is presenting (See Figure 5-2).

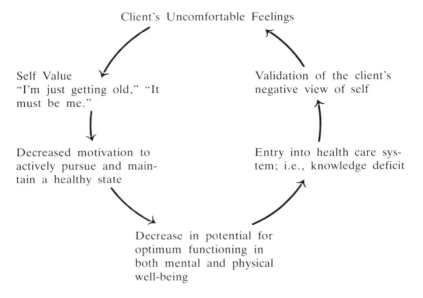

Fig. 5-2. Client's Feelings

Health care becomes cyclic in nature, rarely moving beyond the
stated limitations. This system not only represents clients as being
unable to meet their own needs, but expects them to become passive
in that system. Figure 5-3 shows an assessment with corresponding
diagnoses derived from the current health system. This assessment
focuses on Mona's shortcomings. It is typical of what is seen in most
health care organizations. Each of the interventions are trite as well
as power-limiting.

In setting up a plan of intervention, most health care professionals
see the care plan's as indicating that the professional "takes care of"
the client. The moment the client steps into the system she is expected
to become the passive or weak member of the system. The client is
quickly divested of her personal power. More power is taken away

when the plan of care is devised, as it is rarely created with the input of the client.

The health care system has predetermined criteria for meeting the needs of the client. For example: knowledge deficit will be followed by a mode of educational intervention designed to inform the client of what the health care system believes she needs to know. This is where the health care system sets the client up to either fail or become passive. If the client's value of self or belief system is different from that of the health care organization, she will be coerced into compliance or will be neglected by the system. If Mona does not follow her prescribed diet, the system then perceives her as a noncompliant and a poor investment risk.

1. Obesity/Excess weight

2. Increased family demands
   a. special needs child
   b. husband's layoff
   c. part-time to full time
   d. recovering parent
   e. new school year
   f. adolescent issues

3. Physical/Somatic Difficulties
   a. low energy level
   b. increased use of physical energy
   c. care of body discomforts

1. Nutrition; alteration in more than body requirements; body image disturbance; impaired potential (home) health maintenance management

2. Anxiety, moderate; knowledge deficit; ineffective individual coping; diversional activity deficit; sleep pattern disturbance; parenting, alteration in potential

3. Alteration in comfort: pain; health management deficit

Fig. 5-3. Nursing Diagnoses from Negative Viewpoint

The conventional system of the health care organization is set up to function in the following way:

Medicine	**Nursing**	**Client**
Diagnosis	Follow Through	Passive Acceptance
Prescription →	Care Taking →	of Treatment

Fig. 5-4. Traditional Expectations in Health Care

Figure 5-5 shows change that needs to occur to give the client back her personal power and responsibility.

Medicine	Nursing	Client
Options	Mentor	Decision Maker
Knowledge →	Manager →	Follow Through
Advisor	Support System	

Fig. 5-5. Recommended Change in Perception

In recent years, many health care professionals have begun to build a system that focuses on the positive entities of the client. Decisions must be made from a positive value system, empowering the client, not the professional. A growth-promoting diagnostic process could be measured in steps forward instead of steps remade, validating and promoting positive behavior and the personal power of the client. The following are examples of diagnoses that promote growth and personal power:

1. Effective reality testing
2. Potential for increased self esteem
3. Increased effective coping (potential, actual)
4. Potential for increased quality of life
5. Increased intimacy; individual, family or couple (potential, actual)
6. Increased learning abilities

Fig. 5-6. Positive Nursing Diagnoses for Mona

The key to helping Mona is strengthening her existing resources, building a positive experience of the system and providing support. The practitioner is on the inside of the system and has the ability to manipulate the system to provide efficient plans to meet the stated needs of the client.

Possible interventions that the health care professional could provide include:

Offer daily/hourly health promotion groups while clients wait for family members, doctors' appointments, and treatments

Do evening classes

Go out to schools, businesses, and hospitals to teach programs during lunch hours

Supply written materials for such things as employee programs in businesses

Employ active teen groups/volunteer groups for babysitting/-chores; e.g. Candy Stripers

Recruit other women in the community to make sure health care issues are addressed at social events: exercise, cooking-good nutrition, dinner clubs, recipe books, stress release weekend retreats, community centers

With physician support, provide incentives such as free visit for
child when Mom or Dad gets a physical
Token economy—with business participation—free lunch coupons
for getting BP checked; weight loss programs
Screening clinics that travel to businesses and work areas in the
community
Extended clinic hours
Provide list of videos/audiotapes for use in car and at home
Newsletter on current health issues

One option for meeting Mona's needs may be finding cost efficient
child care services for one or two evenings per week, allowing her
to sleep, exercise or spend time with her husband. This may be a
needed step in meeting her multitude of other needs. The health care
provider in this situation can be the resource person or the empowering
force for the client. She could connect many clients with the same
difficulties to help facilitate a group support system. For example,
she could help Mona, as well as other clients experiencing weight
management changes, form a dance club with an exercise focus. The
nurse might also help Mona find recreational activities in the local
area suitable for families to help her increase her activity level.

It is of utmost importance for the client to experience the health care
system as a positive experience: encouraging the client to maintain her
own autonomy, make her own self satisfying decisions and resume her
health care responsibilities. This will help to ensure that movement
through the health care system will be a positive experience for the
client. A positive experience can be described as one in which all
participants are able to maintain a favorable view of themselves and
the world around them. If the health care provider will manipulate
the system to produce what the client needs, both will experience
the interaction as positive. For example, the nurse in this situation
has access to many people and community agencies. If the nurse
manipulates the system by connecting clients to increase the number
of mothers available to help car pool, all will experience the system
as positive, supportive and a place for helpful networking.

The nurse in this situation can be an effective manager, resourceful
and invested, but if the clients themselves are not motivated to take
back their personal power, the system will work for neither. It will
also continue to be experienced by all participants as negative.

Health Promotion Measures

Self-Responsibility. The most significant aspect of health is well
within the control of each individual. That he has elected not to
exercise his powers of preventive health care amounts to nothing less

than self-destructive behavior. The consequences of not taking personal responsibility for preventive health measures are the diseases that have plagued western society. These diseases require a medium where the roots of illness can take hold and flourish, eventually producing that bitter fruit known by many mysterious medical names. That medium is the lifestyle, to which is added the needed ingredients to produce any particular illness. Each individual is responsible for his lack of health, and believing otherwise is to accept powerlessness. Why have they entrusted their health to others?

It is of interest to note that society has been encouraged, from a myriad of sources, to accept illness as a natural and inevitable process. How often is it heard, "Your doctor knows best." The prevailing message has been that the treatment of disease and dysfunction are the sole realm of health care practitioners. Clients have come to expect magic potions called medicine and feel untreated if they do not receive at least one cryptically written prescription.

Paradigm shifts are increasingly evident in society in the areas of health, environment, and education. These can be seen in the ever-widening personal involvement by the individual questioning previously unquestioned practices and beliefs. It is the intention of this chapter to promote this practice, to invite dissatisfaction and unrest with an imperfect and self-promoting health care system and encourage the sense of self-responsibility for health.

The paradigm shift has been to take more responsibility for one's own health and to rely less on the science of medicine. What is needed is a complete or whole approach to health. Hence, the concept of *holistic* health has arisen, but it is hardly a new or novel idea. Where science has resorted to a reductionist viewpoint, holistic health practitioners are returning to the whole.

Specialists have narrowed the view of the individual to a specific disorder or body system. To treat a disorder that has a host of causative factors with a single and simplistic approach is partial treatment, not recognizing the client as a whole person with parts that interrelate.

Advances in technology have enabled the science of diagnostics to produced wondrous results. The client is quickly informed that he has heart disease. *Question: Why did I have a heart attack? Answer: Because an artery in your heart became blocked. Solution: Coronary bypass surgery.* The question that demands an answer is: How has the client caused or allowed this health problem to occur? Was he a smoker? Did he eat a diet high in saturated fats? Did he have a sedantary life style? Was he a heavy drinker? This places the responsibility with the client. This question also addresses the concept of power and powerlessness. It is powerlessness to subscribe to external sources of illness and remedies. It is empowering to increase knowledge and use internal powers to forge the destiny of one's own health. The importance of knowledge or education cannot be overstated.

If the individual is on a serious quest for health, some basic concepts must be understood. Some of these can be found in the popular literature of today. For example, Ferguson (*The Aquarian Conspiracy*, 1980) suggests a quiet revolution aimed at reclaiming personal power, and Mendelsohn (*Male Practice*, 1981) provides a chilling view of remaining powerless. Other concepts upon which holistic and preventive health movements have been built include: natural is better, use your body for what it was designed for, wear clothing for comfort and warmth, and avoid all mind-altering substances.

Holistic health practice covers a wide range of behavior, knowledge, and beliefs. This chapter does not cover everything in this field. However, the goal is to emphasize the potential for increased personal control through the application of health promotion measures.

Nutrition. One health promotion measure is to adopt a healthier mode of eating. Central to society is the need to eat, with a proportionate amount of time and energy directed at meeting that need. Eating rates high on a survival hierarchy, as demonstrated by the effortless yet urgent suckling of an infant at his mother's breast.

Food is a separate issue and must not be confused with eating. Selection of food is a conscious behavior choice directed at satisfying a need. The choice may be affected by many different factors. These factors can include social and cultural aspects, type and amount of knowledge of food or even a response to one of the senses. The food dilemma is confused even further and more deliberately by various agencies and interested parties. The food industry has spent millions of dollars to influence the individual buyer's choice. Massive amounts of research time and money have been spent determining which packaging color schemes are the most attractive. Every psychological ploy is undertaken to compete for the food dollar. Does it outrage society to find out that the minds of children are being used to influence the buyer's choice? The final indignity is that this occurs on quiet Saturday mornings while the parent sleeps late, feeling safe from intrusion. Television commercials selling sugarcoated, nutritionless cereals are clever, power-robbing devices aimed at children.

There are government agencies set up to regulate the food industry and protect consumers, but many see the government's requirements for fortified or enriched grain products as ludicrous, leaving what was once a nutritious substance an empty package of calories. The bastardization of the food supply is indeed tragic. The question is raised regarding choices and power. What effect do contributions of large sums of money by a major industry to governmental candidates have on the government's decisions about these same industries later on? Personal health is being affected by these governmental decisions every day. It is impossible to not discuss these influences in regard to nutritional choice and power.

In *Sugar Blues*, Dufty (1975) reports the methods used by a former president of the United States to decrease the effectiveness of the Pure Food and Drug Laws. The use of the dangerous coal tar product, saccharin, was a direct result of this intervention. Saccharin was finally banned, but only after use by millions of people for decades. Dufty's book has the potential to dramatically alter the individual's outlook on the food industry and adds to his power base of knowledge.

Essential nutrients have been systematically removed from food in an effort to retard spoilage and prolong shelf life. This can be seen most dramatically in bread that has been processed to the stage where it can sit on an unrefrigerated shelf for weeks without any sign of spoilage. Most reconstituted foods have had a number of chemicals added to enhance flavor, replace lost vitamins and minerals and enhance the color or flavor of the product. What is the effect on the human body by all of these chemicals? Multiply these different chemicals hundreds of times and they add up to an amazing amount of non food substances entering the body daily. Even though the human body has mechanisms to rid itself of these unwanted chemicals, it can only handle a certain amount.

The F & G Emporium, as in fast and greasy, requires brief mention at this point. The average American now eats one third of his meals away from home, often in this type of establishment. Unfortunately, the human body cannot survive on greasy, nutritionally empty sticks that were once potatoes, white processed bread and fatty meat. Add a caffeinated, highly sugared drink, and the results are an obese society afflicted with malnutrition and riddled with disease.

Mental Health. Health is a many faceted concept. One of those is mental health, which is inseparable from physical health. The viewpoint that separates mind and body compartmentalizes not only the individual's illness process, but also the treatment of the whole individual. A cognitive event results in various bodily systems interacting in an orchestrated fashion. The brain produces a thought in much the same way as the heart provides blood circulation. Both are contingent on the whole individual for producing an end result. The body is a system made up of a number of subsystems providing for the whole. The brain is considered to be the least understood organ of the body. It is exceedingly complex in its function and structure.

The brain is regarded as the domain of mental health. There are a variety of drugs that are prescribed to treat "mental illness" such as schizophrenia and bipolar illness, commonly known as manic depressive illness. These two mental illnesses are now recognized as having a physiological basis. Parkinson's Disease, another brain disorder, is characterized by muscular rigidity, tremor and a diminished ability to make voluntary movements. Autopsy studies of these patients have shown that the portion of the brain that produces a substance known as dopamine degenerated. Parkinsons Disease is treated with a chemical substance L-Dopa which is converted to dopamine in the brain. Neural function, as with any cellular function, is a complex electrical and chemical process which requires equally complex chemicals. In the aforementioned disorders, treatment is by replacement of chemicals endogenous to the brain.

In addition, several opiate-like substances have been discovered in the brain. The jogging craze has produced the well known "runner's high." This is a result of the production of endorphins and enkephalins. These chemicals are known to affect pain relief and mood. The unspoken statement here is that the physical state of the brain affects the mind. It is a fact that the deficiency or the availability of certain brain chemicals can produce mental illness or sustain mental health (Travis and Ryan, 1988). These complex chemicals are manufactured from the available nutrients in the body. It also follows that if these nutrients are not available, the quality of vital brain chemicals is affected.

The mind/body concept requires a look at how the mind affects the body. The emphasis in recent years on stress management has been seen as a panacea to today's modern ills. There is unquestionably a state of sensory overload in this increasingly complex society.

There has been an outpouring of mental health books in recent years. A diversity of readings is suggested by experts to avoid linear thinking. Cultivate personal power to make it grow. As awareness expands, powerlessness diminishes.

Meditation. Meditation speaks directly to the power of the individual, the wholeness of man and humanity, the universe, the cosmos. It is not surprising that the men who have had the most affect on the world have been those who have practiced meditation: Jesus Christ, Mahatma Gandhi, K'ung-fu-tzu (Confucius), Buddha (Siddartha Gautama) and Lao-Tse, founder of Taoism.

In his book, *The Tao of Pooh*, Hoff (1982) presents some principles of Taoism. Tao, (pronounced Dao) can be roughly translated as "The Way." The Way is that which is behind everything in the cosmos. It is a harmonious flow which when upset by mankind causes disharmony. From the holistic viewpoint this might be demonstrated by the forests of the earth. They serve to clean the air, produce oxygen, and provide a habitat for other animals of the earth. They are being destroyed or cut down at an alarming rate. The biosphere is at risk, endangering every living thing on the Earth. Although the infinite relationship of the forest to everything else can never be fully stated, it can be understood. Some American Indians worshipped the sun, the moon, plants and animals. They understood Tao, and the hunting of the buffalo to near extinction must have been seen as the act of primitive minds. As with Tao, the power of the mind cannot be fully stated, but it can be understood through the practice of meditation.

Although there are many variations of meditation techniques, the results are similar. There are no rules about the timing of meditation, but the period of sleep preparation is an excellent time to meditate. The benefits of meditation include: decreased blood pressure and pulse, increased tolerance of stress, increased oxygen uptake, increased relaxation response and increased creativity. As with all activities, an excess of time spent in meditation removes the individual from the real world and can become a negative, or unhealthy, addictive behavior.

Physical Improvement. Physical power is no less important than any other aspect of power. The ability to wake up in the morning and feel physically well is a feeling of power. If the body is viewed as the vehicle for the essence called life then the importance of care for the vehicle is evident. What needs to be emphasized is a total body form of physical activity such as swimming or walking. A physically healthy body radiates power in the form of energy.

Rest. One of the most astounding abilities of the human body is one that is commonly taken for granted, the altered state of consciousness called sleep. Sleep is a time when the conscious mind is at rest and the unconscious mind has freedom to roam wherever our dreams take us. It is a dimension of total possibility. For the physical body, the sleep cycle is a time for healing, rebuilding and purification. Muscle relaxing exercises can be important for restful sleep. It is possible to go to sleep in a tense state and awaken feeling tired.

Summary

This chapter examined the empowerment found in the process of health promotion. It was advocated that clients increase their levels of personal power by taking charge of their health maintenance and becoming partners with their health care providers, rather than passive recipients of care. The dilemma of the ruination of food supplies was addressed, as were the issues of mental health and the need for rest. A case study provides examples of more positive assessment of clients, with an emphasis on health rather than illness.

References

Ardell, Donald. *High Level Wellness: An Alternative To Doctors, Drugs and Disease.* New York: Bantam Books, (1977).
Barry, Patricia. *Psychosocial Nursing Assessment and Intervention.* Philadelphia: J.B.Lippincott Company, (1984).

Dufty, William. *Sugar Blues*. New York: Warner Books, Inc, (1975).

Ferguson, Marilyn. *The Aquarian Conspiracy*. Los Angeles: J.P. Tarch, Inc, (1980).

Flynn, Janet-Beth and Aeffron, Phyllis. *Nursing: From Concept To Practice*. Bowie, MD: Brady Communications Company, (1984).

Glasser, William. *Positive Addiction*. New York: Harper & Row, (1976).

Glasser, William. *Take Effective Control of Your Life*. New York: Harper & Row, (1984).

Hoff, Benjamin. *The Tao of Pooh*. New York: Penguin Books, (1982).

Hill, Lyda and Smith, Nancy. *Self-Care Nursing: Promotion of Health*. Englewood Cliffs, NJ: Prentice-Hall, Inc, (1985).

Lao-tse. *Tao Te Ching*. Penguin Books: Harmondsworth, Middlesex, England, (1963).

Lappe, Frances Moore. *Diet for a Small Planet*. New York: Ballantine Books, (1971).

Mendelsohn, Robert S. *Male Practice*. Chicago: Contemporary Books, Inc, (1981).

Miller, Judith. *Coping With Chronic Illness: Overcoming Powerlessness*. Philadelphia: F.A. Davis Company, (1983).

Rice, Edward. *Eastern Definitions*. New York: Doubleday & Company, Inc, (1978).

Riehl-Siska, Joan. *The Science and Art of Self-Care*. Norwalk, CN: Appleton-Century-Crofts, (1985).

Sattilaro, Anthony J. *Living Well Naturally*. Boston: Houghton Mifflin Company, (1984).

Sattilaro, Anthony J. *Recalled by Life*. Boston: Houghton Mifflin Company, (1982).

Sehnert, Kenneth. *SelfCare/WellCare*. Minneapolis: Augsburg Publishing House, (1985).

Selye, Hans. *Stress Without Distress*. New York: Signet, (1974).

Selye, Hans. *The Stress of Life*. NY: McGraw-Hill, (1976).

Stanhope, Marcia and Lancaster, Jeanette. *Community Health Nursing: Process and Practice for Promoting Health*. St. Louis: C.V. Mosby, (1984).

Steiger, Nancy and Lipson, Juliene. *Self-Care Nursing: Theory & Practice*. Bowie, MD: Brady Communications Company, Inc, (1985).

Toffler, Alvin. *The Third Wave*. New York: Banton Books, Inc., (1980).

Travis, John and Ryan, Regina. *Wellness Workbook* (2nd edition). Berkeley, CA: Ten Speed Press, (1988).

Vithaldas, Yogi. *The Yoga System of Health & Relief from Tension*. New York: Cornerstone Library, (1957).

6

Power and the Family

N. Rinehart and L. Samenfeld

Introduction

A family is two or more people who have emotional ties to each other and have, at some point, lived together. A family is the most influential factor in the development of a person's personality and is the base from which everyone learns about the outside world (Johnston. 1980). The degree of affection and support within the family for each member influences the person for the rest of his life (Jones, 1980). Weinhold (1987) believes that most, if not all, emotional and physical disease originates from a dysfunctional family. The family has a distinct personality of its own, as well as being a collective of individual pesrsonalities. A unit with its own judgments and feelings, the family is a complicated composite of its members (Jones, 1980). It also molds the beliefs of each member about personal power. A family's interpretation of its power is reflective of not only each individual and his perception of personal power, but the sense of power of the whole family. Each member of the family contributes his or her own personality to blend in with the others' for the benefit or detriment of all.

Parenting requires no formal education yet makes the biggest impact on a person's life of any job available to mankind. Parenting styles are learned from one's parents. With the best intentions, each person passes the heritage of his ancestors on to his children (Tapia, 1980).

In the case of an individual not eager to pass along certain parenting styles to his children, change is possible, although difficult. There are support groups to help parents work on parenting skills and on themselves to resist old patterns of parenting. For example, Toughlove parent groups support parents with troublesome adolescents. Reality Therapy parent training sessions identify the difference between punishment and discipline similar to that seen in Figure 6-1. These groups enhance feelings of power, control and responsibility in the parent and thus, his child (York and York, 1987). Parenting occurs in a variety of situations.

There are many diverse family compositions in today's society. Although the traditional family is composed of a mother, father and children, the changing family structure in recent years necessitates the inclusion of this nontraditional family, which includes several types of families: blended, single heads of the household, gay couples, and heterosexual couples without children.

Family secrets indicate some of the power that can be found within a family. These secrets may involve a wide range of subjects: that the mother has a drinking problem, Tommy is retarded, Sally has had an abortion or that great-grandmother was a different race from the rest of the family. "It is well documented that family attitudes and actions affect the timing of the initial identification of illness, the therapeutic process, the type and length of hospitalization, and the patient's placement in the community" (Dimond and Jones, 1983, p. 93). Changes within the family structure can promote power struggles. The members of the family will resist any disruption in the pattern of behaviors they have become comfortable with. Ineffective as they may be, patterns of behavior in the family are familiar, and new and unknown behaviors are therefore threatening.

Systems Theory

As an open system, the family functions in the training and protection of its members, but it is less open than many other systems. The knowledge that within this system one can expect love and acceptance draws a person back throughout his life, seeking that expected comfort not found in other groups or systems outside of the family. The family is influenced by other systems outside of its boundaries, but it tends to resist any abrupt changes, selectively choosing those influences which are allowed to enter and alter the members of the family system.

PUNISHMENT	DISCIPLINE
1. As a result of anger.	1. Friendly approach.
2. Punisher takes the responsibility.	2. Behaver has the responsibility.
3. Authority has power to choose resultant punishment.	3. Logical consequences are allowed to occur.
4. The behaver has no options.	4. The behaver knows the options.
5. Increases the behaver's sense of failure.	5. Increases behaver's sense of personal power and success.
6. Easy for authority figure.	6. More difficult to remain consistent.
7. Spontaneous, no thought of consequences of punishment choice.	7. Planned with consequences considered.

Fig. 6-1. Comparison of Discipline and Punishment

Divisions of Family

Duvall (1971) stated that each stage of the family system must go through eight tasks: 1) attending to physical needs; 2) distribution of resources; 3) task assignment; 4) meeting members' social needs; 5) procreation, addition of members and release of offspring into society; 6) establishing order; 7) sending members out into society; and 8) source of morale and motivation. The family provides food and shelter for all its members and ensures that the resources will be divided evenly, thus avoiding the probability that the smaller members will go without adequate physical resources. The jobs of home maintenance are assigned, sometimes by society, sometimes by a formal agreement between partners. Mankind is a social species; without socialization the basic needs are not met, which leads to a malfunctioning individual. Families need to replenish themselves, by procreation or attracting members from outside the home, or they become nonexistent as members grow older and leave the home or eventually die. Another task of the family is to prepare children for adulthood and the eventual leave-taking to establish a home on their own. As a small section of society each family serves to instruct its members in the rules established within the family, which reflects the rules present in society, such as not stealing from one another or telling the truth.

Minuchin (1974) lists two family functions: the psychosocial protection of its members; and accommodation to, and transmission of, the culture of the society the family belongs to. Fulfillment of these tasks depends on the members' perceptions of the family as having power. If the family perceives itself as having no power or control when in the health care setting, the members will also see themselves as powerless.

McCubbin (1983) lists the following six guidelines to promote optimal family function: 1) believe that a family and its members can control life situations, 2) seek social support, 3) develop gentle communication, 4) maintain an optimistic view of life situations, 5) encourage family esteem, and 6) aim for balance. The first of McCubbin's suggestions is basic to improving the perception of personal power. The remaining five support and strengthen the first function listed–encouraging responsibility for one's own actions which promotes personal feelings of control. Families that isolate themselves from society have less potential for power than those who have the support of neighbors, church members, club members, etc. Developing gentle communication, communicating with an emphasis on listening to another person and addressing each other with respect are strengths that the family members will take with them in their dealings with individuals outside the home. Encouraging the perception of events in a positive rather than negative light promotes mental health in the family members. It is more likely that a child will reach his goals if he sees lack of success as a challenge rather than seeing it, and himself, as a failure. Positive family esteem is pride in belonging to a family that envelops each member in love, support and security; families with positive esteem produce members with positive, loving self-esteem. Aiming for balance in the family results in a balance between recreation and work, attention paid to one child as much as the other, and reinforcing moderation in all activities.

Married Couple. The married couple is traditionally defined as a man and woman who have sworn a commitment to each other through a ceremony or contract. This pact usually follows a courtship period, during which the two individuals ideally learn about each other and evaluate the possibility of a successful union (Clatworthy, 1980). The reality, however, is that during courtship most couples are so mutually infatuated that they fail to judge the probability of compatibility in a variety of situations which are common in a marriage. Each member believes that he or she can change the other person or tolerate any little "quirks" the other may have. As long as there is love, anything can be overcome; in other words, the couple has "anticipatory mastery."

Adjustment to sharing a home with another person can be overwhelming to a man who values his independence and privacy then finds himself married to a woman who invades his "space." His spouse may not have an equal sense of personal power. She may only feel "complete" when with her husband, or she may have learned from her family dynamics to manipulate her husband by using tactics of helplessness: inability to make a decision without her husband's input, expressing fear at the thought of going places without him.

The majority of marital conflicts are based on power struggles (Glasser, 1984). The need for recognition and praise is another way of stating a need for power, according to Glasser (1984). The behaviors chosen to meet this need can also cause conflict in satisfying love and belonging needs, but a fulfilling relationship will meet most of each member's needs (Good, 1986, See Figure 6-2).

A couple who has worked through the possible approaches to life and blended into unity—such as a couple who has successfully completed a Marriage Encounter weekend—appears as though they look at the world around them with the same mind. Is this an example of compromise or enmeshment? Does each member still maintain individuality? This meld could be either of those things, negative or positive.

Most families have some difficulties in adjusting to the developmental stages that they must pass through (Wegscheider, 1979). The family can either work through these stages, ignore them and stay together for convenience sake, or the couple can separate and fragment the family.

The married couple must come to several decisions about its future: whether to have children, to support each member's career and future goals, and how to plan for future expenditures. The outcome of these decisions reflects the perceived power of the family unit and its members.

Couples who are unable to have children may feel betrayed by their body's refusal to perform what is accepted as normal, leading to a sense of powerlessness. They have the choice between adoption or adaptation (Schuster, 1980). The couple can discuss the possibility of adoption and be placed on a waiting list. They can also channel their parental energies into activities with the children of relatives, neighbors, hospitals or special school settings, or via some other contact with children through which they can share their affection for them in their struggle to normalize.

The married couple without children, whether by choice or infertility, must withstand much outside pressure (Schuster, 1980). Family members and friends continue to ask when the couple is going to have a child. Even the media fails to support the decision to not have children, filling prime-time television hours with dramas of families with children. Perpetuation of the species is, after all, a mammalian drive.

Family With Children. The family with children has taken on the responsibility of the offsprings' welfare: physical, emotional, spritual, cultural, and intellectual. The goal for this family is to meet those needs while nurturing and empowering each member of the family. Generally, this family type is composed of young adult parents and their children. However, there are increasing numbers of couples who choose not to have children until they are in their thirties or forties, often related to a late or second marriage.

Love

Does this person meet my needs?
Does this person love me unconditionally?
Does this person behave in a manner that enhances feelings of belonging and closeness in me?
Does this person care about me and what happens to me?
Is this person available for bad times as well as good times?

Power

Do I believe this person respects my opinions?
Do I feel important when I am with this person?
Does this person recognize and respect my competence and skills?
Does this person give me recognition and praise?

Fun

> Does this person laugh with me?
> Do we play together?
> Do we share good times?
> Do we learn together?
> Do we make discoveries together?
> Do we have adventures?

Freedom

> Does this person promote my independence?
> Does this person encourage me to make my own decisions?
> Do I feel free with this person?
> Do I share in the decision making about what we are going to do?

Fig. 6-2. Fulfilling Relationships (Good, 1986)

One of the tasks of this family is to prepare its members for interaction with the outside world, satisfying each member's social needs. Personal empowerment—an atmosphere of acceptance and support for each member encourages the assumption of individual control and responsibility—is one such need (Wegscheider, 1979). Without support and encouragement of its members, the family is seen as dysfunctional, not meeting its expected tasks or responsibilities.

Parents can either assume responsibility *for* or responsibility *to* their children. Being responsible to one's children is an empowering position in parenthood, identifying the responsibility of the parent to allow the child's attempts to reach his goals within a safe and accepting environment. Being responsible for children is noted in many parents who live for and hover over the child in a smothering love rather than a freeing and empowering love. This suffocation and overprotection can be as harmful to the child as absent parental involvement.

Another couple with children may include the woman who makes the effort to be everything to everybody—the "superwoman syndrome" (Shaevitz, 1984). In addition to the tasks that she has been raised to believe are expected as wife and mother, she tackles a full-time job outside the home. The accusation of raising "latch-key" children is often directed at this mother (and the single parent). This criticism increases the stress of maintaining the many roles she feels burdened with, adding guilt to her already overloaded sense of responsibility and amplifying her feelings of powerlessness. With a harried schedule, this mother is quickly overtaxed when illness strikes some member of the family; seeking personal health care assumes a low priority for her. According to Scarf (1980), many of these women become depressed as a result of the human inability to continue to meet all the self-imposed expectations of the "superwoman."

The realization of the tremendous responsibility of a house, mortgage, and dependent children seems much more overwhelming when combined with a "milestone" birthday, such as the fortieth or fiftieth birthday. Both men and women identify these events as stressors in their lives (Johnston, 1980; Sheehy. 1981). With the awareness of such long-term responsibilities, the feelings of powerlessness can increase (Paul and Paul, 1983).

The blended family, one with "yours, mine, and ours" children, faces unique difficulties. The children may resent the step-parent, the step-parent may resent the stepchild, the couple may conflict in their childrearing practices, and ex-spouses inject additional stressors into a family structure that has been imposed rather than evolved (Landis, 1970).

"Empty Nest" Family. The "empty nest" family has matriculated children—grown up and free of parental structure—leaving the couple alone in the home. However, there may be some unexpected additional roles—although their children have moved on, the couple is faced with the responsibility for their elderly parents. The vicarious pleasure from the achievements of grown children, the task of guidance and love for grandchildren, and the emotional support tendered to their children striving toward their full potential, rekindles the couple relationship—no longer centered around children, fulfilling both members through attainment of goals as they plan for the retirement years ahead. But with increasing frequency, adult children are returning home, often accompanied by children from a broken marriage. The freedom the couple has looked forward to may be postponed with these added burdens.

Each member must come to grips with the physical changes of late middle age. With the perceived psychological trauma of decreased physical prowess, the late middle-aged person may fantasize about missed opportunities outside the family. This is reflected in the increasing occurrence of divorce in persons who have been married between 20 and 30 years (Conway, 1985; Paul, 1983). A hopeful side to this phenomenon is that many of these persons return to school, learn new skills, launch a new career, or enjoy a renewed awareness of and attraction toward each other (Christenson, 1977). The willingness to try new avenues and reach new goals is an important factor in building personal power, with each effort potentiating self-esteem.

The late middle-aged couple finds more time available for community projects (Peale, 1971). Without the necessity for childcare and supervision, the couple is free to join interest groups, work as volunteers for organizations and interact with other couples whose children are grown. These activities emphasize the usefulness of the couple, which can increase self-esteem.

Nontraditional Family. This family is comprised of members not meeting the definition of the traditional nuclear family, such as single parents, men and women living together outside legal marriage, and gay couples.

The single parent family has become increasingly common. Within the single parent family, the location of power may be poorly defined. Upon the break-up of a marriage, the perception of power shifts, as it is now only one parent making decisions and shouldering the responsibilities for maintaining the family's function. The single mother may feel helpless in view of having been unemployed outside the home for several years and, in perceiving herself as powerless, communicates that feeling of powerlessness to the children she now has responsibility for, which increases their feelings of insecurity (Beattie, 1987). The stressors are many: raising the children without the benefit of another adult to share in the decision making, shaky financial resources, increased caretaking responsibilities, and providing for the child's learning needs for achieving appropriate growth and developmental tasks.

The man and woman living together outside contractual marriage sometimes have difficulty assigning individual responsibility. Without any formal commitment, the members are able to move in and out of the relationship, which may increase the feelings of insecurity and powerlessness for one or both partners. Meeting the need for love and belonging is threatened if the partners perceive little sense of control and compassion (Stanhope and Lancaster. 1984). There are financial responsibilities and ownership problems that must be worked out for the couple who buy a house together. However, there are many couples that believe this lifestyle suits them well and so maintain a stable environment for meeting the tasks of the family. Success is, as in every family system, dependent upon the input, commitment, and health of its members (Wegscheider, 1979).

Even though an estimated 10% of the population is homosexual, the gay couple (male) has more difficulties around the issue of cultural acceptance than any of the other families. Being gay is not a generally accepted lifestyle, which leads these couples to gather into a subculture of society comprised of other gay couples, and to restrict contact with the outside world except in the work setting. The advent of AIDS has caused many more gay couples to adopt a monogamous relationship (Mims and Swenson, 1980). Lesbians have long practiced monogamy, while too often suffering societal ostracism, even though the primary reason for their relationship is companionship, in contrast to the physical bond between men. The sexual preference of a person has no effect on work ability and potential contribution to society. In addition, children raised by gay or lesbian couples usually choose a heterosexual partner, dispelling the myth that these children are tainted or restricted in their choices.

Dysfunctional Families

Rules and attitudes of family members become encoded through the years as they grow up. Many of these rules are emotionally crippling, leading to an estimated 96% of all families being emotionally impaired (Bradshaw, 1988). Support and encouragement of the members is a family task which is often neglected or accomplished in an unhealthy manner. The development of a positive and wholesome self-esteem is the result of healthy support and encouragement in the family, one of the family's basic functions (Clarke, 1978).

Financial restrictions place a certain amount of limitation on the dysfunctional family's ability to seek assistance. The poor can send their children in for emotional treatment at the expense of the taxpayer. The wealthy can afford the astronomical expense of private psychiatric care. The middle class family, however, cannot afford even the twenty percent left after insurance coverage without extreme indebtedness or bankruptcy. There are still many insurance companies that do not provide any coverage for psychiatric care. If these barriers are not overcome, there is a majority of the population that will continue to be denied the assistance available for helping the dysfunctional family.

The order of birth can have a strong impact on the children of the family, as well as the behavior of the adults in the family (Leman, 1985). The addition of another child can change the older children's approach to the world and their siblings, as well as affecting the self-esteem of each child (Clarke, 1978; Leman, 1985).

Abusive families are reflective of powerlessness among the family members. Child abuse and incest are reported in increasing numbers and have received much public attention (Wegscheider, 1979). Some types of abuse are more difficult to document, such as emotional and sibling abuse; they are, however, just as deadly and damaging for the victims. Abusive relationships, whether sexual, emotional or physical, have devastating effects on the family members' behavioral styles for the rest of their lives. All types of abuse exacerbate a decreased perception of control in the children, increased guilt in the adults, and lowered self-esteem within all members of the family, all of which contribute to powerlessness.

Sexual Abuse. The victim of sexual abuse might not be as easily identified as the child with burns and broken bones, but the spirit of the child becomes fractured, and the child develops a warped sense of sexuality.

CASE STUDY

Amy, at age ten, had come to the recent discovery that things occurring in her home did not occur in the homes of her friends. She told her seventeen-year-old brother, Don, what their dad had been doing to her since she was eight. Don was shocked and alarmed, and talked with his school guidance counselor. After a few phone calls, a social worker arrived at the family home to remove Amy from what was considered an unsafe family situation.

Frightened, Amy was examined by doctors and interviewed by the police, social services workers, and numerous other people in every division of the legal and health care system. She was then placed in a group home for her own protection.

Meanwhile, both parents were appalled by the accusations. Where did Amy ever get such nonsense? She had always had a vivid imagination. Dad denied everything and Mom contended that nothing of this nature could possibly have occurred—how could it without her knowing? Don kept his mouth shut; little brother Luke was unaware.

The parents had been having marital difficulties off and on for years. Dad often stayed at work late and came home smelling of liquor or perfume. It had only been recently that they had begun trying to repair their relationship. Mom was not about to let anything get in the way of the progress they had made.

Amy, feeling alone and scared, ran away from the group home several times. She couldn't understand why her mother had not come to visit her and take her home. She missed her little brother, Luke. She wondered why Don hadn't called her. She began to cut on her arms and considered killing herself. Her social worker became increasingly concerned about her self-destructive behaviors and recommended inpatient hospitalization.

Dad was charged with sexual assault of his daughter, but he refused to seek therapy, and continued to deny any wrongdoing; and Mom believed him. Don began to doubt the reality of Amy's accusations.

Amy, with her therapist and the milieu staff, disclosed more and more of what had happened to her. Her self-destructive behaviors continued as she turned all her anger inward.

As the court date approached, her mother began to visit and have family meetings with Amy. Mom began to doubt her husband's word and over the next few weeks her support of Amy increased. Several times during this period, Dad and Mom separated only to reunite. When Luke came to visit Amy, he was frightened and would hide under chairs. A five-year-old, it was recommended that he begin play therapy sessions.

Amy became able to identify the sources of her anger: Dad for what he had done, and Mom for not protecting her. The trial was painful, but Amy bravely told the closed courtroom about the horrors that had occurred. Dad took the stand and denied any wrongdoing; he was acquitted.

Amy returned to the hospital after the verdict had been read. She became increasingly suicidal and self-abusive. She told the staff that all

*she wanted was for Dad to admit what he had done to her—in or out
of court, it didn't matter.*

*Months later, Dad did admit that he had sexually abused his daughter,
and sought therapy. Amy felt a sense of relief that her story was finally
validated. She knew her counselors believed her, but it was important
for her family to know the truth. Her parents separated and Mom
became a support for Amy, who left the hospital to live with her
mother and younger brother; Don had turned eighteen, graduated and
moved out of the house.*

*The family had been shattered in some ways and reunited in others.
Amy continued to be involved with the mental health care system.*

A family in which sexual abuse has occurred is a difficult one in
which to sort out the facts. There are many secrets and loyalties that
need to be deciphered.

In this case, Amy, as the identified victim. was the first to receive
attention and help. This type of situation will require years of treatment
as new pieces of the puzzle are resorted and processed. Initially,
Amy needed to express her anger toward her perpetrator (her father)
and accept him for who he was, rather than accept self-blame and
internalize her anger. Another step will be to express her anger toward
her mother for not protecting her against her father, and then for
siding with him after the truth unfolded. Amy also experienced anger
toward other family members who fluctuated in their support for her.
In general, Amy has very little trust in relationships or in adults who
are supposed to keep her safe. She also learned that the legal system
cannot be trusted, having taken a major risk to bear her soul in public
only the see her father found not guilty. Amy felt powerless in her
relationships with adults.

The best course of treatment for Amy will be to find a consistent
adult with whom she can develop a trusting relationship and receive
support as she deals with her damaging past. She will need to be
guided toward a positive future by supporting and building on her
strengths. Bright and headstrong, Amy is a fighter who can survive.
One option may be an emancipation home.

This type of family situation is a complex one. Amy's older brother,
Don, needs some outlet to vent his feelings. Since he has moved out
of the home and is a legal adult, he probably will seek comfort from a
close friend, at some point seeking professional help. Amy may invite
him to participate in a sibling group or a sibling session with her.
Other options for him might include sibling support groups. The issues
he will need to confront include his changing loyalties after initially
getting the authorities involved with Amy, how this has affected the
family, his changed relationships with each family member, and his
sense of inability or powerlessness to protect his sister from his father.

Amy's younger brother, Luke, is experiencing some degree of

disturbance, but it is unclear what this stems from. Mom was able to recognize Luke's distress and involve him in play therapy on an individual basis, which is the most appropriate modality for a young child unable to verbalize his inner conflicts.

Until the issue was forced by the mental health and legal systems, Mom chose to take a powerless stance regarding what was occurring around her. Her lack of attention to her child's requests for help, added to Dad's control over her, supported the continuance of his abusive behaviors. She will need to learn to feel comfortable taking control in what occurs in her life.

Dad, as the abuser, first admits all he has done, for only then can he begin to process the pathology that allowed him to abuse his daughter and continue to deny it once exposed. Whether he is capable of feeling guilt and remorse for what he has done determines the course of his therapy. He also has a long history of family abuse and pent-up feelings which he needs to resolve. His relationship with each of his family members has been altered and may be irreparable. He will need to evaluate his identity and come to some acceptance of his new self, finding qualities within himself to substitute in place of the abusive power he exerted within his family.

A family that is dysfunctional to this degree may not be able to ever reunite due to the damage and pain that has been mutually experienced. The older children (Amy and Don) are old enough to care for themselves to some degree and may move away, trying to leave the pain behind. There is hope that Mom can rebuild her life and grow in her parenting responsibilities to provide a better atmosphere for Luke. She may feel the need to reunite with her husband, in which case the social service workers should monitor the family for indicators of any further difficulties. The members of this family may continue for many years to be in and out of both the mental health and social service systems.

Physical Abuse. Seeing physical evidence of trauma on children's bodies substantiates these abuse cases. Often the wheels of justice move too slowly in the case of physically abused children, resulting in their return home and further abuse. Most abuse is believed by the lay public to be administered by the adults in the child's life, but what about siblings? Abuse among siblings is prevalent within many families, but is rarely addressed by the experts.

CASE STUDY

Marsha was unwed with an adolescent son, Rick. Rick had never known his real father—Marsha didn't even know his name. Marsha had many come-and-go boyfriends for varying lengths of time. Some stayed only a few weeks, some a few years. Some beat her, some didn't.

Rick had watched his mother get knocked around when one of his "step-fathers" would come home drunk. They would yell and scream at each other and then fists or objects would begin to fly. Rick ran and hid. On occasion, some of the men would go after Rick, who would cover his face and pray that it would soon end. As he became older, he would fight back, only making the fights more intense.

When Rick asked Marsha why this was happening, she shrugged her shoulders and said that some things had to be tolerated if they were going to have a man around the house. Rick spent a lot of time wondering why this was occurring. He had difficulty identifying the cause for his mother's beatings and certainly couldn't for his own. He became more and more confused and angry. Rick felt powerless to help his mother. Marsha felt powerless to help herself and Rick.

Marsha often went to work with bruises on her face and arms. She told her co-workers that she was clumsy and fell down the stairs when they asked her about the marks. Occasionally, Marsha went to the emergency clinic for stitches or fracture care.

As a teen, Rick was reckless, driving too fast and drinking too much. School had never been a priority—money was. Rick and his friends were out looking for money and items they could easily sell. Rick became well known at police headquarters; he was tough, cold, and hardened—headed for a youth detention center. He figured it couldn't be all that bad, and maybe even predictable.

Marsha eventually ended up in intensive care with multiple fractures and a head injury. Rick had fought her attacker and had required stitches on his fist and a cast for a broken wrist. Social services moved him to a group home with mental health facilities.

Rick had been introduced to the mental health system through his many encounters with the judicial system. In and out of youth detention centers and experiencing varying degrees of counseling such as group confrontation and brief one-to-one crisis intervention, he was wary of authority figures. In general, so-called professionals had been of little help to Rick, who maintained the position that in the end, he is the only one he can depend on.

Rick doesn't trust adults and certainly does not see them as helpers. Without redirection, Rick's years of anger, confusion, and bitterness will stay pent up inside and will probably trigger continued run-ins with the law until he is sent to prison where, he believes, he will feel safe. All his delinquent behaviors are cries for help, but at the same time, he finds it difficult to accept that help. Admitting that he may not be as powerful as he appears to be will break down the defense that he has used to maintain his functioning, hiding his true feelings of powerlessness. It may take a major crisis to scare him enough to accept help. Rick needs a therapist who is tough and who will be clear with both limits and expectations; he needs boundaries and to feel the safety he did not experience as a child.

Marsha received counseling from the battered women shelter during her recovery. She calls Rick often and discusses their future with him. Rick pleads with her to leave her current boyfriend and let Rick take care of her. He begs her not to let any more men hurt them.

Marsha will require support and counseling to change her pattern of entering abusive relationships. Her affection for Rick may be the motivator that convinces her to alter her lifestyle. However, her low self-esteem and belief that she cannot function without a man to protect her, may keep her in a pattern of behavior choices that can end in her death.

Inpatient hospitalization may be indicated for Rick so that he can be encouraged to deal with his feelings and discover that adults can provide a safe environment for him no matter how angry he gets. The structure of the unit can provide support for him as he learns to take more responsibility and effective control of his life struggles.

During hospitalization, family therapy will be necessary to assess Mom's ability to provide a safe environment for Rick. This will be a long process, beginning with both Mom and Rick learning to share their feelings with each other. The process will hopefully move to varying lengths of home passes, with specific goals to identify and establish a healthier home environment. During this process, Mom can be assisted through her own individual therapy to discuss her feelings of inadequacy and learn more effective parenting skills. Many inpatient units have parent or multi-family groups where parents can share their common experiences and receive support from their peers as well as from professionals.

A Big Brother may provide Rick with a positive male figure. It is also important to re-establish Rick in school and develop some positive after-school activities. Competitive athletics can be an acceptable outlet for pent-up aggression. If Rick is not athletically inclined, an afterschool job may be helpful. It is important to discover what talents he has and help him to cultivate then in order to find a sense of personal power in a more socially acceptable activity.

Rick will carry his pain throughout his life, but with the earliest and most intense interventions possible, he can change the direction of his life. If Mom is unable to provide a healthy environment, it may be necessary to look at group home placement after hospitalization. There are many emancipation programs that are designed to help adolescents finish school and learn a trade, as well as teach them daily living skills. Rick will have a long road ahead of him no matter which route he takes, but with the consistent support of adults, he can lead a productive life and not repeat the experiences of his past as an adult with his own children.

Emotional Abuse. The wounds of emotionally abused children as adults are not as easily noticed, they are deeper and more pervasive. The child being abused felt powerless to stop the barrage of hurtful words hurled at him throughout his childhood. A result of unidentified emotional abuse is the perpetuation of the abusive style of parenting from one generation to the next.

CASE STUDY

Donna and Jack sat down to have Sunday dinner with their two small children and Donna's mother, who came to dinner every Sunday. As they began to eat, Jack yelled across the table, "Where's the salt and pepper? That dumb broad never does anything right." Donna had spent the best part of the day preparing the meal and carefully setting the table so that everything would be perfect.

A few minutes of light conversation continued and again, there was a loud oath as Jack yelled, "What is this slop? Some fancy thing I can't even identify." Donna's mother looked at Donna and said, "Dear, you know Jack is a meat and potatoes man, a good wife should feed her man what he wants." The intermittent demands and put-downs continued throughout the meal. By the end, the children had eaten little and were anxious to leave the table; this type of constant bickering was the norm.

Donna had high hopes for her marriage when she was a newlywed at 18. She left an overbearing, perfectionist mother to make a home of her own with the man she loved. Soon after Jack and Donna were married, she became pregnant. The baby cried a lot and Donna knew little about mothering. Both Jack and her mother criticized her frequently. She had never had much confidence in her own abilities and now, six years later, with the children in school, she continued to doubt herself. She saw herself as dumb and inadequate. When she stood in the kitchen after clearing the table, she began to cry. As the children ran outside she heard one say, "I wish Mom would get it right just once."

Donna, not willing to fight back with the adults who criticized her, found herself yelling and belittling the children more and more often.

It is likely that Donna will be the family member to seek help for her situation. Neither Jack nor Donna's mother are experiencing any discomfort in the situation, and together, they support a destructive form of communication. It is the way that they exercise strength and power—leaving Donna the powerless nonconfident member.

In her efforts to seek help, Donna has begun to take power and control over her future. To continue this process, she will most likely need to leave behind her destructive family members in order to build a new, healthy self image. She may move in and out of treatment as new and painful ground is uncovered. The tendency of dominated individuals is to return to the unhealthy situation rather than learn to integrate new patterns of behavior.

If Donna chooses to stay within her present environment while she seeks out her new self she will receive little, if any, support for her efforts and will probably be met with increased criticism from her mother and husband. Her children will also be confused by the new Donna who is not accepted by their adult role models.

The treatment of choice will include both individual and group support. It is important for Donna to learn that she is not alone in her struggle, and that her efforts will eventually be rewarded. She has probably received encouragement from a close friend to begin this process in the first place.

In individual therapy it will be essential to identify goals for treatment which must be attainable and limited to one or two items. A reasonable time frame should be established to promote movement toward the identified goals, as guided by the counselor. As goals are met, new ones may be added only if Donna and the therapist feel this will be helpful. Initially, it is important to help Donna identify what *she* would like to change in her life. If the goals are not her own. she will have little motivation to change or work toward them. This may by a very scary time for Donna; she is now in a new situation where people value her as a human being and praise her strengths. Her identity will go through a transformation, forcing a decision as to whether she will be a happier person if she values herself and her abilities. Is it worth leaving behind the things she knows and counts on? As she begins the process of change, her treatment modalities will change. She will need to seek independence, but she may come back to the group "nest" for support, reaching out again to try on her own. As Donna puts her new life together, she will need to consider what her future will be. She has many things to consider: pursuing a career, whether or not to engage in marital therapy with Jack, whether or not to confront her mother's lack of support, and how her children will fit into her new lifestyle.

With Donna out of the home the dynamics of the remaining family constellation will change. Donna served a specific role in the family that kept it functioning. Without Donna as the focus as the incompetent member, the bond between Jack and Donna's mother may disintegrate. Jack may seek out another female to meet his needs and restore his sense of vitality and power. Donna's mother may focus her attention on raising the children in the absence of their mother.

These children are now at risk, experiencing feelings of loss and abandonment by both their mother and father as the family unit breaks apart. The attitudes and behaviors they are used to are no longer active. Depending on their developmental levels and the explanations and support they receive, the children will develop their own beliefs and feelings about their changing situation. They may have difficulty recognizing and accepting their "new" mother, and may feel anger at the changes they are being confronted with.

It will be helpful if Donna's mother, as the children's temporary caretaker, can be engaged in a positive mode and learn to support her daughter's changes. The children need to be included in group therapy to voice their feelings and concerns about what has taken place within their family unit. They will probably need support of one type or another for years to come as they deal with new understandings of their childhood experiences. It is hoped they can learn to support their mother's growth as she seeks a more positive role for herself.

Family in Crisis. The family in crisis may function in a healthy manner most of the time. However, in a crisis situation the family structure weakens, each member is afloat in the world without the firm support of the others as a result of the imposed crisis in the family unit. This situation can lead to one problem piling on top of another. For example, the effect of one child being in intensive care may be an increased financial strain on the father, the mother working full-time instead of part-time to help out, the older brother getting drunk with his friends, and the younger sister expressing the lack of familial attention by engaging in sexual intercourse for the first time to assure her of feeling loved. A crisis with one member of the family becomes a crisis to every member and has a ripple effect for the family, then spreads out into society.

CASE STUDY

June 29th had been a sunny day—summer vacation was in full swing. The park was full of children at play, but the sounds of laughter all came to a halt as the screeching of brakes was followed by a loud crash. A small child lay still on the pavement. Sirens and emergency vehicles followed.

At the hospital, Sue and Tom constantly sat beside Ginger's bed. From the outset, the prognosis had not been favorable—Ginger had sustained extensive head injuries and there were indications that she had sustained extensive brain damage. As the doctor's hope became less and less, so did Tom's. He thought about the fun times they had shared, the laughter, and Ginger's vibrant smile. He was coming to terms with the reality of the tragedy. Sue spent hours reading to Ginger and fixing her hair; she talked to her as if they were having a playful conversation. This made Tom's pain worse. He spent more time away from the hospital.

As the months passed, Sue and Tom became more distant from each other. What had, until now, been a strong and warm relationship was deteriorating into distance. Sue continued to focus all her attention on Ginger's future; Tom's efforts to help her see reality were only met with anger and frustration. He began to seek comfort outside of their home, eventually moving out in hopes of salvaging what was left of his own life.

In a crisis situation that brings a family to a health care facility, the family's first encounter with the mental health system will probably be with the hospital's social service department or chaplain. A family with a disabled member will require involvement with many allied health professionals: physical therapy, occupational therapy and psychological counseling. Along with the many stressors that occur as a result of an accident, the family must cope with all the highly technical experiences that surround them. They must deal with new sights, sounds and smells that overload their senses, They may miss sleep in the hopes that their child will suddenly show some degree of improvement. The sleep deprivation is followed by attitude and behavior changes that will affect their coping strategies.

The clinical nurse caring for the family is in an optimal position to assess each family member's degree of functioning. During a crisis it is common to regress to a level that is comfortable and does not require a lot of thought or higher critical functioning. Initially the family members will be experiencing their own personal shock. It is helpful for the practitioner to keep in mind the possibility that things will be said in anger, so she does not make inaccurate judgments about the family's ability to cope with the situation. As the members move through the grief process, their coping strategies will change and they will be able to function at a higher level. The powerlessness of the family to alter the crisis situation places all family members in a state of powerlessness.

Tom and Sue are both in need of support, Sue is more visibly in distress due to her inability to accept her daughter's prognosis. In this situation she is experiencing a high degree of powerlessness since all her hoping, physical care, attention and willpower may not change her daughter's physiological status. Through her single focusing she neglects the needs of her other children, although she may not intend this.

When approaching the family, the practitioner must keep in mind the individual's desire for, and acceptance of, support outside the family system. Their views of health care practitioners will be dependent upon their past experiences, attitudes and knowledge of health care systems.

Tom may be more approachable in this setting as his tendency is to look at things more realistically and to seek the support of others. It will be important to assess not only his need for support but his willingness to engage in a therapeutic relationship. Offering services by making short contacts in a nonthreatening manner may be helpful.

A crisis situation can strengthen already strong bonds or shatter tenuous ones. Each individual's reaction and coping ability will be unique and be either supportive of the family members or not. A crisis may cause a shift in the roles the members have played within the family as the delicate balance is upset.

In the case of Tom and Sue, a once strong bond has been changed by the crisis, resulting in their choice to no longer maintain their marital relationship. In this case, the parents as well as the siblings and significant others may require professional intervention. Everyone involved has experienced a loss. Before accepting a new role and future for Ginger, each family member must grieve the loss of the old Ginger. While going through this grief process they must all be supportive and available to the incapacitated child. Each family member will move through the grief process at their own rate and will need to come to terms with their feelings, as well as those of the rest of the family. This may cause more stress on the family unit; one member may see another as being uncaring or self-centered if they have accepted the loss while the other member is still denying it.

Therapeutic intervention in a crisis is limited to assisting the individual through the crisis. At this point, the practitioner needs to promote the strengths of the individual while cultivating others that will help him adjust. It will also be important to make the experience positive so that the client will feel free to approach the practitioner as future needs arise.

Sue is less able to reach out to those around her, angered by anyone who tries to alter her view of reality. A supportive approach is most useful in establishing rapport. Short visits to allow her to ventilate can help establish the relationship. As the relationship between the practitioner and Sue strengthens, a more confrontive stance may be attempted. This must be carefully gauged or the entire relationship will be lost. It may be helpful to have representatives from a parents' support group visit Sue. She may reject these attempts, but letting her know that resources are available will assist her in making decisions when she is ready to do so. The practitioner must keep in mind that Sue will seek out the person with whom she feels the most comfortable. This may not be a mental health professional but a neighbor or the parent of another hospitalized client. It is important to be aware of this type of relationship to make sure that it is supportive of healthy attitudes and behaviors rather than unrealistic beliefs.

All members of the family in crisis are experiencing some degree of pain and need to modify their role within the family system. A child may take on the parental role as the caretaker of other siblings. Depending on the sibling's age and maturity, a younger child may feel they somehow caused the accident (after an argument he may have wished that his sibling was dead). The siblings will need to be evaluated individually to assess their level of coping. Sibling support groups or individual short term therapy may be indicated. Grandparents may need support through such a crisis too. They also experience varying degrees of helplessness and powerlessness as they see their adult child in distress.

A crisis may turn into a long term need for support as the family needs change. With the now disabled child, the family experiences other crises such as surgeries, regressions and homecomings. The anniversary date of the accident or the child's birthday may be particularly painful times for the family. This family needs frequent reminders of the support and therapy that are open to them for as long as they perceive the need. Issues may be dealt with repetitively, while others may be kept suppressed until the individual is strong enough to deal with them.

Additional Interventions

Choosing and effecting the appropriate intervention takes much skill and knowledge. Many things must be considered: the client's desire to engage in treatment, the perceived severity of the situation, the client's financial resources, and available support systems. One must consider what other options have been tried and have been successful. If the client has been in treatment before, it will be helpful to obtain any past records and test results. Many children, as well as adults, have learning dysfunctions that may range from comprehension to processing difficulties. Knowledge of any and all of these factors will assist the practitioner in making the most effective choice possible.

Unfortunately, the practitioner may have her hands tied due to the resources available within the community and factors such as the ability of social services to fund extensive treatment. The best choice may not always be available, so second or third choices may be best. This is the reality of the system.

Treatment modalities offer much variety. The therapist's or treatment center's philosophy will affect the methods chosen. Approaches vary from those that are behaviorally based to those based strictly on psychoanalytical techniques. The client's needs and comfort with the therapeutic modality will determine its success. For example, a client of below average intelligence who has a learning disability will not benefit from strictly insightful therapy. Children, as would be expected, benefit greatly from behaviorally based approaches such as positive reinforcement. Due to a child's lack of verbal skills, play therapy is extremely effective in helping them express their inner conflicts. Adolescents can benefit from a more insight oriented approach, as this gives them some control and power over what they would like to discover and explore about themselves.

Groups are an effective modality in many cases. This is also a good option when funding is limited, as group therapy or support groups are generally less expensive than one-to-one interventions. There are support groups for alcoholics, gamblers, people with AIDS, people with various handicaps and illnesses, and incest victims. Groups have also been developed to support the needs of families who are experiencing difficulties or who have a member who has a special need or difficulty such as dyslexia, anorexia, cancer, Alzheimer's, or attention deficit disorders. More confrontational groups are also available, such as Tough Love parenting groups that help families experiencing problems with their adolescents.

Treatment approaches are available from community-based therapy to hospital-based therapy. When considering the appropriate modality, one must keep in mind the client's rights and first consider the least restrictive therapy. Only when the individual's behavior indicates the need for in-house treatment should this approach be used.

Other resources are also available. Whether or not the behavioral problems the client displays are caused by medical problems such as sleep deprivation, chemical imbalance, or other pathophysiological disorders dictates the need for a medical work-up. Speech and language consultants may also be helpful, while psychologists provide insight into other aspects of the client's level of functioning.

Therapeutic modalities include art therapy, dance therapy and recreation therapy. Educational programs can be helpful in helping the client and/or his family understand various problems and to teach new skills in coping and interventions.

As well as having many modalities to choose from, there are many factors that influence the success or failure of the therapeutic modality: client-practitioner rapport, the client's willingness to engage in therapy, and the identified goals of therapy. If one intervention does not seem to be effective, the practitioner should consider consultation with another practitioner. The therapist should provide the client with a positive experience whenever possible in order to increase the likelihood of the client reengaging with health care practitioners should the need arise. Unfortunately, as with most health care, individuals do not seek preventive intervention.

Summary

The family is the base from which all individuals draw their initial impression of the world, learn the skills with which to function, and seek comfort and support when society exhibits less than friendly acceptance of the person. As a safe haven and training ground, the family has great impact on the personality formation of the individual.

The majority of families have some degree of dysfunction which occurs intermittently. Even those families that operate in healthy patterns may become dysfunctional when an unforeseen crisis occurs.

The issue of power within the family and the family message about personal control has an impact on family members for the rest of their lives. Identifying interventions for increasing or maintaining personal power in a variety of situations has been discussed.

References

Beattie, Melody. *Codependent No More*. New York: Harper and Row, (1987).

Bradshaw, John. *Bradshaw On: The Family*. Deerfield Beach, FL: Health Communications, Inc., (1988).

Christenson, Larry and Christenson, Nordis. *The Christian Couple*. Minneapolis: Bethany Fellowship, Inc., (1977).

Clarke, Jean Illsley. *Self-Esteem: A Family Affair*. New York: Harper and Row, Publishers, (1978).

Clatworthy, Nancy. Initiating a family unit. In: Schuster, *A Holistic Approach*. Boston: Little, Brown and Company, (1980).

Conway, Jim and Conway, Sally. *Women in Mid-Life Crisis*. Wheaton, IL: Tyndale House Publishers, Inc., (1985).

Dimond, Margaret and Jones, Susan Lynn. *Chronic Illness Across The Life Span*. Norwalk, CN: Appleton-Century-Crofts, (1983).

Glasser, William. *Reality Therapy for Parents*. Long Beach, CA: Educator Training Center, Institute of Reality Therapy, (1978).

Glasser, William. *Take Effective Control of Your Life*. New York: Harper and Row, (1984).

Good, E. Perry. *In Pursuit of Happiness: Knowing What You Want, Getting What You Want*. Chapel Hill, NC: New View Publications, (1986).

Jones, Susan. *Family Therapy: A Comparison of Approaches*. Bowie, MD: Robert J. Brady Co., (1980).

Landis, Paul. *Making the Most of Marriage*. New York: Appleton-Century-Crofts, (1970).

Leman, Kevin. *The Birth Order Book*. New York: Dell Publishing Company, (1985).

McCubbin, Hamilton. *Family Stress and Family Coping*. Booklet 6, Well To Do Series. Appleton, WI: Aid Association for Lutherans, (1983).

Mims, Fern and Swenson, Melinda. *Sexuality: A Nursing Perspective*. New York: McGraw-Hill Book Company, (1980).

Minuchin, Salvador. *Families & Family Therapy*. Cambridge, MA: Harvard University Press, (1974).

Paul, Jordan and Paul, Margaret. *Do I Have To Give Up Me To Be Loved By You?* Minneapolis: CompCare Publications, (1983).

Peale, Ruth. *The Adventure of Being a Wife*. Greenwich, CN: Fawcett Publications, Inc., (1971).

Scarf, Maggie. *Unfinished Business: Pressure Points in the Lives of Women*. New York: Ballantine Books, (1980).

Schuster, Clara and Ashburn, Shirley. *The Process of Human Development: A Holistic Approach*. Boston: Little, Brown and Company, (1980).

Shaevitz, Marjorie Haines. *The Superwoman Syndrome*. New York: Warner

Books, Inc., (1984).

Sheehy, Gail. *Pathfinders*. New York: Bantam Books, (1981).

Stanhope, Marcia and Lancaster, Jeanette. *Community Health Nursing: Process and Practice for Promoting Health*. St. Louis: The C.V. Mosby Company, (1984).

Tapia, Jayne. Fractionalization of the family unit. In: Schuster, Clara and Ashburn, Shirley (eds.). *The Process of Human Development: A Holistic Approach*. Boston: Little, Brown and Company, (1980).

Wegscheider, Don. *If Only My Family Understood Me...A Family Can Find New Balance Through Stress*. Minneapolis: CompCare Publications, (1979).

Weinhold, Barry. *Breaking Family Patterns: A Guide for Adult Children of Dysfunctional Families*. Colorado Springs, CO: Circle Press, (1987).

York, Phyllis and York, David. *Toughlove*. Doylestown, PA: Toughlove, (1980).

7

Power and the Child

D. Ault, N. Rinehart, and L. Samenfeld

Introduction

Children express their need for power in ways appropriate to their age. They need to feel in control of their universe as much as an adult does. Children's communication skills are not as sophisticated as the adult's, but also not as indirect. Whether by crying, temper tantrums or resistance, the child expresses his desire to have personal power. In the health care setting, the child's and parents' powerlessness need to be addressed.

As the parents are the ultimate decision-makers in the care given to the child, health care professionals must incorporate parental participation in the plan of care. Clinicians who talk down to or belittle the parent concerning the needs and care of the child will not be as effective in receiving compliance with suggested care regimens as the professional who takes the time to develop a partnership with the parents of the child. Parental acceptance of the treatment regimen is reassuring for the child.

The ill child is often frightened by strange places, personnel and treatments. In spite of all the efforts to combat discomfort in treatments, the child is often subjected to painful and invasive procedures. Diminishing fear decreases pain, as has been demonstrated for years in obstetrics. When dealing with an older child the relaxation methods of obstetrics are easily learned. However, in working with young children, explanations are not as effective. The health care professional must be creative and patient in finding a method of relaxing the child and building trust in the client/caregiver relationship.

It is important to exert maximum effort in promoting comfort and control for each child in the pediatric setting. Once past fear and pain, the child can more easily be helped in perceiving himself as having some control. But until these two elements of the pediatric health care setting are dealt with, the powerless feelings of the child cannot be changed.

ASSESSMENT OF CHILD POWERLESSNESS

Obviously, the empowerment approach used is different with each pediatric age group. Each of the power resource areas can be evaluated.

Parental information is often the most common source of information about the child. It is important, though, to assess the nonverbal and verbal messages from the child as well (See Figure 7-1). They are, after all, the recipients of the health care and the highest authority about what is comfortable and acceptable for them. The children discussed in this chapter are those in the infant, toddler, preschool and school age groups.

ASSESSMENT TOOL

Physical

Does the child perform any of his own self-care? Is he able to hold his own bottle? Is he used to feeding himself? Is he toilet-trained? Is his muscular strength comparable to other children of his age? Can he walk? Does he climb out of bed? Does he cry when examined? Does he appear frightened when procedures are being performed? How does his growth and developmental level compare to that of other children his age?

Intellectual

What vocabulary does the child have? Can he understand simple instructions? What are his favorite stories? Does he identify his parents? Does he follow bright lights? What does he claim to understand?

Emotional

How does he respond to separation from his parents? What defense mechanisms does he use? How does he handle frustration? Is he affectionate or isolative? Is he boisterous or shy? Does he cry when approached by strangers?

Cultural

What traditions are carried out on a frequent basis at home (e.i., mealtime prayers, singing at the table, nothing to drink before bed, hair curled on Saturday night)? What is the family composition (siblings, only child, grandparents in home)? Does he like to be held on a lap? Does he have a favorite blanket or toy?

Spiritual

Do the adults in his home express optimism or pessimism? What does he think about being ill? What religious needs does he/parent have? Does he look forlorn when his parents are not nearby?

Figure 7-1. Assessment Tool

CASE STUDY: Infant

Sally was seven weeks old when she was first seen on the pediatric unit. She was the first child born to a couple in their mid-twenties. She was a full-term, small-for-gestational-age baby who had had a difficult delivery with a period of anoxia. Shortly after birth she had been transferred to a Neonatal Unit sixty miles away.

Sally developed seizures, had feeding problems and muscle rigidity. She stayed in the neonatal unit for four weeks and was discharged home on gavage feedings due to poor sucking and given physical therapy to increase her motor ability. For the past two weeks she had been taking formula from a bottle, but was having difficulty retaining her feedings. She was on Phenobarbital for seizure control.

The initial assessment of Sally revealed an infant who was not easily consoled. She held her body rigidly in one's arms and responded best to a rocking motion. Her parents reported that when they attempted to feed her it took much coaxing to achieve sucking, but once started she would take the feeding.

When a young infant is admitted to a pediatric unit, it is helpful to learn about the parents' prior experiences with, and knowledge of, their infant. The course of the pregnancy, the labor and delivery experience and the postpartum events for the mother may reveal important information. The immediate newborn period may be contributory to the present problem. Certainly the parents' view of the entire childbearing experience may help identify problem areas and therefore contribute to a plan for the future.

Sally's parents visited on a regular basis but did not room-in. They were both willing to share their experiences with Sally and demonstrate the techniques that were most successful for them when feeding or consoling their tiny daughter. They asked many questions and were anxious for concrete answers regarding Sally's future.

Sally had diagnostic testing done during her hospitalization to rule out reflux. She also underwent a neurological work-up. The results did not identify any specific new problems and Sally was discharged after several days of hospitalization.

Parents of high-risk infants need ongoing support in order to reinforce positive parenting behaviors. A key parental task during infancy is learning cues and interpreting the infant's needs (Mitchell, 1985). The ability of parents to correctly interpret the communications from their infant may require periodic assessment. Nurses should be alert to parent-infant interactions during hospitalization. They provide parent teaching and make appropriate referrals for follow-up. Listening with sensitivity to what the parents are saying, both verbally and nonverbally, helps to build a trusting relationship. Acknowledging that the role of parenting is sometimes a difficult one and recognizing the positive aspects that the parents demonstrate with their infant may reduce anxiety and guilt feelings, therefore powerlessness.

In order to achieve the best possible outcomes for Sally, it was important that her parents be provided psychological and emotional support. It is well established that preparation for parenting begins with one's own childhood experiences. Good parenting depends on the parents' level of self esteem, maturity and the kind of infant born to them (Marlow and Redding, 1988). The development of maternal and paternal roles during pregnancy has been documented by many authors (Jensen and Bobak, 1985; Mercer, 1985; Rubin, 1967; Rubin, 1984; Sherwin, 1987). Even the most prepared parents, however, find the birth of a "high-risk" infant to be a crisis situation (Steele, 1987; Lemon, 1980). Issues facing these parents include coping with the loss of the fantasized child, overcoming barriers to bonding, and becoming knowledgeable about the infant's present and future needs (Steele, 1987).

The fact that Sally required transfer to an Intensive Care Nursery shortly after birth indicates disruption in the early attachment process that is known to be beneficial to infants and their parents (Greenberg and Morris, 1974; Horowitz, Hughes and Perdue, 1982; Klaus and Kennell, 1982). The behaviors of new parents toward their infant are predictable and are repeatedly observed in the delivery room and on the postpartum units of family-centered maternity units. New parents touch and explore their infant with their fingertips and then hands, establish eye contact with the infant, and talk softly while the infant is in a quiet alert state immediately following delivery. The infant reciprocates with a wide-eyed gaze, intermittent crying followed by calming, and by grasping the parents finger. Some newborns suck their fist or may suckle at their mother's breast. Following birth, the perpetuation and strengthening of the parent-infant attachment depends on a system of correctly interpreted reciprocal cues (Horowitz, et al., 1982).

In addition to early contact between infant and parents for the purpose of establishing beginning attachment, a thorough newborn assessment that includes behavior aspects of the infant as well as physical attributes fosters optimal parent-infant interactions.

It is imperative to examine the newborn for physiologic status soon after birth. Early detection of physical anomalies allows for optimal management. A systematic assessment should be part of routine newborn care (Erickson,1978; Buckner, 1983; Judd, 1985; Kiernan and Scoloveno, 1986; Parker and Brazelton, 1981). The aspect of behavioral assessment of the newborn takes on increasing importance as babies survive what used to be devastating birth experiences. Behavioral assessment can identify potential problem areas and offer interventions that may prove helpful to the parents. Parents need a repertoire of techniques to try with their newborn.

It was difficult to share early assessment data with Sally's parents because she was transferred to a regional Neonatal Intensive Care

Unit. Under normal circumstances, the newborn spends much of his first few days of life with his mother and father in the hospital setting. Parents can look, listen, touch and smell their newborn and learn about the baby's capabilities from the staff. In circumstances that involve separation of parents and newborn, those early experiences are not possible. The sick newborn cannot demonstrate his wonderful capabilities for his parents when they come to visit since he must conserve his energy for life-sustaining tasks.

Prior to discharge from a Neonatal Intensive Care Unit, parents should be involved in the care of their infant. Behaviors should be familiar to them. Performing the Neonatal Behavioral Assessment Scale (Parker and Brazelton, 1981) in the parents' presence should help to identify expectations for the infant. For example: discussing consolability with parents and demonstrating techniques that are helpful; facilitating hand-to-mouth movements for the infant; talking softly to the infant; and providing visual stimulation, particularly a human face, are helpful activities for many babies (Jensen and Bobak, 1985; Brazelton,1984). Swaddling is a useful method for consoling some babies (Ramanko and Brost, 1982).

Temperament is described by Marlow and Redding (1988) as "the very core of each individual's personality" (p. 579). Temperament is genetically determined, with infants being classified as "easy," "slow-to-warm-up" and "difficult" (Jensen and Bobak, 1985; Sevronsky and Opas, 1987; Peery and Mott, 1985). Sally had been described by her parents as being "difficult" and their perceptions needed to be heard. Their observations were confirmed by the nursing staff who attempted to hold, console and feed her. Through observation and innovation, those caretaking behaviors most satisfactory to Sally were identified. With guidance and support, Sally's parents were able to gain skill in their parenting abilities and confidently take Sally home.

CASE STUDY: Toddler

Twenty month old Jeremy was admitted via the emergency department after receiving burns on his chest, neck and upper arms from spilled hot coffee. His parents related that Jeremy knocked a full coffee cup off the table as he was climbing up on a chair to get some cookies that were on the table. His mother had just poured the coffee for herself and had turned to put the pot back on the stove. It was determined that Jeremy had first and second degree burns over 15% of his body. Intravenous fluid replacement was initiated and sulfadine was applied to his burns before dressings were applied. Jeremy had been medicated in the Emergency Room and was drowsy from the effects of the medication when he arrived on the pediatric unit.

Jeremy's parents were visibly upset on arrival to the unit. Mom was softly crying and Dad hesitated outside the room. During and following the admission interview both parents quietly sat by Jeremy's bed. They didn't ask any questions or offer to touch or hold Jeremy. They were unsure, upon questioning, if they could, or should, room-in with their son. They had two older children at home.

The nurse planning care for Jeremy identified several nursing priorities during the admission assessment such as maintaining adequate fluid and electrolyte balance and aseptic wound care. In addition, nursing care needed to respond to the psychosocial needs of Jeremy and his family.

Jeremy's sense of powerlessness must be acknowledged. He was restrained so as not to dislodge his intravenous (IV) line, which added to his loss of control. Toddlers are struggling to gain autonomy, and Jeremy's declarations of "No" had to be respected and dealt with. It is easy for adults to simply move the toddler about and constrain him to acquiesce to adult plans. This is extremely traumatic for the child and may lead him to despair and a give-up attitude about life.

Parents also have emotional needs in this situation. Parents often feel powerless to help their child and are afraid to approach him for fear of causing him further distress. Recognition and identification of feelings that predictably occur when young children receive accidental injuries help parents verbalize their fears, concerns, and guilt or powerlessness. Any anticipatory guidance must be offered after the feelings of guilt, fear and anxiety have been resolved to some degree.

It is imperative to family-centered care to make parents feel welcome and explain the benefits of rooming-in for this age group. If neither parent is able to stay, explore other sources of support for the child. Extended family members may be able to assist with other children at home. Another option is to encourage frequent telephone contact with the child. Provide explanations for unasked questions, along with general statements such as "You must feel overwhelmed to be here," followed by a pause. If no response is forthcoming, it may help to assure them that many parents stay with their children. It is helpful to show parents around the unit, explain the rules and expectations, and provide written information concerning the pediatric unit.

Issues of separation anxiety need to be explored with the parents. The literature indicates that with optimal interventions there usually are no long-term ill effects from hospitalization experiences (Vernon, Schulman, and Foley, 1966; Mene, 1980; Baxter, and Mishel, 1983).

However, a study done by Vernon et al. (1966) demonstrated that children between the ages of six months and four years are the ages most likely to be upset following hospitalization. Separation from parents was the most pronounced factor in their study. Family-centered care has evolved over the past two decades. Even in institutions offering family-centered care, not all hospitalized children and their families have their needs met for reducing post-hospital upset. Meeting the child's need for power or control is one of the most challenging goals of care.

The hospitalized child with burn dressings and intravenous fluids needs assistance with feeding and modified play activities. As much independence as possible for the child is maintained through creative and unique planning. Whenever possible, hands and fingers should be free for manipulation of toys. Games can be improvised that are age appropriate.

Dressing changes create stress for the child and parents. Some parents can participate with this procedure early in the hospitalization. Others may be participant observers. For those who are too upset to be a support for the child and/or to learn techniques for home care, additional interventions should be employed. Teaching dressing changes with a doll might be an appropriate forerunner to actually observing the child and later doing the dressing. It is helpful to provide continuity of care through primary nursing assignments. Written materials and public health nurse follow-up can also be used.

Determining baseline parameters for the child prior to the accident is helpful in minimizing the regression that frequently results with an illness or injury involving hospitalization. The review of normal growth and development milestones with parents during the course of the hospital stay may be useful to them as the child regains mastery and moves on following discharge.

The concept of self-care can be easily utilized with the young pediatric client in family-centered health care facilities. Self-care is defined as the ability or potential of the client to perform behaviors that promote health and well-being (Orem, 1985). Self-care deficits emerge when individuals cannot meet the demands placed on them and the desired self-care behavior is not produced (Joseph, 1980). The infant and young child do not have the ability to perform self-care from a purely developmental standpoint. However, infants begin the process of communicating their needs to their parents from the moment of birth. Parenting involves providing care for dependent children while gradually providing opportunities for the child to develop self-care behaviors. This is evidenced by the infant eating finger foods as motor skills develop and by the toddler learning to walk and dress himself.

Nursing, as viewed by Orem (1985), assists clients who are unable to provide care for themselves or others in order to meet health care needs. In situations involving young children, nursing involves the parent(s) in both the decision-making aspect and the interventions needed (Eichelberger et al., 1980). The nurse who encourages the parent to provide care for the child can assess caretaking abilities and provide necessary interventions or referrals as needed to enhance parenting skills. The nurse who observes parental strategies for feeding, comforting, and playing with their child can then plan similar care activities to meet the child's needs when the parent is not present, thereby providing consistency in the provision of care.

Care should be planned to minimize the disruption in the parent-child relationship and support attachment (Gill, 1987). Parent participation in caring for their children is recognized as beneficial, but not all nurses encourage or support this notion. Some nurses may feel that they lose "control" when the parent bathes, feeds and nurtures their child (Gill, 1987). However, nurses can play a vital role during the hospitalization of a child. Assessing parent-child interactions, role modeling for parents when necessary, and providing teaching related to the health problem, developmental issues and anticipatory guidance are appropriate nursing interventions and promote feelings of power in the parent.

CASE STUDY: Preschool

David and Joan have been married for five years and have a three-year-old girl, Melanie. Two months ago David received an offer of a promotion and transfer with his company. Before accepting the new position, David and Joan thoroughly examined the area that they would be moving to. Health care options were important considerations to them.

After researching the options and finding out that the new town had a well-known medical center, David accepted the transfer. After getting settled, Joan talked to her new neighbors and acquaintances through work and narrowed her choices of pediatricians down to three. She then went to their offices and talked with some of their clients to determine satisfaction with the services. She questioned other parents about the physician's approach with children and how the parents perceived the doctor's expertise. She interviewed each physician and chose one, resulting in an educated choice.

Joan wanted the option of having well-child care performed by a nurse practitioner, so she looked for one that was affiliated with the pediatrician she had chosen. The nurse practitioner's qualifications were examined and Joan made a well-informed choice.

At the first scheduled well-child visit, the nurse practitioner greeted Melanie and gave her a choice of which color gown she would like to wear during her examination. Melanie smiled and chose the lime green one. The nurse practitioner left the room while Joan helped Melanie put on the gown, allowing her privacy for undressing. During the examination, the nurse practitioner took time to explain to both Melanie and Joan what she was doing and why. She allowed time for questions and let Melanie handle the equipment such as the stethoscope and thermometer. When the examination was over, the nurse practitioner again left while Melanie dressed. She returned to explain her findings and gave Melanie a bright colored sticker for being so cooperative during the examination. Both Melanie and Joan left the office feeling positive about the visit.

That evening, when David was playing with Melanie, she said, "Come to my office." David wasn't quite sure what to expect, but went along. Melanie took a pencil and put it under his arm. "I think you're sick," she said. "What should I do?" asked David. Melanie said, "I'll be right back," and off she went. Several minutes later she returned with her doll's bottle. She put the bottle up to David's ear and pretended to put in ear drops. She then handed him some imaginary pills and said, "Take these until they are gone and you'll feel better." She then handed David a piece of paper on which she had scribbled. David said, "What's this?" Melanie answered, "The bill." She placed the sticker she had received on David's shirt.

By making a thoughtful choice, Melanie experienced her visit to the nurse practitioner as a positive one. She demonstrated, through her play with her father, that health care practitioners were helpers and made people feel better. Because of her positive experience she will not be as fearful if she needs to go to the the nurse practitioner or doctor when she is ill. She is learning that adults can be trusted to take care of children. David and Joan also had a positive experience in validating their ability to make a good choice in providing health care for their child.

Melanie's parents experienced empowerment in this situation because they had a favorable experience as a result of their concern and increased knowledge base that helped them come to a satisfactory solution to the problem of providing good health care for their daughter. They improved their feelings of self-esteem, a component of personal power.

Melanie also received a boost in self-esteem from this situation. Being given a choice of apparel and participating with the equipment, as well as having her privacy respected, increased Melanie's sense of control in the situation. This enhanced her perception of herself as a worthwhile person, which was reflected in the respect and consideration shown to her by an adult. Her trust in her parents to care for her, or to take her to someone who could, was validated by this experience; her support network was thus also strengthened.

Preschool children who develop a sense of control in their lives tend to behave cooperatively with others in their environment. If the child perceives his parents as in control and reliable, he then is more willing to work with them and other adults toward a common goal. Parents need to provide the pre-schooler with opportunities for supervised independence, but realize that the child may lose self-control often and needs to have parental limitations set on his behavior.

CASE STUDY: School Age

After the death of his wife, Sam moved himself and his ten-year-old daughter, Janey, to a new town so that they could be near his family. Janey was enrolled in the fifth grade and easily made friends. Her father encouraged her to have her friends over to the house so that he could meet them.

One Friday afternoon after school Janey invited her two new friends, Lori and Katie, over to listen to records. Upon entering the house, Janey introduced her friends to her father. They look startled as his "hello" was somewhat garbled. Sam smiled and asked them how school had gone that day. Janey noticed that the girls looked uncomfortable and excused the threesome to the family room. Janey went to the kitchen to get some refreshments and when she returned she heard the girls giggling and making fun of the way her father talked. After her friends left the house Janey went to her room and cried. She felt so helpless.

In her old home town, everyone knew and loved Sam. It didn't matter to them that he was deaf. Sam lipread and was able to speak, although unclearly. He made every effort to hold interesting conversations with his friends. Sam was of above average intelligence and his family had never allowed his hearing loss to lessen his goals. Janey had grown up in a positive and growth-inducing environment. She was shocked by her experience with her new friends.

Sam noticed that Janey had been crying and asked what was wrong. She hesitated to tell him as she didn't want to hurt his feelings.

At school, Janey refused to talk in class and began crying when the teacher approached her about her silence. The teacher sent Janey to the school nurse. In a quiet, unhurried fashion, the school nurse encouraged Janey to talk about her feelings and soon learned the reason for Janey's lack of participation in school. She set aside time for Janey to come talk with her three times a week, assessing that Janey needed to have an adult woman to talk to. She also urged Janey to speak with her father about the problem with her friends, saying that her father would have some suggestions and that he had had to adjust to this world of hearing people and could help her understand that experience.

That evening Sam again asked Janey what was the problem. Janey and her father had always been close and honesty had been stressed, so Janey went ahead and described her experience. Sam assured Janey that this was not a new experience for him. They talked about how some people are scared by others who are different or embarrassed by their own discomfort. Sam encouraged Janey to be open about his deafness and prompted her to have her friends over again.

The next day, Janey asked Lori and Katie to come to her house again. Lori declined and told Katie to do the same. Katie enjoyed playing with Janey so she agreed to come. When they arrived, Sam met them at the door with some fruit and juice. Sam explained to Katie why his speech was unclear. She had read about Helen Keller and thought it was wonderful that he could speak as well as he could. They had an enjoyable afternoon and Janey's faith in humans was restored.

The school nurse recognized Janey's need to verbalize her feelings and helped strengthen Janey's self-esteem by planning time to devote solely to her. She also encouraged Janey to talk to her father, helping her to identify a resource for strength and power in her father, her chief support system. Identifying some of her other power resources helped decrease Janey's feelings of powerlessness and gave her the confidence or positive self-worth to approach her peers again in an offer of friendship. Sam strengthened Janey's power resource of intellectual abilities by assisting her in adding to her knowledge and understanding of certain human behaviors.

Janey had been exposed to prejudice for the first time. She decided at that point that she would be an advocate for the disabled, not realizing that she already was by treating them as she would anyone else.

In the process of adapting to the outside world, school age children may have some difficulties. It is typical of this age group to become aware of the differences between their home situation and that found in other homes and settings. More comfortable with the familiar, the school age child is tentatively exploring the unfamiliar aspects of their environment. The attitudes of the child toward an uncommon situation are similar to to those reactions he has noticed in the members of his family, but beginning to resemble those of his peers. The school age years are a time of identifying oneself as separate from the family and a member of the larger community.

Summary

Children express their needs for power differently than the adults in their environment but just as persistently. The power needs for children in the age groups of infant, toddler, pre-school and school age are discussed. A sample assessment tool for powerlessness in children is provided. Suggestions are made for potentially empowering interventions to use in the effort to meet the power needs of children in the health care setting.

References

Baxter, P. Frustration felt by a mother and her child during the child's hospitalization. *MEW* 1 (3) 159-161, (1976).

Buckner, E. Use of Brazelton Neonatal behavioral assessment in planning care for parents and newborns. *Journal of Obstetrics, Gynecology and*

Neonatal Nursing 12 (1) 26-30, (1983).

Erickson, M. Trends in assessing the newborn and his parents. *Maternal Child Nursing.* March/April 99-103, (1978).

Gill, K. Parent participation with a family focus nurses' attitudes. *Pediatric Nursing* 13 (2) 94-96, (1987).

Greenberg M, and Morris, N. Engrossment: the newborn's impact upon the father. *American Journal of Orthopsychiatry* 44 520-531, (1974).

Horowitz, J., Hughes, C., and Perdue, B. *Parenting Reassessed: A Nursing Perspective.* Englewood Cliffs, N.J.: Prentice-Hall, Incorporated, (1982).

Judd, J. Assessing the newborn from head to toe. *Nursing 85* 15 (12) 34-41, (1985).

Kiernan, B, and Scoloveno, M. Assessment of the Neonate. *Topics in Clinical Nursing* 8 (1) 1-10, (1986).

Klaus, M., and Kennell, J. *Parent-Infant Bonding* (2nd Ed.) Saint Louis: The C.V. Mosby Company, (1982).

Lemons, P. The family of the high-risk newborn. In Perez, Rosanne (ed.) *Protocols for Perinatal Nursing Practice.* Saint Louis: The C. V. Mosby Company, (1981).

Marlow, D., and Redding, B. *Textbook of Pediatric Nursing* (6th Ed.) Philadelphia: W. B. Saunders Company, (1988).

Meng, A. Parents' and childrens' reactions toward impending hospitalization for surgery. *Maternal-Child Nursing Journal* 9 (2) 83-98, (1980).

Mishel, M. Parents' perception of uncertainty concerning their hospitalized child. *Nursing Research* 32 (6) 324-330, (1983).

Mercer, R. Relationship of the birth experience to later mothering behavior. *Journal of Nurse Midwifery* 30 (40) 204-11, (1985).

Mott, S., Fazekas, N., and James, S. *Nursing Care of Children and Families; a Holistic Approach.* Menlo Park, California: Addison-Wesley Publishing Co., (1988).

Orem, Dorothea E. *Nursing: Concepts of Practice* (3rd Ed.). New York: McGraw-Hill Book Company, (1985).

Parker S., and Brazelton, T. Newborn behavioral assessment *Children Today.* July/August 2-5, (1981).

Peery, J., and Mott, S. Infancy. In: *Nursing Care of Children and Families: A Holistic Approach.* Menlo Park, CA: Addison-Wesley Publishing Co., (1988).

Romanko, M., and Broct, B. Swaddling: an effective interaction for pacifying infants. *Pediatric Nursing* 8 (4) 259-261, (1982).

Rubin, R. Attainment of the maternal role part I: process. *Nursing Research* 16 237-245, (1967).

Rubin, R. *Maternal Identity and the Maternal Experience.* New York: Springer Publishing Co., (1984).

Schuster, C., and Asborn, S. *The Process of Human Development: A Holistic Approach.* Boston: Little, Brown and Company, (1980).

Servonsky, J. and Opos, S. *Nursing Management of Children.* Monterey, CA: Jones and Bentlett Publishers Incorporated, (1987).

Tulman, L. Theories of maternal attachment. *Advances in Nursing Science* 3 (4) 7-14, (1981).

Vernon, D., Schulman, J., and Foley, J. Changes in children's behavior after hospitalization. *American Journal of Diseases in Childhood.* III (6) 581-593, (1966).

8

Power and the Adolescent

N. Rinehart

Introduction

According to Erikson (1950), adolescence is the period of life devoted to establishing self-identity. According to Simons (1984), this involves 1) seeking independence from parental ties, 2) achieving capable heterosexual relationships outside family confines, and 3) consolidating a firm sense of identity. Seeking a sense of separateness, the adolescent asks "Who am I?" and "Where do I fit in?" Piaget wrote that during the ages of 11 through 15, the adolescent's cognitive skills refine themselves to include formal operations (Schuster, 1980). Formal operations include true logical thought and manipulation of abstract concepts, hypothetical deductive thought development, the ability to plan and implement the scientific approach to problem-solving, and the handling of all kinds of combinations in a systematic way. In other words, the adolescent desires to "do his/her own thing" unsupervised, to find structure and meaning in life via discovering rules, regulations and how things happen. Salk (1977) stated that the main task of the adolescent is to covertly seek adult guidance (Hine, 1972). The adolescent may experience similar feelings to those of childhood, but must learn new controls and ways of coping with and expressing these often frightening feelings, resulting in displacement (e.g., sports) or intellectualization (Simons, 1984).

Attempting to define what may be called his/her locus of control and to clarify values, the adolescent must totally reprocess earlier identifications and values, and reform them into a new whole; any unresolved issues from childhood will resurface to be reckoned with (Simons, 1984). Erikson (1950) called this "psychosocial moratorium" or "normative crisis." The adolescent struggles to separate out the values of friends, family and church, and form his/her own values, often opting for peers' over parental standards (especially with dress and music). Feedback, in the form of attention, is sought by the adolescent in this sorting process, and is "tried on for size"—if the feed-back does not match the self-image, ego or role diffusion results (Hines, 1972). The adolescent may either drop out (e.g., turns to drugs) or develop a negative identity (e.g., becomes delinquent). The chronicity of the positive or negative response depends on previous experiences with success and failure, and upon gender. Dweck (1978) found that females tend to view failure as indicative of an innate lack of ability, whereas males are taught that failure is due to a personal lack of motivation. If failure is repetitive, and seems to be independent of behavior, the adolescent learns helplessness, wrote Seligman (1975). This perceived loss of control over life events is displayed as an external locus of control, according to Arakelian (1980), and the adolescent may view the world as "doing unto them." Dweck also stated that females will suffer long-term effects of helplessness, whereas males will tend to develop conduct and behavior disorders. Adolescents with an internal locus of control exhibit more compliant behaviors, and are better able to forego immediate rewards (Arakelian, 1980). For the adolescent, it is often easier to know what is *not* wanted, rather than what is. Delayed gratification from achieving positive behavior is often met with frustration, for most adolescents seek immediate acceptance and recognition.

Isolated incidents that threaten or block goals may be met with frustration leading to anger (Janis, 1969). Resultant aggressive behavior in the adolescent is an attempt to elicit some response from the environment. When the response is obtained, whether it is positive or negative, it is still a reward to the adolescent, who achieves an ensuing sense of power or control. Lack of response is met with withdrawal, passivity and a decreased expectancy of any goal gratification (Janis, 1969; Seligman, 1975). And, according to Seligman (1975), expectancy is the key variable. When an adolescent *expects* to control some aspect of the environment, there is an absence or decreased sense of helplessness. Likewise, the degree to which an adolescent expects acceptance or rejection determines whether he/she will develop passive-submissive or active-dominant traits, Janis (1969) found. These traits may be translated into Arakelian's (1980) internal and external locus of control. The degree to which an adolescent is internally or externally controlled depends on his developmental age. The younger the adolescent, the more externally controlled he tends to be.

Smith (1985) equates powerlessness to feeling unable to perform certain activities, or as a failure to do so. Therefore, writes Macdonald (1984), failure is a feeling of inadequate control. This frustration from failure can lead to desperation behaviors, such as the grandiose story-telling by some adolescents, or the angry outbursts and resultant property destruction or personal injury by others. In this way, they see that they can change or manipulate their environment. Other undesirable outcomes of an adolescent's inability to accept seeming inevitable results may also include depression and suicidal ideation, antisocial personality, delinquency, anorexia nervosa and schizophrenia (Simons, 1984). These are the adolescents who have failed to have the following self-identified needs met: 1) increased respect from adults, 2) increased quality time with adults, 3) constructive opportunities to experiment with life, 4) help in developing social competence, 5) qualified youth leaders, 6) increased opportunity for moral development, and 7) help in finding meaning in life (MacDonald, 1984). Compare the above list to Havighurst's (Schuster, 1980) list of developmental tasks of adolescence: 1) to achieve new and more mature relationships with peers, 2) achieve a masculine or feminine social role, 3) accept one's own physique and use the body effectively, 4) achieve emotional independence of parents and other adults, 5) prepare for marriage and family life, 6) prepare for economic careers, 7) develop an ideology— a set of values and an ethical system as a guide to behavior, and 8) achieve socially responsible behavior. The difference in perspective between what the adolescent sees as necessary and what the adult view is is apparent.

For purposes of further discussion, adolescence has been divided into three groups: early (12-13 years), middle (14-16 years) and late (17-19 years). Late adolescents have little in common with early adolescents, yet health care systems frequently put them together in care settings for extended exposure to each other. Although there may be adolescents who do not exactly fit into their age group characteristics, treating all adolescents as the same leads to unrealistically high expectations for early adolescents and low ones for the older members of the group. There is the hazard that early adolescents will learn behaviors beyond their capabilities or maturity and that late adolescents will regress to behaviors long since grown out of.

Therefore, it is suggested that the adolescent population be divided into subgroups that have common features. The five sources of power (physical, emotional, intellectual, cultural and spiritual) will be discussed as experienced by the "textbook" adolescent in each age group, followed by a case study and discussion of the plan of care for the example client.

EARLY ADOLESCENCE (12-13 years old)

Physical

The early adolescent experiences rapid changes in body size, body abilities and secondary sex characteristics. Fascinated, yet embarrassed, by these changes, the adolescent may feel betrayed by, though proud of, his developing body. Illness, both physical and emotional, seems an affirmation that forces beyond his control are ruling his body.

The female adolescent begins to assume the physical proportions of the woman she is to become. Her breasts and hips enlarge and menses begin. Her body is becoming adult far ahead of the necessary mental processes which guide a mature use of growing womanhood.

The male adolescent is taking on some of the characteristics of adult manhood. His chest broadens, his penis grows and hair begins to appear where it has never been before. The voice is inconsistent, ranging from deeper tones to high squeaks. He is often clumsy and not sure of a safe place for his extremities that seem too large for his frame.

Physical energy, or stamina, is affected by illness. The early adolescent is growing rapidly and using up a great deal of metabolic energy in the growth process. Limitations and abilities of the adolescent must be realistically assessed. If illness has left their physical resources depleted, energy must be reserved for meeting necessary demands. The ill adolescent has a need for support and understanding from the adults around them as they additionally attempt to deal with the awkwardness of their bodies. If physical exercise is not contraindicated, it will increase the adolescent's feelings of control and power and sublimate feelings of anxiety.

Besides increased physical exercise, proper nutrition and rest must be encouraged. Adolescents may need to work with the dietitian to establish a diet that will provide the necessary nutrition and still be appealing to them. Rest periods help conserve physical and emotional energy, and allow time for integration of information.

Members of this group of adolescents identify their locus of control as being external, as manifested by their behavior. This adolescent sees the changes in his body as being centered in himself, but from forces he cannot control. Afraid of further alteration in his body image, the adolescent should be included in decisions concerning his body.

Choices regarding care and compliance need to be encouraged. To make decisions about the plan of care, he should be encouraged to increase his self-care agency. However, care must be taken not to overwhelm him with too many choices.

Activities must be planned that incorporate his abilities and limitations. As previously stated, his energy is drained through the process of growing, and illness makes further demands on his body; some energy must be reserved for necessary activities, such as mild to moderate exercise.

If the adolescent does not readily participate in the plan of his care, involve him in it as much as possible, gradually adding to his responsibilities with time. He may come from a home where decisions have always been made for him. If such is the case, sudden responsibility for choices about his own care may be frightening and places too much of a demand on what he feels his resources are. Since he has learned to be dependent, he will also be unable to operate decision-making behavior.

Teaching regarding treatment and the course of the illness is important. Encouragement to participate in self-care will increase the patient's sense of control. In order to see the external world as being controlled by him, he must be urged to participate in choices for his care, as well as healing activities, such as visualization. This enhances the sense of control over one's body.

The involvement of other adolescents in the health education of the client is important. As peers are often more credible to the adolescent than adults, it is important to seek the assistance of other adolescents in teaching regarding treatment and illness.

It is vitally important to praise the adolescent for activities he can do well. Feedback for positive behaviors will increase his acceptance of himself and enhance self-esteem. Encourage the adolescent to give feedback about his perceived limitations and help him see how to decrease those limitations. Ask him about his preferences in diversional activities (Table 8-1), and honor those requests. His perception of control in his health care situation will become more internal the more support in decision-making he is given.

Table 8-1. Summary of Interventions for Adolescent Powerlessness

Physical
Environment modification to increase self-care (wheelchair ramps)
Rest periods
Good nutrition
Isometric exercises
Weight lifting
Walking
Basketball
Relaxation Tapes/ Meditation
Baseball
Swimming
Puzzles
Hand-held video games
Bedspread from home

Intellectual
Teaching regarding illness and treatment
Setting realistic goals
Word games (Scrabble)
Puzzles
Decision-making games (Risk, Chess, Monopoly)
Reality testing
Relapse prevention (situational role play)
Informative t.v. programs (Nat'l. Geographic)
Trivia games

Emotional
Verbalization of feelings
The Ungame

Behavior modification
Values clarification exercises
Review alternative coping strategies
Role play-expression of feelings in acceptable manner
Watch any activity (from window or via TV)

Cultural

Involvement of significant others
Posters
Music
Telephone
Clothing
Activities with peers
Arrange for work situations
Opportunity for grooming (curling iron or shaver)
Drug Rehabilitation Program

Spiritual

Encounters with others
Refer to clergy
Provide for religious rituals
Provide privacy for religious practices
Plan future activities
Values clarification exercises

Determination of the physical source of power in the early adolescent is based on the feedback from the client as well as observations of objective data from the nurse. Listen to the statements made by the client.

Are the statements internally focused? For example, does the client talk about what he is able to do rather than what he is allowed to do? If this is occurring in his speech, he is beginning to view himself as responsible for his own physical performance. However, the majority of early adolescents' perceptions will not reflect an internal locus.

Intellectual

The 12 and 13-year-olds are usually concrete thinkers with little abstract thinking ability. As they venture into the world of adolescence, they are bewildered by the contradictions they see from their concrete vantage points. Abstract thought, handling hypothetical situations and thoughts, and other hallmarks of formal operational thinking are the cognitive goals of adolescence. For the early adolescent, these abilities are the exception rather than the rule.

Abstract expressions usually puzzle the early adolescent. The ability of deductive reasoning, such as "if A does this, then B will happen," is only starting to appear. Comprehending the implied meaning of "it's raining cats and dogs" may be difficult, as their speech is "black and white." They say what they mean without the added innuendoes found in the speech of older adolescents and adults. They tend to see their parents as suffering the consequences of their behavior: "It would kill my folks if they knew what I was doing."

Introspection is another difficult area for early adolescents. The gaining of introspection assists the individual in handling frustration and refining social behaviors. It also accounts for the inability to accept delayed gratification. An early adolescent does not have this ability; he is often bewildered by his powerlessness to control his frustration and, in fact, may resort to childlike responses (i.e., temper tantrums). His social skills are rudimentary and not as refined as they will become later on. He looks at those people he wishes to emulate and wonders why the envied social skills of these revered others are not easily part of his repertoire. A main source of frustration is the way he is treated by adults—more like a child than a "real teenager."

The use of concrete and abstract statements, and requesting the client's interpretation, will assist the health care professional in evaluating the status of the adolescent's intellectual functioning. Most early adolescents will have difficulty explaining such statements as "a bird in the hand is worth two in the bush," but will easily tell the assessor that robins are a type of bird. Ability may be assessed with simple math problems, although serial sevens may be difficult. Assess the knowledge deficits in the client, and determine the teaching methods that are most appropriate.

The staff member must not expect more of the adolescent than he is able to give. Communication must be kept at the concrete level; for example, what is going to happen next, what objects are used for, what the relationship is between two events, and rudimentary explanations to clarify plans of care.

Power is related to knowledge. Education regarding the disease process and the treatment for it should be included in the plan of care for this adolescent. Increased knowledge enhances the power to understand.

Ask the adolescent to repeat instructions and explanations to validate his understanding. Ask him to demonstrate self-care procedures he has learned, and praise him on his successes. If the client is unable to follow through with self-care, or is too embarrassed, do not belittle his inability to do so, but patiently try an alternative plan, with a statement such as "Good! Now we know one way that won't work," or, "That way didn't work too well, so how else might we arrange things so that the job will get done?" This is the "try another way" philosophy employed so successfully in special education (Haring, 1978).

Carry out planned client teaching and frequently assess the comprehension of the client. Alter teaching techniques to provide variety and avoid boredom by the adolescent. Using current visual aids is a help and increases retention by one-third (Morse and Wingo, 1969).

Emotional

Emotional stability is a difficult thing to assess in the adolescent as he normally exhibits a labile affect and wide variations of behavior. The early adolescent will exhibit more childlike behaviors than an adult, but will fluctuate between those and his attempts at more controlled behavior. He is adding to his repertoire of defense mechanisms.

The defense mechanisms of this age group include few of the adult ones but many of the child including: acting out, denial, rationalization, avoidance, hypochondriasis, passive-aggressive behavior, projection, displacement, dissociation and regression (Barry, 1984). These are more readily used than the more mature defense mechanisms of sublimation, suppression and compensation.

Coping styles in the early adolescent are often a reflection of the way they see adults about them coping with the world. For instance, they may see their father having a drink to "unwind" after a long day's work and may secretively copy the behavior. The adolescent may also see his mother take a diet pill for energy or to control her eating. This results in implicit permission for the adolescent to take pills, drink, or begin anorexic behaviors to gain the approval of, or seek attention from, parents or peers. If these behaviors are not countered, the adolescent feels "they don't care;" or, if confronted, responds with "you do it!" Tragically, this is when an inadvertent successful suicide often occurs, while self-esteem and self-worth are low.

The self-esteem of the early adolescent is based on his assessment of himself, as well as what he perceives others think about him. Heavily influenced by his perceptions of others' evaluations of him, the early adolescent is affected more by peer pressure than any influences of home and adult society. The emotional motivation of the early adolescent hinges on self-esteem. How he feels about himself and his sense of self-worth relates to the amount of motivation he feels in working toward improvement in his quality of life. Lack of motivation, distorted cognition and emotional disturbance result in feelings of powerlessness or hopelessness in adolescents, sometimes leading to suicidal ideation and acting out. If an adolescent actually cannot control the traumatic experiences he may have endured, any motivation to respond in the face of subsequent trauma will wane. Even if the adolescent responds and succeeds, he will have trouble learning from the results, and believing that his response worked. This cycle contributes to depression and anxiety (Seligman, 1975). He commonly expresses an external locus of control.

To internalize the client's locus of control, and thereby increase the adolescent's sense of power, incorporate the three techniques developed by Arakelian (1980). These include: reconstrual of stimuli, action-oriented approach and counseling (Table 8-2).

Reconstrual of stimuli is the process of helping the individual alter his perception of particular life situations. The person's perceptions are modified from that of being a victim to one of effecting control. For instance, rather than seeing the inability to perform a certain sporting skill as failure, the nurse encourages the client to see the task as a goal to meet.

The action-oriented approach entails the implementation of new behaviors resulting from altered perceptions and attitudes. This involves the identification of specific and attainable goals. However, if the adolescent is unable to exhibit new behaviors, do not criticize him. Offer alternative behaviors to encourage success.

The third technique is counseling, and requires the health care professional to challenge externally oriented verbalizations and excuses, and to either acknowledge internally oriented statements or help to identify personal needs or wants. This approach includes the identification of consequences of various behaviors. In considering the consequences, the adolescent may begin to "own" his behavior.

Table 8-2. Internalization of Locus of Control, (Arakelian, 1980)

Intervention	Examples
1. Reconstrual of Stimuli "Pollyanna" (See things in a positive light rather than the negative–Perception)	Lose a game, but see the challenge to improve. Fail to accomplish a goal, but able to identify smaller goals within it that have been accomplished and see remainder of goal as something to be completed.
2. Action-oriented approach "Silver Lining" (New behaviors resulting from altered attitudes–Action)	Being friendly to a frightened younger child rather than being angry about having to cope with the irritation of having a younger child around.
3. Counseling "Rose Garden" (Challenge of external locus of control statements–Speech)	If *you* break a window you must pay for it. "Brian did not *make* you do anything, you chose to respond with anger."

Ask the adolescent for feedback concerning his perceptions of things going on in his environment. If the nurse exhibits caring and genuine interest, the adolescent will usually make an honest attempt to validate the nurse's perceptions of events. Internalization of locus of control will yield more emotional stamina for the adolescent.

Emotional stamina or energy is related to the adolescent's evaluation of himself, as well as to the emotional reserves with which he tackles each confusing day. With so many physical and psychological demands made upon the energy levels of the adolescent, he may exhibit low tolerance to frustrations and stressors and, as a result, spend a great deal of the time frustrated or angry about situations over which he feels has no control. The amount of energy required to deal with these upsetting circumstances further depletes his reserves of emotional energy and often leads to additional blowups. If he maintains an external locus of control, he may end his day in an explosion of hurt feelings or temper tantrums, and feel that "if only" this or that had not "made" him upset, it "never would have ended up this way."

Considering the often extreme emotional lability of the adolescent, occasions should be provided for the client to release feelings in an accepted and structured environment. Different methods of coping with stressors must be discussed with the adolescent in a manner that promotes his choice of behavior rather than being dictatorial. Discuss alternative coping strategies with the adolescent. Building a list of possible behavior alternatives is empowering for the adolescent. Encourage the verbalization of feelings to decrease the probability of acting-out behaviors (Barry, 1984).

Cultural

Peers are the greatest influence for adolescents and the source of their cultural behavior. The reasoning used by adolescents for most behavior at this age is that "everyone else does it," reflecting the great influence of peers on their behavior. Not being like peers can lead to increased feelings of powerlessness.

Female members of the early adolescent group are beginning to display interest in social relationships with male adolescents, although these are generally "crushes." Parents often complain about the girls being "boy-crazy," yet they have close ties with other girls. The social behavior in this age group includes hours on the phone, sharing secrets, giggling and writing notes. Experimentation with make-up may be distressing to the parents, but it is important to the adolescent.

Boys are not as socially mature as girls. They are more interested in hanging around with their male friends and participating in all-boy activities. They begin to look at girls in this age group, but rarely participate in social activities with them. Strongly influenced by their peers, boys tend to want to be seen with the girls that their peer group admires. Male adolescents are not as likely to live on the telephone, but do dress and act like each other as much as possible. For these teenagers, what is currently in vogue dictates their musical taste and attire.

In assessing the cultural resources of power in this adolescent, the health care professional must also examine his cultural background. A strong peer support network may be intact, but little as he may like to admit it, the adolescent wants to have a strong family support system to depend on also. If he comes from a family that has split apart or has parents (or a parent) who have given up trying to provide him with a secure and well-disciplined home, he may not express the emotional strength that would increase his sense of self-worth. (This is most evidenced in the "throw-aways" who, though they hang together in a pseudo-family, continue to telephone home.)

The continuance of contact with his support group is important. Visitation by peers is vital to a sense of well-being and control by the client. He also needs to have opportunities to see his family members, if he chooses. Providing access to a telephone and writing materials will assist the client in maintaining his network of support outside of the hospital. Radios and tape decks will provide the environmental music that assure contact with his world. (The piped-in music in a hospital is often referred to as "funeral music" by adolescents.) However, limits may have to be set on volume, and sometimes, inappropriate selections if it interferes with another client's preferences. With the adolescent's input, the staff should provide a social environment as closely resembling that of the adolescent as is feasible.

Spiritual

Spiritually, the early adolescent is relatively immature. As mentioned previously, his thought processes are mostly concrete, and spirituality is an abstract pattern of thought. This age is the beginning of a critical view of the spiritual values of his parents and the dawn of the formation of his own.

Paying close attention to the behaviors of adults in his environment, the adolescent notices any contradictions between the adults' actions and what they tell him he must follow. He questions the values that he feels have been forced on him by family, church and society, and begins a search to define the values he will hold as an adult. In helping the client identify these values, the nurse can assess the following facets of the spiritual source of power: belief system, expectations, motivations, and support network.

In determining the presence and depth of the above elements of spiritual power, the health care professional can identify which ones are weakened and which are absent. Spiritual illness does not assist the client in regaining health, but retards it. In some instances, it can be dangerous (as in Satanic worship).

The practice of appropriate and healthy religious rituals should be facilitated. Even though hospitalized, the adolescent should be given the opportunity to participate in the religious service to which he is accustomed, if practical. Have the client participate in the planning of these activities. If he wishes, allow his family to participate with him.

It may be necessary to provide experiences to encourage support network awareness; these would include peer or family involvement. Values clarification exercises (Table 8-3) can be implemented and the resultant feelings discussed with the adolescent. It may be more appropriate, however, to utilize the ministerial staff in this domain.

Table 8-3. Values Clarification Exercises (Simon, 1974)

1. **Values Journal**
   Write some conclusive statements in answer to:
   How do I, taking an average day as an example, generally spend my time?
   What are the things (at least five) that really interest me?
   How do I view life as a whole?
   What are my commitments in life?
   What five things do I most value about my life?
   What conflicts or problems do I have about my life?

2. **Answer the following seven questions to determine if something is a value or an opinion** (all seven must be 'yes' to qualify as a value):
   Was my decision made freely without external force or coercion?
   Do I cherish the position that I have taken?
   Did I carefully consider the advantages and disadvantages of my decision and thoughtfully consider the consequences?
   Did I make my decision after examining all the possible options?
   Have I applied and acted on my convictions and beliefs?
   Have I given public affirmation to what I believe?
   Does my behavior indicate that I act on these beliefs repeatedly and does it reveal a definite pattern and personal commitment?

3. **Who Are All Those Others?**
   Draw a circle in the middle of a piece of paper labeled "ME." Draw eight large boxes around the circle. Label each box with one of the following categories: peer leader, parent-guardian or favorite aunt or uncle, important teacher, parent-guardian, best friend, person you are in love with, important neighbor, other. Put the initials of those who fit those categories in the appropriate box. List four or five things each of these significant others *want* you to value (What do they want you to be? What do they count on you for? What do

they want you to think? What demands do they place on you?).
Make a list in the ME box that states those things you also want
for yourself. What do you do with the rest of the things listed that
are not what you want? Learn to state clearly what *you* want and
how to gently say "no."

4. **Data Diary**

Of the following list, choose one or two to write about specifically for
one or two weeks:

1) Daily Diary—How do I spend my 24 hours?

2) Confidence Diary—Record your varying levels of confidence and
insecurity.

3) Success Diary—List days you consider successful and some things
that made your day a success.

4) "Bad Day" Diary—Record events on days when it would have been
better to stay in bed.

5) Affirmation Diary—Record nice things done for you and said about
you.

6) Depression Diary—List the things and people who may have dragged
you down.

7) "I Gotta Be Me" Diary—Keep a record of where and how your
actions showed your individuality.

8) Role Play Diary—Review your day in search of the times and
situations when you were pretending, playing a role rather than
being openly and honestly yourself.

9) "Go To Hell" Diary—Some people and situations spawn anger and
even hatred. Keeping a record might reveal a pattern.

10) "Special Moments" Diary—List the persons or situations that evoked
affectionate feelings and thoughts because they were pleasant, intimate, and thoughtful.

11) "I Learned" Diary—Are you growing? This record may give you a
hint.

CASE STUDY

*C.T. is a 12-year-old female admitted to an Adolescent Development
Unit for "conduct disorder and family dysfunction." She has a younger
sister, five years old, by her stepfather and natural mother, with whom
she lives. Her natural father and stepmother are active in her life, but
agreed to the hospitalization following the client's suicidal ideation in
the wake of the death of a close cousin. She appears angry, sullen,
and verbally abusive to non-allied adults and peers.*

*During the course of hospitalization, a strict behavior modification
contract had to be instituted to help control her outbursts of rage,
including profuse profanity and property destruction. One of her peer
allies shares in her devotion to "heavy metal" rock groups (e.g., Motley*

Crue). These two patients share the "devil's handshake" and frequent reference is made in C.T.'s speech to Satan as having "real power." Her mother refuses to take her out on passes, even though ordered, unless C. talks with the hospital chaplain each day. Her dress and make-up frequently mirror the "punkers." She often requests "space from staff" and relates that she gets more support from her peers. Primary among them is a 17-year-old male who happens to be the tallest client in residence, whom she refers to as "Dad."

After an unsuccessful trial of Dexedrine for a presumed Attention Deficit Disorder, she has exhibited more controlled behavior on Desipramine (150mg/d) and Mellaril (50mg/d), the latter she regularly refuses because "it's my right."

Assessment

Physical. C.T. is physically healthy, although her eating is not regular and she refuses at least one meal a day.

Intellectual. Intellectually, C.T. is bright and quickly demonstrates comprehension for those issues that are interesting to her.

Emotional. C.T.'s suicidal ideations indicate a low sense of self-worth and a disbelief in alternative behaviors being effective. C.T. demonstrated difficulty controlling her anger, indicating the need to work on her repertoire of acceptable coping strategies.

Cultural. She has firmly established her core of significant others among her peers. Her behavior indicates the need to belong by dressing like, and staying close to, her peers in the hospital setting. Because the adults in her world do not appreciate heavy metal music, C.T. claims to adore it.

Spiritual. C.T. demonstrates interest in Satanism and its power. Her suicidal ideations indicate a lack in feelings of hope for life to be worthwhile in the present and future.

Plan

Physical. Provide her several opportunities during each day to expend some of her physical energy. Have the dietitian speak with her about what foods she would like to eat. Therapy dealing with her feelings will likely cause an improvement in her self-care, including eating patterns.

Intellectual. Assess areas of C.T.'s interest and arrange setting goals around rewards and consequences dealing with these. Provide puzzles and informational programs for C.T. Arrange for continuance of school. Encourage decision-making games with staff and peers, i.e., Monopoly. Identify areas of weakness as challenges rather than failures. Remind her of her right to refuse medications, but also assess for her understanding of the purpose for the medication and educate for any deficits noted.

Emotional. Encourage C.T. to verbalize her feelings appropriately. Work through a program of rewards and consequences in establishing socially acceptable methods for expressing emotions. Play the Ungame with her, asking her opinion and sharing those of peers and staff. Discuss alternative coping styles with C.T. Role play some new behavior choices. Challenge her external statements about her behavior; i.e. "no one can make you angry, C."

Cultural. Encourage C.T.'s interactions with the younger clients on the unit without obviously restricting her from her 17-year-old friend. Allow posters and music other than those with a Satanic or substance abuse message. Explain to C.T. that these rules were created for the safety of everyone on the unit and no other peer could have these things either. Clothing without Satanic, drug, alcohol or anarchy messages are acceptable and, unless sexually provocative, C.T. is welcome to wear her own clothing. Allowable music was encouraged, but at a volume that did not interfere with the freedom of other peers and staff to listen to their choices of music. Request her assistance in planning the activities for the peers during the next week, such as movies, bowling, pizza night and go-cart riding. Provide time and facilities for C.T. to meet her grooming needs.

Spiritual. Review values clarification exercises with C.T. Encourage her to plan her activities for the next day, perhaps the next week. Promote interactions with clients who are exhibiting hopeful behaviors. Discourage any Satanic practices among the client population. Because of its influence on suicidal and hallucinating children, Satanist literature is forbidden on the unit. Offer the services of the chaplain, but respect C.T.'s wishes. Discuss her adolescent behaviors with her family and encourage them to not make demands on C. that she cannot tolerate, such as having to talk with the chaplain.

Interventions and Evaluation

Physical. C.T. talked with the dietitian and chose foods she liked but still refused to eat at times, especially when she was depressed. She enjoyed the activities that allowed her to run and jump, showing physical coordination and prowess in sports.

Intellectual. C.T. enjoyed the more difficult puzzles, but became frustrated if she could not figure out the solution within ten minutes. She resisted going to school, but agreed after discovering that her 17-year-old friend enjoyed classes. C.T. knew what her medications were for and continued to sporadically refuse them; however, as she felt better and enjoyed the rewards for her improved behavior, she refused her medications less often. She began talking about enjoying the challenge of solving the problems in her day and expressed pleasure in being able to conquer them.

Emotional. C.T. was encouraged to express her feelings; at first this was extremely difficult for her and she became angry when she was approached by the staff to talk. She initially refused to role play alternative methods for coping with her anger but enjoyed doing this when it was presented as a game for the peers to participate in. When the expectations of the the staff concerning her behavior were explained, C.T. stated that they might as well just put her in isolation for life. However, she recognized that the others were not tolerant of her destructive outbursts of anger and that they encouraged her to handle herself with more control. C.T. enjoyed the privileges accorded her when her behavior was appropriate, such as going with a staff member to select a video for her peers to watch on movie night.

Cultural. C.T. sulked when her unacceptable clothes and posters were sent home with her parents. She found the other peers agreeable with her complaints of the unfairness of this rule, but they were not allowed to have these things on the unit either and had come to accept it as "just another senseless rule made up by adults." C.T. expressed happiness in the acceptance of her by the peers. She checked out her clothing, viewpoints and speech with her peers for their approval. She helped plan the week's activities and received positive feedback about coming up with acceptable activity ideas that had not been thought of before. C.T. and her peers experimented with hairstyles and make-up, within the limits of the unit. She continued to spend time with the 17-year-old peer, but the time shortened and she spent more time with the peers closer to her own age.

Spiritual. C.T. refused to speak with the chaplain and remained angry with her parents for several days after they made their demands known to her. She began to talk positively about what she wanted to do when she got out of the hospital. She discussed the hope that things could get better for her. She expressed anger over the restriction of Satanic practices, but complied with the staff rules. She enjoyed the values clarification exercises and told the staff members that it was nice to have someone interested in what she thought was right for her, rather than what she should do because some adults said so. She was encouraged to apply her identified values to the rules of the unit and the staff's explanation of them. She was encouraged to arrive at a different solution that would accomplish the same thing and could not do so, thus increasing her compliance with the unit rules.

Outcome

C.T. was eventually discharged to her mother's care. The family had attended biweekly family therapy sessions and expressed their intention for continuing to attend therapy in the future. C.T. was to continue her individual therapy on an out-patient basis at her county mental health center. She could list several behavior choices with which to cope with anger. She had demonstrated her ability to use these on the unit. C.T. was voicing her life goals with optimism. She had taken her medication regularly for an appropriate period of time.

MIDDLE ADOLESCENCE (14-16 years old)

Physical

Middle adolescence is the in-between stage, away from childhood but not yet adult. Neither the adolescent nor society know quite what to expect. Their bodies continue to change and social skills are refined. Adult height is nearly accomplished in the females of this age group and the males are catching up to and growing beyond the height of the female.

Energy is a problem area for this adolescent. His body is growing so rapidly and his activities involve him in so much expenditure of energy, physical exhaustion becomes a risk. Upon seeing their child draped across the furniture and too tired to help with the chores, parents may accuse him of laziness. Parents often express fury when the "tired" adolescent finds the physical resources to go out with friends.

Interventions useful in increasing the sense of power in the physical realm include focusing on energy conservation, activities of daily living, and time organization.

Adolescents need to learn about energy conservation and to follow a nutritious diet. A well-balanced diet, coupled with adequate rest, will give the adolescent a good source of energy. Discussing the "here and now" effects of nutrition will enhance compliance, as the adolescent has little concept of "when you're old" problems.

Coordination of their extremities increases throughout these years. Yet with rapid growth spurts, the adolescent may have difficulty in maintaining an appearance of balance and coordination.

Many adolescents of this age group have acquired the secondary sexual characteristics of adulthood. Long before their minds have matured enough to use prudence, their bodies are sending out signals about urges they are eager to explore. There is much unconscious sublimation of these drives.

Contrary to the seeming opinion of the adults around them, the adolescents see themselves as old enough to control their own destiny, and take themselves very seriously. Independence as a goal is sought fervently, and the major conflict is to sort out and cope with love and anger.

Independence with supervision is important for these adolescents. They should be urged to perform their own self-care and activities of daily living, if at all possible. Still uncomfortable with their bodies, they will do the more intimate aspects of their care readily, as opposed to having the nurse do it for them.

Organization of physical power resources is important for the adolescent. As their world is frequently full of unexpected happenings, they need a sense of order in their lives. Schedules are valuable aids in this goal.

Planned activities should include such things as games, outings, listening to music or watching a chosen television program or video. Exercise is planned for the improvement or maintenance of physical strength. Isometric exercise is used with the adolescent in traction. Passive or active range of motion is a must with the immobilized teenager. If ambulatory, as in a psychiatric setting, the adolescent's participation in morning exercises, outings to a health club, and walks are encouraged. A gymnasium within or near the facility will provide space for the adolescent to move about and release energy, decreasing the build-up of stress.

Schedules for activities and rest times will assist in conservation of energy. The adolescent will respond positively to choosing which activity to participate in, but will not be comfortable in planning his entire day's schedule. Freedom within boundaries is a useful goal with the adolescent in this age group.

The health care provider should reassess the abilities and limitations of the client after trying each new level of activity. The adolescent may overstate his physical abilities or assess himself as being able to do less than an assessment of him reveals.

If the adolescent is not active enough, he will be restless and irritable. On the other hand, to have the adolescent do too much is not desirable. In attempting secondary level nursing, the nurse must frequently assess the energy level of the client to keep disease from affecting or damaging any more self-care abilities.

Intellectual

Adolescents of this age group (14-16) are beginning to use abstract thinking. They can more easily report the consequences of certain behaviors. The future does not seem forever away for them any longer, although it may stop at age thirty.

The adolescent's perception of himself in relation to the world affects his recovery or rehabilitation rate. The adolescent who believes himself to be stupid will relate differently to his environment from the adolescent who feels he is capable of learning and understanding whatever he wishes.

Relationships with others are affected by the adolescent's view of his intellectual abilities. The class clown may feel his behavior is necessary because he is not smart enough to be the "brain." On the other hand, the adolescent who is very bright may keep his intelligence a secret in order to fit in with his peers.

Knowledge of his condition leads the adolescent to make informed choices and have increased feelings of power. Adolescents tend to be relieved when they receive information about their bodies and the treatment that is planned. However, the nurse must continually be sensitive to how much information it is appropriate to relay.

The adolescent will cooperate much better with a teaching plan if you ask for his input: when he would like to discuss his illness, what this instruction should cover, and how the information should be delivered. Watching tapes, slides or videos about a topic may be sufficient for understanding. If he is a "hands-on" learner, examining models of organs, practicing a self-care procedure or showing him the equipment that is to be used in his treatment will make the teaching plan more successful. The assessed deficits in knowledge about himself should be deemphasized, as the adolescent may not take kindly to a plan that is called teaching.

Assertiveness training will assist the adolescent in expressing his desires in a more tactful way and enhancing his sense of control. Self-image is often a problem for the adolescent, so communicating acceptance is important. Feeling good about oneself is necessary for a positive self-image. The stronger the adolescent's feelings of self-worth, the greater his sense of power. Use of the techniques described in Table 8-2 will help the adolescent accomplish a feeling of control.

An increased internalization of control will lead to a feeling of responsibility, which is a goal of self-care. Complete compliance or submission without resistance is a form of perceived helplessness which reflects the perception that any success or failure is independent of the adolescent's own skills and responsibility.

Client responsibility is enhanced via learning assertiveness techniques. Practice assertiveness training using situations and role playing to aid the adolescent in working through difficult problems with peers and parents.

Emotional

This is a very labile and fluctuating period for the adolescent, trying to balance what his head knows versus what he feels. He has trouble being the adult he wants to be while still feeling childlike in his heart.

Journal writing is appealing to the adolescent and useful to help understand "where he is coming from." It may be used to aid the client in gaining some introspection into his behavior, and as an aid in evaluating teaching plans. Review the contents of the journal with the adolescent as a further indication of interest in him.

One-to-one counseling expresses adult interest in the adolescent. Although not too keen on talking things over with his parents, the adolescent sees individual attention given to him by another adult as empowering and important. Stable relationships with health care professionals are crucial as a tool in building trust.

Continuity of care, using the same nurse for the client whenever possible, and good communication between shifts aid in building trust between the adolescent and the nursing staff. It also promotes awareness that staff-splitting is unacceptable.

Teaching healthy coping mechanisms is a process which takes time and patience, especially if negative coping behavior has involved all of the adolescent's friends. Situational role playing will assist the adolescent in identifying alternative behaviors related to his peers.

During the process of evaluating the motivating factors for a behavior, it is vital to share these observations with the client. This allows him to clarify or validate the assessment as well as to let him hear what he seems to be saying. Motivation is assessed by examining the needs met by the client's behavior. Cultural

The teenager perceives himself to be omnipotent at this age. The adolescent functions in a world of "supposed-to's;" rules bend for them, but not for adults. What is "kosher" is dependent upon what is in vogue. Life is generally intense.

To enhance the client's availability for communication with with peers, provide telephones, if possible, and paper and envelopes for correspondence. Encourage his friends to come see him during his hospitalization.

Arrange activities for a group of adolescents which will encourage bonding of the group. This can be accomplished with the aid of a recreational therapist, if available.

Encourage interactions with other members of the same sex. Discuss with the adolescent roles and attitudes that he employs to feel part of the group, and provide opportunities for these interactions.

In listening to the adolescent's favorite music, the nurse may find a basis for discussion with the adolescent in who performs it and what the words mean to him.

Determine what can facilitate communication with the other members of the adolescent's family. Provide times for visiting with family members, if the adolescent wishes.

Offer information and means for birth control measures, if the adolescent is sexually active. The adolescent's confidentiality must be respected. Ask the adolescent whether or not he has talked with his parents about his sexual activities.

Create a comfortable environment, allowing the placement of posters, as is reasonable. If possible, allow the client to choose the placement of furniture in his room.

As attention is essential to the adolescent, the nurse should provide occasions for one-to-ones. Be sensitive to an adolescent's mood swings. In consulting with the health care team, the team members should relay any information about the adolescent's school history or drug problems that might be helpful in the overall treatment plan. This would also include any inferences of suicide.

Spiritual

Whether conscious or unconscious, the middle adolescent is trying to build a foundation for his belief system. It is unlikely that most adolescents will embrace their parents' religious standards, although participation may be an overt symbol of seeming compliance. What their peers think and believe is much more influential at this age.

It is important for the health care professional to incorporate into her care plans any religious rituals that may positively influence the client's health and recovery. Values clarification exercises (Table 8-3) may also be helpful in this area. Most importantly, be available to talk, and refer when necessary. It may be necessary to contact the ministerial staff to provide another support option for the adolescent, especially if family is not available.

CASE STUDY

J.S. is an attractive, somewhat precocious 14-year-old admitted for family problems and alcohol abuse. She lives with both natural parents, and has an 11 year old brother. Five years earlier, her mother was diagnosed with cancer, and there were real concerns over her surviving surgery and subsequent treatment. J.S. dates her problems back to this time, during which she assumed many of her mother's tasks (i.e., cooking and cleaning). She recently expressed fear of her father's affection toward her as bordering on sexual interest. It is interesting that this allegation came within one week of her roommate's discharge, the roommate had been hospitalized following several sexual assaults by her stepfather. Previously, J.S. had expressed suicidal preoccupation while rooming with another client admitted for multiple suicidal gestures.

During her hospitalization, J.S. frequently took charge in community meetings, and was often voted president. She developed a relationship with the oldest client, and when he was placed on Dexedrine, she immediately requested some "to help my concentration too." She came to be one of the longest hospitalized patients, and frequently used that longevity as a means for telling colorful and exaggerated stories of previous patients' escapades. Many of the inpatient population held her in awe, and often fed into her perceptions. When this bubble of esteem burst, J.S.'s response was to withdraw and become extremely compliant with the unit routine she had earlier so often criticized and fought. This behavior was short-lived, as her goal for the compliance was to net special dispensations—a reward not realized. She then vowed to return to her previous behaviors as "all the changes I've made don't count with my parents—they want some nice little girl, and I can't do that fakiness anymore." She also complained about her parents' "new church" and her inability to understand why they gave up Catholicism for it, which she continues to practice.

After several reportedly difficult family meetings, J.S. was convinced she would not be returned home to live, but be sent instead to "some sort of placement—a group home."

Assessment

Physical. J.S. has no physical weakness or activity restrictions. Her alcoholism has led to an imbalanced diet with a heavy emphasis on carbohydrate intake which is typical of alcoholics who are not allowed free access to alcohol (Anonymous, 1974).

Intellectual. She has the ability to understand whatever is of interest to her at the moment. J.S. is also quick to arrive at the rationalizations of the alcoholic and has a vivid imagination, both of which indicate the potential for comprehension and adaptation to daily occurrences.

Emotional. J.S. is an emotional "porcupine," sensitive and touchy, coping at one moment and devastated the next. She borrows the coping styles of her peers, seeking the attention she craves. She is in a "good place" emotionally while she is the center of attention, then becomes angry and resentful when the attention shifts away from her.

Cultural. Her striving for acceptance is not based on her own adequacy but on how much she can be like her peers. By copying them, she can gain acceptability. In her chameleon-like shifts, J.S.'s individuality is lost. She works at pleasing her peers and gaining their approval, as reflected by their voting her in as president of the group. J.S. gains a certain superiority by being a long-term client on the unit.

Spiritual. J.S. expresses confusion with her parents' switch from one faith to another. She states her intention to continue in her practice of Catholicism. In demonstrating her non-personness, picking up the other peers' problems, J.S. is clearly indicating a low self-esteem. Her defeat over difficulties reflects a lack of hopefulness on her part.

Planning

Physical. Provide plenty of situations for J.S. to move and develop some prowess. Encourage a well-balanced meal plan and have the dietitian come to the unit to speak with her about her predilection for sweets. Encourage her participation in A.A. meetings.

Intellectual. Provide opportunities to learn about her alcoholism; promote attendance at teen A.A. meetings. Assist J.S. in identifying excuses versus the truth. Encourage her to write about her understanding of situations, to be reviewed by staff with her and teen A.A. sponsor. Provide her with games and puzzles that challenge her but for which she can find the solution or win at with practice.

Emotional. Encourage J.S. to express her own feelings, not those of others. Urge her to write down her feelings about things as they occur. Play the Ungame or Scruples with her, seeking her opinion and feelings about different situations in life. Work with J.S. on methods for expressing herself assertively without the need to impose her feelings or judgments on anyone else. Practice options of behavior in response to a variety of feelings.

Cultural. Give J.S. positive feedback for her expression of her own decisions. Provide her with opportunities to share with other adolescents with a similar background, as in Teen A.A. and a support group for children of cancer victims or a hospice program. Investigate her interests in music and movies and discuss them with her at various times. Acknowledge clothes that she looks attractive in. Encourage her participation in group activities.

Spiritual. Provide opportunity for her to participate in her faith's practices. Offer to call a clergyman for her to talk with. Discuss her past successes with her. Encourage the redefinition of problems as being challenges. Promote the discussion of her parents' spiritual choices, and hers, as individual rights.

Intervention and Evaluation

Physical. J.S. enjoyed the daily exercise and game periods. With time, she increased her skill in playing volleyball and bowling. She attended Teen A.A. meetings twice a week. She cut down on her consumption of sweets and ate a more balanced diet.

Intellectual. She read her A.A. literature thoroughly, underlining those statements that meant something special to her. She began to identify those times when she used rationalizations, or excuses, rather than name the true feeling she had and acknowledge the situation without blaming others or conditions outside herself. She enjoyed working with the puzzles and helped the younger clients on the unit find the solutions as well.

Emotional. Assigned the task of writing her own feelings and identifying those of others. Scheduled time to discuss her writings in her journal and practiced voicing her own feelings in a nonthreatening manner. Played games with peers and staff expressing pleasure in making her own decisions and stating her reasons behind her choices. Practiced and adapted various behavioral choices for various feelings. J.S. built a large supply of coping behaviors to choose from. She maintained control of her behavior and assisted other peers in gaining control of their own behavior.

Cultural. J.S. continued to be looked upon as a leader by the other peers, but demonstrated the ability to increasingly allow the group to focus on someone other than herself without any disruption in her compliance with appropriate behavior standards on the unit. She began selecting clothing that looked at- tractive on her without as much expressed need to be exactly like the other peers, indicating an increased ability to see herself as an individual worthy of style and attention. J.S. regularly attended the Teen A.A. meeting and the adolescents-of-hospice program, forming several new relationships with other adolescents.

Spiritual. J.S. attended services and routinely practiced her faith. She had a family meeting to discuss her choice of faith as opposed to her parents.' They managed to reach an agreement that each was capable of making their own decision and could respect that right for the others in the family as well. J.S. talked about her successes in the past and the possibility of having more in the future. She began to express the urge to meet some of the challenges in her life rather than to flee from them.

Outcome

The majority of the problems present on admission had been worked through, involvement in A.A. had been established, and J.S. was discharged home with her parents.

LATE ADOLESCENCE

Physical

In late adolescence physical attributes closely resemble those of the adult. The height of the adolescent is nearing that which he will maintain for his adult life. He continues to develop more muscle mass and his voice is consistently lower.

The adolescent female in this group is at her adult height and weight. Her menses are regular, her breasts are mature and her hips have become rounded.

Having better control of his body, the adolescent exhibits coordination of movement, reaching that of adults. Sure of his body's position, he has fine motor control and dexterity more often than not. There is a great need for privacy with this client, and he may seem embarrassed at times by the necessity of the health care provider to examine parts of his uncovered body.

Although adult in appearance, the late adolescent needs to be assessed for his individual physical traits rather than for those expected of an adult. Due to his physical dimensions, adults often expect more physical control or ability than is reasonable. Because he has a longer attention span, he does not need the variety of activity required in earlier years. Though his strength may not be as developed as it will be later in his life, his level of energy is often greater than that of an adult.

His metabolic rate is considerably higher than an adult's, leading to an ability for the male to consume large quantities of food without weight gain. This is not always true of the female adolescent of this group and she may have anorexic or bulemic behaviors.

The late adolescent is in the process of selecting a mate or learning to be intimate with or attached to members of the opposite sex. Therefore, appearance is important to him, especially if being seen by a member of the opposite sex is a possibility.

With a more mature level of testosterone, the male client may be concerned with maintaining or enhancing his muscular proportions. Activities that include the use and exercise of muscle groups may appeal to this client. The female adolescent may also be interested in sculpting her body to meet her ideal standards. However, she may express reluctance to participate in any contact sports, or those deemed unfeminine by society.

Male adolescents often enjoy such activities as basketball, baseball and football. If the client has a limited activity tolerance or allowance, related to a disease process, isometric exercises and active range of motion of the unimpaired extremities would be appropriate. Physical exercise will help the client to feel that he is doing something for his own recovery, as well as decreasing his anxiety. Help the client choose those activities that diminish his feelings of stress and encourage those activities that fall within the realm of his allowed activity level. Teaching needs to be aimed at helping the adolescent to assess his own limitations and abilities and how to set realistic goals for himself.

Availability of grooming tools, or the provision of grooming, is important. The adolescent may well have determined what his best colors are and have a preference for a particular color of clothing, even in hospital gowns.

Letting the client know whether he has a choice in apparel is helpful. If he has his own clothing that he wishes to wear, oblige him as much as possible. If the client's self-care agency is not such that he can shave himself, offer to do it for him. Female clients who are immobilized in traction, for instance, are grateful when the nurse offers to shave their legs and/or underarms. The application of make-up or aftershave will increase the client's positive self-image.

Involve the adolescent in the planning of his care as much as possible. If he chooses self-care activities for himself, he is more likely to follow through with these behaviors. Contracting for his expected behaviors and those of the staff member further enhance his feeling of being in control, or of having power.

The tolerance of the client for the activities in his care needs to be assessed. The adolescent may not admit to being tired or weak, so the nurse must assess his activity tolerance by careful observation and monitoring of the client's vital signs.

The late adolescent will give the nurse feedback concerning his care that is often nonverbal. The nurse must look for expressions of satisfaction or dissatisfaction from the client; this may be as subtle as facial expressions, or as obvious as food being thrown across the room.

Intellectual

The 17 to 19-year-old is able to think abstractly. He is refining his ability to find possible solutions and alternatives for problems. He can handle hypothetical information and identify any relationship to him. He sees the world in its many shadings of gray, as well as the absolute blacks and whites. Included in the results of formal operational thinking comes the foundation of the adolescent's own set of values.

The late adolescent should be able to use deductive reasoning. He is able to use introspective thinking by this time in his life. A mental status examination will identify the stage of the adolescent's intellectual ability.

Having some idea of what he wants for his life's work, the late adolescent has begun to set his priorities related to marriage and family life. He has a part-time job if he is still in high school or college, or a full-time job if he has graduated or left high school. He may be concerned about his financial status related to his hospitalization. He often worries about losing his job or missing class.

Arrange assistance for this adolescent to work out his finances, such as a meeting with the hospital social worker or a financial assistant. As this group's financial difficulties run the gamut from losing a part-time job to paying for a new baby, the client's needs are quite individualized.

The nurse must be alert to the nonverbal communications of the late adolescent. He has learned to use the subtleties of language with its hidden messages. He may not express what he wants to say, fearful that his meaning may be unclear, misunderstood or unacceptable.

This client's health values must be assessed to assist the nurse in understanding what is behind any noncompliance. Meeting self-care requisites may not be on the top of his list of priorities.

Assist him in meeting his self-care needs. Help him find alternative methods to perform self-care if he is unable to succeed using the formulated plan. Ask the client to repeat the teaching information given.

The late adolescent is busy with the process of maturation and his feeling of control or seeming lack of it. Able to identify the fact that he does have control of himself when asked, on a reasoning level, he may act as if this is not true. Speech habits, such as "you make me so mad" will continue to abound in his conversations. The counseling portion of Arakelian's (1980) internalization steps is particularly important in dealing with this age group (Table 8-1). As this client becomes able to identify cause and effect, he will adopt a manner of speech that more closely reflects his rational appraisal of a situation.

Validation of implied or interpreted meanings of his communication must be carried out by the health care provider if the client is to be understood. The adolescent may express irritation with the nurse's inability to understand what he says, but will attempt to communicate more clearly if the nurse continues to express care for and concern about him.

Emotional

The late adolescent is more sure of himself, with a stronger self-esteem than he had in his earlier years of adolescence. He does not depend on the opinions of his peers so much as on his own judgment. By this age, he learns from his mistakes and successes. The adolescent is nearly, or entirely, independent of parental supervision. Emotional stability is easier to assess, as the wide mood swings of adolescence have become narrower with the advancement of age. The behavior and defense mechanisms utilized by the late adolescent should be more nearly those of an adult. He should resort to such defense mechanisms as rationalization only when under extreme stress.

Short-term coping behaviors, such as smoking, drinking and drugs, are often firmly established by the time the adolescent reaches this age. He may feel that his adult size calls for "adult" behaviors to impress others with his maturity.

Emotional stamina continues to reflect the evaluation he has of his own abilities. He deals more effectively with frustrations in his daily life, handling postponed gratification in a mature manner. The late adolescent may continue to look only at "today," having the optimism of youth that life will go on forever; however, he is usually willing to wait for rewards for his behavior. Illness may have a direct influence on the client's emotional energy. Physical and emotional illness are psychologically taxing, and the adolescent may be dismayed when his behavior is not as mature as he wishes, so he may exhibit regression, which further depletes his energy resources.

Female late adolescents will generally portray more mature behavior than the males in this group. The female adolescent may demonstrate more tolerance for frustration than does her male counterpart.

The emotional age of the client must be considered when planning care for him. He will not like being treated the same as a young adolescent. However, his chronological age may be more advanced than his emotional age.

Talking with the client about his feelings should be part of the plan of care. Discussions concerning his methods for coping with his feelings and alternative patterns of behavior must be incorporated into his plan of care. This would include an assessment of any suicidal ideation, whether implied or episodic, as an expression of coping behavior. Encourage the verbalization of the adolescent's feelings. Provide a safe and accepting atmosphere in which he can express himself and not fear any consequences.

This client is more adaptable than the younger adolescent and can build relationships with more than one staff member. Of course it is ideal to have the same nurse care for the client every day, but the late adolescent is more able to tolerate changes in his environment, including a different nurse occasionally. He sees adults as people who will soon be his peers, and therefore exhibits a willingness to adapt to changes in staff assignments.

Cultural

The late adolescent does not depend on his peers for approval, nor does he act consistently like his peers and do things because "everyone does it." Members of both sexes have been dating and are often more involved with members of the opposite sex than during their younger teen years. One of the tasks of this age group is to maintain satisfactory feelings of intimacy with the opposite sex. Being sexually active in this age group is common. The pressure to act a particular way because others behave that way has diminished, but still may be present in intimate relationships. The possibility of pregnancy or capability of impregnation is not as fearful as in earlier teen years. With increased knowledge and maturity, more responsible choices concerning fertility and procreation are made.

It is important to assess the social activities of the late adolescent and the presence or lack of significant others. Relationships with others of the same sex are not as strong as they were in earlier adolescence, and the presence of an important attachment to a member of the opposite sex has become the norm rather than the exception. Preoccupation with the love object may supersede any other interest or responsibility to others. Much time is spent talking of marriage, families, homes and the future.

Support networks consisting of family and friends are accepted with tolerance, with a preference for the support of one special person. If the family rules are too inhibiting for the adolescent, rebellion is not uncommon. The late adolescent likes to think of himself as quite independent, but grudgingly recognizes the security of knowing that home can always be returned to.

As a consequence of illness, the client may feel his sexuality threatened and make overtures to young staff members in his environment. Acceptance of the adolescent in setting limits while encouraging the continuation of his social network is important. It requires coordination among the staff to provide consistency in their approach to this client.

Maintaining his accustomed environment is not as crucial at this age, though the provision of a stereo or tape-deck would be appreciated by the adolescent. He may also want posters brought in from his room at home. As long as he does not infringe on others' rights, the adolescent may require an environment closely resembling that which he is used to.

Spiritual

With the acquisition of more abstract thought processes, the adolescent's spiritual life is more easily defined. He may have decided that the faith in which he was raised is no longer appropriate. On the other hand, he may have decided that his parents were not involved enough in spiritual areas. Whatever his decision about spirituality, the late adolescent will have firm viewpoints to express.

Besides the faith aspect of spirituality, there is the realm of hope. Not only does it include the hope for total recovery, but also includes such areas as hope for a more meaningful future, hope for doing something constructive or helpful to others, and the anticipation of pleasurable experiences yet to come. As a result of the ability to think abstractly, the late adolescent experiences these hopes for the future.

The expectations, or hopes, of the adolescent are a reflection of his opinion of society. If he cannot see things improving in his life, or cannot anticipate such a change, he is less likely to express hopefulness. An expression of hopelessness may forewarn health care professionals of future difficulties with this client and his recovery potential.

It may be helpful to arrange with the chaplain of the hospital, or private clergy, to visit the client and perform those rituals that are important to him, allowing for privacy during the service.

CASE STUDY

B.D. is a 17-year-old male admitted to the orthopedic unit for multiple fractures sustained in a motor vehicle accident. He was arrested for stealing a vehicle, crossing state lines, and driving while intoxicated. He has been court-ordered to a drug rehabilitation facility following this hospitalization. The oldest of three children, he lives with both natural parents. He has failed his sophomore year three times, and denies multi-drug problems, although by history he admits to alcohol, marijuana and occasional LSD use.

B.D. talks of wanting to become a physician, and "really enjoys anatomy–isn't that the bone stuff?" He says he has "never been able to do anything right, not like my brother, the preppie. Guess that's why I got into dealing and dressing like a punker...." He grins when asked about his sexual experience.

At home, his parents have sanctioned his beer drinking, although they supposedly deny knowledge of his marijuana and LSD use. At present, as he looks over his fractured femur and dislocated-fracture shoulder, he vows to discontinue using all drugs. After treatment he plans to obtain an apartment of his own and attend A.A., "even if I'm still on crutches! After all," he says, "I guess it's time to grow up..."

Assessment

Physical. B.D. is currently in traction and is limited in his ability to perform his daily care. He has a history of drug and alcohol abuse. He is experiencing pain from his various fractures and contusions. His activities are restricted to bedrest. He reports having had flashbacks upon occasion.

Intellectual He considers himself intelligent enough to set a medical career as his goal, though he has not demonstrated this with his repeated failure of tenth grade. He acknowledges the importance of attending a support group.

Emotional. B.D. has a police record and an upcoming court date that can be a source of stress for him. He expresses a low self-esteem, as related while discussing his brother. Also, his plans for the future include his comments about the importance for him to "grow up."

Cultural. He alludes to relationships with females via his grin when asked about his sexual experiences. He confesses to dealing drugs, which indicates a membership in some social group and a need for spending money. Perhaps he learned to "hot wire" cars from his social peers.

Spiritual. B.D. has not indicated a religious preference. He expresses hope for himself through his statements about growing up and going on to school.

Planning

Physical. B.D. is encouraged to do as much as possible for himself. For instance, his equipment for his bath is arranged close to his bed, with the caregivers completing his bath. His call-light, phone, radio and television remote control should all be within his reach. His favorite posters can be posted on his walls.

Intellectual. B.D. has high aspirations about his future and needs to assess these carefully and realistically. He is provided with reading materials about the drug rehabilitation program he will be attending. A tutor is provided to help him meet his schooling needs at this time.

Emotional. Arrange for B.D.'s lawyer to visit him periodically and inform him of the proceedings concerning his case. Provide him with a journal and encourage him to write daily entries about his best moment during the day and his worst, and what precipitated these.

Cultural. Provide a telephone and writing materials for his communication with his social group. Encourage visitors during times when B.D. is rested and available for uninterrupted meetings. Discuss the importance of choosing "new playmates and new playtoys" if he is to remain sober and clean from his addictive behaviors. Promote relationships with B.D.'s nonaddict friends. Do values clarification worksheet with B.D., encouraging him to identify the consequences of his behavior choices in the past and what is possible for him now. Provide sex education brochures and opportunities to discuss his sexuality and safe and responsible sexual practices.

Spiritual. Promote discussions of his feelings of hope for his improvement and future achievements. Identify short-term goals that he can accomplish each day or two, aiding his identification of his ability to reach goals and increase his feelings of success.

Intervention and Evaluation

Physical. B.D. resisted doing his own self-care, but admitted it was better to do his own shaving and bathing than to have "some woman do it" for him. His jacket hangs on the end of his traction apparatus, where B.D. requested it, and two of his posters are posted on the wall next to his bed. He can reach and use all communication and entertainment equipment in his room. His "boom box" is at his bedside and he enjoys controlling what shows are on his television screen.

Intellectual. Testing provided the information that B.D. is quite intelligent. He discussed his ambitions and the work necessary to attain them. He agreed to begin work with the tutor hired by the hospital for bedridden adolescent clients. He has contacted and visited with members of the A.A. group he will attend while awaiting sufficient recovery to be transferred to the drug rehabilitation center.

Emotional. Discussed forthcoming court case with his lawyer and reported less tension concerning this event, now that he knew what to expect. Complained about the staff's expectations that he write in a journal, but within five days he was writing several pages each day and discussing his responsibility for his own behavior. He reported looking forward to the time set aside each day for his caregiver to sit down and discuss his journal entry for the day.

Cultural. B.D.'s old friends came to visit him and brought him some marijuana, even after being informed of the rules regarding the smuggling in of "contraband" substances onto the hospital unit. Thereafter, with B.D.'s cooperation, his friends' packages and coats were searched for drugs and alcohol. The friends who used to "do drugs and drink" with B.D. gradually stopped coming in to see him. His friends who were willing to obey the rules of the unit were encouraged to continue to visit and did so. After doing values clarification exercises he began to identify the choices he had made in the past and their consequences. He also looked at those alternatives for behavior that he had for the present and future. With a male nurse, he freely discussed his sexual practices and the information provided for him on safe and responsible sexual relationships.

Spiritual. He is able to set daily goals and achieve them, expressing an improving sense of successfulness or personal control. He remains optimistic concerning his ability to achieve those long-term goals he perceives as important.

Outcome

Upon release from the hospital orthopedic unit, B.D. was transferred to a drug rehabilitation center. During his court case, it was decided to place him on probation as long as he stayed away from his addictive behaviors. He was eventually sent to an emancipation home, finished his G.E.D. exam and began evening classes at a community college. He got a job in a fast food place during the day.

Summary

This age of transition is a difficult one without the complications of illness or other familial dysfunctions. Being sensitive to needs and supportive of feelings, the health care professional can have a positive impact on the adolescent's life. These interventions, coupled with the adolescent's support systems, will ensure a more successful course of healing. Being available and concerned is often as effective as the doing part of medicine.

Adolescence was divided into three age and developmental groups. It is noted that 12-year-olds have little in common with 17-year-olds, yet these children are usually placed together in constant interaction situations by the health care system.

One of the major developmental tasks for the adolescent is to gain of control in his life. The conflict between being a child and becoming an adult makes this task difficult to achieve.

References

Aguilera, Donna C. and Messick, J. M. *Crisis Intervention: Theory and Methodology*. St. Louis: Mosby, (1978).

Arakelian, Maureen. An assessment and nursing application of the concept of locus of control. *Advances in Nursing Science*, 3, 25-42, (1980).

Blos, Peter. *On Adolescence*. Glencoe, NY: Free Press, (1962).

Dweck, C., Davidson, W., and Nelson, S. et al. Sex differences in learned helplessness: II. The contingencies of evaluative feedback in the classroom: III. An experimental analysis. *Developmental Psychology*, 14, 268-276.

Erikson, E. H. *Childhood and Society*. NY: Norton, (1950).

Haring, Norris G. (ed.). *Behavior of Exceptional Children*. Columbus: Merrill Pub. Co., (1978).

Hine, F.R., Pfeiffer, E., Maddox, G., et al. *Behavioral Science: A Selective View*. Boston: Little Brown & Company, (1972).

Janis, I.L., Mahl, G. F., Kagan, J. et al. *Personality*. NY: Harcourt Brace & World, (1969).

Johnson, S. H. *High Risk Parenting: Assessment and Strategies for the Family at Risk*. Philadelphia: Lippincott, (1979).

Konstantareas, M. and Homatidis, S. Dominance hierarchies in normal and conduct disordered children. *Journal of Abnormal Child Psychology*. 13, 259-268, (1985).

Kritek, P. B. Patient Power and Powerlessness. *Supervisor Nurse*. 12, 26-34, (1981).

Macdonald, D. *Drugs, Drinking and Adolescents*. Chicago: Year Book Medical Publishers, (1984).

Salk, L. *What Every Child Would Like His Parents to Know*. NY: Warner Books, (1977).

Schuster, C. and Ashburn, S. *The Process of Human Development: A Holistic Approach*. Boston: Little, Brown and Company, (1980).

Seligman, M. *Helplessness*. San Francisco: Freeman and Company, (1975).

Shillinger, F. Locus of control: implications for clinical nursing practice. *Image: Journal of Nursing Scholarship*. 15, 58-63, (1983).

Simon, S. *Meeting Yourself Halfway*. Niles, IL: Argus Communications, (1974).

Simons, R. (ed.). *Understanding Human Behavior in Health and Illness*. Baltimore: Williams and Wilkins, (1974).

Smith, F. Patient Power. *AJN*. 11, 1260-1262, (1985).

Snyder, M. *Independent Nursing Interventions*. NY: John Wiley and Sons, (1985).

Thornburg, H., Thornburg, E., and Ellis-Schwabe, M. Assignment of personal values among adolescents. *Journal of Psychology*. 9, 65-70, (1984).

9

Power and the Obstetric Family

N. Rinehart and C. Wrasper

Introduction

Whether pregnancy is planned or not, the expectant client undergoes many physical changes and hormonal fluctuations. Psychologically she "tries on" her new role as mother. She may feel power in giving birth to a new human being. If she already has children, the addition of another child can require further adjustment. Her body changes, as do her interests and social contacts. She may seek out other mothers, or reflect on the parenting skills of her own parents. She feels separate from her changing body and behaves in ways that bewilder her (Olds, London, and Ladewig, 1988). Each day, there is an increasing sense of the other person within her and its subsequent physiological demands.

The expectant woman and her significant others have many decisions to make concerning the birth experience and the process of parenting the infant (Schuster, 1980). Obstetrics, perhaps more than any other health care area, has worked to promote the sense of personal power in the client. Even so, there is still room for improvement. Many childbirth experiences can be improved to increase the positive feelings of control and bonding of mother and child.

The Expectant Father

According to Olds et al. (1988), pregnancy is a psychologically stressful time for the expectant father because he too is facing the transition from nonparent to parent or from parent of one or more to parent of two or more.

For most men there is initial excitement and pride in their proven virility. This may be accompanied by feelings of ambivalence. Olds et al. (1988) assert that the extent of the ambivalence depends on many factors, such as whether the pregnancy was planned, his relationship with his partner, his previous experiences with pregnancy, his age and, finally, his financial stability.

Lederman (1984) found that expectant fathers must establish a fatherhood role just as the woman develops a concept of herself as a mother. Lederman also found that fathers who were most successful at this generally liked children, were excited about the prospect of fatherhood, were eager to nurture a child, had confidence in their ability to be a parent, and shared in the experiences of pregnancy and delivery with their partners.

Some fathers experience "mitleiden" (suffering along) and develop symptoms similar to those of the expectant mother: weight gain, nausea, vomiting, backache, and other physical complaints.

After the initial excitement of the confirmed pregnancy, the father may feel left out. He may be upset and confused by his partner's frequent mood swings and, as the mother's physical shape changes, he may be uncertain about what is happening. He may feel powerless and resent all the attention that is directed toward the mother. Changes in sexual activity and desire may create frustration and anger. He may also have financial concerns. All of a sudden his life has changed drastically and he may feel little if no control. The father may have concerns and fears that continue throughout the pregnancy regarding the well-being of both the mother and the unborn child.

According to McKay (1983), today's father is becoming more interested in taking an active role in the process of childbirth. Nurses must identify his concerns and assist him to become actively involved. Through education, he is provided with information so that he too can make informed choices. He must be assisted so that he can utilize his resources of power.

Control Theory

Although a woman's choices may not be those preferred by the health care professional, she must have support in her efforts, and gentle nonjudgemental suggestions for improvement or alternative methods for providing for herself and her newborn. Glasser (1984) emphasizes that individuals make the best choices they can at the moment.

Control Theory does not advocate that the care provider take control. Rather it is suggested that the client be given information that will assist her in making more effective choices for herself. She has to make her own decisions, not those of her health care providers. After all, she is the one who will take the newborn home. If she is ridiculed for her clumsy handling of the infant, her self-confidence is undermined and she may not bond well with the newborn feeling ineffective as a mother, and subsequently turn her child's care over to others.

Health Belief Model

The amount of prenatal care a woman receives is a direct result of the variables that contribute toward her health beliefs. What she has been taught about childbirth, what she hears from her friends or the media, coupled with her previous personal experiences or those of significant others in her life all combine to determine the importance she places on prenatal care. Orque, Bloch and Monrcoy (1983) advocate the assessment of each individual, rather than assuming understanding of the client's needs and beliefs because she is a member of a specific ethnic or racial group. The history of the client's health beliefs will assist the health care professional in instituting a plan of care that meets the needs of each client. See Figure 9-1.

The same variables influence the woman's interpretation of labor, delivery and postpartum experiences as well as the value she places on whatever teaching she receives during these times.

There is a positive correlation between the amount of education of the client and the prenatal information she seeks (Humenick, 1981). Lederman (1984) indicates a strong relationship between the health beliefs of the client and her ability to adapt to and accept her pregnant state.

Antepartum

The antepartal period is one of upheaval. With the planned pregnancy, the woman may experience feelings of creative omnipotence, carrying the creation of an act of love. On the other hand, the unplanned pregnancy may cause feelings of betrayal by her body, her significant other and God for finding herself burdened by an unwanted pregnancy. During this time, the mother-to-be experiences many periods of powerlessness as well as powerfulness. She can delight in the power of her procreative function while bemoaning the ungainly and out-of-control feelings of an expanding abdomen. Either interpretation of her pregnancy experience is normal (Olds et al., 1988).

ASSESSMENT TOOL

1. What cultural group do you consider yourself a member of?
2. What type of information do the women in your cultural group seek?
3. What preparation do you think is necessary for childbirth?
4. What did your mother do when she went into labor?
5. What did the women in your family tell you about labor and delivery?
6. What experiences have you had with childbirth?
7. What do you expect to happen in the delivery room?
8. What position were the women in your family in when they delivered (on table flat, squatting, kneeling, on their side)?
9. Who would you like to be with you in the delivery room?
10. Can you control anything about being in labor?
11. How do you respond to pain?
12. Who told you the most about childbirth?
13. What is your impression of being in labor?

14. Where did you get these impressions (movies, mother, books, relatives, friends)?
15. What happened to the baby after delivery in your family members' experiences?
16. How do you feel about breastfeeding? bottle feeding?
17. What do you expect it to be like after you deliver?
18. Have you taken care of many babies?
19. Do you think it is important to see a physician or midwife before you are ready to have the baby?
20. Whose advice do you listen to the most (mother, friend, grandmother, doctor)?

Figure 9-1. Assessment Of Childbirth Beliefs and Cultural Background

CASE STUDY: Antepartum

Alison is a 27-year-old gravida 1 para 0. She is a CPA with a local accounting firm and plans to continue to work as long as possible. Her husband, Kent, age 31, is a successful attorney. They have been married for 5 years. They have bought their home, are financially comfortable, and are active in their church. A year ago, they decided to start a family so Alison stopped taking her birth control pills. Ten days after missing her menstrual period, Alison checked her urine with an over-the-counter pregnancy test. The test was positive so she made an appointment with a local obstetrician and was seen for her first prenatal visit at eight weeks gestation. Alison told the nurse that the pregnancy was planned and both she and her husband were eager to learn all they could about "their" pregnancy. Alison stated that she planned to breastfeed her baby, to take off three months after the birth and then return to work full-time. The nurse obtained a comprehensive health history, checked Alison's vital signs, weight, urine specimen and drew blood for studies. The nurse determined that there was nothing in Alison's lifestyle that posed a threat to her pregnancy. The doctor reported that her physical exam was normal and that her pelvis appeared adequate for a vaginal delivery, and started Alison on a vitamin and iron supplement. The nurse discussed the signs of potential problems during pregnancy, gave Alison some literature and suggested that the couple enroll in the "early bird" classes that were conducted by a local hospital. Alison agreed and they began attending the class two weeks later. She returned to the clinic every four weeks for routine care. Both Alison's and Kent's parents were delighted at the thought of a grandchild, and although the in-laws lived quite a distance away, they planned to visit after the baby was born. Alison's mother would stay and help as long as she was needed.

During the first trimester Alison experienced some nausea and vomiting

which subsided by the fourth month. She began wearing maternity clothes, and continued to exercise in moderation as she had done before getting pregnant.

At 19 weeks, Alison experienced quickening, and a week later the fetal heart tones (FHT) were auscultated. Kent attended this prenatal visit and was excited to hear the FHT's with the Doppler.

In her seventh month, Alison developed constipation and hemorrhoids, making sitting at her desk increasingly uncomfortable. The nurse suggested that Alison increase fluids, roughage and bulk in her diet, emphasizing the benefits of exercise and allowing enough time after breakfast for the natural action of the body to defecate. Alison followed all the suggestions but the constipation continued to be a problem. The doctor was consulted and prescribed a mild stool softener. The medication plus the suggested lifestyle changes corrected the problem. When the constipation was relieved the hemorrhoids no longer bothered Alison.

At 34 weeks Kent and Alison attended labor and delivery preparation classes, as both of them wanted to be active participants in their child's birth. At 37 weeks, Alison reported urinary frequency and leg cramps; the doctor's exam revealed that lightening had occurred. Alison continued to work until two days prior to her estimated date of confinement (EDC) at which time she began having regular contractions and bloody show, and was admitted to the hospital.

Assessment

A nursing assessment of the five resources of power reveals that this client demonstrates assets in each of the following areas: strength, motivation, networking, coping, knowledge, perceptions, self-esteem and energy reserves or stamina. These assets assist her to maintain power and control in her life. It is the responsibility of the nurse to first identify the assets and second to assure that the client is encouraged to utilize these assets as a source of power and control.

Strength. This client is a healthy 27-year-old whose lifestyle is focused toward wellness. She is emotionally stable and demonstrates no behaviors that would interfere with her maintaining this level of wellness during her pregnancy. Her intelligence and career success indicate that she has the strength to both set and meet challenges. Her spiritual background also gives her comfort. These strengths will assist her to maintain, control, and utilize personal power during her pregnancy, labor, and postpartum period.

Motivation. She possesses the energy necessary to be self-directed. She has an internal locus of control. She revealed that her pregnancy was planned and she is eager to learn all she can about the pregnancy. She attended both "early bird" and "labor preparation" classes.

Networking. Alison received support from her husband and family. Her attendance at classes allowed her to meet others, get involved, and establish an external support system. The nurse at the antepartum clinic also provided a source of support for her.

Coping. Her past coping style indicates her ability to effectively deal with challenges. She possessed protective devices that maintained her emotional stability and homeostasis.

Knowledge. This client realized that knowledge and information was necessary for her to maintain control. She enrolled in classes and did a lot of reading in order to prepare herself to meet the challenges and changes that occur during pregnancy, labor, delivery, and motherhood. Her decision-making style involved having all pertinent information before making an informed choice.

Perceptions. Her perception of pregnancy was that it was a health state that was manageable and challenging. With this view she was able to mobilize her strengths in order to exhibit control over this life event.

Self-Esteem. This client's self-esteem is high. She views herself as a person of worth. Her accomplishments and successes (e.g., career and marital) along with her physical strength reinforce her positive self-image.

Energy Reserves/Stamina. This client possessed physical, emotional, and intellectual stamina. This was evidenced by her healthy, physically fit body, emotional stability, and intellectual capabilities. Her resources of power (physical, emotional, spiritual, cultural, and intellectual) had sufficient reserves that allowed her to mobilize her forces and meet challenging stressful situations.

Interventions

Alison is a healthy person who is adjusting to her pregnancy in a positive manner. She does not display any behaviors that suggest powerlessness. Therefore it is the responsibility of the nurse to assist her to utilize her resources of power and support her self-care behaviors. The main focus of nursing interventions would be to present information and options and allow the client to make informed choices regarding her care. According to McKay (1983) this would be labeled the "assertive approach." McKay affirms that the assertive couple understands the need to thoughtfully survey birth alternatives during pregnancy. When they clearly understand various options, they seek consultation with their health care provider to plan as closely as possible the events of their baby's birth. The assertive stance provides the opportunity for a joint partnership between expectant parents and members of the health care team. It denotes mutual respect and concern.

The nurse serves as a: resource person, advocate, teacher, and external support system. Olds, London and Ladewig (1988) suggest that the health care information should focus on:

1. The right of the woman to know her own health status and that of the fetus/baby.
2. The parents' options.
3. Their participation in decision-making.
4. Responsibilities in self-care.
5. Treatments and rationale.
6. Maintenance of family support systems.
7. Consideration and respect of each individual's needs.

Many decisions must be made when a couple becomes pregnant. Decisions as to who will deliver the baby, where the birth will take place, whether or not the couple participates in classes, who will attend the birth, whether anesthesia or analgesia be used, what will be the position for birth, the need for an enema, IV, prep, monitor, or episiotomy, support for nursing baby immediately after delivery, etc. In order to be aware of the various options available to the client a birth plan can be designed (see Figure 9-2). This plan is a communication tool used between clients and the health care providers who assist the couple during labor, delivery, and the postpartal period. It allows for individualization of care and enhances the use of the client's power and decision-making processes.

The intervention methods most used during the antepartal period include therapeutic communication and teaching/learning strategies. The nursing diagnoses most applicable to a healthy pregnancy, which reflect power/powerlessness include:

· Knowledge deficit
· Alteration in sexuality patterns (self-esteem)
· Alteration in rest and sleep patterns
· Anxiety
· Self-Care Deficit
· Ineffective personal coping

Olds, London and Ladewig (1988) suggest the following goals for care during the antepartal period:

1. Promote family adaptation.
2. Provide anticipatory guidance.
3. Integrate cultural factors influencing pregnancy.
4. Relieve common discomforts during pregnancy.
5. Promote maternal/fetal well-being.

Using this framework for nursing care the power resources of the client will be enhanced and her power will be maintained. Lederman (1984) stated that the acceptance of pregnancy referred to a woman's adaptive responses to the changes inherent in prenatal growth and development. Acceptance was characterized by feelings of happiness and enjoyment of the pregnancy, relatively little physical discomfort or high tolerance of the discomfort by the third trimester, moderate mood swings, and relatively little reported ambivalence during the first trimester. The challenges precipitated by the pregnancy were readily acknowledged and a general sense of hope and self-confidence prevailed. Thus, the generalization can be made that if a woman accepts the pregnancy, she is typically in a happy state of mind despite bodily discomfort, changed shape, mood swings, or some financial worries.

Lederman (1984) asserted that the acceptance of pregnancy related partially to fears about labor concerning helplessness, pain, loss of control, and loss of self-esteem. If the client does not accept the pregnancy, she tends to despair and be depressed, and both physical and emotional disruptions occur. According to Lederman, total acceptance is rare, some ambivalence is 'normal.' Ambivalence was found to be expressed overtly in two prime areas: financial security and changed lifestyle, which included the motherhood-career conflict. Therefore, if a client does not accept her pregnancy, she is a prime candidate for the nursing diagnosis of powerlessness. The nurse in the antepartal clinic must make a sound assessment of the mother's psychological adaptation to her pregnancy, abnormalities must be identified and appropriate interventions instituted.

BIRTH PLAN

Name: _____ Coach's Name: _____

CHOICE — I WOULD LIKE TO HAVE:	YES	NO
BIRTH PLACE		
a. Birth Center	___	___
b. Hospital birthing room	___	___
c. Hospital delivery room	___	___
d. Home	___	___
BIRTH ATTENDANT		
a. Obstetrician	___	___
b. Certified Midwife	___	___
c. Lay Midwife	___	___
d. Family Practitioner	___	___
CHILDBIRTH PREPARATION		
a. Bradley	___	___
b. Lamaze	___	___

c. Read   _____ _____
d. Kitzinger   _____ _____
e. Hypnosis   _____ _____
f. Hospital classes   _____ _____
g. Sibling classes   _____ _____
h. Cesarean classes   _____ _____

FAMILY INVOLVEMENT

a. Partner present during:
    labor   _____ _____
    delivery   _____ _____
    cesarean section   _____ _____
    postpartum period   _____ _____
b. Sibling(s) visitation during:
    labor   _____ _____
    delivery   _____ _____
    postpartum period   _____ _____

DURING LABOR I WOULD LIKE:

a. To ambulate as desired   _____ _____
b. Shower if desired   _____ _____
c. Wear my own clothes   _____ _____
d. Use a hot tub if available   _____ _____
e. Use a rocking chair   _____ _____
f. To listen to my own music   _____ _____
g. To have an enema   _____ _____
h. To have a mini shave   _____ _____
i. To have an IV only if needed   _____ _____
j. To have electronic monitoring only if needed   _____ _____
k. To naturally rupture membranes   _____ _____
l. To have labor stimulation if needed   _____ _____
m. To have limited vaginal exams   _____ _____
n. Ice chips if possible   _____ _____
o. To have medication (type desired)
_____   _____ _____

DURING DELIVERY I WOULD LIKE:

a. To deliver:
    on my side   _____ _____
    kneeling   _____ _____
    squatting   _____ _____
    on my hands and knees   _____ _____
    in a birthing chair   _____ _____
    in a birthing bed   _____ _____
    other _____   _____ _____
b. _____ present   _____ _____
c. To have birth filmed   _____ _____
d. To have the LeBoyer method   _____ _____
e. To have an episiotomy only if needed   _____ _____

f. _____ to cut cord   _____   _____
g. To hold baby immediately   _____   _____
h. To nurse as soon as possible   _____   _____
i. To have the baby as long as possible   _____   _____

CESAREAN BIRTH I WOULD LIKE:

a. To be admitted the day of surgery   _____   _____
b. _____ present   _____   _____
c. Anesthesia:
   spinal   _____   _____
   epidural   _____   _____
   general   _____   _____
   other _____   _____   _____
d. The anesthesia screen down during birth   _____   _____
e. To hold the baby as soon as possible   _____   _____
f. To breast feed in recovery room   _____   _____
g. Early removal of catheter   _____   _____
h. To use the PCA machine   _____   _____

CARE OF THE NEWBORN I WOULD LIKE:

a. To have the eye treatment delayed   _____   _____
b. To breast feed immediately   _____   _____
c. To bottle feed   _____   _____
d. To supplement
   Type of Supplement _____   _____   _____
e. To room-in continually   _____   _____
   only during day   _____   _____
f. My son circumcised   _____   _____
g. Newborn pictures taken   _____   _____

POSTPARTUM CARE I WOULD LIKE:

a. Family-centered program
   father-unrestricted visiting   _____   _____
   sibling visitation   _____   _____
   extended family visits   _____   _____
   friends Visit   _____   _____
b. Educational information on:
   self-care   _____   _____
   newborn care   _____   _____
   breast feeding   _____   _____
c. To be discharged as early as possible   _____   _____
d. To have home visit or follow-up by member
   of birth facility or public health nurse   _____   _____

ADDITIONAL REQUESTS/COMMENTS:

_____

_____

Figure 9-2. Birth Plan

Labor

Our society has recognized the feelings of powerlessness experienced by families in the labor and delivery areas. The increasing popularity of Lamaze and other natural childbirth practices indicates a movement toward control through knowledge and behavior practice to diminish the powerlessness evident in the laboring mother. Through classes, friends, family, hospital tours, and books, a woman is encouraged to prepare for maintaining control during this ordeal (Olds et al., 1984). As waves of contractions crash in upon her, it is with extreme difficulty that the woman maintains a semblance of control. It is an important function for her labor coach to keep her on task and concentrating on relaxation. Relaxation through the contractions is accomplished through using focal points and concentrating on breathing patterns, as the birth coach encourages relaxation of muscle groups and reminds the laboring client to maintain the rhythm of her breathing.

Without any preparation, the woman is often thrown into panic resulting from the wrenching uncontrollable pain. The labor experience is one during which a woman can be made to feel totally powerless. The major thrust of childbirth preparation classes however is to provide a woman with techniques that help her maintain a sense of control. Through practice, the expectant woman learns that labor pain is lessened by the use of relaxation techniques and that preparedness also lessens the pain through a decrease in anxiety. Knowledge of the labor process allows the laboring woman to identify the stages and decrease anxiety by eliminating the unknown aspects of the birth process.

CASE STUDY: LABOR

Amy and Dan O. are expecting their first child. Amy is a secretary for the public school system and Dan is an English teacher. The pregnancy was planned and they attended prenatal classes at the local hospital, which has a birthing room that they planned to use. Amy's prenatal course was uncomplicated.

Five days before her due date, Amy started having regular contractions. After four and a half hours of regular labor, her contractions were five minutes apart, lasting 45 to 60 seconds. As she was getting uncomfortable, especially in her lower back, the couple decided to go to the hospital to be examined. There they were greeted by the nurse who had conducted the prenatal classes they had attended. This reassured them as they knew the nurse would be supportive during labor. During their prenatal classes the O's had prepared a "birth plan" that would assist the hospital personnel in individualizing the labor and delivery experience. The nurse did a sterile vaginal exam and found the following: dilatation of the cervix to 5 centimeters, the membranes were intact, the cervix was 100% effaced, and the head of the fetus was presenting at a right occiput posterior position at a +1 station in the birth canal. The fetal heart rate (FHR) was 144, strong and regular. The contractions were soon 2 to 3 minutes apart, lasting 45 to 60 seconds. The nurse notified their doctor of the admission, then helped Amy and Dan settle in to complete the admission process. The nurse provided a warm, caring, quiet, unhurried and supportive environment. Amy was attached to a fetal monitor with both the FHR and contractions were monitored externally. With each contraction Amy focused her attention on a picture of her pet cocker spaniel, Jackson, using her slow breathing pattern. Dan assumed the role of coach without hesitation and provided constant encouragement. With each contraction he placed firm pressure in Amy's sacral area, helping to relieve her back discomfort. Dan unpacked the "goodie" bag and got out the tape recorder, soft music tapes, knee socks, talcum powder, suckers, lip ice, and extra pillows. As the labor continued Dan and Amy worked well together. The nurse provided support and encouragement, her periodic assessments revealed a normally progressing labor. As Amy entered transition the need for nursing support was more apparent and the nurse stayed with the O's constantly. Amy found it increasingly difficult to relax between her contractions, stating that she didn't think she could take it much longer. Dan offered reassurance and helped Amy with her breathing and relaxation. The doctor's exam revealed that a rim of cervix remained, the vertex was at a +3 station and the position had rotated to ROA. He performed an amniotomy with clear fluid returned and FHR remaining strong and regular. Amy had an uncontrollable urge to push. An exam revealed that Amy was fully dilated. Dan and the nurse assisted Amy in her pushing efforts. The birthing bed was positioned for the birth.

Assessment

It is fairly well accepted that women who take prepared childbirth classes rate their childbirth experiences more positively than those who do not participate in classes. Humenick (1981) suggests mastery (control) not pain management is the key to perceived satisfaction during the childbirth experience. Humenick asserts that pain is just one of the many potential stressors during childbirth. Others include fear, fatigue, loss of ability to participate, loss of dignity, aloneness, and threats to the health of the mother and the baby. These and many other fears and stressors play a role in pregnancy. For those women to whom mastery is important, mobilizing inner resources and learning coping skills in classes may lead to a significantly more positive perception of the birth experience. According to Humenick (1981), the degree of mastery these women feel they have attained may relate to changes in self-esteem, whether they experience depression, changes in locus of control, and in assertiveness.

Strength. This client is a physically healthy young woman experiencing her first pregnancy. The pregnancy was planned and except for the usual psychological changes associated with pregnancy, she is emotionally healthy. She has experienced no complications with her pregnancy. She attended a junior college and has a degree in career studies. She continues to enjoy her work as a secretary for the public school system. Even though the O's do not attend church, they hold a belief in a higher being which is a source of comfort for them. These physical, emotional, and spiritual strengths will assist this client to utilize power and maintain control during her labor.

Motivation. Amy has the energy necessary to be self-directed. She has an internal locus of control. During her labor she uses a focal point as a source of diversion and control over the discomfort of the contractions. The breathing patterns assist her to use her inner strengths. This pregnancy was planned, she has read material and taken classes to prepare herself. She and Don prepared a "birth plan" which will assist the health care workers to provide individualized care during labor.

Networking. Amy receives support from her husband, family, and others. Through classes she has developed an external support system both with her peers and with the nurse/instructor. During the labor, Amy utilizes the resources of others. Dan and the nurse assist her with relaxation and allow her to maintain control and use her own strengths with each contraction.

Coping. This client's past coping styles suggest that she is able to deal with life's challenges. She has a happy marriage and a satisfying career. This indicates that she has protective devices that allow her to maintain emotional stability and homeostasis when faced with challenge.

Knowledge. Amy was aware that knowledge was the key to maintaining control during her pregnancy, labor, and delivery. She participated in prenatal classes, read material, and asked questions. She realized that the best decisions are made when all pertinent information is available.

Perceptions. This client viewed pregnancy as a healthy life event that was both challenging and manageable. With this opinion, she was able to activate her strengths to maintain control.

Self-Esteem. From the assessment there is no reason to believe that this client's self-esteem is not high. She has demonstrated successes in her life and she is both physically and emotionally healthy.

Energy Reserves/Stamina. Amy demonstrates that she has energy reserves and stamina in the physical, emotional, and intellectual realms. Her resources of power (physical, emotional, spiritual, cultural, and intellectual) have sufficient reserves that allow her to mobilize her forces and meet challenging stressful situations.

Interventions

This is a healthy young woman who is handling her labor in a positive manner. She is able to use her resources for power to maintain her power and control. She exhibits no behaviors that suggest powerlessness thus, it is the responsibility of the nurse to assist her to continue to use her resources and promote self-care behaviors. Olds,London, and Ladewig (1988) assert that the common nursing diagnoses for the healthy woman during the intrapartal period might include:

Alternation in comfort: pain
Potential for ineffective individual coping
Knowledge deficit

Having prepared herself, this client is knowledgeable and able to cope effectively with her labor, she requires minimal support from the nurse. The main goal for the nurse would be assurrance that the mother and fetus are both in a safe and secure environment that is conducive to a positive rewarding experience. To be effective, the nurse must utilize both technical and expressive interventions. Open communication and reinforcement of information learned is of utmost importance. Olds et al. (1988) assert that nursing care during the first stage of labor is influenced by the physical, psychologic, and cultural data. The primary goals of care are:

To integrate the couple's cultural beliefs
To promote maternal and fetal well-being
To promote maternal comfort

Using this as a framework for nursing care the five resources of power that the client has available would be utilized and power and control would be maintained.

Delivery

The multitude of childbirth centers is witness to the realization by health care professionals of the importance of providing choices and control to the parents during childbirth. No longer are women strapped into a supine position with their legs dangling from stirrups, to be given general anesthesia and have their babies pulled from their unconscious bodies. The change in birthing methods reflects the need of the client to maintain some control of her laboring body.

CASE STUDY: DELIVERY

Kelly has been in labor for eight and a half hours. This, her second pregnancy, was not planned, but has been uncomplicated. Kelly, age 20, is a Shoshone Indian; she has worked as a waitress for the past two years, and moved to this town six months ago. Her boyfriend is not aware of this pregnancy and has not visited her since her move to the city. She is at 41 weeks gestation and has seen the physician twice in the past month—her only prenatal care. She has never taken a childbirth class. Her last child was born three years ago at home with the women of her family in attendance. The Shoshone midwife delivered her child.

Kelly was admitted with a cervical dilatation of 6 cm. The nurse assessed Kelly as being in control of her labor, as Kelly denied her offered presence at her bedside to assist her during labor. Kelly's membranes ruptured spontaneously with clear fluid a strong FHR and a cervix dilated to 8 cm. Half an hour later Kelly began to push. The nurse heard her grunting, performed an exam, found Kelly's cervix to be complete and prepared her bed for delivery.

During the delivery, Kelly made no sound to indicate discomfort to the nurses, who positively responded to Kelly's continued silence. Kelly did not stop pushing, even though instructed to, and the nurses delivered her new daughter over her intact perineum with a periurethral tear. The doctor, arriving one minute after delivery, scolded Kelly for her insistence on pushing as he stitched her perineum, failing to notice the twinge of Kelly's eyelid as he stitched tissue that had not been numbed with local anesthetic.

Kelly did not protest when the nursery nurse came in to take her daughter to the nursery to be weighed and measured. Kelly had not expressed her desire to the nurse to breastfeed immediately after delivery. The nurses did not make any effort to bridge the culture gap between themselves and Kelly and assumed she was satisfied with the way her delivery was handled, although they did not validate this assumption with Kelly. Assessment and adaptation of the environment to meet the client's cultural needs is important if the client is to have as positive a delivery experience as possible (Orque et al., 1983).

Assessment

A nursing assessment of the power resources reveals that this client lacks assets in some areas. This lack of attributes interferes with Kelly's ability to maintain power and control during her labor and delivery. The lack of these assets may be the result of cultural differences and expectations between the client and the caregivers.

According to Olds et al. (1988), "knowledge of values, customs, and practices of different cultures is as important during labor as it is during the prenatal period. Without this knowledge, a nurse is less likely to understand a woman's behavior and may impose personal values and beliefs upon the woman" (p. 652).

There are three areas where cultural diversity is apparent during the labor and delivery process; these include: modesty, pain expression, and the role of the father (Olds et al., 1988; Orque et al., 1983). For most cultures modesty is important during childbirth; according to Farris (1978), most American Indians view it as "female business." Pain expression is culturally specific. Some women openly exhibit an emotional response to pain, some exhibit physical signs and symptoms, and still others are very stoic. Understanding pain behavior helps lead to accurate assessment of the mother's needs and most often the nonverbal behaviors are the best indicators. The role of the father cannot be assumed, his participation varies among cultures.

Strength. This client is a 20-year-old gravida II. Although currently not working, she has been a waitress for the past two years. She finds herself tired most of the time, especially when trying to keep up with her active three year old daughter. She dropped out of school at age 16. She does not attend church, but holds to some of her cultural spiritual beliefs. The lack of physical strength at this time adds to her feelings of powerlessness.

Motivation. Her motivation for action is externally controlled. She was not motivated to protect herself from pregnancy as this pregnancy was not planned. Kelly does not value prenatal care and has had only two visits during her pregnancy. She views labor as an uncontrollable event and did not see the need to prepare herself for it.

Networking. She has been isolated from her boyfriend, family and friends since her move six months ago. She lives in an apartment which she rarely leaves. Because of her pregnancy, she has recently been unable to find employment. She periodically sees a social worker at the Department of Public Assistance and Social Services (DPASS).

Coping. Her past coping skills indicate that she has made some ineffective choices. Pregnant at age 16, she dropped out of school. Finding herself pregnant again, she left her home and her external support system. Even though she rarely expresses her feelings, her behaviors indicate that she lacks emotional stability, if evaluated by Anglo-American standards. Perhaps, to Kelly, it is desirable to stand alone, to be brave and silent, not to burden her family and friends with her problems. However this possibility was not validated by the staff.

Knowledge. Kelly was an average student in school, lacking the motivation to succeed. She did not know anyone, among her relatives, who had gone on to school after high school, and very few who had finished high school. She has no plans to finish high school at this time.

She did act on a need to gain information concerning her pregnancy. She apparently made most of her decisions without any foresight.

Perceptions. Kelly's perception of labor and delivery is that it is an uncontrollable event, one that will "just happen." She can identify no reason to try to interfere with nature. During the birth process Kelly does not listen to the nurse when asked to stop pushing, possibly related to her perception of labor as uncontrollable.

Self-Esteem. Kelly's self-esteem is low, if evaluated by the caregivers' standards. She does not appear to view herself as a person of worth. Kelly did not complain when she felt the suturing during the repair of her laceration. Was this due to her lack of self-worth or because she values tolerance of pain without expression as a sign of bravery? She has had few accomplishments in her life. She is proud of her daughter and her success as a waitress for two years. It may be that Kelly has a great deal of self-esteem as she has managed to support herself and her daughter until recently.

Energy Reserve/Stamina. At this time the energy reserves of this single mother are limited. She finds herself tired and without her usual support system.

Interventions

This single mother does display behaviors that suggest she is experiencing powerlessness. Even though she is reluctant to verbalize her concerns, her actions indicate that she has lost control in her life. The nursing diagnosis of powerlessness would be appropriate for her.

In order to work effectively with women from another culture the nurse must have an awareness of the beliefs, values and practices of that culture. As cultural sensitivity increases, so does the likelihood of providing high quality individualized care.

Olds et al. (1988) suggest that the primary nursing goals during the second stage of labor is to: assist the woman with pushing and prepare the mother for delivery. This client denied the offered presence and support of the nurse.

The key to the selection of appropriate nursing interventions would be to first have accurate knowledge of the culture of the client. This is difficult for the nurse who has met the client for the first time during the admission to the labor suite.

Some suggestions for nursing interventions for this client are:

1. Use therapeutic communication to assist the client in explaining her feelings about her situation.
2. Assist the client to identify factors that may contribute to her feelings of powerlessness.
3. Allow the client as much control over her situation as possible.

4. Give accurate updated information regarding the process of labor.
5. Involve the client in decision-making (e.g., prep, enema, medications, support persons, position of delivery, involvement with baby after delivery, etc.).
6. Provide explanations for realistic options in care.
7. Provide flexibility in care and routines.
8. Offer self and display attending behaviors.

Evaluation

Evaluation is an ongoing process during health care and the health care provider is continually readjusting the plan of care according to the responses of the client. However, in Kelly's case, no antepartal assessment of health beliefs was done or sent on to the delivery area. Even in the most hurried situation it is possible to do a short version of the assessment seen in Figure 9-1. Did the health care team fail to meet Kelly's needs and encourage her in a sense of control? Did the disapproval of the health care team members (her unmarried status and minimal antepartal care) make this a less than positive experience for Kelly? Seeking Kelly's feedback is the only means of knowing what she thought of her experience in the delivery area.

Postpartum

The postpartum period includes the taking hold process essential to bonding between mother and infant. It is important to encourage the mother to voice her preferences in performing newborn care to promote this bonding.

The postpartum period is marked by the additional responsibility to meet the newborn's needs and the loss of the doting attention poured on the woman during the antepartal period. These changes can lead to an enhanced sense of control and power, or they can create a nagging feeling of loss of control. Either perception is within normal parameters during the postpartum period (Olds, 1988). In fact, this apparent dichotomy is variously portrayed in most women.

CASE STUDY: Postpartum

Ann and Jerry are a black married couple with one child, Ben. Jerry is a college student and garage mechanic and Ann works as a babysitter in their home. Their families live in the same town and provide a solid base of support for the expectant couple. They have a strong Baptist church family.

Ann and Jerry had their second child 16 hours ago. After two hours in the labor area, Ann delivered the eight pound four ounce Jason over a midline episiotomy. Four hours after delivery, having no complications, Ann was transferred to the postpartum area.

Ann chose early discharge, allowing her a total of 48 hours in the hospital from admission. Included were two follow-up home visits for Ann and the baby. She attended the patient education classes presented by the staff nurses on the unit that included such topics as breast feeding techniques, baby bath options, sibling rivalry, and supplementation. Ann opted for "24 hour rooming-in" and fed Jason on demand, requesting that he not receive a supplement. The decision was made not to have Jason circumcised at this time. Sibling and extended family visiting was permitted and Jason's brother Ben, and his grandparents visited several times. After instructions were given, Ann was encouraged to use her sitz bath as needed. Ann's medications were placed at her bedside to be taken as needed.

Assessment

A nursing assessment of the power resources reveals the presence of many assets that assist in Ann's maintenance of power and control. These assets contribute toward a positive postpartum experience for Ann.

Strength. Ann is a 24-year-old gravida II. She was healthy when she got pregnant and she experienced no complications during her pregnancy, labor or delivery. Her immediate postpartum recovery time was normal. Ann is emotionally stable. She is very content with her role as a mother, enjoys her baby-sitting job with three other children in her home and finds great pleasure and comfort in her church affiliation where she serves as choir director.

Motivation. Ann considers herself to be self-directed. She has a high school education and plans to pursue a college degree when Jerry is finished. This pregnancy was planned, she and Jerry attended "labor refresher classes." Ann also had Ben attend sibling classes to prepare him for the arrival of his new brother.

Networking. This client has a well developed external support system. Through her family and friends, Ann receives encouragement and comfort. She attended her prenatal appointments on schedule and received support from the nurse. In preparation for early discharge, Ann has arranged to have her mother spend 10 days assisting with the household responsibilities.

Coping. Ann's past coping styles indicate that she is able to effectively maintain emotional stability and homeostasis. Her first labor was 12 hours and she states it was a satisfying experience. She breastfed Ben for ten months and considered her-self a success as a nursing mother. She has encouraged her first child to cope with the new arrival via sibling classes and family discussions about his new position and ability to help care for the new baby (Bradshaw, 1988).

Knowledge. This client realizes that information and knowledge are necessary for her to maintain control. She attended labor refresher courses and read several books in order to prepare herself to meet the challenges of a second pregnancy, labor and delivery. She is particularly interested in the integration of a second child into the household.

Perceptions. Ann viewed childbirth as a normal healthy time in her life. She did have some concerns about having a second child, but she was eager to prepare herself, Jerry and Ben for the experience. She does not foresee any difficulties in integrating the new baby into the family unit.

Self-Esteem. This client's self-esteem is high. She views herself as a person of worth. She is satisfied with her life, content in her marriage and enjoys motherhood.

Energy Reserves/Stamina. Ann possesses physical, emotional and intellectual stamina. Her resources of power have sufficient reserves that allow her to mobilize her forces and meet stressful life situations. She does acknowledge that the care of her older child as well as the new baby will take additional energy and effort until the members of the family establish a comfortable pattern or schedule of care that suits them.

Interventions

This is a healthy young woman who is adjusting to her postpartal period in a positive manner. She does not display any behaviors that suggest powerlessness. Therefore, it is the responsibility of the health care professional to assist her in utilizing her resources of power and to support her in her self-care behaviors.

According to Olds et al. (1988), the best postpartal care is family centered and disrupts the family unit as little as possible. Suggested nursing goals for the postpartal mother include:

1. Promote comfort and relieve pain.
2. Promote rest and graded activity.
3. Promote maternal psychologic well-being.
4. Provide effective parent education.
5. Provide anticipatory guidance about sexual activity and family planning.
6. Promote successful infant feeding.
7. Enhance parent-infant attachment.
8. Prepare for discharge.

Additional Situations: Appropriate Interventions

Even though pregnancy is a normal process, it is both physiologically and psychologically stressful to normal healthy clients. For other clients there are additional stresses which increase the chance of loss of control and the diagnosis of powerlessness. Included in this group would be: the adolescent mother, the mother who must have a cesarean birth, the older primigravida, and the mother who has a "surprise" or preterm labor with little time for preparation. This section will deal with these situations.

The nursing assessment focuses on the five resources of power and examines the client's strength, motivation, networking, coping mechanisms, knowledge level, perceptions, self-esteem, and energy reserves or stamina. In each case the normal stressors of pregnancy, labor, delivery, and the postpartum period would be considered along with the additional stressors of each unique situation.

Adolescent. In 1981 the Guttmacher Institute reported one in every ten pregnancies are adolescents (Creasy and Resnik, 1984). Pregnancy is a developmental challenge no matter what the age of the individual client. However, many factors make it more complicated for the adolescent. Her physical development is incomplete; she has not yet completed the developmental tasks for her age group. Her education is unfinished and the chance of completion is jeopardized. Her support systems are limited. A nursing assessment of the five resources of power reveal that this client has the potential for a sense of loss of control and powerlessness.

In terms of strength, it is highly unlikely that this client would possess the attributes necessary. Her body has not completed its growth, making pregnancy a risk factor for mother and child. Her body is working on her growth and the demands of the fetus rob the mother of nutrients her own body needs. The older the adolescent is the more chance there is for the outcome of the pregnancy to be a healthy baby and mother.

Her motivation to prepare herself for labor, delivery, and motherhood is probably compromised. The adolescent mother is most often focused only in the here and now and is not interested in the future. Immediate gratification is her main concern. The networking that she does have may or may not be supportive. At one extreme, her friends may think it is wonderful that she is pregnant and daydream about becoming pregnant themselves or they may respond in the opposite direction and reject the client for being pregnant.

Her coping style has not developed enough to be growth facilitating and she finds herself using methods that are inappropriate. Usually her knowledge is limited and the information that she does have may be faulty. Her perceptions of pregnancy may focus on illness rather than health aspects. Most often her self esteem is very low and she feels that her self worth is questionable. Often a pregnancy is a cry to be accepted as an adult or to insure that she will have someone who loves her in her life.

The one asset she may have is her energy level and stamina, however, this is not true of all adolescents. For some adolescents, their nutritional state and lifestyle does not support wellness. The nursing diagnoses appropriate for this client will vary according to her age, maturity, support systems, and current health status. The appropriate nursing diagnoses often reflect an assessment of a loss of control, poor self-esteem and a sense of powerlessness. These include:

Altered growth and development
Alteration in family processes
Knowledge deficit
Noncompliance with prenatal appointments
Ineffective individual coping

Nursing interventions may include the following:
Develop a trusting relationship
Promote self-esteem, decision-making and problem-solving skills
Promote physical well-being
Promote family adaptation
Facilitate prenatal education

Cesarean Birth. One in every five births is via cesarean section (Olds et al., 1988). Whether it is scheduled or an emergency, the client who has a cesarean section often perceives herself to be powerless and less in control than her peers who manage to have vaginal deliveries. The mother experiencing her first pregnancy has anticipated and prepared for a vaginal delivery when suddenly, for some reason (CPD, breech presentation, failure to progress, fetal/maternal distress or malpresentation), her plans are dramatically changed. Decisions are made, often very quickly, with little input from her. Surgical consent forms are thrust at her for her signature, her abdomen is prepped, a urinary catheter is inserted, and an intravenous line is started. The choices she may have include: the type of anesthesia used and whether or not her significant other will attend the birth.

For the multigravida, an emergency or repeat cesarean section is also stressful. If previous labors and deliveries were uneventful and this labor involves complications that necessitate a cesarean section, she feels out of control and fearful. For the mother faced with a repeat cesarean, there is the concern that it will be a repeat of the first time. If the first experience was unpleasant she is especially concerned.

With few choices available to her, the client faced with a cesarean birth certainly does have a perceived lack of control over the current situation, thus validating the nursing diagnosis of powerlessness. Due to the emergency aspects of the unplanned surgery, the nurse is challenged to initiate appropriate intervention that will diminish the powerless position of this client. Nursing interventions might include:

· Use therapeutic communication to assist the client to express her feelings about the situation.
· Assist the client to identify factors that may contribute to powerlessness.
· Allow the client as much control over the situation as possible.
· Involve the client in decision-making about care as much as possible.
· Inform the client of realistic options available.
· Provide explanations for care and procedures.
· Keep client informed of changes in plan of care and rationale for changes.
· Include significant other(s) in plan of care.
· Allow flexibility in plan of care as appropriate.

Older Primigravida. Olds (1988) states that medical professionals consider that women who are over 30, especially those who are 35 or older at the time of their first pregnancy, are at higher risk for maternal and fetal complications than younger women. The risk of conceiving a child with Down Syndrome increases significantly with age (Creasy and Resnik, 1984). The incidence of medical conditions such as diabetes and hypertension, which can be serious complications during any pregnancy, increases for women over the age of 35 (Olds et al., 1988).

No matter what her age, most expectant mothers have concerns regarding the well-being of her fetus and her ability to be a "good" mother. But for the older mother/couple this may be an even greater issue. Most older couples are concerned with being able to meet the needs of a child as their age progresses. Will they be financially ready for a college student when they are ready for retirement? Will they be able to cope with a teenager when they are in their fifties or sixties? They may also find themselves socially isolated from their peers, who may already be grandparents, have children who are almost grown or have decided to have no children.

Health care professionals may treat the older expectant couple differently than they would a younger couple (Olds et al., 1988). The medical profession tends to view the older pregnant client as high-risk. Older women may be asked to submit to more medical procedures than the younger client, such as amniocentesis and ultrasound. An older client may be denied the use of the birthing room or birthing center even if she is healthy because her age is considered to put her at risk.

Olds et al. (1988) state that once an older couple has made the decision to have a child, it is the responsibility of the health care professional to respect and support the couple in this decision. As with any client, it is important that risks are discussed, concerns identified, and strengths promoted. The client's age should not be the only issue. To promote a sense of well-being, the nurse must treat the pregnancy as 'normal' unless otherwise indicated. The older woman who has made a conscious decision to become pregnant often has thought through potential problems and may have fewer concerns than the younger mother.

Since a loss of previous lifestyle does occur with pregnancy, this mother may experience some grief. This grief may promote a sense of loss of control and powerlessness.

Preterm Labor. Labor that occurs between 20 and 37 completed weeks of pregnancy is referred to as preterm labor (Creasy and Resnik, 1984). Major risks for the mother relate to psychologic stress factors involving her concern for her unborn child. With the onset of labor the woman finds herself involved in a situation that she has very little control over. She is worried about the baby's ability to survive if delivered preterm. She is concerned because her body has begun the process of labor well before the baby is mature enough to survive in the extrauterine environment. Fear is a predominating feeling and leads to the sense of powerlessness.

If she is being managed for preterm labor on an outpatient basis her medical treatment demands that she be well in tune with her body. She will regulate her activity level and medication dosage based on her uterine activity.

Whether the preterm labor is stopped or continues, the client and her significant other will experience intense psychologic stress. Decreasing the fear and anxiety associated with the unknown and the risk of a preterm baby is a major concern of the health care professional. Common behavioral responses include feelings of anxiety and guilt about the preterm onset of labor. A feeling of loss of control and powerlessness prevails. It is vital that the responsibility of awareness of body signals be emphasized without increasing any perceptions of guilt in this client. Accomplishing this goal is a challenge for all members of the health care team.

Summary

Health care professionals in the obstetrical field have done much in an attempt to encourage client control of the maternity experience. Thorough assessment of the client's locus of control and health beliefs will assist the health care team in providing as positive a childbirth experience as is currently possible. Assessment tools for cultural needs and writing a birth plan are included in this chapter.

A variety of childbirth experiences are presented with suggested interventions to promote personal power in the childbirth situation. The suggested interventions are by no means the only available interventions but should be seen as a starting place for developing plans of care that will meet the individual needs of each maternity client.

References

Bradshaw, J. *Bradshaw On The Family: A Revolutionary Way of Self-Discovery.* Deerfield Beach, FL: Health Communications, Inc. (1988).

Clarke, J. *Self-Esteem: A Family Affair.* NY: Harper & Row, Publishers, (1978).

Clatworthy, N. Initiating a family unit. In Schuster, Clara and Ashburn, Shirley (eds.). *The Process of Human Development: A Holistic Approach.* Boston: Little, Brown and Company, (1980).

Creasy, R.K. and Resnik, R. *Maternal Fetal Medicine: Principles and Practice.* Philadelphia: Saunders, (1984).

Ginott, H. *Between Parent and Child.* NY: Avon Books, (1965).

Henderson, G. and Primeaux, M. *Transcultural Nursing Care.* Menlo Park, CA: Addison-Wesley Publishing Company, (1981).

Humenick, S. Mastery: the key to childbirth satsfaction? A review. *Birth and Family Journal* 8(2). 79-90, (1981).

Lederman, R. *Psychosocial Adaptation in Pregnancy: Assessment of Seven Dimensions of Maternal Development.* Englewood Cliffs, NJ: Prentice-Hall, Inc., (1984).

Leman, K. *The Birth Order Book.* NY: Dell Publishing Co., Inc., (1985).

McKay, S. *Assertive Childbirth: The Future Parents' Guide to a Positive Pregnancy.* Englewood Cliffs, NJ; Prentice-Hall, Inc., (1983).

Olds, S., London, M. and Ladewig, P. *Maternal-Newborn Nursing: A Family-Centered Approach* (3rd Ed.). Menlo Park, CA: Addison-Wesley Publishing Company, (1988).

Orque, M., Bloch, B. and Monrcoy, L. *Ethnic Nursing Care.* St. Louis: The C.V.Mosby Company, (1983).

Schuster, C. The decison to be or not to be parents. In Schuster, Clara and Ashburn, Shirley (eds). *The Process of Human Development: A Holistic Approach.* Boston: Little, Brown and Company, (1980).

10

Power and the Geriatric Client

C. Hannon and N. Rinehart

Introduction

The word elderly typically brings forth thoughts of the infirm and disabled. In reality, only a small (5%) (Hing, 1987) percentage of the elderly are in nursing homes or are bedridden, although they do stand the chance of one in every six being in the hospital each year (Schuster and Ashburn, 1980). The elderly may be plagued by chronic physical ailments, but this does not need to stop their late years from being fulfilling and joyful. As it has been said, you are only as old as you think you are. As with any other population, the values and motivating factors are important to assess when attempting to maintain or increase the geriatric client's sense of control.

The quality of life can be good, no matter what limitations age and illness have placed on the elderly client. He can contribute to society offering the wisdom and experience of his years. Many of the elderly are able to continue physically active lives, enjoying their leisure hours by playing tennis, golf, swimming, and riding bicycles (Schuster and Ashburn, 1980). For those who think of retirement as a reward for work well done rather than as punishment for getting old, pleasure and personal control await (Reibel, 1980). Those elderly who are not able to enjoy full activity levels can create things of beauty to pass on to the younger generations, teach information that will be valued through the years, reminisce and write their memoirs, intervene with wisdom in conflicts that occur with younger individuals and provide a different perspective on issues (Bornstein, 1980). All techniques for contributing to society are empowering as they feed the self-esteem, build strong support networks, provide valuing expressions of cultural and spiritual beliefs, and encourage positive life-review. The elderly client may be pleased about his life. He has come to terms with the changes in himself and the world and accepts them peacefully. The elderly client is a member of a much more heterogeneous group than any other age group of humans.

On the other hand, the elderly client is surrounded by change. He is forcibly retired from what, to him, may be the only activity that reflects his worth (Lerner, 1986). His body is changing in ways he cannot combat (Flynn, 1980). He may feel unimportant and unwanted. His family is grown and no longer looks to him for wisdom and guidance.

His own self-esteem drops with the uselessness he feels. He may feel helpless in a society that idolizes youth and physical abilities. Balked in these confrontations he may become apathetic, perceiving society as against him and condemning him for his advanced years of experience and physical degeneration. In this case, the client has a low perception of personal power and credits the rest of the world with power instead of himself (Lerner, 1986).

Many are the issues of control for the elderly client. Insurance forms seem to be created solely for the purpose of frustrating him. Employers choose to enforce mandatory retirement at the age of 65 in a time when the elderly are living longer and there are fewer and fewer young people to take their places in the work force. Driving a car is a hazard and, rather than encourage defensive driving lessons, the family or city community are quick to deny driving privileges to the elderly (this occurs less often in small towns and rural areas where the majority of the population is over 65). When they do become ill, they are rushed out of the hospital far too quickly for their comfort and adjustment. The day of receiving one's Social Security check becomes hazardous for the elderly as muggers with less age and more muscle are ready to prey upon them as they walk to the market.

The ultimate control issue for the elderly is the conflict between life and death. With age comes the knowledge that life must end eventually and the individual either comes to accept his certain death at some point or spends an enormous amount of energy fighting the inevitable and reinforcing his feelings of powerlessness. Another perception of this conflict is to decide to enjoy what time there is left and plan for the future to promote peace about death (Bornstein, 1980).

Holistic care of the elderly is the hallmark of gerontological nursing. There is a general agreement about the role of self-responsibility in wellness. The elderly also agree that wellness includes mental aspects as well as physical (Kutlenios, 1987).

It is not uncommon for an elderly person to enter the hospital functionally capable in spite of the presence of acute illness, various chronic conditions, and normal age-related physiological changes (Lueckenotte, 1987). The older individual is, however, highly vulnerable to a loss of control over his life through imposed rules, politics, and seeming mysterious language of the healthcare institution. Carnevali (1980) describes the advent of feelings of powerlessness as an expectancy that the outcome of a situation is beyond one's control. Due to the provider's responsibilities in health care, it is seen as advisable to have circumstances under control. "However, all of us professionals need to consider carefully whether our relationships with patients demonstrate need for control that is rational or irrational" (Jahraus, 1974, p. 6).

Whether young or old, health at the 100% level is usually unattainable by many due to the stressors of daily life (Butler, 1987). Old people are old survivors! Golander (1987) exclaims: "The aged succeed in reaching old age because of their strengths and their ability to cope with stressors and changes throughout their long lives" (p. 27).

The majority of the elderly are reported to be functional, active, and enjoy feeling quite well most of the time. Yet within this group, 86% are known to have one or more chronic diseases. Thus, the presence of pathology per se cannot define the level of health for the older person. Ford (1988) states, "Self reported health status, based on a lifetime of experience, may be more accurate than the physician's impressions and has in fact been shown to be a better predictor of mortality" (p. 192).

Locus of Control

Figure 10-1 illustrates the struggle for personal control, or an internal locus of control, among the elderly. The global components rely on maintaining a network of family and friends while the reality is that many of them die, leaving the client alone and feeling deserted and helpless. Many elderly clients are in dependent positions regarding their health care, such as needing funding for medications, treatments, surgery, and food. This dependence leads to the fear of retaliation by withdrawal of assistance if they irritate someone in a position of control. This fear cycle then leads to despair and death.

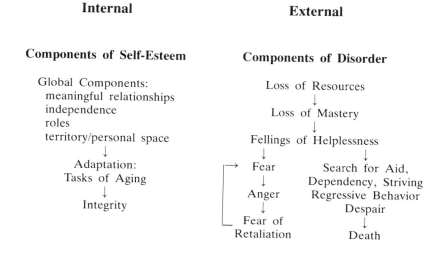

LOCUS OF CONTROL

Internal

External

Components of Self-Esteem

Components of Disorder

Global Components:
 meaningful relationships
 independence
 roles
 territory/personal space
          ↓
     Adaptation:
     Tasks of Aging
          ↓
      Integrity

Loss of Resources
          ↓
Loss of Mastery
          ↓
Fellings of Helplessness
   ↓   ↓
  Fear   Search for Aid,
   ↓   Dependency, Striving
  Anger   Regressive Behavior
   ↓   Despair
 Fear of   ↓
 Retaliation   Death

Fig. 10-1. Locus of Control Conflict for Elderly

The internal or external locus of control of the client has a great influence on his acceptance of the aging process with peace and secure knowledge of his having control of his life. Obviously, the client who is external is not going to perceive himself as having any power and will blame or bless the outside world, fate, God, or whatever for placing him in the situations he encounters. This client would exhibit behaviors indicated in the components of disorder part of Figure 10-1.

The internally controlled client would present a much different picture of himself, though he may be the same age and has gone through similar experiences to the external client mentioned above. The internally controlled client manifests his adaptation to aging through his meeting the global components listed in Figure 10-1: companionship, touch, meaningful relationships, independence roles, and territory or personal space. He is in control and though his every moment may not be joyful, the majority of his time is spent as he chooses, in the mood he chooses. He has intact personal power.

Control Theory

Glasser describes perception as being the process of altering the messages to the brain so there will or will not be a sharp frustration signal sent to the behavioral system as a result of comparison with the individual's idea of what is need-fulfilling for them (1985). The perception of an event is influential during the process of choosing behaviors. This viewpoint may indicate either a wide variance between what the individual is experiencing and what he wants, or little or no difference between the two.

The elderly person who is in effective control of his life makes behavior choices that satisfy his needs and do not harm himself or others. The client who is in ineffective control is dissatisfied with his life and is meeting his needs the best way he can, though his behavior choice may be harmful to himself or others.

Perceptions of events, places, persons and things can be altered. It is possible to change the way a person evaluates a situation. (Consider going to the doctor and knowing he is going to yell at you for not taking your medications correctly while he stands there, stern and knowledgeable in his white lab coat and suit pants. Now, alter that perception by visualizing him in a playpen with a rattle in his hand and his thumb in his mouth.) With some effort on the part of the health care professional and the client, perceptions of the situation which used to cause feelings of powerlessness in the client can become the perception of a challenge to conquer or "just one of those things."

Wholly Compensatory Clients

The client who can no longer perform his self-care and must depend on others to do those tasks for him is classified as needing wholly compensatory care (Orem, 1985). This client may express his lack of control, or powerlessness, in a variety of ways. He might use the capabilities he still has to try and control his environment. For instance, he may well refuse to open his mouth and eat if he is in despair about not being able to feed himself. Or he may knock everything off his bedside table from frustration in trying to do something for himself. As illustrated in Figure 10-1, anger is sandwiched between fear and fear of retaliation. This anger really may be aimed at himself or external factors over which he perceives no control. But what often happens is that the care giver becomes the target for the expression of his anger. After yelling or hitting or throwing something at the care giver, the client feels ashamed of his behavior and further envelops himself in a cloud of gloom over his powerless position.

CASE STUDY: Wholly Compensatory Client

Thirty years ago, Mr. C. immigrated from Japan and established a very successful landscaping business. At age 81, he lives with his only son's family, enjoying the status of revered patriarch. Grandchildren and their parents seek and receive religious guidance (Shinto-Buddhism) from Mr. C. as well as instruction regarding the native culture and regional philosophy (Confucianism). Thus inspired by religion and occupation, Mr. C. has great respect for nature and loves the outdoors. He continued to manage the annual garden until a hip fracture one year ago. His daughter-in-law resigned her job at that time to provide Mr. C. with increased assistance and care.

Recently, he experienced a severe right cerebrovascular accident with resulting left hemiparesis. The subsequent disability of this event necessitated nursing home placement for stabilization and rehabilitation. Mobility is now limited to a wheelchair which Mr. C. cannot control. He is incontinent of urine induced by a bladder infection. Bathing, dressing, and eating require assistance due to Mr. C's weakness, one-handedness, and visual impairment. Embarrassed by an inability to care for their elderly parent, supportive family visits begin to dwindle. Mr. C. has become increasingly withdrawn and passive during much of his daily care. During feeding attempts, he takes very little, then shakes his head "No" proclaiming, "A man who has lost his family should die." He is beginning to lose weight. The staff fear he may require supplemental nutrition via a nasogastric tube. Mr. C. wears an external catheter for his incontinence. He frequently removes this device remarking angrily, "Unclean." Mr. C's only positive response when approached is the request for a "Bath" or frequent "Backrub."

Assessment

To understand the older Asian, especially a first generation immigrant, the health care provider must appreciate the impact of religious and Confusian influences which are deeply ingrained in his cultural traditions (Chae, 1987; Murray and Zentner, 1975; Rajewski, 1988). Therefore, cultural and spiritual power resources deserve special attention in determining Mr. C's assets or strengths.

The interrelationship of body-mind-spirit is strongly reflected in the health beliefs and practices of Mr. C. These cultural attitudes are demonstrated through self-discipline in one's daily habits, a respect for physical fitness, and reserve in expressing emotion and/or pain (Murray and Zentner, 1975). Also highly valued are the concepts of group achievement, the extended family, determination, cleanliness and education (Chae, 1987). These beliefs remain equally important to the sick Asian person. They deserve recognition as assets in the pursuit of Mr. C's self-care goals. Murray and Zentner (1975) stated, "what the person has learned from his culture determines how and what you will be able to teach him, as well as your approach to him during care" (p. 275).

While Mr. C. suffers left hemiparesis, physical viability remains intact on the right side. The cultural assets which emphasize physical fitness, determination and education further support rehabilitation efforts. His requests for frequent backrubs signifies a motivational power towards physical and emotional comfort. Golander (1987) reports that the elderly invest a great deal of effort, time and energy searching for modes of action to avoid discomfort or to minimize its effects. It is a complex task to achieve this goal without altering their self-image or threatening relationships with staff and/or family. "It demands that the beholder be a scholar as well as an implementor of the decision-making process, to have the change agent's skills and the negotiator's expertise" (p. 2). Furthermore, Hirst and Metcalf (1984) identify that the perception and/or knowledge that one is worthy of touch - fosters self-esteem. As closeness by family and friends declines, the elderly, like Mr. C., often become "touch hungry" (Moriwaki, 1976). An overt expression of closeness, non-threatening touch says, "You are worthy, I care." Seeking and receiving this "caring touch" provides an opportunity for Mr. C. to assert behavioral control and soften the perceived female dominance if it exists.

As Confucianism teaches, "filial piety" is of key importance in many Asian families (Chae, 1987; Rajewski, 1988). To be unable to care for one's "honorable" parent regardless of disability may be viewed from a cultural standpoint as a "loss of face." Yet, the family's continued concern and visitation is a networking strength, a ray of hope.

Mr. C's decreased food intake has several references related to the maintenance of personal power. First, it is an action of behavioral control; a step towards self-determination and/or self-destiny regarding what and how much he will eat. Secondly, there is an element of cognitive control, perhaps designed to stimulate feelings of guilt in family members who are no longer meeting his needs. Further, it is improper to assume that Mr. C's "withdrawn and passive" behaviors are totally indicative of depression and/or reactions to grief. A portion of this behavior may stem from the cultural posture of aloofness to strangers and a philosophy of reserve in emotional matters (Murray and Zentner, 1975). Golander (1987) found "a great deal of activity under the mantle of passivity" (p. 28). Intellectual and coping skills are marshaled to identify and act upon vital survival strategies. For example, careful planning is required to decide which type of help to ask for, when to ask, by whom, and what is the proper approach. Present and future energy costs and potential reinforcements must also be considered in this process (Golander, 1987).

Lastly, Mr. C's perception of the external condom catheter as "unclean" and his subsequent removal of it may also have as their foundation cultural-spiritual beliefs (Murray and Zentner, 1975). Personal aesthetics and cleanliness are highly valued by Mr. C. The presence of urine in close proximity to body parts is viewed with distress. Mr. C's actions are designed to bring this perceived situation into agreement with his value system.

Rajewski (1988) reflects, "It becomes extremely difficult for individuals steeped in this tradition and heritage to enter a system devoid of anything faintly resembling the practice of filial piety, status and reverential respect. Is it any wonder why Asian "elderly" feel they have few choices "and/or control" when ill?" (p. 89).

Plan

The nursing diagnoses identified through the assessment process are:

1. Grief related to losses of function, family, and possessions.
2. Self-care deficit related to difficulty performing ADL's.

The vast majority of elderly persons have accommodated grief in their life experiences. However, even these enlightened individuals may feel a profound grief when their losses are numerous and occur within a short period of time. Garrett, 1987, described the phenomenon experienced as "bereavement overload" or "an overwhelming grief precipitated by the occurrence of multiple losses with little allowance for separate grieving time" (p. 8). The emotional crisis imposed by this phenomenon can lead to depression and disorientation. The highly vulnerable, relocated individual often feels that everyone and everything of importance to him has been taken away. The precipitating loss of continuity with life history and loss of identity or sense of self fosters feelings of loneliness and helplessness that may even threaten their own survival (McCracken, 1987).

The psychosocial and nursing literature emphasize the significance of "power resources" which enhance the person's ability to cope with grief such as: a) the griever's general state of health, b) the ability to maintain a sense of control over some of the factors relevant to the loss, c) the existence and use of support systems, and d) the belief in a power greater than oneself. Mr. C. possesses each of these power resources in varying degrees. The plan of care requires these strengths be recognized, fostered and built upon in designing intervention strategies that minimize limitations. Furthermore, to address the nursing diagnoses for Mr. C., the health care provider must highlight "care negotiation" as the focal point of each plan of action. Specific goals should include, but are not limited to:

1. To improve and maintain mobility, nutrition and continence for enhanced independence and self-esteem.
2. To provide appropriate sensory stimulation for the maintenance of communication and cognitive abilities.
3. To counsel the family in order to provide necessary reassurance and foster participation.

Interventions

Institutionalization may have placed Mr. C in a situation that decreases his opportunity to act in a self-directed way. Sometimes as an act of kindness or in order to speed up the process of care, the practitioner performs many tasks for the older client that if given the opportunity, time or special instruction, they could do for themselves. Lacking personal growth and being deprived of identity are demonstrated in two ways: 1) no longer doing or having what made him a unique individual, and 2) the perceived loss of respect through others. Thus, Mr. C finds it difficult to view himself in a positive way (Dressler and Carnes, 1973). As illness interferes with a person's sense of worth to himself and value to others, helping Mr. C overcome these negative perceptions is an important practitioner responsibility.

Aasen (1987) identified six intervention strategies geared to foster perceived or actual control for the institutionalized elderly in behavioral, cognitive, and decisional spheres. These strategies can be used as a framework for Mr. C's rehabilitation.

To begin, one must consider and promote awareness of areas of personal control which include the right to make preferences known. Mr. C is very concerned with personal cleanliness. His "bathing customs stem from Shinto purification rites, and baths are taken in the evening before eating not only for cleanliness but for ceremony and relaxation as well" (Murray and Zentner, 1975, p. 293). Simple flexibility in accommodating an evening bath schedule would support Mr. C's control resources in the areas of culture and religion. Eliciting his participation in a continence program could also make use of this motivational strength.

Aasen's (1987) second strategy is to "provide realistic opportunities to make choices regarding personal care and daily activities possible" (p. 26). Mr. C's frequent requests for a backrub can be used to enhance overall well-being. The task-oriented touching of a back rub promotes relaxation, but also demonstrates the concern and caring associated with effective touch (Burnside, 1981). Aside from providing occasional short backrubs upon request, the practitioner can utilize this motivational asset as a care-negotiation tool. For example, the practitioner agrees to rub Mr. C's back while he takes his medication. Aasen (1987) states the literature supports the premise that illusionary control is equally effective as actual control in facilitating perceptions of personal power. Likewise she suggests that simple, decisional options may be even more meaningful in maintaining feelings of power for the mentally alert, physically disabled such as Mr. C.

The third intervention proposed by Aasen centers around "opportunities to participate in activities consistent with personal talents, values and interests" (p. 26). Strategies for Mr. C could include: a) Care of personal plants and/or those within the home; b) Taping his memoirs or philosophy; c) Assembling large piece nature scene puzzles; d) Listening to recordings of cultural music or family members reading special ethnic books. The last technique also enhances Mr. C's emotional resources through nonthreatening family contact and caring.

The fourth intervention focuses on reinterpretation of stressors within the environment to reflect reality. Mr. C's immobility could be altered by the use of an electric wheelchair. Opportunities to ventilate feelings or participate in group activities may change his perception of social isolation.

Intervention number five concerns providing counseling and information wherein the client and/or family can recognize the relationship between past and present behavior outcomes. One could assist Mr. C's recall of feelings and thoughts associated with his initial immigration process and then reflect upon what resources and skills he utilized in adapting to that situation. This reminiscence might offer insight into Mr. C's present strengths necessary for adaptation and rehabilitation. Family therapy should include reassurance related to feelings of inadequacy and understanding of Mr. C's behavior plus rehabilitation needs.

Lastly, there is the requirement for reinforcement of achievements. Positive interactions and advances in self-care must be verbally validated by the care provider. This recognition serves as an external motivator of internal control practices.

Evaluation

Through rehabilitative techniques, care-negotiation, and reinforcement of achievement, Mr. C progressed to a partially-compensatory level of care. At this point he was able to return home with his family, continent, able to assist with transfers and mobile via the electric wheelchair. Professional involvement included ongoing telephone reassurance and clinic visits.

Partly Compensatory Clients

The client who performs his own self-care in some areas but needs assistance in others, is said to need partly-compensatory nursing care (Orem, 1985). The health care professional performs those functions that are no longer possible for the client, such as monitoring the temperature of an electric heating pad on a client whose peripheral nervous system is no longer acute to heat or cold. This type of nursing care also involves revising the environment of the client who can no longer walk very well by placing necessary or desired items within the client's reach (Miller, 1983). His perception of himself as deteriorating or becoming useless is directly proportionate to his feelings of powerlessness (Miller, 1983). Having to depend on others to do some of his care can lead to depression and hopelessness.

It is no easier for the elderly than any other age group to accept favors rather than to give. The individual's perception of receiving reflects power or powerlessness. The person with personal power welcomes the giving of others without a threat to their self-esteem. In denying the pleasure to others in giving to him, the client often fears that allowing another person to help them would establish the validity of his fear, that he is no longer useful, that he can't control his own life (Good, 1987).

CASE STUDY: Partly Compensatory Clients

At age 87, Mr. F. has a six year history of using intermittent supplemental oxygen to compensate for his moderately severe chronic obstructive pulmonary disease. A former industrial supervisor, he feels a sense of pride in successfully managing this disability by participation in pulmonary rehabilitation instruction, structured exercise classes, and compliance with prescribed medical regime. Indeed, he maintains a productive lifestyle through volunteer work in numerous organizations. Mr. F. enjoys a very satisfying relationship with his wife of 25 years. Twenty years younger, she actively supports his continued community involvement as well as the exercise and medical programs. As an Irish Catholic, Mr. F. has strong religious ties. He firmly believes that, "God helps those that help themselves."

Mr. F. had thought it was just a "winter cold" when first experiencing a hacking cough and malaise. However, these symptoms progressed to include diarrhea, nausea, anorexia, and increased lethargy. Reluctantly, he agreed to hospitalization; the diagnosis, Pneumococcal Pneumonia. Now debilitated by severe exertional dyspnea and hampered by intravenous lines, he relies on the nursing staff to assist with his care.

The first night, Mr. F. becomes increasingly restless and agitated secondary to his compromised respiratory status and Theolair toxicity. The nursing staff, fearing he might remove his intravenous lines and attempt to get out of bed unattended, applied soft restraints and secured an order for sedation. By morning, Mr. F. is weak, but quite alert. He agitatedly requests, "Get these restraints off me, I'm not a prisoner, I'm okay now!" While deciding on a course of action, the staff is called away by another medical emergency. Meanwhile, Mr. F., unable to get to a urinal, becomes incontinent. Experiencing feelings of defeat from his illness, he reports to the returning nurse with teary eyes, "I'm not going to make it this time. Where is my wife? If she doesn't get here soon, it may be too late!" Mr. F. allows the nurse to assist with his morning care and transfer him to a reclining chair. However, he becomes increasingly despondent throughout the day, eats very little and finally refuses his medications. Attempts by his doctor to complete a mental status exam are greeted negatively. Later, Mr. F. questions the nurse, "Why doesn't someone tell me what's going on? All that burly, young doctor does is ask me stupid questions. I don't know what day it is and I don't care. I'm just trying to breathe!"

Assessment

While Mr. F's sense of control has been threatened by restraints, incontinence, delirium, and the ultimate loss of self through death, his "solid self" maintains the desire for independence, competence, and the right to self-determination. Solid self is "that part of self that accepts responsibility for decisions about issues significant in one's life" (Nowakowski, 1980, p. 198). In recognizing the capabilities of all disoriented persons, this "solid self" is a very important phenomenon. Nowakowski (1980) suggests talking to the person behind the dysfunction and finding meaningful thoughts to support their care. To move towards recovery, Mr. F. identified his ethicolegal right of health education. This insight proclaims that it is impossible to be truly autonomous without knowledge of one's present and future health care situation (Phillips, 1987).

Mr. F's cultural-spiritual philosophy also fosters an internal locus of control orientation. Aasen (1987) remarks, an "individual learns what to expect for a reinforcement as a result of specific social experiences and subsequently expects that a similar reinforcement will occur in related or similar situations" (p. 24). Mr. F's participative belief is inherent in the concept of "helping oneself" towards recovery, not merely expecting others to provide cures. His remaining physical strength and stamina support this activity if programmed wisely by each health care provider. "Family, friends and significant others play an extremely important role in the care of the hospitalized aged patient, a fact not always recognized by staff" (Lueckenotte, 1987, p. 14). Self-esteem, continuity, and thus cognitive control are fostered through this valued outreach network offering hope, love, comfort and reassurance.

Fear is a normal reaction in situations in which one has no skills, understanding or knowledge base to call upon. Many of today's hospital staff have limited education in gerontological principles of care. "Reflections of fear can be observed in the reluctance to touch or talk to aged patients; a ridiculous notion when one considers that assessment requires communication with the client" (Lueckenotte, 1987, p. 14).

Plan

Mr. F's assessment stimulates a multitude of nursing diagnoses including:

a. Anxiety related to death vs. recovery
b. Noncompliance related to medications
c. Anger related to restraints, mental status exam
d. Self-Care deficit related to knowledge of current disease state
e. Decreased self-esteem related to feelings of inadequacy

Everyone strives to achieve and maintain self-esteem as it is the foundation of psychosocial health. It is understood that the physical and psychosocial requirements of the elderly are closely interrelated and that it is often difficult to separate the two. The influence of this interrelationship is often magnified when an aged individual enters an institution. Hirst and Metcalf (1984) report "self-esteem, in the form of a high evaluation of one's self, comes first from acceptance by others; only then can an individual accept and respect himself. Without self-esteem one lacks the courage to attempt new challenges and is hesitant to interact with others" (p. 72).

Fostering independence through knowledge is a treatment modality that can result in an increase in self-esteem. Of primary concern in this interaction is client involvement in the decision-making process. Thus, the health practitioner collaboratively establishes care priorities and identifies specific objectives as performance (outcome) criteria (Joseph, 1980). The goal for Mr. F. is to provide health related knowledge and emotional support towards the resolution of feelings of anxiety, anger and inadequacy.

Interventions

It is probably unrealistic to attempt extensive problem-solving and/or patient education with a client whose basic needs are unmet, according to Maslow (1954). Thus, for Mr. F, priority interventions are directed toward restoring physiologic and psychologic homeostasis.

Physical needs are predominant in sustaining and motivating human behavior. Treatment of medical problems under poor control is obviously imperative. However, emotional pain is as real and uncomfortable as physical dysfunction. It is frequently the main motivator of behavior patterns and consequently an area of primary therapeutic importance. Mr. F's physical comfort and emotional well-being can be fostered by attention to skin care, grooming and appropriate attire. Likewise, assistance with activities of daily living should be provided with attention directed towards encouragement of self-care abilities, i.e., call bells and urinal easily within reach.

Closely aligned to one's physical needs is the desire to protect oneself and feel free from harm. Mr F's lack of psychological safety stems from a perception of being not in control of his emotions, life and/or future. The practitioner's actions should strive to support a predictable, lawful and orderly world. Limited mobility and alterations in sensory perception increase the chance of accidents. Manipulating the environment and adaptive equipment may compensate for these impairments and enhance feelings of personal security and control. Restraints, conversely, can enhance insecurity through sensory deprivation and the perception of being punished. They should be used with care and removed as quickly as possible.

Mr. F's confusion may be associated with his depression as well as his altered physical state (Haggerty, 1988). The resulting sense of insecurity may lead to unsafe behaviors such as his noncompliance with prescribed medications. Furthermore, what appears to be confusion may actually be apathy—Mr. F simply does not care enough to make the effort to eat or to know the day's date. Consistency should be the hallmark of care via stable space, routine, and caregivers (Wolanin and Phillips, 1981).

The third of Maslow's (1954) hierarchial needs "belonging" overlaps somewhat with the fourth need of "self-esteem." Persons like Mr. F whose powerlessness seems to stem from feelings of inadequacy and an unwarranted pessimism about the future are often future despondent about their depression. Mr. F and his family require reassurance that situational depression and normal grieving are understandable and treatable. Support for the family and friends could in turn enhance their effectiveness in providing love and affection which often is more meaningful from those to whom the elderly feel close. A long-term trusted health professional is also very useful in this role. Regardless of the source, the most important intervention is to communicate to Mr. F a sense of being unconditionally accepted as a unique individual. This nonjudgemental relationship includes opportunities for Mr. F to ventilate feelings and to know his feelings are acknowledged as acceptable. Telling Mr. F that one has five to ten minutes and then giving him undivided attention for that time-frame is far better than ignoring his need for interaction due to concern with a "lack of time." It is quality, not quantity, that fosters trust.

The practitioner is able to understand nonverbal behavior and recognize it in conversation through attention to observation skills. Providing Mr. F with feedback will support him in defining his own problems and recognizing the appropriate solution. Control in choosing preferable therapeutic modalities is facilitated by client teaching regarding Mr. F's disease process. One must be mindful that perhaps only the first four levels of Maslow's needs hierarchy (1954) can be met while Mr. F is in the hospital. Further support, education and counseling can be provided through follow-up outpatient visits and referrals to community health agencies.

Evaluation

The simultaneous provision of medical, cognitive and behavioral therapies as well as enhanced problem solving skills fostered Mr. F's sense of wellness, mastery, achievement, and control. As he developed physical and psychological strength, his sense of self-confidence and capability to deal with his disease was rejuvenated. This sense of power extended into other areas of his recovery and life. Mr. F verbalized the goal to be home for Christmas and responded affirmatively to treatment regimes geared to this objective. With team support, Mr. F achieved his discharge goal. Through continued follow-up therapy, Mr. F was back pursuing voluntary occupational services in a nearby nursing home within three months of his discharge from the hospital.

Supportive-Educative Clients

This group of elderly clients is functionally active and capable of self-care. Seeking assistance from the health care professional involves meeting the client's needs for more information about their health care, preventive behaviors that they can adopt, and support for their current level of functioning (Orem, 1985). Even though this age group sees health professionals more often than other age groups, insurance tends to pay for illness rather than prevention so the elderly client waits until he is ill before seeking any health care. Preventive health teaching is necessary to save the client from a severe illness. However, with no insurance coverage and few wealthy elderly, the self-care needs are taught in less than ideal situations while the client is ill. Health care professionals can help by lobbying for health promotion coverage through Medicare, write and call the insurance companies and offer to educate administrators concerning the financial benefit of preventing illness rather than promoting it.

CASE STUDY: Supportive-Educative Clients

Mrs. J., a 72-year-old heavyset, black widow has a medical history of adult onset type II diabetes, stress incontinence, and degenerative joint disease of her hips, knees, and lower spine. The mother of five grown children, she takes pride in maintaining an immaculate apartment within a senior housing complex. A deeply religious, retired teacher, Mrs. J. devotes many hours to her Baptist church activities. She loves to cook and her socialization need is met through sharing her delicious creations with neighbors and family.

For several weeks, Mrs. J. has experienced moderately severe right leg pain and numbness. She has attempted bedrest, as ordered by her physician. Today, she comes to the clinic regarding a left shoulder injury sustained during a slip in the bathtub. Mrs. J. confides, "I'm not minding so much staying at home because the urine leakage problems have increased." An X-Ray reveals no broken bones. The urine specimen shows + glucose, but no bacteria. Mrs. J. will be discharged home on Tylenol with Codeine. The nurse is requested to provide medication and continence instruction.

Upon greeting the nurse, Mrs. J. half-heartedly proclaims, "I'm glad nothing is broken, but what am I supposed to do to make it get better? My home is already becoming a mess with all this lying around! And by the way, I forgot to tell the doctor about my sore left big toe." Examination reveals unevenly cut toenails, a small blood blister anterior to the right lateral great toe surface. When questioned about footcare, Mrs. J. states bluntly, "I don't like those small clippers, I use scissors, and besides the problem's an ingrown toenail!"

Assessment

The key ingredient of "health and well-being" for persons of Mrs. J's age or older, is the ability to perform their activities of daily living (ADL's) and "instrumental" functions (IADL's) with relative ease. It is no surprise, therefore, that Mrs. J. is much less concerned with the medical diagnosis since independence and personal power are contingent upon her level of performance in meeting personal and household chores, to participate in social activities, and complete necessary errands. Mrs. J. and other "quite" healthy elders are referred to by Sloane (1984) as the "well-derly."

Butler (1987) reports that a "significant number of elderly with one or more chronic diseases do not stay under regular medical supervision, but seek medical care only during acute illness episodes and emergencies" (p. 24). Mrs. J. comes to the clinic seeking acute care for her injured shoulder and sore big toe. Her cognitive strengths request assistance from knowledgeable "powerful" others to support her own recognized responsibility to take part in the treatment process. Rauckhorst (1987) studied 84 community-dwelling elderly widows; the majority (71%) were black. As a group, they remained just as "internally controlled" as that seen by Wallston, Wallston and Devillis (1978) in a larger sample of healthy adults. However, these women were likewise more realistic in viewing their health as more dependent while still retaining this sense of responsibility for their health (Wallston et al., 1978).

Mrs. J's assertive action to seek help in the resolution of her health problems demonstrates the resource strength of hope. An important component of self-esteem is hope for future achievements and the resolution of current difficulties. "Hope is essential for action" (Carnevali and Patrick, 1980, p. 230).

As one ages, the individual's heritage is emphasized. Aging blacks command a high status in their culture, more than half seeing their children at least twice weekly (Rajewski, 1988). Mrs. J. enjoys such a supportive relationship with her family and can call upon them as well as fellow church members for help and encouragement. Koenig (1988) found that religious attitudes and activities may influence complex interactions of health and sociodemographic factors affecting morale and well-being. They found that religiosity represents a significant correlate of morale among sick and healthy older people, especially women (Koenig et al., 1988).

"Health providers need knowledge about the practice of health habits by elderly women so as to facilitate self-regulatory health behavior among this older population" (Rauckhorst, 1987, p. 19).

Plan

The self-care approach for Mrs. J. is guided by the two following major nursing diagnoses:

A. Self-care deficit related to:
1. care of injured left shoulder
2. pain medications
3. management of urinary incontinence
4. diabetic glucose control and footcare
5. environmental safety issues
B. Decreased self-esteem related to:
1. control of continence
2. perceived "messy" home environment

The premise of the supportive-educative category lends itself easily to a wellness promotion conceptual framework. Within this structure the elderly person is supported and guided toward her own self-care choices and activities. In doing so, the practitioner recognizes the individual's age, environment, culture, and lifestyle to maximize her potential, optimal functioning and/or health.

To foster this high level wellness, a behavioral self-management approach is most appropriate. This treatment modality involves teaching the client to use procedures to change her own problematic health-related behaviors. More specifically, Butler (1987) suggests that the nurse involve the elderly in improving their coping skills, developing self-control strategies geared toward reducing detrimental behaviors while encouraging beneficial activities, fostering knowledge through formal and informal educational programs, and participating in collaborative problem solving and decision making.

Interventions

The value of any medical intervention, especially for the older person, must be judged in terms of its effect on the individual's subjective quality of life. The personal act of giving recognized "worth" to the client's value judgment or primary health concern is the key to establishing professional credibility and rapport necessary for health promotion. Thorne and Robinson (1988) observed that "whether they approach us with cheerful compliance or as a militant consumer, elder citizens seek relationships in health care that acknowledge their personhood more than their pathology" (p. 26). Therefore, the practitioner's initial interventions should address Mrs. J's "sore toe" and left shoulder rehabilitation regardless of the potential significance other health issues may seem to pose.

Three additional important intervention strategies have been identified by Thorne and Robinson (1988). First, while each practitioner recognizes and values their autonomous role, the elderly continue to find meaning in the traditional role structure. Consequently, one must emphasize the continuous communication and collaboration among the health care team, and, most especially, with Mrs. J's physician. This verbalization supports the comfort and security developed in that relationship while establishing one's own therapeutic relationship.

The second intervention technique Thorne and Robinson (1988) recognize is that the maintenance of professional distance seems particularly rough on the older client even if perceived appropriate in some health care contexts. "By strategic disclosure of information about ourselves, we may be able to foster trust and confidence in the health care services we provide" (p. 26).

The last strategy acknowledges that in a more formal sense, the elder client expects from this relationship "not cure or medical treatment, as much as reassurance that they have someone who will advocate on their own behalf" (Thorne and Robinson, 1988, p. 26). The self-care concept demands such a role as one facilitates attainment of the following:

1. Support of life processes and promotion of functioning;
2. Maintenance of normal growth and development;
3. Prevention and control of disease processes and injuries and;
4. Prevention of or compensation for disability (Butler, 1987, p. 24).

As health promoter, teacher and advocate within the supportive-educative model it is helpful for interventions of the practitioner to include the components of daily self monitoring and reinforcement. Written instruction, charts and/or graphs which guide and maintain Mrs. J's participation and compliance foster self-care achievement and self-actualization.

Special adaptive equipment such as an automatic glucometer and/or the use of continence pads also facilitate personal control and independence. Community referrals, support groups, appropriate literature, and a scheduled return clinic appointment further enhance Mrs. J's confidence in the health care system and her own "active power" within it.

Evaluation

Mrs. J's podiatry consult fostered treatment of her infected great toe and established the mechanism for on-going foot care. Referrals to a visiting nurse service including physical therapy and a home health aid supported her needs for health promotion, back and shoulder therapy, and short term assistance with bathing and home maintenance. On her return visit to the clinic, Mrs. J expressed gratitude for the myriad of services fostering her progress towards good health and continued independence. By using Kegel exercises and continence pads she stated renewed confidence in pursuing social involvement with family, friends and church. Mrs. J was especially proud to share her glucose monitoring chart which reflected therapeutic levels, thus demonstrating compliance with diet and activity through newly acquired knowledge.

Summary

As has been illustrated, the elderly client does not desire nor thrive in an environment of powerlessness. The despair from powerlessness that leads to death is seen far too often in the elderly population. The sources of feeling out of control of one's own life situations are many, such as physical changes, loss of loved ones and societal attitudes toward the elderly population. Powerlessness in regard to health is an avoidable addition to the present societal influences.

Case studies describing the assessment of powerlessness and the nursing process in counteracting this problem are given for the supportive-educative, partly compensatory and wholly compensatory clients. Interventions for increasing power in the elderly client are listed.

References

Aasen, N. Interventions to facilitate personal control. *Journal of Gerontological Nursing.* 13(6) 21-28, (1987).

Bornstein, R. Cognitive and psycho-social development in the older adult. In Schuster, Clara and Ashburn, Shirley (eds.). *The Process of Human Development: A Holistic Approach.* Boston: Little, Brown and Company, (1980).

Burnside, I.M. *Nursing and the Aged.* New York: McGraw-Hill Book Co., (1981).

Butler, F. Old people are survivors! *Journal of Gerontological Nursing.* 13 (8) 23-28, (1987).

Carnevali, D. and Patrick, M. *Nursing Management for the Elderly.* New York: Lippincott, (1980).

Chae, M. Older Asians. *Journal of Gerontological Nursing.* 13(11). 11-17, (1987).

Dressler, D. and Carnes, S. *Sociology, The Study of Human Interaction.* New York: Alfred A. Knopf, Inc., (1973).

Duvall, E. R. M. *Family Development* (4th Ed.). Philadelphia: Lippincott, (1971).

Erikson, E. H. *Childhood and Society* (nd Ed.). New York: Norton, (1963).

Flynn, J. Biophysical development of later adulthood. In Schuster, Clara and Ashburn, Shirley (eds.). *The Process of Human Development: A Holistic Approach.* Boston: Little, Brown and Company, (1980).

Ford, A., Folmar, B., Steven, A., Salmon, R., Medalie, J., Roy, A.W., Galozka, and Sim S. Health and function in the old and very old. *Journal of American Geriatrics Society* 36(3) 187-197, (1988).

Golander, H. Under the guise of passivity. *Journal of Gerontological Nursing.* 13(2). 26-31, (1987).

Good, E. P. *In Pursuit of Happiness: Knowing What You Want and Getting What You Need.* Chapel Hill, NC: New View Publications, (1987).

Havighurst, R. J. *Developmental Tasks and Education* (3rd Ed.). New York: McKay, (1972).

Hing, E. Use of nursing homes by the elderly: preliminary data from the 1985 National Nursing Home Survey. *New Horizons, National Gerontological Nursing Association.* June-July.p.1, (1987).

Hirst, S. and Metcalf, B. Promoting self-esteem. *Journal of Gerontological Nursing* 10(2). 72-77, (1984).

Jahraus, A. Who is confused. *Nursing Homes.* August-September. 6-9, (1974).

Koenig, H.G., Koale, J., and Ferrel, C. Religion and well-being in later life. *The Gerontologist.* 28(1). 18-28, (1988).

Kutlenios, R. Healing mind and body: a holistic perspective. *Journal of Gerontological Nursing* 13(12). 9-13, (1987).

Lerner, M. *Surplus Powerlessness.* Oakland, CA: Institute for Labor Mental Health, (1986).

Lueckenotte, A. Sharpen skills in hospital settings. *Journal of Gerontological Nursing.* 13(3). 12-19, (1987).

Maslow, A.H. *Motivation and Personality.* New York: Harper and Row, (1954).

Miller, J. *Coping With Chronic Illness: Overcoming Powerlessness.* Philadelphia: F.A.Davis Company, (1983).

Moriwaki, S. Ethnicity and aging. In Burnside, I.M. (ed). *Nursing and The Aged.* New York: McGraw-Hill, (1976).

Murray, R. and Zentner, J. *Nursing Concepts for Health Promotion.* New Jersey: Prentice-Hall, Inc., (1975).

Nowakowski, L. Disorientation-signal or diagnosis. *Journal of Gerontological Nursing.* 6(4). 197-202, (1980).

Orem, D. *Nursing: Concepts of Practice* (3rd Ed.). New York: McGraw-Hill Book Company, (1985).

Phillips, L. Respect basic human rights. *Journal of Gerontological Nursing.* 13(6). 21-28, (1987).

Rajewski, G. Minority elderly in the V.A. *VA Practitioner. February.* 85-92, (1988).

Rauckhorst, L. Health habits of elderly widows. *Journal of Gerontological Nursing.* 13(8). 19-22, (1987).

Reibel, E. Retirement. In Schuster, Clara and Ashburn, Shirley (eds.). *The Process of Human Development: A Holistic Approach.* Boston: Little, Brown and Company, (1980).

Sloane, P.D. How to maintain the health of the independent elderly. *Geriatrics.* 39(10) 93-104, (1984).

Thorne, S. and Robinson, C. Legacy of the country doctor. *Journal of Geriatric Nursing* 14(5) 23-26, (1988).

Wallston, K.A., Wallston, B.S., and Devillis, R. Development of the multidimensional health locus of control (MHLC) scales. *Health Education Monographs.* Vol.6. 16-17, (1978).

Wolanin, M. and Phillips, L. *Confusion Prevention and Care*. St. Louis: C.V.Mosby, (1981).

11

Power and the Acutely Ill Client

J. Cavanah Turner and N. Rinehart

Introduction

Acute illness denies the individual time to adjust to the changes in his body and promotes a sense of powerlessness. The acutely ill client relinquishes the role of a healthy functioning adult adopting that of an ill person, unable to effectively function in his usual manner. He has physical symptoms that overwhelm him, pain that is constant or altered body functions. He seeks assistance from the health care professional in gaining control over the illness. In his admission of the need for assistance, the client perceives his personal power as diminished.

Whatever the diagnosis, the perception of himself as powerless prolongs the client's recovery time (Kneisl and Ames, 1986). To expedite his recovery, the client must retrieve his personal power. He acknowledges his body alterations and decides to assess and use his own self-care capabilities. "Studies indicate that persons show less anxiety and physiologic response in aversive situations in which they believe that personal competence and action affect the outcome" (McFarland and McCann, 1986, p. 1827).

In the acute care setting clients need support from the health care professional to move from the receipt of care to that of care participation (Long and Phipps, 1985). Clients should be encouraged to join in a partnership with the health care professional. "The goal of nursing practice is always to encourage and facilitate patient independence" (Luckmann and Sorensen, 1980, p. 9). Changing his perception of the care provider from one who does things to him, to a partner with suggestions for alternative health behaviors is vital in meeting the goal of increasing his personal power.

Control Theory

The basic concept of Control Theory is that all individuals have the power of choice, whether it be a choice of action or perception (Glasser, 1984). In the medical-surgical areas of health care, the client often does not evaluate himself as having much control over his body and therefore, his choice of actions. However, he does have the choice of his perceptions. Through emphasizing the areas in which the client has control, his perception of being powerless alters. His perception of powerlessness lessens when he is encouraged to participate in decision-making and carry out as much of his own self-care as possible.

The client's perceptions change when he is given additional information about his condition and procedures that are planned. Then he chooses to perceive a procedure as frightening or as less anxiety provoking. Awareness of self-responsibility for perceptions leads to a gain in the client's sense of personal power.

Systems Theory

The individual with the acute illness affects, and is affected by, many other people. Those who work with the client notice his absence and often are expected to do his job as well as theirs. The client's family members experience alterations in their lifestyles. His role tasks in the family are left for others to fulfill. It does not require more than a few days in the hospital to run up a bill that will demand the making of sacrifices and the worry of endless monthly payments.

In each of these situations the client is part of a system. If one member of a system is not functioning optimally, the entire system will change. The rapidity with which hospitalized clients are discharged further upsets the efficiency of each of the client's systems. Clients leave the hospital, still in a state of ill health, with the hospital staff's expectation that the client and his family can and will perform the required nursing care. Clients socialized to meekly accept and obey whatever the health care professional suggests for him do not expect to be responsible for their own care. It is an abrupt reverse in societal norms for self-care to be performed by the client or his family. Education and support facilitate a smoother transition from hospital to care at home. The client and his family need frequent reassurance that they can increasingly take control of the illness care needs of the client.

Medical

The medical client's body no longer functions efficiently. He depends on the health care professional to discover some method for the improvement of his current state of health. Although considered less invasive than surgery, the medical treatments and diagnostic techniques used on the client in the medical setting encourage the client to consider himself at the mercy of his caregivers and powerless to protect himself from their ministrations.

CASE STUDY

John F. was a 34-year-old client admitted to the hospital medical unit with a diagnosis of subacute bacterial endocarditis. As the nurse collected the admission nursing data from John, she found that he had been experiencing symptoms of malaise, fatigue, and anorexia for approximately three weeks prior to admission after having two wisdom teeth extracted. As John was a Certified Public Accountant and tax time was drawing near, he attributed the symptoms to the pressures of work. However, during the previous week John noticed intermittent fever and a weight loss of two pounds. Because of these symptoms, which he interpreted as "flu," John sought medical attention from his family physician. The physician discovered a heart murmer that had not been present previously and a palpable, enlarged spleen. John was referred to a cardiologist who, on echocardiography, found evidence of valvular vegetations. Blood cultures revealed the presence of Streptococcus viridans. The cardiologist admitted John to the hospital for four to six weeks of intravenous penicillin therapy.

John told the admitting nurse that he had just recently graduated from college and received his certification. He was in business for himself and had been able to manage his meager income carefully enough to plan marriage to his long-time fiance. The wedding was to take place in two weeks. Although John had been told by his physician that long-term intravenous antibiotic therapy was to be initiated, John laughed with the nurse about his condition, stating that he would be in "tip top" shape in time for the wedding. The nurse replied, "I'm sure you will be" and continued with the admission.

Initial treatment for John began with antibiotic therapy and bedrest. Although John had been told he was to stay in bed he insisted upon getting up to the bathroom. When confronted with this behavior, John stated "there isn't that much wrong with me; I can make it to the bathroom just fine." The nurse scolded John and repeated that he was to stay in bed. She noted that every time he got up his temperature elevated and his lethargy became more pronounced.

For the first forty-eight hours past admission, John continued to joke about his illness with the staff. To each staff member he came in contact with he said, "I'm starting a pool; how soon do you think I'll be out of here?" When confronted about getting out of bed, he indicated that he didn't need bedrest. When asked, "Why don't you feel you need restricted activity?" John replied that he was beginning to feel better. After the nurse took the time to explain the rationale for limited activity in the early phases of the illness, John was more compliant with the order. He continued to grumble, however, about the unit policy of bathing all clients in the morning, stating that he would rather bathe immediately prior to visiting hours. None of the staff arranged for him to do so.

After a few more days of treatment, John's fever subsided and he began to gain weight. He attributed this fact to his overall good physical condition. He seemed to become more restless as he began to feel better and complained frequently that he needed to be in his office "making a living as a man's supposed to do." He confided to the nurse that he was concerned about the additional financial burden of hospitalization postponing his marriage even longer. Soon after, John appeared listless. His appetite, which had been improving, decreased. When asked if he was depressed, John replied "What do you care? Nobody around here cares what happens to me." The nurse became upset and told the charge nurse that John was "mad" at her. The charge nurse talked with John and assured him that his feelings of depression were normal.

John looked forward to the frequent visits made by his fiance and family but was often withdrawn and hostile to the staff after they left. He resumed his previous pattern of ignoring the physician's order for limited activity even though the importance of the order had been frequently reinforced. When the physician found John doing business with a client in the lounge, he changed the activity order back to strict bedrest without informing John. Furious at not being consulted, John threatened to sign out of the hospital against medical advice (A.M.A.). He became increasingly agitated when the charge nurse tried to calm him. He yelled at the staff, blaming them for the interruptions in his life, for enforcing restricted activity, and for his current health problem.

Application of the Nursing Process

The nurse responsible for John's care at this point in his hospitalization scheduled a patient care conference in an attempt to help the staff meet John's needs. Together, they arrived at several nursing diagnoses based on the assessment data. Among them was powerlessness related to the perceived loss of control over his life events. The manifestations of this diagnosis included the many examples of his early denial of the situation such as his minimizing the situation to the admission nurse, asking each staff member the same question about the time necessary for treatment, and his repudiation of restrictions. Other manifestations include: 1) his later depression, indicated by his listlessness and appetite loss, which evolved into overt anger as demonstrated by his hostility to staff and accusing them of not caring, 2) violating his activity restrictions and 3) threatening to sign out A.M.A.

The expected outcome for the resolution of this nursing diagnosis was that John perceive that he could regain personal control over his life during the course of this illness. The application of control theory was appropriate in this particular situation. The staff planned to encourage him to alter his perception of the situation from one of impossibility to one of challenge, thereby lower his stress and contribute to his sense of control (see Figure 11-1). John was consulted by the staff to validate the assessment of powerlessness and to inform him of the staff's plans for decreasing this. Talking with him as his care was being performed reinforced the message that his opinion was valid.

The staff assessed his power resources to arrive at an appropriate plan for assisting John toward recovery. The staff found that physically he had, and perceived himself as having, strength because of his youth and good physical condition. His physical reserves were depleted to some extent because of his illness, but he retained the ability for complete recovery if the course of the illness continued without complications.

John was emotionally stable in terms of his occupation, family, and significant other. His emotional stamina, self-concept, and coping mechanisms were altered because of the stress of illness. John experienced a difficult emotional adjustment to the role of being the health care client, hospitalized, and his postponed normal lifestyle from that of wage earner and independent male.

John had a highly developed intellectual ability that served to promote understanding of imparted knowledge. The major impairment in this realm was John's self-perception. John did not have complete knowledge of his situation and limitations, so he perceived himself as having fewer choices than he actually had.

In the cultural and spiritual areas, John had a fully functioning support network. His expressions of hopelessness indicated powerlessness. He also lacked the motivation necessary to participate in ordered therapy, thus indicated no acknowledgment that such participation would be need-fulfilling for him.

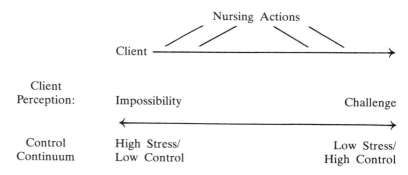

Fig. 11-1. Goal of Care

The staff's plan of care for John was based upon the acceptance of power as a basic need and the goal to provide assistance to him in altering his perception of the situation as illustrated in Figure 11-1. The nursing actions were to be directed toward strengthening

John's physical, emotional, spiritual, intellectual, and cultural power resources (see Figure 11-2).

PHYSICAL	INTELLECTUAL
Reserves	Self-perception
EMOTIONAL	**CULTURAL**
Stamina	Support network
Self-concept	
Motivation	**SPIRITUAL**
Coping	Hope

Fig. 11-2. Power Resources to be Enhanced by Nursing Actions

In the physical realm, the staff sought to rebuild John's depleted reserves by emphasizing a high protein, high carbohydrate diet and reinforced the importance of compliance with the antibiotic regimen. They also continued to assess his physical condition and response to therapy (conservation of strength, isotonic exercises, passive-assistive range of motion exercises, and provision for self-care tasks still allowed, e.g. oral hygiene and hair care).

The staff encouraged John to verbalize his thoughts and feelings thereby assisting him to increase his emotional stamina (Phipps et al., 1983). Whether John's feelings were denial, depression, or anger, the encouragement to verbalize them promoted feelings of acceptance of him and his right to his feelings without reinforcing them. The staff planned to appropriately reassure him that these feelings are normal in the situation in which he found himself. They provided positive caring and concern to reinforce his self concept and motivation. Allotting adequate time to deal with questions and to seek John's input into decision making, strengthened his self-concept and motivation. He was consulted about his preferences for aspects of his hospital routine such as when to bathe, exercise, eat, and rest. The staff accepted his anger without personalizing it. John's coping skills were improved by discussing alternative methods possible for him to use in coping and what had worked for him in the past and encouraging him to practice or role-play new behaviors. Finally, the charge nurse bolstered his motivation by consulting with the physician about the possibility of beginning teaching for John so he might soon be discharged with home intravenous therapy.

To build John's intellectual power resources, the staff promoted readjustment of John's self-perception by conferring with the physician about the possibility of John's conducting a limited amount of business in the hospital predicated upon his physical response to such activity. Accommodating John's cultural needs, the staff scheduled his care so he had maximal time to spend with his fiancee and family and arranged staff-visits at intervals when the family was not present.

The partial nursing care plan for John is reflected in Figure 11-3.

John was discharged after two and a half weeks of hospitalization in stable condition. He and his fiancee were to be responsible for continuing his intravenous therapy under the direction of a home health nurse.

DATE	NURSING DIAGNOSIS	NURSING ACTION	RESPONSE
3/15	Powerlessness related to perceived loss of control.	1. Encourage hi pro, hi CHO diet selections.	3/17 Client selecting appropriately;
	Expected Outcome: client will regain sense of control during this illness.	2. Reinforce importance of antibiotic regimen.	appetite good; weight gain of 1#.
		3. Assess VS, activity tolerance.	3/18 VS with in normal limits; tires easily with activity.
		4. Monitor ECG results.	3/20 stable.
		5. Encourage verbalization of feelings.	3/19 Able to verbalize feelings of anger are lessening.
		6. Reassure that negative feelings are normal.	
		7. Convey caring and concern.	3/21 receptive to staff; friendly; no further angry outbursts.
		8. Take time to explain and answer questions.	
		9. Consult about preferences for times of hospital routines.	3/15 Requests bath at 1300; rest from 1200 to 1300 up in room 1400-1600.
		10. Accept anger matter-of-factly; do not personalize.	3/16 Angry outbursts dissipate rapidly when allowed to vent.
		11. Confer with physician regarding possibility of home IV therapy & of conducting limited business.	3/15 Obtained permission to begin teaching in "a few days" if stable.

DATE	NURSING DIAGNOSIS	NURSING ACTION	RESPONSE
		12. Organize nursing care to allot maximal visiting time.	3/17 Spends all of visiting time with family & friends; cheerful.
		13. Visit at frequent intervals without tiring him.	
3/18		1. Begin teaching for home IV care to client and fiancee.	3/18 Client and fiancee receptive, eager; pleased with their success.
		a. A&P of circulatory system	3/22 No breaks in technique noted.
		b. Site care	3/23 Client and fiancee doing each procedure correctly.
		c. Asepsis	
		d. Piggy-back procedure	3/24 Tolerates 2 hours of activity/day with no change in VS, activity tolerance; sleeping well.
		2. Allot 2 hours in a.m. for work; assess response.	

Fig. 11-3. Nursing Care Plan

Surgical

The surgical client is not only betrayed by his body functions, he faces the loss of control of his body while strangers cut away his tissue. Having a local anesthetic promotes a sense of control for the client. However, even a local anesthetic increases the client's perception of being out of control, as the surgical area of his body is numbed and he can no longer move or function as the surgical staff expose the inner workings of his body (Luckmann and Sorensen, 1980).

CASE STUDY

Mrs. S., a 67 year old hispanic woman, has been a client on the hospital surgical unit for four days. She was admitted in the early evening hours with acute right upper quadrant and subscapular pain. She was given a narcotic for pain about every four hours during the first night of hospitalization because of extreme discomfort. During the night, she experienced several episodes of nausea and vomiting for which she was given intramuscular antiemetics. The next day biliary ultrasonography revealed acute cholecystitis and cholelithiasis. Mrs. S. continued to experience acute pain and vomiting for which she was medicated.

Mrs. S., a heavy smoker in the past, had a moderate degree of emphysema for which she received no medication. In addition she had a mild degree of congestive heart failure.

During the second evening of hospitalization, Mrs. S. placed a frantic call to her daughter asking her to come to the hospital immediately because the "television set is climbing down the wall." When the unit staff was alerted, they discovered Mrs. S. cowering in her room, fearful and crying because she was experiencing visual hallucinations. Her surgeon was notified and a different narcotic ordered. Mrs. S. began refusing the narcotic at intervals even when she was obviously in pain because she had been told that it was the cause of her hallucinations. She remained anxious and depressed, and on frequent occasions told the nursing staff that the pain prevented her from "being my own person." While doing preoperative teaching about the use of an incentive inspirometer the respiratory therapist told Mrs. S. that she shouldn't be "silly" but should take the medication as often as she needed it for pain.

The nursing staff explained to Mrs. S. that her surgeon planned to perform a cholecystectomy after the acute inflammation had subsided somewhat, and urged her to take the narcotic as indicated. Mrs. S. generally refused, saying that she feared the medication because it prevented her from "thinking straight." In the meantime, she became increasingly apathetic when the pain or worry prevented her from carrying on her usual activities and grooming measures.

Two of Mrs. S.'s children lived in the city and visited frequently, as did her elderly husband. Mrs. S. fretted over the fact that she was not at home to care for her husband as she had been doing for forty-five years. Mrs. S.'s children voiced concern about the fact that their mother, who had always been so strong, was now seemingly so helpless. The only comfort Mrs. S. appeared to experience was during her priest's brief visits.

Preoperative teaching was begun for Mrs. S. She was concerned about the instructions for the Patient Controlled Anesthesia (PCA) pump and the Transcutaneous Electrical Nerve Stimulator (TENS) unit she would use later in her postoperative course, afraid that she would not know how to manage the devices after surgery. Her roommate, who had been listening avidly to the instructions, told her not to be "such a baby."

As she was being prepared for surgery, Mrs. S. told the nurse that she dreaded the upcoming procedure since she would have even less control over what happened to her postoperatively. She was received back onto the primary care surgical unit with a nasogastric tube in place after a cholecystectomy had been performed. She had an uneventful course in the post-anesthesia unit.

Application of the Nursing Process

Because of Mrs. S.'s stormy preoperative course, the clinical director assigns Mary as her primary nurse. After careful assessment of Mrs. S.'s preoperative course, she decides to plan her nursing care from a systems approach. She views the client as an organized system composed of subsystems in the physical, emotional, cultural, spiritual, and intellectual realms. This system is being influenced by internal and external stimuli which could ultimately result in either stability or instability (Brunner and Suddarth, 1988) depending on the effectiveness of nursing action (see Figure 11-4).

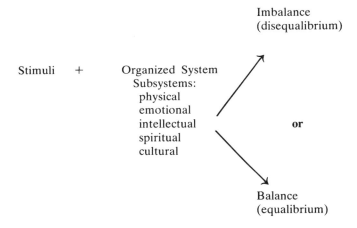

Fig. 11-4. The client as a system

From analysis of the assessment data, one nursing diagnosis arrived at is powerlessness related to feared lack of pain control manifested by anxiety and depression, fears of inability to manage pain control devices and verbalization of dread concerning postoperative pain control.

Each of the subsystems is examined, with the finding that in the physical realm, Mrs. S. has depleted reserves and strength due to a history of smoking and chronic illness and having just had general anesthesia and surgery. In general, however, she finds that Mrs. S. has more abilities than disabilities in the physical realm.

GOALS	NURSING ORDERS

#1: Assist the client to minimize the impact of post-a operative pain and discomfort.

1. Assess the NG tube for patency:
   a. Irrigate as ordered prn.
   b. Assess for return of bowel sounds.
   c. Administer ordered throat lozenges prn.
2. Turn, cough, and deep breathe every 2-4 hours:
   a. Assess breath sounds.
   b. Splint incision with pillow.
   c. Reinforce previous teaching for use of incentive spirometer; assist prn.
3. Progress from dangling at bedside to ambulation in room first 24 hours:
   a. Assist to turn every 1-2 hours.
   b. Plan kind and timing of activity with client.
   c. Do not rush client.
   d. Praise efforts.
4. Encourage use of PCA and (later) TENS unit:
   a. Reinforce preoperative teaching.
   b. Assist as necessary.
   c. Monitor client response and adapt accordingly.

#2: Assist the client to minimize impact of environmental stimuli.

1. Build a trust relationship:
   a. Use primary nursing.
   b. Use minimal number of associates for care.
2. Encourage visits from family, priest, church members, friends:
3. Place call light, telephone, and bedside table, within reach:
   a. Emphasize that objects form part of client's territory.
   b. Respect her right to exert control over her territory.

"continued"

GOALS	NURSING ORDERS

GOALS   NURSING ORDERS

4. Promote partnership in decision-making:
   a. Seek client's input for time and type of routines.
   b. Provide choices.
   c. Give verbal and non-verbal positive reinforcement for performing own ADLs and setting goals.
5. Assess learning needs and provide information.

Fig. 11-5. Nursing Orders to Control Stimuli

According to her family, Mrs. S. usually is emotionally stable, although at present, her emotional stamina is altered due to fright and depression. Her poor self concept is related to her perceived lack of control and dread of postoperative pain. Mrs. S's coping style is ineffective although it is her best possible effort in this situation. As a result of not seeing herself as her "own person" or capable of meeting others' expectations, Mrs. S. lacks the motivation to take control of her own situation.

The greatest power resource in the intellectual realm for Mrs. S. is her perception of having always been in control in the past. She possesses normal cognitive abilities which can be enhanced.

Additional sources for development of power for Mrs. S. are in her spiritual and cultural subsystems. She has a strong and consoling religious belief and an intact network of support systems by way of husband, family, and church affiliation.

Since the subsystems of any open system are constantly in a state of interdependence, Mary bases the nursing plan for Mrs. S. on strengthening each of the subsystems and reducing the impact of the environmental stimuli, particularly the pain. Nursing orders in Figure 11-5 reflect Mary's plans.

Mrs. S. responded well to the primary care setting and was discharged six days postoperatively with no pain or fever, solid food tolerance, a healing surgical would, and normal bowel function — the usual desirable criteria (Brodt, 1986). She verbalized understanding and feelings of control over her discharge instructions.

General Measures For Powerlessness In The Medical-Surgical Client

1. Build a trust relationship.
2. Encourage expression of feelings and concerns; reassure that negative feelings are normal.
3. Solicit opinions, likes, dislikes, and wishes and apply these in the care plan.
4. Promote active participation in simple decision making; assess readiness for complex decision making.
5. Provide situations in which the client can take control.
6. Provide positive reinforcement and acknowledgment for active participation in planning care.
7. Assess knowledge and perception of treatment program.
8. Encourage questions.
9. Assess communication patterns.
10. Approach client calmly and with confidence.
11. Be sensitive to situations which might precipitate feelings of powerlessness.
12. Teach self monitoring by diary, log, etc.
13. Avoid hurrying the client.
14. Provide consistent caretakers whenever possible.
15. Modify the environment so that client can participate in self-care as much as possible.
16. Provide for privacy.
17. Inform client prior to scheduled tests and procedures.
18. Provide relevant audio-visual aids.
19. Help client recognize strengths, potential, improvement in condition, mastery of skills, coping mechanisms, specific stressors.
20. Alleviate physical discomfort.
21. Involve significant others in the plan of care.

Summary

Awareness of the power needs of the client by the health care professional is required in the promotion of personal power in the client. Without the efforts of the medical-surgical staff members in assisting the client to be more responsible for his care, the client can fight against the feelings of powerlessness and cause extensive harm to himself or, at least, prolong his recuperation period.

Case studies are discussed for clients in the medical and surgical settings. Appropriate interventions are suggested through the use of the nursing process.

References

Brodt, D. *Medical-Surgical Nursing and the Nursing Process: A Study and Review Book*. Boston: Little, Brown, and Company, (1986).

Brunner, L. and Suddarth, D. *Textbook of Medical-Surgical Nursing* (6th ed.). Philadelphia: J.B.Lippincott Company, (1988).

Fanslow, J. Do we have too much power over our patients? *RN* 49(6), 17, (1986).

Glasser, W. *Take Effective Control of Your Life*. New York: Harper and Row, (1984).

Kneisl, C. and Ames, S. *Adult Health Nursing: A Biopsychosocial Approach*. Menlo Park, CA: Addison-Wesley Publishing Company, (1986).

Lambert, V. and Lambert, C. *The Impact of Physical Illness and Related Mental Health Concepts*. Englewood Cliffs, NJ: Prentice-Hall, Inc., (1979).

Leonard, B. and Redland, A. *Process in Clinical Nursing*. Englewood Cliffs, NJ: Prentice-Hall, Inc., (1981).

Long, B. and Phipps, W. *Essentials of Medical-Surgical Nursing: A Nursing Process Approach* (3rd ed). Philadelphia: W.B. Saunders Company, (1985).

Luckmann, J. and Sorensen, K. *Medical-Surgical Nursing: A Psychophysiologic Approach* (3rd ed). Philadelphia: W.B. Saunders Company, (1987).

Phipps, W.; Long, B.; and Woods, N. *Medical-Surgical Nursing: Concepts and Clinical Practice*. St. Louis: C.V.Mosby Company, (1983).

Smith, F. Patient power. *American Journal of Nursing*. 85(11), 1260-1262, (1985).

Thompson, J.; McFarland, G.; Hirsch, J.; Tucker, S.; and Bowers, A. *Clinical Nursing*. St. Louis: C.V. Mosby Company, (1986).

Tucker, S.; Canobbio, M.; Paquette, E.; and Wells, M. *Patient Care Standards: Nursing Process, Diagnosis, and Outcome* (4th ed). St.. Louis: C.V.Mosby Company, (1988).

12

Power and the Critically Ill Client

S. Garman and N. Rinehart

Introduction

The client who is admitted to the critical care setting has not calmly walked into the hospital and decided to be admitted. Because of the critical, life-threatening nature of his illness, he has been rapidly shunted through the emergency room and into the critical care unit with little input by himself. He has been the victim of a motor vehicle accident or a physical crisis, such as a myocardial infarction. In the critical care setting, he finds himself surrounded by strange sounds and sights, with tubes and machines attached to his body.

In this strange world of machines, medications, discomfort and strangers controlling his bodily functions, the client perceives himself as having little or no power. Furthermore, caregivers increase the client's perception of helplessness through the use of technical and undefined language and the control issues of the health care professional. If this client is not to become a dependent, psychologically crippled person, the health care professional must assess for strengths in his available resources of power and assist the client in enhancing these. The client must be helped to increase his sense of power and develop his inherent capabilities and rights of power to improve his chances of recovery and resumption of a relatively normal and productive lifestyle (Driver and Gallo, 1977).

The health care professional perceives the environment as necessitating the extinction of one crisis after another (Claus and Bailey, 1980). This calls for quick and logical thinking, an indepth knowledge base and rapid reflexes. Somehow, in this tense and frenzied atmosphere, the client's emotional and spiritual needs tend to become ignored. The nurse spends so much time "stomping out small brush fires," or handling one crisis after another, she has difficulty seeing the client with anything other than physical problems.

Early in the client's critical care experience, certain elements that indicate powerlessness can be recognized. Zschoche (1976) identified the following in clients: acute fear, sustained tension and agitated depression. If these are dealt with in a timely manner the frequency of psychotic reactions in critical care clients may be decreased.

A concern in the critical care situation must be the identification and treatment of "intensive care psychosis," according to Wilson (1977).

He advocates the use of reorientation methods for combating this syndrome but states that "a confident, concerned physician and nursing staff who communicate well with the patient are most important" (p. 122).

Diminishing the client's perception of powerlessness is urgent from the initial contact with critical care practitioners to his discharge in a stable condition. The methods available to implement an increase in client control are as individualized as the client situations. Figure 12-1 lists some of the possible interventions.

The client faces many dilemmas, not the least of which is physical status. Other conflicts that occur are: lack of identity in the rapid-paced critical care unit with its unisex gowns, lack of privacy and invasion of the client's personal space; the influence-power-control struggle (Who has power? The client? The doctor? The nurse? Who has authority?); and the incongruence of client needs and the goals of the health care team.

It is necessary for all professionals caring for the client to be concerned about the client's mental status because "to traumatize the body is to traumatize the mind" (Kenner, 1985, p. 1152). The client's feelings of powerlessness in the critical care setting influence his physical as well as emotional health. When the client perceives that all of his control is gone, he may initially struggle against his helplessness, but eventually "gives up," which affects the parasympathetic system of the client and leads to deterioration of the physical systems of the body (Kenner, 1985).

Physical
Provide choices in scheduling care activities.
Promote participation in ADL's.
Perform hygiene and grooming needs as desired.
Keep area clean and attractive.
Avoid machine noise as much as possible.
Explain all procedures.
Alert client before touching him.
Educate concerning illness and treatment plans.
Encourage family members to perform personal care.
Include family in discussions regarding care plan.

Intellectual
Talk to client while performing care tasks.
Orient to time and place as needed (clock, calendar, copy of care schedule).
Provide reading or listening material.
Evaluate for knowledge deficit of client and family.
Use appropriate teaching methods for client and family.
Discuss outside world occurrences.
Assess for and share common topics of interest.

Emotional

Assess for fears and discuss them.
Ask what helps client cope in stressful situations.
Reinforce situation as challenge rather than defeat.
Provide as peaceful an environment as possible.
Encourage family visitation as appropriate.
Maintain caring and supportive attitude.
Use disclosure judiciously.

Cultural

Assess for cultural needs (i.e.,privacy, food, and traditions).
Identify role in family and assist in adapting to altered role.
Encourage contact with cultural support system.
Contact members of cultural group to visit if from another town.
Provide translator as necessary.

Spiritual

Ask if clergy visit is desired.
Provide atmosphere appropriate for religious rituals.
Encourage family participation in spiritual needs.
Read to client from religious literature if desired.
Allow space for religious symbols and equipment as appropriate.
Assess need of client to discuss feelings of hope.
Discuss death and dying as indicated by client and family.
Support spiritual requests as desired.

Fig. 12-1. Empowerment Interventions in Critical Care

Locus of Control and the Critically Ill Client

In the emergency room environment, the client is often placed in the victim role. Not only has his body or society betrayed him by initiating a health crisis, the emergency room and ambulance staff are focused on saving his life and make decisions about his life without any input from him or his family. They command him to stay quiet, hold still, open his mouth, turn over, lift his arm, flex his ankle. The client becomes a possible ruptured appendix, head injury or coronary in bed three, which further isolates him and increases his feelings of powerlessness. It is a challenge for the emergency room staff to identify independent behaviors available to the client. What is he allowed to do to hold onto any remaining self-image of being in control? Aguilera and Messick (1986) state that the illness of the the client "threatens his total integrity as well as his sense of personal adequacy and worth to others" (p. 118).

The emergency room staff needs to be aware of the client's rights. He should have as much input as possible in the administration of his emergency care. It is important that he be informed of the reason for all treatments. The client's wishes need to be respected. If he is unable to communicate, his family must be involved in decision-making concerning his care. If he has religious beliefs that do not allow certain procedures, the staff should present the rationale for the suggested procedure, listing the possible choices and the consequences of each without any attempt to change the client's mind. The client should not be badgered or harassed about his informed choice. If the health care provider becomes too agitated, she must stop and assess whose needs she is meeting.

In the critical care unit, the client and his family must be included in treatment plans. Not only do restrictions need to be explained, it is important to emphasize the independent behaviors the client still has access to. If it is not stressed that the client does have some responsibility, some choices, the client will quickly identify the locus of control as outside of himself. He will exhibit an external locus of control. As the client progresses through his illness, he needs to be supported in becoming more internally controlled. If his physical crisis is to be resolved as much as possible, it is important for the caregivers to identify and assist the client in working through the emotional crisis as well, leading to relief from the stressors he perceives and restoring him to his precrisis functioning level (Garland and Bush, 1982).

In encouraging a more internal locus of control in the client, the health care professionals must combat the urge to do things "the easy way" by taking the control away from the client. Nurses, doctors and other health care professionals must deal with their own control issues and arrive at a comfortable stance that provides support and encouragement for themselves as well as the client. After all, if the client is informed about the possibilities for his care, and thus makes a truly informed choice, what guarantee is there that the client will choose to cooperate? For many health care professionals, turning the power of choice over to the client is not an easy task.

Change Theory and the Critically Ill Client

Changes brought about by a critical illness should be kept to a minimum. The client has had all control of his body taken away by an unplanned-for crisis. The coronary client who states that he is still going hunting next month, no matter what the staff suggests, is possibly speaking from the stage of denial in the grieving process or he is merely reflecting a personal value for quality rather than quantity of living. Suggesting a lifestyle change for the client will, in most cases, meet with a great deal of resistance. This resistance is almost always encountered by the health care professional if the steps of change theory are not recognized and worked through with the client. This process is time-consuming and unpalatable for staff members who are used to everything being done quickly. Decisiveness and expediency are desirable traits in critical care staff members, but these same traits may hinder progression through the change theory and most often they will provoke resistance from the client.

Until the client is receptive to the necessity of change, it is futile to argue or plead with him about these changes. Initially, the health care professional must work on unfreezing. Rather than demand that the client make changes in his lifestyle, discuss the possibility of alternative methods for the continuation of meeting his needs. If he can begin to agree to the possibility of there being other means for achieving satisfaction of his needs, the stage is set for finding an acceptable plan of action.

Instilling the idea of a new way to achieve life goals is an important phase of the change theory. If the client is in despair about the necessity of change, it may take a great deal of effort to get the client to accept the idea that he has changes that have occurred and now must regroup and have input about his future plans. However, if the caregivers provide a consistent message of optimism for the client, the reward of encouraging the client to envision the possibility of options or changes of behavior will be actualized (McNeil, 1985).

Refreezing, or fixing the new plan firmly with the client, may occur after the client has left the critical care unit. Being unable to see the client get well and go home is yet another stressor for the critical care staff (Jacobson and McGrath, 1983). Role-playing and discussion of the plan of action are possible activities that can occur in the critical care unit. It is possible to see the whole process of change occur in the critical care unit. It is, however, also possible that the client will still be in denial upon discharge from the unit. Rather than barging into a client's life with demands that he change, critical care staff need to assess the client's affect, arrange for slower approaches to possible life changes, and, most important of all, it is necessary to remember that the client's choices are his own.

Client Power and Staff Burn-Out

Burn-out is a major problem among critical care staff members, and emotional care is often perceived as one more demand on already overstressed employees. In an environment that rewards quick action in a crisis and familiarity with advanced technology, what are the dividends for staff members who give emotional care to clients? All nurses were taught about the biopsychosocial view of clients. Ignoring two-thirds of each client and delivering clinical care to just the physical component of her client promotes dissatisfaction for the nurse, perceiving herself as not as good as she could be. This dissatisfaction leads to the increased incidence of burn-out.

In a study by Claus and Bailey (1980), the greatest job satisfaction for critical care nurses came from seeing client improvement and recovery. An atmosphere that encourages emotional care of clients will promote more rapid recovery for the client and job satisfaction for staff members (Fuszard, 1984). The improved rate of recovery by clients becomes reinforcing for continued provision of emotional care by the nurse. This alteration in perception of the priorities in the client care environment is called reframing.

Reframing is a preventive measure against burn-out. Grout (1980) suggests that the reframing of the staff's perception of a situation will result in less stress. Reframing does not change the situation, but it does alter its significance. Perceiving emotional care as a challenge and benefit rather than a hassle will promote a decrease in staff member burn-out.

Exposure to stress also leads to burn-out. Focusing on client teaching, thereby increasing client power, reduces stress in clients and staff (Moran, 1980). The nurse benefits through decreased stress as she receives the client's positive responses during and after teaching. The client's favorable reactions also build the nurse's self-esteem.

Building self-esteem leads to diminished burn-out and increased job satisfaction. According to Goble (1984), self-esteem needs can be broken down into two elements: 1) desire for self-approval (resulting from mastery, competence, confidence and independence) and 2) respect from others (acceptance, recognition, and appreciation). The critical care nurse often does well in identifying that her self-approval needs are met, but she gets even less respect from others than nurses in other areas. Because critical care nurses are competent and independent, characteristics of the self-approval portion of self-esteem, they rarely take the time to give positive feedback to each other and the clients are too sick to do so. However, meeting the self-esteem needs of the client and other nurses can be empowering for the nurse as she receives back what she gives away. Meeting self-esteem needs in other nurses and the client will build personal power. Through enhancing the personal power of the client and others, the nurse further adds to her own and becomes a role model for other nurses.

Critical care staff members are role models for coping skills (Garland and Bush, 1982). The methods of coping used by the staff are watched and copied by the client, his family and others. Staff members who remain calm, use healthy coping mechanisms, and who present a caring attitude, add to the ability of the client and family to remain calm in and accepting of the critical care situation. Maintenance of the perception of the client as a whole person and his family as concerned and frightened individuals helps the staff promote recovery. A caring and concerned environment is established by the nurse who sees the client as more than a set of organs, unfortunately, a far too frequent occurrence in critical care units (Shelly, 1980).

Seeing a client as a heart or a set of lungs is a form of distancing. Distancing oneself from the client is a symptom of impending burn-out (Jacobson and McGrath, 1983). The nurse who does not cope well, provide emotional care for the client and/or distances herself from the client adds to his powerlessness as well as her own.

Feelings of powerlessness are almost unbearable to humans (Ujhely, 1963). Rather than continue to experience the powerless/hopeless feeling, the individual will adopt an attitude of hopelessness or withdraw from the situation. Either of these responses will afford short-term relief from the powerless feelings, but neither will contribute to the solution of the problem (Ujhely, 1963). Nurse powerlessness promotes client powerlessness, just as anxiety is contagious. Burn-out is enhanced by feelings of powerlessness. The amount of staff burn-out will be decreased if a climate of client empowerment is established and maintained.

Divisions of Clients

The clients in this chapter are identified by the location in which they are found more than by the severity of illness. The client in each setting is different from the clients in the other areas, yet the same in that they are all in critical condition and, therefore, placed in an enforced powerless position.

Emergency Room. The client who is brought to the emergency room, often by ambulance, may or may not be conscious. It is understood that not all clients who enter the emergency room are critical, but for the purposes of this chapter, those are the clients who will be discussed.

The more anxious a client is, the more difficulty there will be in treating him, eliciting information, teaching him and determining his health status. Therefore, it behooves the care provider to initiate measures to calm the client and to provide an environment that is as conducive as possible to client feelings of acceptance and power of choice.

CASE STUDY

Tyrone is a 32-year-old Black man who was brought to the Emergency Department of a small private hospital in the back seat of his mother's car. He had sustained a stab wound to the abdomen, inflicted by his brother during an argument at a barbecue in his mother's back yard. "It was a family matter," his mother explained. "It was over a girl they'd both dated, and we didn't want to involve the police. It wasn't serious. They'd both had a fair amount of beer to drink and we all

*just wanted them both to calm down a little. They're both nice boys—
neither has given me a minute's trouble. Just sew him up and let me
get them both back home again. We're sorry for all the bother."*

*Two carloads of brothers, sisters, relatives and other interested parties
from the barbecue accompanied the family to the Emergency Department.
There were many individual interpretations of the event, and each was
loudly refuted by other members in the party. The family was unable
to supply information about Tyrone's possible drug allergies, current
medications he might have been taking, or any significant health history
that the staff needed to know. Noisy arguments, and eventually a fight,
ensued in the waiting area about who did what to whom and why.
The hospital security guards were summoned to intervene.*

*While this took place, Tyrone was extricated from the back seat of the
car, placed on a cart and rushed into the trauma room. He was awake,
frightened and smelled of alcohol. (A subsequent blood alcohol level
of 230 substantiated a high level of intoxication.) He was diaphoretic,
shivering, incoherent, and both pupils were dilated. He had a 2 cm
laceration lateral to the umbilicus, but no other external evidence of
trauma. His abdomen was distended and he was vomiting undigested
food. His only verbal response to questions was, "I'm sorry, I'm sorry."*

*Though inaudible, his blood pressure was palpable at 70 mm Hg.
His pulse was regular at 146. His rectal temperature was 97.0° F.*

*To aid in rapid assessment, his clothes were cut from around his
body so that he was lying naked and exposed amid a room full of busy
strangers. A well-trained trauma team worked smoothly to apply monitor
electrodes, start nasal oxygen, draw blood, place large angiocaths in
both arms, insert a Foley catheter and nasogastric tube, and apply
MAST pants to his legs and lower abdomen. The monitor showed sinus
tachycardia. An X-Ray of his abdomen was taken and a Dopamine
drip begun. The surgical resident was summoned and the surgical team
alerted. Tyrone began yelling, "Help me! Help me!" as the trauma team
worked frantically to stabilize his falling blood pressure and increase
his peripheral tissue perfusion.*

*Two hours following his injury found Tyrone anesthetized and
undergoing an exploratory laparotomy in the operating room to repair
a tear in his gastric artery and to evacuate the blood clot that filled
his abdomen.*

Initially, the needs of Tyrone's family and friends in the waiting
room were subject to the interventions of the hospital's security force.
Later, a nurse and physician from the trauma team talked briefly with
Tyrone's mother and obtained signatures for permission for anesthesia
and surgery. Tyrone's mother was not kept informed concerning his
condition and the events in the trauma room. Adding to the family's
feelings of powerlessness was the involvement with security and the
local police (all stabbings had to be reported to the authorities).

Tyrone had been restless and hysterical, which made teaching him about the various procedures difficult, and the staff gave up trying after a short time. He was told frequently to "Lie still, and don't pull on that tube." Eventually, soft restraints were applied to his wrists, securing his arms to the sides of the cart.

Tyrone's powerlessness increased throughout this situation. Client teaching and attainment of cooperation was attempted then discontinued. Tyrone's privacy was ignored, promoting an interpretation by the client of his lack of worth in the eyes of the trauma staff. Team members did not speak to him except to command him not to do things. Restraints decreased the control he had over his body position. The catheter removed Tyrone's bladder control. He had been invaded through almost every bodily orifice and had needles piercing his skin for intravenous fluids.

Even with the urgency of the situation, an assigned communication staff member would have been of assistance in this instance. A staff member who can communicate with the family members in the waiting area could have decreased some of the tension and confusion in that area. A continued and calm attempt to communicate with Tyrone to keep him informed and gain his participation would also have been helpful. Until the client was stable, the crisis situation demanded speed and efficiency, but communication with Tyrone and his mother would not have influenced or slowed the process.

Medical Intensive Care. The client in the MICU may find himself in restraints, with tubes in his throat, nose, arms, bladder and chest. He is surrounded by noises twenty-four hours a day so that his normal sleep pattern is disrupted. With the lights on and noisy machines going all the time, he cannot keep track of the time of day, becoming disoriented and irritable. He feels that his control of his own life situations is gone, that he is in a strange place where his language is not the same as the doctors and nurses, his opinion is not sought, and strange machines and tubes have taken over his most intimate bodily functions.

CASE STUDY

To Gayle, it seemed that the last year or so of her life had been one big downward spiral. Her graduation in the top two percent of her law school class had brought a once-in-a-lifetime invitation to join a prestigious law firm. The extra workload in the new firm brought about her divorce. A settlement with her ex-husband left her with the cat and a broken-down Volkswagen. A poorly handled rape case led to public and peer disdain. She had moved to a new city to join the law firm and knew no one other than her ex-husband.

Feeling deserted and alone, Gayle found a room-mate to share her apartment. The other woman was rarely home, though, and Gayle felt lonely and helpless.

One rainy Friday evening, the prospect of another dreary Monday and all it heralded grew too much for Gayle. She swallowed a handful of antidepressants not so much from a desire to kill herself as from simply wanting to feel better and have things be different somehow. She became dizzy, then sleepy. When her room-mate came home late Saturday afternoon, Gayle was unresponsive and barely breathing. Her room-mate dialed 911 and the Rescue Squad arrived shortly thereafter.

Gayle was admitted to the Medical Intensive Care Unit by way of the Emergency Department of a large metropolitan hospital. She was shocky and required continuation of the mechanical ventilation that had been initiated by the Rescue Squad. During her assessment in the Emergency Department, a nasogastric tube had been inserted and gastric lavage performed along with the administration of charcoal. A Foley catheter had been inserted with only a scant amount of urine returned. Owing to her arterial blood gases and the appearance of her lungs on a portable chest X-Ray, it was judged that she had probably aspirated vomitus a short time before she was discovered by her room-mate. Gayle's mother was called by the physician and notified of her condition.

The critical care staff told Gayle what was happening to her at all times, though she did not give any observable response to their communications. Even with the use of warming blankets, Gayle's temperature remained subnormal. She exhibited bradycardia as well as hypotension. IV fluid, diuretics and vaso-active support did help stabilize her blood pressure, but there was no appreciable response in her urinary output. Additionally, a rising BUN, creatinine, and urine electrolyte level began to suggest a picture of acute renal failure. Such being the case, an A-V shunt was placed in her wrist and hemodialysis begun.

Following her second dialysis, Gayle began to show some neurological improvement. She seemed to arouse more easily to less painful stimuli and would follow some simple commands at times. Her pulmonary picture remained questionable. She began to require less hemodynamic support, but concern remained about the recovery of her renal function. Gayle's mother arrived from the airport and visited Gayle every hour, talking to her about the family and how much she loved Gayle. The staff encouraged Gayle's mother to perform some of Gayle's grooming and hygiene activities while she talked to her.

A third dialysis left Gayle awake but lethargic. Her kidneys at last began to show a slow but definitely improved response. By this time, she was aware of her surroundings and began to make some attempts to communicate, using hand gestures and simple pantomime. She was given a Magic Slate and a picture board to assist her efforts. Her first legible response was, "Where am I? Where is my mother?"

Gayle was feeling powerless before she arrived at the hospital. The environment of the critical care unit could have added to her powerlessness. However, with the staff talking to Gayle, keeping her informed and involving her mother in her care, Gayle was not likely to feel any more helpless than at the time of her overdose.

Other interventions could include asking for Gayle's input concerning when and how to carry out her grooming and hygiene, provision of a counselor to begin work on her depression, and assessing for any other desired support or activity.

Surgical Intensive Care. The surgical client in the critical care area has the stressors identified for the MICU client as well as the added lack of control of self in the operating room suite and the resultant pain experienced afterwards. Most individuals are afraid of anesthesia and the loss of personal control of their body that is experienced during surgery. In the surgical client there are the additional stressors of knowing that it is critical to have the surgery, that there is a chance of death during the surgery and that the surgery may not successfully prolong the client's life or correct the life-threatening problem for which the surgery was performed.

CASE STUDY

When George turned 50, he resolved to put the experiences of his two previous myocardial infarctions behind him and make a successful adjustment to the changes in his life that had come as a result of their occurrence. George watched his diet, walked every day, took his medicine as prescribed and enrolled in a cardiac rehabilitation program. He enjoyed tending his garden of radishes, cucumbers and sweet corn. He and his wife of 30 years bought a camper and planned a trip to the Grand Tetons to celebrate the honeymoon they had never quite managed to take.

Shortly after Thanksgiving, George came back to the Cardiac outpatient clinic with complaints of shortness of breath and some chest pain while doing little more than the Sunday crossword puzzle in his recliner. He stated that he got "huffy" while walking to answer the telephone, and a persistent pressure in his chest had caused him to walk out on his granddaughter's ballet recital.

Following another cardiac catheterization, George admitted that he wasn't surprised by the doctor's recommendation for heart surgery. After a discussion of his options with his physician, George agreed that there were no reasonable alternatives, but he did admit to some worries and reservations about the prospect of surgery on his heart. He had his son promise to pack straw around the strawberries and to be sure to winterize the camper. Arrangements were made for George's *immediate hospital admission with surgery the next day.*

Toward the close of the revascularization procedure, the surgical team was unable to wean George's heart from the pump. Owing to the two previous MI's, his heart had little myocardial reserve and it would not pump effectively. Ventricular arrhythmias further complicated the picture. The decision was made to insert the Intra Aortic Balloon Pump as it was felt that George would not make it out of surgery without it.

When George woke up he was hazily aware of the Surgical Intensive Care Unit and a distant fuzzy shape telling him, "your operation is all over, George, and you're doing okay." He felt chilly and cold. He felt weighed down in his arms and legs by the tubes lying across his body at all angles. He discovered he could not talk and he had an uncontrollable urge to cough or swallow away the lump in his throat. He couldn't close his mouth or lick his dry lips because of the tube in his throat. Some machine was making him take deep breaths that made his chest hurt. He wanted to turn over, but couldn't. His legs hurt. His nose itched. There was a stinging sensation in his penis that made him want to urinate. He felt nauseated.

The more awake he became, the more aware he was of all the "things" going into and coming out of his body. The pain wasn't too bad—mainly a dull ache everywhere with a few "hot spots." But the noises were awful—hisses, bubbles, beeps, droning voices and a distant thump-thump-thump. The commands were unending—"Don't pull on the tube, George." "Don't bite down." "Lie still." "Wiggle your toes." "This will make you cough." He realized he was naked but for a single sheet.

"You'll feel a little drowsy, now. It's okay to go to sleep. My name is Tom. I'm a nurse and I'll stay here with you. Your wife and son know your surgery is over and that you're waking up."

George's powerlessness could have been lessened by preoperative teaching. His physician had discussed alternatives of treatment with him, which is important. However, he was not given enough emotional preparation prior to surgery, such as a thorough discussion of his fear and anxiety as well as a family meeting in which to talk over his desires and feelings.

Summary

Critical care clients were divided into those seen in the emergency, medical intensive care and surgical intensive care units. Clients in all three areas are in great need of support and assistance from the health care team in finding areas of control that are practical to provide for the client. If this is not done, there is a strong chance that the client will become less tractable towards his plan of care and will not recover as quickly or thoroughly as possible.

References

Aguilera, D. and Messick, J. *Crisis Intervention: Theory and Methodology* (5th Ed.). St. Louis: The C.V. Mosby Company, (1986).

Claus, K. and Bailey, J. *Living with Stress and Promoting Well-being: A Handbook for Nurses.* St. Louis: The C.V. Mosby Company, (1980).

Driver, K. and Gallo, B. In: Hudak, C., Lohr, T., and Gallo, B. (eds.). *Critical Care Nursing* (2nd Ed.). New York: J.B.Lippincott, (1977).

Garland, L. and Bush, C. *Coping Behaviors and Nursing.* Reston, VA: Reston Publishing Company, Inc., (1982).

Goble, F. The esteem needs. In: Fuszard, B. (ed.) *Self-Actualization for Nurses: Issues, Trends, and Strategies for Job Enrichment.* Rockville, MD: Aspen Systems Corporation, (1984).

Grout, J. Stress and the ICU nurse: a review of nursing studies. In: Claus, K. and Bailey, J. (eds.) *Living With Stress and Promoting Well-being: A Handbook for Nurses.* St. Louis: The C.V. Mosby Company, (1980).

Hudak, C., Lohr, T. and Gallo, B. *Critical Care Nursing* (2nd Ed.). New York: J.B.Lippincott, (1977).

Jacobson, S. and McGrath, M. *Nurses Under Stress.* New York: John Wiley and Sons, (1983).

Kenner, C., Guzzetta, C. and Dossey, B. *Critical Care Nursing: Body-Mind-Spirit* (2nd Ed.). Boston: Little, Brown and Company, (1985).

McNeil, D. Depression. In: Jacobs, M. and Geeks, W. (Eds.). *Signs and Symptoms in Nursing: Interpretation and Management.* Philadelphia: J.B. Lippincott Company, (1985).

Moran, J. From distress and worry to awareness and fulfillment: perspectives of a critical care nurse. In: Claus, K. and Bailey, J.(eds.). *Living With Stress and Promoting Well-Being.* St. Louis: C.V. Mosby, (1980).

Shelly, J. *Dilemma: A Nurse's Guide for Making Ethical Decisions.* Downers Grove, IL: InterVarsity Press, (1980).

Steffen, S. Perceptions of stress: 1800 nurses tell their stories. In: Claus, K. and Bailey, J. (eds.) *Living With Stress and Promoting Well-Being: A Handbook for Nurses.* St. Louis: C.V. Mosby Company, (1980).

Ujhely, Gertrud Bertrand. *The Nurse and Her Problem Patients.* NY: Springer Publishing Company, Inc., (1963).

Wilson, R. *Principles and Techniques of Critical Care.* Detroit: Upjohn Company, (1977).

Zschoche, D. *Comprehensive Review of Critical Care.* St. Louis: C.V. Mosby Company, (1976).

13

Power and
The Chemically Dependent Client

V. Doucet and N. Rinehart

Introduction

Control, or its lack, is a major theme found in the behavior analysis of addictive individuals (Schaef, 1987). The chemically dependent client begins his behavior for the initial effect of the particular substance: to escape, feel more powerful, more in control, and/or seek relief from the anxieties of his environment (Miller, 1980). Several other factors contribute toward the formation of an addiction: heredity, addiction physiology, intellectualization, socialization, and frustration intolerance (Miller, 1980). What starts as a temporary escape soon becomes a repetitive behavior pattern and subsequently an addiction. As the addiction progresses, the substance may fail to work effectively for the client, so he increases the intake of the substance, while denying he has a problem. When no amount of the substance works any longer, the addict may choose another substance to use as well as the original one. But soon the substance becomes the controller and has gone from being a perceived comfort to being an enemy with a death-grip on him. The client experiences bewilderment when his substance of abuse, his friend, fails him, and then he has an increased feeling of loss of control, or powerlessness. It is this very lack of control, or self-perception of being externally controlled, and the resultant fight to regain personal control that is addressed in this chapter.

THE POWERLESSNESS OF ADDICTION

Addiction has been likened to diabetes. Consider what happens when a diabetic denies that he is different and must live his life with some alterations in lifestyle. It is easier to see this physical deterioration than to understand the substance abuse which, like diabetes, can lead to disability and death. Like the diabetic, the addict must admit that he needs to make some changes in his lifestyle in order to survive.

It is often thought that if the addict would just stop his addiction behavior all would be well. Although the diabetic is not asked to control his insulin output, it has been presumed the addict could control his behavior. Health care professionals who think the addict can control his behavior, that addiction is a moral issue rather than an illness, further strengthen the guilt, worthlessness and powerlessness feelings of the addicted, or impaired, client. To treat the illness of addiction, the disease and recovery process must be thoroughly understood. Control, or personal power, is found to be at the root of the addictive behavior.

The individual abuses his chosen substance to control his feelings or sensations. Milkman and Sunderwirth (1983) designate all addictive substances as capable of causing arousal or satiation. Rather than using a substance with satiating properties, the normally excitable addictive individual will use substances which cause more arousal, heightening his perception of having control over his moods and the addictive or potentiating substance. The low-key style of personality is made even more "laid-back" via a satiating substance and enhances the feeling of control (Milkman and Sunderwirth, 1983).

While the chemically dependent person is attempting to gain control through the use of substances, he labors through intricate patterns of rationalization, giving power to persons, places and things outside his control (Schaef, 1987; Twerski, 1982). Addiction has been called the disease of denial. Common statements of addicts include: "I don't have a problem." "I don't have any fears about my life or what I'm doing." and "There's no way I have a disease."

The chemically dependent client has cut a wide path of destruction through the lives that he has touched (Anderson, 1981). He either wallows in guilt, helplessness and grief or he may seek to rectify the damage and regain some personal power. It is vital that the health care professional offer the hope and confidence that recovery is available, as well as acceptance of the client (Silverstein, 1977).

It is common for a client to enter treatment with overwhelming negativity and denial. The breakdown of denial reveals four steps: victimization, defeat, anxiety, and loss identification (Anderson, 1981). The client often perceives himself as a victim of society. He thinks he is defeated by the world and himself. For years it was believed that a client had to "bottom out," to physically and mentally "lose it all," to be willing to accept help. Those in the treatment of addiction now know, however, that an emotional "bottom" can just as effectively open up a client to willingness to change and work with the therapeutic milieu.

Therapeutic Milieu

It is easy for the health care professional to act as a codependent or enabler. Therefore, it is imperative that the staff members of the addiction rehabilitation units are able to let go of control and encourage clients to develop their personal power by guided direction.

This guided direction is given in the safety of a controlled milieu, or a therapeutic environment. In this environment, the staff is responsible for providing space for clients to express and act out feelings but yet not act out or express them in a manner that is threatening to other clients. The staff must have open and honest communication between themselves and clients. This behavior is evidenced by consistency and structure within the facility. In other words, nursing, counseling and all other staff must relay the same messages with similar expectations.

The initial design of milieu management starts with a structured day. Clients need to know what is going to happen throughout the day to decrease anxiety. It becomes simple for the client to focus his feelings on anxiety about "What's going to happen after lunch?" rather than "I am afraid to feel angry," or work his prescribed treatment program. A planned schedule and clear rules are necessary to deflect this tendency in the addicted client.

Thus, rules are necessary in the treatment program. Clients who have been isolated and self-centered because of their disease process need guidance and regulation in order to live in community with others. Rules establish guidelines for behavior in treatment as well as society in general. Staff members reinforce this healthier behavior through role modeling and consistency.

A condemning and belittling attitude on the part of the health care provider causes more injury to the person's already low self-esteem and reinforces his perception of lack of control (Anderson, 1981). Acceptance does not mean approval and it is this problem with semantics that trips up many health care professionals.

Most addicted, or impaired, clients find it easy to accept the fact that they have a genetic predisposition for intolerance to specific substances. However, in early recovery this leads to blaming external substances and ancestors for the disease. The client views the disease in an oversimplified way as simply an allergy to alcohol, sugar, drugs and so forth. It is easy then to dismiss the emotional and spiritual components of the disease and to abdicate any responsibility for any further change.

If knowledge alone would increase the chemically dependent person's sense of power, more treatment program participants would be successful (Glasser, 1976). However, without the client gaining a healthier dependence on a Higher Power, he will only fail, turn to the addiction once more, and damn himself for his lack of willpower and control (Silverstein, 1977).

In treatment the client is first asked to give up false control—the illusion that he has control over the substance of abuse. The client is asked to accept that he has a disease. This surrender is facilitated through the use of intellectual and experiential learning. In the anonymous programs, the person first admits to this powerlessness before moving forward and gaining more power through working the 12 step program with a reliance on a Higher Power (Anonymous, 1986).

The 12 Step Programs

The "Big Book" of A.A. states that a "lack of power" is the dilemma of alcoholics (Anonymous, 1976). Through the years, other anonymous groups have developed, using the same Twelve Steps that are used by A.A. The participants in these other groups use the Big Book without any difficulty, which leads addiction counselors to point out the many similarities between the addictions (Miller, 1980).

However, some conflict may arise between different anonymous groups when one group does not believe that the other group has a valid addictive problem. An example of this conflict is the alcoholics who scoff at the idea that refined carbohydrates, discussed in O.A. (Overeaters Anonymous), are addicting. The O.A. view is that alcohol is a liquid form of refined carbohydrates, the same substance of abuse, one solid and the other liquid, but the same chemical nonetheless (Miller, 1980). There has been a recent movement in some of the anonymous groups to exclude those individuals who have more than one addiction. This conflict within recovery programs stems from lack of knowledge about the etiology of the physical, emotional and spiritual aspects of addictive disease. The disease of addiction is described as a threefold disease, physical, emotional, and spiritual (Anonymous, 1976).

The purpose of A.A. is, according to the Big Book (Anonymous, 1976), to help recovering alcoholics find the power by which they can live. Glasser (1984) lists behaviors indicative of personal power as: competing, achieving and gaining importance. These behaviors, in combination with the A.A. approach of spiritual growth, then become major foci of treatment.

Control Theory

In Control Theory, Glasser (1986) describes the process through which the individual makes choices which result in specific behavior. The addicted client often communicates the choices for his behavior as being external to himself with statements like, "I wouldn't drink if my boss were human" and "If only my wife would do things the way I tell her to, things would be better." With such an attitude, simply telling the client he has choices will not accomplish much. However, with an explanation of the process of behavior choices as given in Control Theory, the client will eventually begin to identify his choices of behavior that have no connection with what others are doing.

Glasser (1985) discusses the essential needs of all persons: survival, belonging, fun, power and freedom (1985). Survival is the most basic need identified. Treatment centers fulfill the survival needs for the client. Safe housing, nutritious food and a protective environment are necessities that these centers must provide in order to enhance client learning about meeting their needs in a healthy fashion.

The belonging need is met through treatment centers as the client enters to find himself surrounded by acceptance and cooperation. The staff as well, as the other clients, express this acceptance of the client. He may be assigned a buddy to help introduce him to the program schedule and expectations. All groups focus on increasing his personal power and taking responsibility for his own behavior. With such needy and rationalizing clients, the staff must refuse to assume the power the clients continually hand them.

The basic need for fun is incorporated into the daily schedule of the treatment program. The client learns that it is socially acceptable to have fun within the limits of the law; it can be enjoyable and it is possible to have fun without the artificial feelings produced by his choice of abuse substance. The learning component of fun is identified by Glasser (1987), but may be resisted by the client. For an event to be fun, however, there must be a chance for learning an improved method of participation.

Personal power, as defined by Glasser (1983), includes competition, achievement and importance. It is a challenge for the client to compete for the sake of trying and to enjoy the knowledge that he tried. Achievements need to be pointed out to the client who believes himself a failure. What the client has control of, those things directly influenced by him, must be repeatedly identified to encourage him in acknowledgment of his personal power. The addict client may not believe himself to be worthy or important in any of the scenarios of his life. If he can be encouraged to see himself as important to himself and others, his sense of power will be increased.

Freedom is a right and a need of humankind. However, individuals may not assess themselves as either having freedom or being worthy of it. The freedom to choose an opinion and to voice it is highly valued, yet the addicted client frequently gives the power of choice over to his addictive substance or another person. Therefore, he experiences powerlessness that is self-induced, with his rejection of internal control and his choice to be externally controlled instead.

Locus of Control

As previously stated, most addictive clients give their personal power to the substance they abuse and perceive persons, places and things as out of their control. These clients respond well to therapy that incorporates external factors such as some of those listed in the Alcoholics Anonymous booklet, *Living Sober* (1975) or to Methadone. However, not all addicted clients are this external in their perception of the source of power.

Some clients resist efforts to control them, clearly indicating that they perceive themselves as powerful. It is not uncommon to hear these clients talking about being in control, controlling their substance and using that substance to increase their perceptions of control (Ray, 1983). It could be said that this client believes he has an internal locus of control. The reality is that the substance is controlling the client, with demands for more usage and for euphoria only when using it. The internally-controlled client will work better in a recovery program that emphasizes his power of choice and his ability to recover without the assistance of medications such as Antabuse. No matter what type of treatment program the client is in, control is always a major issue exhibited by the need to control and the fear of being out-of-control.

Single Addiction Clients. Clients with only one addiction are difficult to find anymore if most of the potentially addictive substances and situations are assessed for: alcohol, drugs, food, sugar, sex, gambling, nicotine, and caffeine. However, in this chapter, the three most common substances will be addressed: alcohol, drugs, and food (Miller, 1980; Yudkin, 1972). The defined single addiction client only abuses one of these three substances. His behavior has not deteriorated, in the pattern of addiction, to the point of acquiring a large menu of substances with which to cope in his environment.

CASE STUDY

Robin, a thirteen-year-old black female was admitted to treatment for problems with compulsive overeating. The precipitating event leading to admission was confrontation by her mother for eating a whole cake by herself while the rest of the family went to a neighbor's home for a visit. When forced to stand on a scale in front of her family, Robin had gained sixty-seven pounds in four months.

Robin's eating pattern was continual snacking on refined carbohydrates along with three large meals. Robin stated quite firmly that she wouldn't eat any "rabbit food," that she hated all vegetables.

When asked about binging, Robin told the intake counselor that she just couldn't stop when she ate something sweet. She cried and reported eating three batches of cookie dough before any cookies got cooked for her little brother and sister. She assessed herself as a "big, fat slob." She stated she "had no willpower" and that that proved she was stupid and not as good or pretty as her sister.

The client was introduced to her peer group on her first day after admission. Although reserved, Robin seemed to be bonding well with individual peers. At the first meal with her peers she asked why all these skinny girls needed to do anything about their weight. Two of the peers explained that an obsession or addiction to food did not always have to lead to obesity, that some of the clients used laxatives, forced themselves to vomit or were terrified to eat at all. Robin responded by requesting forgiveness for her stupidity and hoping that she hadn't upset anyone.

In her initial assessment, four specific areas were identified as needing treatment: extreme guilt or shamefulness, poor self-esteem, perfectionism and inability to be assertive. All these problems reflected a sense of powerlessness.

Robin's guilt and shamefulness were targeted through education about the disease process in addiction and an emphasis on the principles of the Alcoholics Anonymous Twelve Steps as used in Overeaters Anonymous (O.A.). Additionally, Robin's sense of shame was enhanced by the fact that many mental health programs have a negative reception among blacks. With the acculturation of members of her peer group to strive toward slim perfection, Robin judged herself a total failure.

A plan was formulated to help Robin see herself as a worthy human being. The client was instructed to accept favors, compliments, and hugs without the obligation to give anything back. She began this exercise by being extremely uncomfortable and evasive, but by the end of the first week Robin displayed signs of pleasure and increased self-esteem with her love and acceptance needs beginning to be met.

Robin's perfectionism led her to adopt an all or none approach in her life. Absolute statements made by Robin emphasized this philosophy; either she had to be perfect in dieting or it was hopeless. If she could not make perfect marks in school, she was a failure. If she could not have the starring role in the school play, she would have none. If she could be mean enough to force her peers to avoid her, that reinforced her opinion that she was not lovable at all.

The challenge of assisting Robin in accepting her human frailties, and those of others, became a major goal in her treatment. She was given a writing assignment to identify faults in those individuals she most respected and to assess herself for similar weaknesses. In this manner Robin could recognize her unrealistic expectations for perfection in herself when those she held in esteem were imperfect.

She went to lectures on basic nutrition and healthy weight control methods; during these lectures realistic self-expectations were stressed. As Robin's eating history revealed poor nutrition and eating habits, these were closely evaluated and discussed with her.

The client's need to be more assertive was addressed in the treatment plan designed by Robin and the staff. The client was able to identify that most times she was not assertive because she did not know what her needs were. She was given the assignment to write in a journal, at the end of each day, about things that aroused uncomfortable feelings and experiences in her. She was then to define what she had felt and needed. The next step in that assignment was for her to stop the next situation she became uneasy in and try to identify the need or feeling at that point. This process enabled her to stop acting so impulsively, begin to know herself and her needs, and become more internally or self-oriented.

Robin was introduced to a concept of building personal power through spiritual growth by attending Overeaters Anonymous meetings. She had a strong religious background and was willing to try this approach to strengthen her spirituality. She was introduced to recovering O.A. members who were black, to facilitate more comfort and acceptance for Robin. The experience of a sense of belonging that occurs with the recognition of others like oneself in similar circumstances facilitates concentration on the principles of the program.

Robin's "anything to please" attitude repeatedly got her in trouble. In the past, Robin stuffed down her feelings with food to expedite compliance, and meanwhile built a large reserve of resentment toward those she sought to please. It was difficult for Robin to express her feelings, but with continuous support and acceptance from the staff and her peers, she began to recognize and voice her feelings. She informed her family that she planned on continuing to express her feelings rather than push them down with food. Her family participated fully in the family program during Robin's treatment and learned to express and deal with their own feelings.

Robin was discharged home after four weeks with a contract indicating her intention to attend at least two OA meetings a week and aftercare meetings three evenings a week. In the unconditional acceptance of the members of O.A., Robin continued to grow in her perception of herself as worthwhile. Her attendance at aftercare meetings promoted a continuing contact with her therapists and support for her efforts in dealing more effectively with life.

Cross-Addiction Client. This client abuses more than one substance, and therefore has a more complex recovery problem. He has added substances through the years, which reinforces his mind-set that external substances will help him cope with his daily activities. The more the client has fortified this belief, the more messages he will need to receive that it is not only possible but desirable to enjoy and cope with life without an external substance supplying his desired sensations.

CASE STUDY

Erik, a 40-year-old Scandinavian Lutheran dentist, admitted himself for treatment of cocaine abuse. He used approximately 4 Gms. of cocaine a week and drank a pint of vodka each evening, but stated his drinking was within social limits.

Erik entered treatment after a conference with his accountant about the status of his finances. The client had a wife and two small children and was behind in house and office payments.

Detoxification involved monitoring the client for signs and symptoms of alcohol as well as cocaine withdrawal. He was medicated with Tranxene during the first 48 hours for slight hypertension and withdrawal-related anxiety. The client refused to see the necessary medication as related to his alcohol consumption.

Initial treatment planning involved teaching Erik about disease and cross-addiction concepts. The client was given the assignment of having a one-to-one (1:1) interaction with a different peer each day to share substance abuse stories. The rationale for the assignment was two-fold: 1)to have the client gain some understanding of his cross-addiction and 2)to help him with his problem of isolation. By hearing the stories of different peers it was hoped that Erik would begin to identify his own cross-addiction pattern. It was hoped he would begin to personalize others' experiences and use this personalization to gain insight into his own pattern. By doing so he could begin to break down the isolation of his disease.

Isolation is a common problem with most addicts entering treatment, but it is pronounced with addicted health care professionals. Dentists, like doctors and nurses, are in a caregiver role and have great difficulty accepting anything from others, thus becoming even more isolated. Health care professionals find it easier to take care of others, keep them at arm's length, and not acknowledge feelings of rejection or loneliness. Also, as a Scandinavian, Erik is much less likely to express his emotions openly in a large group. Therefore these 1:1's also had the goal of helping Erik bond with his peers on an equal level.

The staff met weekly with Erik to review his progress and plan goals for the coming week. The client was very receptive to this mode of treatment and plans were made to help him improve his self-esteem. He was given peer leadership positions and blossomed with the experience, but still struggled with the concept of being "just one of those drug addicts."

Because of his ongoing denial, it was decided at his next treatment planning meeting to focus on involvement in A.A. as well as N.A. It was hoped that this goal would help him overcome his denial and set him up with support systems for long term abstinence. He was encouraged to find an A.A./N.A. sponsor and develop a relationship with him. He was given extra time to go out to meetings with his sponsor, separate from his treatment group. He was introduced to a support group for impaired health care professionals. Through the positive experience of bonding with his sponsor and support group Erik was able to let go of some denial and gain more acceptance of himself and his disease.

Erik and his family spent a week in the family program together. Much of this week concentrated on education for the family about the disease concept and enabling behaviors. The week culminated in a communication exercise. In that exercise Erik and his wife were able to discuss their feelings related to his addiction and build some plans for recovery.

A back-to-work conference was held with Erik and his partners to plan for his ongoing responsibilities and financial future. It was important to Erik that his partners understand what he needed to do for recovery.

Looking at Erik's history and inpatient assessments, a typical picture of the "hero child" of an alcoholic household emerged. Erik gave no direct history of his parents as alcoholics. However, as he let go of some fears he described growing up in a rigid, unemotional, distant family. Since this is such a familiar history, the substance abuse clinicians sought a more detailed familial history. Further investigation showed a repressed but clear picture of alcoholism in both grandfathers.

It has been well-documented that alcoholism/addiction is a multi-generational disease (Black, 1982). Erik gave a history of grandfathers who were distant, physically absent or abusive, erratic and with many "secrets" about how much they drank. Thus Erik's parents' families of origin passed down a legacy of genetic predisposition, lack of healthy coping skills, and inability to communicate and deal with feelings. Erik was perfectly set up for this disease.

As Erik gave more history about his role growing up in this family a clear picture developed of him as the family hero. It is known that in a rigid family environment members take on specific well-defined roles to keep the family running smoothly (Black, 1982). These roles have no relationship, however, to satisfying the normal development needs of its members. He was the perfect codependent. Erik became the fixer, the adult/child whom everyone could rely on to perform well no matter how he felt. What better characteristics to bring into a helping profession (Beattie, 1987)?

Unfortunately, unless Erik developed ways to step out of this rigid role and satisfy his own needs it was doubtful he would be able to maintain sobriety. Like so many impaired helping professionals, he used drugs and alcohol to medicate himself, satisfy his needs to perform at all costs and numb emotional pain (Beattie, 1987; Twerski, 1983).

For Erik, the second phase of recovery was to discover what his needs were and then begin to satisfy them. With Erik, these were basic issues of being responsible for himself, his feelings and his life. Only then could he be in control of how he lived.

Planning this phase of treatment for Erik involved two stages: first, that which took place in the treatment program and secondly, an early return to his normal environment.

The initial plan involved helping Erik experience asking for and getting his needs met. It was decided to start at the most basic physical level and build from there. Erik was given the assignment of asking his peers to meet his physical needs for three days and reporting back at group therapy times about what this felt like.

Erik had peers clean his room, bring him coffee and food and wash his clothes. He reported feelings of warmth and nurturance. Most powerful for Erik were the feelings of vulnerability that he had to deal with in the daily group sessions.

Erik was then able to ask for some emotional needs to be met. This was facilitated by staff in two ways. First, Erik was instructed to ask two peers and one staff for a hug daily. He was to report his reaction to this assignment weekly in a small group meeting. Second, Erik did a communication exercise with his wife in family group. In this exercise he expressed his needs to her and how he would like them met. This exercise was extremely successful, with both Erik and his wife tearfully communicating to each other their love and commitment to his recovery and their life together.

The week before he was to leave treatment, Erik met with the clerical staff to evaluate his progress and discharge plan. The evaluation disclosed that Erik had made excellent progress in treatment. He had come to see his alcoholism and cocaine addiction as diseases and that total abstinence was necessary for him. He had come to realize that he did isolate, both on an emotional and spiritual level. He was now ready to plan to address this problem on a long-term basis. Erik was ready to take responsibility for himself and make plans for controlling the way he would live his life.

The basis for Erik's long-term recovery program would be on-going involvement in A.A., N.A. and family counseling. Through the process of the 12 Steps of Alcoholics Anonymous, Erik would learn to keep his internal focus intact when he dealt with others. He would also learn, through spiritual growth, to start relying on a Higher Power for help in his life. He could give up spiritual isolation gradually, eventually joining others in a spiritual community.

By keeping his internal focus intact Erik was gradually able to decrease his impulsive response to care for others first and could identify and meet his own needs. Thus as a caregiver he did not deplete himself and set himself up for relapse, but was able to give out of a full heart rather than habit. In this way his caregiving satisfied himself as well as others. This gave Erik the control over his choices and destiny that he needed to mature as an adult and to lead a satisfying life.

Erik started his spiritual journey as a child, even though he was chronologically nearing middle age. Spiritual maturation and development is a process of risk taking, decision making and growth through pain and joy. Because of his family history he learned little through his role models. Through his chemical dependency he did little to grow out of his childhood years and beliefs. The steps and fellowship of Alcoholics Anonymous gave Erik the concrete steps to use to grow and the "safe" environment in which to experiment and take risks. The mature A.A. community offered him mentorship and guidance. Because Erik had not been involved in his church for years, he made the decision to concentrate on Alcoholics Anonymous for a period of a year to build basic support for himself before branching out to other groups and/or his church of origin.

Erik, his wife and children had been strongly involved in the family group while he was in treatment. Because this had been such a worthwhile experience for them, and because they identified so many communication problems, they made a family decision to continue family therapy.

Dual Diagnosis Client. This client is addicted to one or more substances as well as having an additional psychiatric diagnosis e.g., the borderline alcoholic. This client has the added difficulty of his psychiatric problem in achieving recovery from his addiction. It is imperative that the health care professional emphasize that the client can recover.

CASE STUDY

A 42-year-old Hispanic male, Mario, was admitted for treatment for his alcohol abuse. He also had a history of major depressive episodes. A private therapist had been working with Mario around multiple life crises, especially his inability to hold a job, although he was a highly qualified technician. The admitting diagnoses were alcoholism and major depressive episode.

Detoxification went well physically, but Mario was isolative and avoided interaction with his peers and the staff. When confronted with his behavior, Mario threatened to leave the treatment program. The staff met with Mario to create a plan for identifying the limits of acceptable behavior on the treatment unit. Mario was successful in maintaining the minimum acceptable behavior in interactions with others. He bonded with two other Hispanic clients. In time he was encouraged to assist in the orientation of new clients in the program. There was a noticeable improvement in his affect; he was brighter and more assertive about his needs. Although improvement was noted, Mario did continue to express depression; the staff met with him to discuss the possibility of placing him on a tricyclic antidepressant. Mario agreed to be assessed by a consulting psychiatrist for this treatment as well as a more in-depth assessment of his depression.

Although Mario had had the usual emotional, behavioral and social assessments, along with a medical assessment early in treatment, the staff felt the need for another assessment at this point in his treatment. The psychiatrist agreed with this need and met with Mario. Mario disclosed to the doctor that early in his teens he had been the victim of multiple sexual assaults by two uncles and stated that he had never revealed this to anyone else. Along with the introduction of a tricyclic antidepressant, the psychiatrist recommended Mario begin to address this abuse in treatment. Mario met with his counselor and the psychiatrist to develop a plan for his treatment stay.

It was decided that Mario would write and present his autobiography to the group, disclosing the sexual abuse along with his alcoholism and what effect these problems had had on his life. Using feedback from the group and crystallizing in small group what he had learned, Mario could then go on to develop a plan of therapeutic action.

At his second evaluation session Mario was able to use what he had learned to identify the hopeless and helpless feelings that led to his depression. The repeated sexual violations had left him at a critical point in life without identity boundaries. The victimization had left him with the feeling of powerlessness. Mario and his counselor listed some goals for him toward increasing his feelings of personal power.

Mario was given assignments to strengthen his internal locus of control and develop behaviors to maintain this personal power. One of Mario's assignments was to learn to meditate. He was given relaxation and meditation tapes to listen to daily. The recreation therapist arranged yoga lessons for Mario. He was to journal his experiences with these methods and report to his small group about his sessions. Thus he could strengthen his internal locus of control. His reports were accepted with enthusiasm from his group, increasing their knowledge bases while increasing Mario's self-esteem, making his initial attempts all the more positive.

With his increased feelings of personal power, Mario began to take on a more assertive role in the community. This reinforced his positive feelings about making decisions for himself and having some control over his recovery.

Mario had made great inroads into his acceptance of his alcoholism. He displayed no difficulty in seeing that he could not control his alcohol consumption and how his drinking had caused problems in his life. Mario had a strong religious background and accepted the concept of working with his higher power to change his behaviors.

Mario's third evaluation meeting with clerical staff centered around discharge planning. All clerical staff, as well as Mario, felt he had done well in treatment but needed a very structured aftercare program because of his secondary diagnosis. It was decided that he should continue in individual therapy with the psychiatrist and have his antidepressant monitored there. He would continue to work on his depression and shame in therapy with the doctor. It was also decided that Mario would be transferred to a structured outpatient program for long-term involvement.

Mario was discharged early from inpatient and transferred to the outpatient program, an anticipated involvement for six months. This plan would serve three purposes for Mario: 1) a structured support group to wean him off his antidepressants, 2) a long-term structure in which to work through his feelings surrounding the sexual abuse and 3) the opportunity to hold a job while maintaining a relationship with a supportive group from which to draw strength.

As part of his program he was required to attend a specific number of A.A. meetings. At these he was to acquire a mentor and work on the steps of the program for spiritual growth.

Addictive clients who do not address their problems of shame and anger regarding their history of sexual abuse will relapse again and again (Black, 1982). They have a high rate of suicide. Much of the structure around Mario's recovery program was to assist him in developing personal power and control in his life.

The clinicians working with this client must understand the need to let go and let this client experience his pain and anger. To try to "fix" this client with advice is futile—to confront him is futile— to let go and allow him to grow is vital. Mario needed an arena in which to experience life and a structural frame to prevent his being overwhelmed by his own pain.

Codependent Client. The addictive client affects many others while practicing his addiction. His significant others often serve as enablers for, or codependents in, his addiction (Beattie, 1987). As the addicted client is frequently from an addictive family, he too may be a participant in codependent behaviors (Beattie, 1987).

CASE STUDY

Rachel, a 52-year-old Italian Catholic housewife was admitted to the outpatient program for treatment of her codependency. The precipitating event for this admission was the client's involvement in family week and family meetings at the treatment center where her husband was being treated for alcoholism. During the family week, Rachel identified feelings of fear, anger, and resentment. She believed these were unresolved feelings stemming from growing up with an alcoholic father and then marrying an alcoholic.

The first phase of treatment was based upon educating Rachel about the disease of codependency. This involved lectures by the staff, personal stories from clients further along in the treatment program and reading assignments. The client continued to defend her denial by remaining confused over the material presented and focusing on her father and husband's alcoholism and behavior problems.

In the weekly staff conference Rachel was given the staff's feedback. She cried and expressed the fear that if she let go of the focus on her father and husband there would be nothing left for her. They had been the focus of her life. She and the staff went on to develop a treatment plan to start to build her own life identity and support systems.

Rachel was introduced into the second phase of treatment. This involved group therapy twice a week to talk about her own fears, problems and solutions. The client bonded well with the group and became an active participant.

Rachel was given the assignment of attending a 12 Step program meeting weekly. The choice was hers whether it was a codependency, adult children of alcoholics, or Alanon meeting. It was suggested that she try each and see where she felt the most comfortable. She was to report back to the therapy group on her progress.

The client had a great deal of difficulty participating in the discussions with the therapy staff about her treatment. She wanted staff to tell her what to do to get "fixed." With her reluctant input, the next phase of therapy was designed to help her develop confidence and self-esteem, especially around choices and decisions. The client was to keep a journal to increase her awareness of decision-making needs that were presented to her, what she did about them, and how it felt to either make or not make conscious decisions. To help her feel in control of what she was doing, the client was to stop and take a short "time out" when faced with a decision and decide on a choice, not to merely react to the situation.

Rachel clearly exhibited victimization, the most common symptom of codependency (Beattie, 1987). She was the victim of her father's alcoholism, her husband's alcoholism and their abusive behaviors. She saw herself as the victim of life and the world. This gave her some advantages—she did not have to make decisions and therefore take responsibility for them—she did not have to control her life. She had drifted along and blamed others for her lack of success and uncomfortable feelings. She had never experienced the joy of personal power and had little confidence in herself. Rachel's life revolved around being angry and powerless. The focus of treatment was to guide her toward some experiences that were joyful and empowering.

Rachel was addicted to the negative feelings she experienced, just as an addict is addicted to drugs. She was comfortable in these feelings and felt out of control and fearful when she felt the positive sensations of love and joy.

In working the 12 Steps, Rachel followed the same program as other members of anonymous groups. She committed to a specified number of meetings weekly and acquired a mentor. As she worked these steps she gave herself permission to change her thinking—she was the one in control of her thoughts, not the outside world. Instead of blaming others for her uncomfortable feelings she was able, through practice, to accept the fact that all adults occasionally experience discomfort. She became more spontaneous in her actions and reactions. Instead of shutting down in confusion when a situation was fearful she was able to step back emotionally and take whatever action she needed for her own self-care. The ultimate goal was for her to accept responsibility for her life and make decisions about what she wanted to do with it.

Rachel learned about relapse in the lecture sessions. Codependency relapse is in many ways more subtle than other types of addictive relapse—there is seldom any concrete physical evidence of relapse. In relapse, the drinker gets drunk, the drug abuser gets high, the compulsive overeater gains weight and the anorexic loses weight. It is much more difficult to identify codependent victim behaviors and thinking (Beattie, 1987). Codependency relapse, like other relapse, is a slow, insidious process. It starts with unrelenting feelings of anger and blaming others for uncomfortable feelings. It ends up with the individual becoming isolative, ill, and as victimized as ever (Beattie, 1987).

Rachel was given this information and her counselor strongly suggested that a way to monitor relapse was to continue to go to meetings. There she would hear others in recovery and assess where she was. She could maintain contact with her mentor for honest feedback on her status.

Rachel chose to do none of these things. She stopped going to meetings regularly and eventually was dropped by her mentor. Although she continued to maintain contact with the treatment program, she was in complete relapse. She eventually dropped all contact with the treatment program.

Additional Interventions

After using his substance for controlling himself and his environment, the addictive client must have something to fill the void. It is not effective to simply take away the addictive substance. Glasser (1985) advocates giving the client something to do, not telling him what not to do. In this way there is something with which the client can fill this emptiness in his life, going to AA meetings, for example, or calling a sponsor.

Bibliotherapy is recommended for use by addicted clients. It is important to remind the client that reading books will not take the place of contact with others and practice of the skills he has learned.

Service is firmly established in the anonymous programs as a method for continuing recovery. Getting the client involved in reaching out to help others will improve his self-esteem and increase his personal sense of power.

Exercise is strongly recommended to the recovering individual for several reasons:

1. To increase endorphin production to replace the addictive substance with natural highs.
2. For the cocaine addict, it gives some of that "thrilling" feeling—get in shape and do some "risky" exercise (Milkman and Sunderwirth, 1982).
3. For stress management.
4. To provide socialization and education regarding acculturation to social situations devoid of substance abuse, which decreases anxiety.

Summary

The definition of addiction indicates powerlessness or a lack of control in the life of the chemically dependent client. Case studies provide examples for interventions appropriate to the different divisions of clients. Clients are divided into four groups: single addiction, cross addiction, dual diagnosis and codependent. Within these divisions are examples of clients abusing themselves with alcohol, drugs and food.

References

Anderson, D. *The Psychopathology of Denial*. Center City, MN: Hazelden, (1981).

Anonymous. *Alcoholics Anonymous* (3rd Ed.). New York: Alcoholics Anonymous World Service, Inc., (1976).

Anonymous. *Living Sober*. New York: Alcoholics Anonymous World Services, Inc., (1975).

Anonymous. *The Twelve Steps: A Healing Journey*. Center City, MN: Hazelden, (1986).

Beattie, M. *Codependent No More*. New York: Harper & Row Publishers, (1987).

Black, C. *It Will Never Happen To Me*. Denver, CO: MAC Printing and Publications Division, (1982).

Dufty, W. *Sugar Blues*. New York: Warner Books, Inc., (1975).

Glasser, W. *Positive Addiction*. New York: Harper & Row Publishers, (1976).

Glasser, W. *Take Effective Control of Your Life*. New York: Harper & Row Publishers, (1984).

Milkman, H. and Sunderwirth, S. *Craving for Ecstasy*. NY: Lexington Books, (1982).

Milkman, H. and Sunderwirth, S. Symposium on Addictions in Denver. October, (1983).

Miller, W. *The Addictive Behaviors*. New York: Pergamon Press, (1980).

Ray, O. *Drugs, Society & Human Behavior* (3rd Ed.). St. Louis: C.V.Mosby Company, (1983).

Silverstein, L. *Consider The Alternative*. Minneapolis: CompCare Publications, (1977).

Schaef, A. *When Society Becomes An Addict*. San Francisco: Harper & Row, Publishers, (1987).

Twerski, A. *It Happens To Doctors, Too*. Center City, MN: Hazelden, (1983).

Yudkin, J. *Sweet and Dangerous*. New York: Bantam Books, (1972).

14

Power and the Chronic/Terminal Client

J. Glover and N. Rinehart

Introduction: The Common Powerlessness

All terminal illnesses are chronic, and many chronic illnesses lead to the termination of life. One difference between these two diagnostic labels is the focus. Chronic illness often represents a long-term illness that places a daily drain on the client's power resources. The diagnosis of a terminal illness often places the emphasis on the forthcoming death. Ideally, the focus of each diagnostic division is to improve the client's sense of personal control each day and assist him to live each day to the fullest possible level of fulfillment.

However, there is often conflict between the client trying to express his need for personal power and the health care system imposing its values and treatment preferences on the client. This conflict adds to the feelings of powerlessness experienced by the client. Clients with chronic and terminal illnesses demonstrate many similarities in behavior which reflect powerlessness.

Fig. 14-1. Characteristics of Powerlessness

The commonalties between chronic and terminal illness include: increased anxiety and anger, decreased self-esteem, ineffective coping, self-care deficit, noncompliance (denial), grief, and fear—in other words, powerlessness (Fig. 14-1). After identifying the predominate occurrence of powerlessness, the health care professional can then concentrate on increasing the client's sense of control, or power.

Although the terminology is different, Kubler-Ross' (1969) stages of dying and Bowlby's (1961) stages of bereavement are easily recognized in the clients' common responses to the diagnosis of a chronic or terminal illness. With an increase in personal control, these eight responses can be resolved and the client can more comfortably face the inevitability of the future and capitalize on his energy for handling the present (Fig. 14-2).

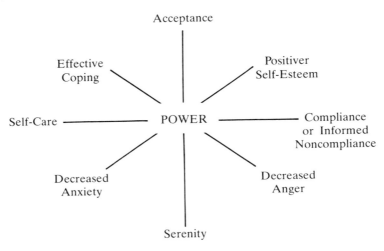

Fig. 14-2. Characteristics of Power

Anxiety is almost always experienced by the client awaiting a diagnosis. The dread of the possible diagnosis can build the client's anxiety level to that of panic (Barry, 1984). The confirmation of the client's diagnosis may initially decrease the client's perception of anxiety. Shortly after the diagnosis, the client is assailed by a barrage of questions: Will I be able to work? How will this affect my lifestyle? How long will I live? What can I expect? These questions and more add to the anxiety of the client. He questions the fairness of life and its meaning. One common response to this anxiety is anger.

The anger of the client is expressed in a myriad of ways. This anger is often displaced and anything can become its target. He may lash out at everyone around him, at those who brought him such bad news, at those who are healthy and seemingly carefree, and at those who love him. Clients experiencing anger are difficult to cope with for both the health care workers and the family. The family responds to the client's anger with sadness, anger, guilt and often communication avoidance, all of which increase the client's anger. With assistance, the family members may alter their perception of the situation and, thus, their behavior towards him. Refusal to believe the diagnosis can be demonstrated in overt anger or in passive-aggressive resistance.

Resistance, or denial, of the diagnosis and its implications may lead to noncompliance with the recommended plan of treatment. Occasionally, clients in denial "shop around" for a cure, a more aggressive physician, or one last course of chemotherapy. Denial is used by almost all clients, not only during the first stages of illness but at intervals throughout the illness. When denial cannot be maintained, it is replaced by feelings of anger, rage, envy and resentment. Denial acts as a buffer after the unexpected shock of diagnosis, allowing the client to collect himself and, with time, mobilize other less radical defenses (Kubler-Ross, 1969). Bargaining is an attempt to postpone the illness. If the client does not agree with or acknowledge the diagnosis he can avoid coping with its reality in his life.

The coping skills of the client are challenged. He has not prepared himself to deal with the overwhelming omnipresence of a chronic or terminal illness. This lack of coping ability leads to a lowered self-esteem, or evaluation of himself as less self-sufficient and personally powerful.

The client's self-esteem is related to the potential he evaluates in himself, his ability to perform well in present and future life situations. The acknowledgment of a chronic or terminal illness places limitations on his future performance, or self-expectations.

He may not know how to go about meeting his altered self-care needs. Without information or skills with which to care for himself, the client identifies his own self-care deficits. He wonders about his self-care needs and grieves for his absent or threatened abilities, seeing himself as powerless.

Grief is multifaceted for this client. He grieves for the losses he sees in his future. He grieves for his altered self-image. He grieves for future plans that may never come to fruition. He experiences the anticipatory grief of separation from his loved ones. The loss of abilities and favorite activities are sources of grief for him and enhance his perception of himself as powerless. Clients recognize their loss—loss of life, family, job, and friendships. The client perceives himself as in the process of losing everything and everybody he loves. Health care professionals should not interfere too quickly with his depression, as it facilitates gradual acceptance (Kubler-Ross, 1969). The client often experiences the six stages of grief: shock, denial, anger, depression, bargaining and acceptance (Kubler-Ross, 1969). Each client experiences some of these stages, in different time frames and not necessarily in order. Each client does not necessarily achieve the acceptance level.

Acceptance is not the same as being happy. It reflects a change in thought rather than emotion. Pain and envy are recognized. The struggle with living is continued or relinquished. Without acceptance, the client grieves for his altered future and fears what it may bring.

The fears of the client increase his perception of powerlessness. He may fear pain, separation, aloneness, sorrow, the unknown, and the loss of self-control, function and identity (Rickel, Pappas, Seidenschnur and Williams, 1984). Fear is one of the greatest motivators of behavior, overshadowing other feelings and diminishing the capacity to learn (Waitley, 1987). The health care professional must therefore, work to calm some of these fears if the client is to experience personal control and the fullness of each day. The attainment of maximum fulfillment for the client depends on his personal values.

Values Clarification

Values are difficult to measure, since they are concepts upon which individuals conduct their daily lives (Simon, 1974). The purpose of values clarification use with the chronic or terminal client is to identify those areas in which the client is willing to work, and to help the care provider and client understand his motivating factors.

The client's motivating factors may be different from those of the health care professional. No matter how knowledgeable the health care professional and how much she thinks she knows what is best for the client, it is necessary that the client's right of choice be honored. Clients must choose the lifestyle they feel most comfortable with (Lewis, 1985). However, it is the health care professional's responsibility to be sure that the client is making his choice from an informed stance. Once that is ascertained, the professional should discuss the client's values, searching for the key that explains the behavior choices of the client.

Sick Role

The client who assumes the role of the sick person has to meet the expectations of society: 1) he must seek out health care, 2) follow the prescribed treatment plan and 3) want to get well. As this client is not going to get well, society may have difficulty coping with his chronic aches, indispositions and limitations (Avery, 1985).

These difficulties keep the client in the sick role indefinitely and place a continuous burden on the client to be always seeking a better, faster, easier way to optimal health. With the chronicity of his disease, the client is placed in a position that can be interpreted as never achieving any mastery or control of the situation. Powerlessness is a constant companion of the chronically or terminally ill client and can lead to attitudes of hopelessness and despair (Miller, 1983) (Fig. 14-3).

Powerlessness Assessment

Physical

Are you able to perform your own self-care?
Are you able to perform part of your self-care?
What activities make you feel independent?
Can you function at your previous normal level?
What activities are difficult for you? Work? Play? Sex? Eating?
What hobbies have you previously enjoyed?

Emotional

How would you rate your coping skills?
Do you view problems as defeats or challenges?
Are you a worrier?
Do you take life seriously? Humorously?

Intellectual

What activities are mentally stimulating for you?
What would you like to achieve during the rest of your life?
What do you not understand about your disease?

Cultural

What is your cultural background?
What traditions are important to you?
Who are the members of your support system?
How often do you interact with your support system?

Spiritual

Do you have a faith preference?
Do you actively participate in your faith?
How hopeful do you feel about your life?
Do you believe you are a worthy person?
What have you accomplished in the past that makes you feel successful?

Fig. 14-3. Tool for Assessing Powerlessness

Chronic Illness. Chronic illness implies a disease that is never cured (Dimond, 1983). It is often associated with the discomfort that occurs during exacerbations. Though it may recede, the pain or dysfunction is ready to spring forth again, disrupting the individual's plans or goals. The diagnosis of chronic illness comes as a blow to the client's perception of himself as in control. The chronicity leads to despair, in a never-ending cycle of recurrence (Fig. 14-4).

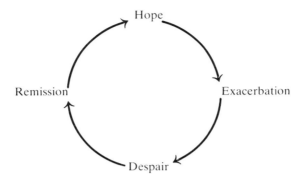

Fig. 14-4. Cycle of Chronicity

The client is no longer able to make firm plans for the next month or day, which strengthens his self-perception as powerless. His disease affects his ability to schedule activities hours or days ahead (Anderson and Bauwens, 1981). The chronic illness may suddenly exacerbate and curtail the attainment of his goals, either for a brief period or forever. This leads him to view the performance of his body as a betrayal of his trust.

The perception by the person with a chronic illness that his body or illness has become his enemy is a chief concern when dealing with this individual's perception of personal power. At odd times his body has made insistent demands that his behavior be altered (Miller, 1983). He is deluged with physical messages that require a change in plans, work schedule, goals and capabilities, the results of which undermine his efforts to retain or gain internal control.

It is possible to remain internally controlled in the face of adversity, but it is difficult (Glasser, 1985). The difficulty would not be hard to tolerate if it were occasional; however, the chronically ill client must face this problem day after day. He is often overwhelmed by the sheer energy drain of battling his body's signals. Exhaustion may lead him to believe himself to be without any strengths or positives in his life.

The health care professional needs to draw the client's attention to his remaining strengths and assist him in altering behaviors so that he can continue as much of his own self-care as possible (Miller, 1983). A care provider who guides the client along new ways to perceive himself and his world will do much to increase the client's perception of personal power. This is augmented through the assessment of his motivation resources.

Assessing motivation resources is of paramount importance when the client is being encouraged to improve his own self-care and to prevent or postpone sequelae of his chronic illness. The strength of the client's motivation for self-care will greatly affect his prognosis (Miller, 1983) (Fig. 14-5).

Terminal Illness. The terminally ill client knows, and must cope with, limitations on his life expectancy. The continuance of hope and maintenance of as much self-care capability as possible are principle concerns of the caretaker working with this type of client. General health care requirements for the terminally ill include the continuous effective meeting of his universal self-care requisites (Orem, 1984). Emphasis on the client's progress through the stages of grief and continuation of a relatively normal existence is vital, since despair will advance his disease, shorten his life, and add to his feelings of powerlessness.

Motivation Assessment

Physical

How well do you tolerate discomfort?
What things indicate wellness to you?
What activities are important in your self-care?

Emotional

Is the way you cope helping?
Do you enjoy each day?
What does feeling depressed/sad do for you?
What does feeling powerless get you?

Intellectual

What activities leave you mentally stimulated?
Do you assess yourself as intelligent?
What mental activities are you good at?

Cultural

Is it important to you to belong to a group?
How do you feel about traditions?
How do you feel when you do not carry on traditions?

Spiritual

Do you participate in a faith to avoid trouble? to express love? to follow the rules?
Do you see any hope for civilization?
Do you believe you are being judged by God for your behavior?

Fig. 14-5. Tool for Assessing Motivation

The client who gives up hope, who dwells for an extended period of time in a depressive state, will die sooner and without the closure of his personal affairs. Despair will fortify his impression of being a victim.

The client who has a terminal illness often views himself as a victim of his disease, experiencing powerlessness in many facets of his life. His diagnosis rings through his head, sounding a death knell. He knows his days are numbered. It is the lack of knowledge regarding the length of one's life, as well as the inability to postpone death, that promotes an interpretation of one's life as out of control. The client's interactions with the health care professional far too often reinforce this perception.

Health care professionals should be aware of the need for personal power in all of their terminally ill clients. Instead of addressing this need in a manner that builds the client's self-confidence, some health care professionals who work with the dying client talk to him as if he were an infant, eager to do things for him, commiserate with him and rob him of the chance for positive self-esteem in his final hours. These behaviors thwart his achievement of a positive end to his life.

The successful completion of the developmental stage of finding purpose and meaning for the client's life is inherent in the achievement of his positive self-esteem. Reminiscence is an important activity for this client and must be explained to his family to encourage their cooperation and support for this phase of dying (Collison & Miller, 1987). In the process of finding worth in his past, the client can cope more effectively with the loss of control he faces moment by moment in the course of his terminal illness.

Assessing Powerlessness

Although decreasing powerlessness is a major concern, it must be validated that the client does indeed feel powerless. Upon ascertaining the client's areas of concern, the health care professional can move forward in helping him arrive at a plan of care that will enhance his perception of being in control. According to Orem (1985) the client must feel he is a partner in his health care and have the maximum possible control of his self-care. Therefore his desires regarding care must be acknowledged and facilitated.

The client's preferences are often ignored. Well-meaning family members and health care professionals have a tendency to shield the client from reality and make plans without his input. This places the client in a childlike position and further enhances his feelings of powerlessness.

Rather than being treated as a child, the client must be encouraged to be a responsible partner in his care and treatment planning. Far too often informed consent is incomplete, with the client being told only what the physician recommends and not what other alternatives for treatment are available to him. Legally, this constitutes a lack of informed consent for treatment. When completely informed about his options, the client will arrive at a decision that is most comfortable for him. The establishment of living wills is one area in which clients attempt to insure their personal choices.

Through their choices of behavior, clients may create a remission of their symptoms. There are many examples of clients working themselves into a healthier state through laughter, distraction, altered perception, imagery, faith and improved coping strategies. All of these methods and more are available to the client and are rarely supported as valid by the health care community. It is vital that the client's needs be met rather than those of the health care professional. Thorough assessment identifies the client's needs.

The client will express his unique needs if these are carefully assessed. Client needs are as varied and individualized as are clients themselves. Each of the following case studies illustrates some of the myriad ways a client can express his need for and assertion of personal power.

CASE STUDY

Terry was a 32-year-old female with the diagnosis of rheumatoid arthritis. She was a first grade teacher and the mother of two preschool-age children. She was active in community and church activities. Terry was a member of a health club and was always dieting, unsuccessfully, as she remained thirty pounds over her recommended weight. She came to the clinic with complaints of bilateral joint pain in her hands, knees and shoulders, with intermittent periods of fatigue.

Upon hearing her diagnosis, Terry asked appropriate questions about what the suggested course of treatment was. Allergic to aspirin, she was given a prescription for a nonsteroidal anti-inflammatory drug. She was told to rest her joints periodically each day and lose thirty pounds. By the time she arrived home, she was in tears, remembering the crippled condition of her grandmother who had had arthritis.

She told her husband about her diagnosis and fears. He read the pamphlets she had picked up in the office regarding rheumatoid arthritis. He urged Terry to put her energy into the present rather than the future and its unknown properties.

The next morning, Terry shared her diagnosis with three of her coworkers, at which point one of them remarked that she would just have to get used to it. Terry was disappointed by her coworkers' response.

She called a close friend during her free period that day. This friend suggested that Terry begin writing in a journal or tape recording how she was feeling, what she wanted to do, what her choices were, and how she could reach her goals.

Terry called the clinic that afternoon and spoke with the nurse about literature available concerning rheumatoid arthritis. The nurse also suggested a support group and some stores specializing in adaptive aids that would help Terry in maintaining her independent self-care. Terry told the nurse about the tremendous amount of anticipatory grief she was feeling because she was certain that she would wind up crippled and wheelchair-bound, as did her grandmother. She cried and stated that she had recently quit going to church since she could no longer tolerate kneeling. The nurse urged Terry to come to the clinic to talk with the counselor about her feelings and to discover ways to cope with them.

Terry met with the counselor for three sessions. Afterwards she expressed the belief that she was capable of dealing with her chronic disease at this point. She concentrated on the positive aspects of each day and worked on increasing her awareness of her perceptions of events.

Terry read every book she could find related to her type of arthritis. She attended meetings of the Arthritis Foundation and took their course on arthritis and self-help. She developed a close, trusting relationship with her nurse practitioner and physician. She began losing weight after starting a sensible diet and exercise program. She went to specialty shops and purchased door handles for her house to replace the doorknobs that caused her pain, a zipper pull for dressing herself, a bottle opener that fastened on the bottom of her top cupboards and allowed her to use both hands to turn the jars, and a grip to slide onto her pen to help her maintain control of her pen without too much pain. Her care plan follows:

Nursing Diagnoses

1. Powerlessness related to expression of lack of control over her disease.
2. Fear related to past experiences of relatives with this disease process.
3. Knowledge deficit related to seeking information about the disease.
4. Low self-esteem related to repeated dieting failures.

Desired Outcomes

Client will:

Identify areas of personal control.
Express a decrease in fear about her future.
Demonstrate knowledge of disease process.
Express more positive self-esteem.

Plan

Physical

1. Assist in adapting difficult activities to be more easily achieved.
2. Educate regarding disease and treatment options

Emotional

1. Decrease fear through education and verbalization of feelings.
2. Increase self-esteem through identification of past successes and establishment of easily obtainable daily goals.
3. Support friend's suggestion to do journal writing.

Intellectual

1. Provide books for bibliotherapy.
2. Stimulate through challenges to problem solve, with assistance, her own areas of difficulty.

Cultural

1. Encourage her to interact with positive and supportive friends.
2. Introduce her to an Arthritis Foundation support group.

Spiritual

1. Encourage hopeful statements about life situations.
2. Provide opportunities to participate in her faith activities without stressing her joints.

Implementation

Physical

1. Attended arthritis self-help classes.
2. Read about and discussed disease and treatment options.

Emotional

1. Expressed a decrease in fear of the future and confidence in handling one day at a time.
2. Set realistic daily goals and met them, expressing pleasure in her achievements.
3. Continued and expressed benefit from journal writing.

Intellectual

1. Read literature available, adding to her knowledge base.
2. Enjoyed the challenge of problem-solving and quickly managed to arrive at effective choices without any assistance from the health care system.

Cultural

1. Nurtured relationships with supportive friends.
2. Established new support system with friends met in the arthritis support group meetings.

Spiritual

1. Began expressing herself in more positive and hopeful terms, as suggested by her husband.
2. Attended church services regularly after discussing concern with clergy and understanding that it was permissible for her not to kneel.

Evaluation

Although the initial reaction to her diagnosis was one of powerlessness, Terry did not stay in a posture of despair for long. This reflects a willingness to improve her situation and build a positive self-esteem and coping system, among other assets. Through the suggestions and support of her husband, friend, physician, nurse and counselor, Terry's sense of personal power was fortified.

CASE STUDY

Loretta was a 59-year-old woman diagnosed with lymphoma eight years ago. She had had three abdominal surgeries secondary to her cancer and a course of chemotherapy three months ago. She asked a cousin to call the Hospice to "get her into the program." She related passing through each of Kubler-Ross' stages (1969) and said she wanted no further treatment, just to be comfortable and to not die at home. When she suffered complications on two separate occasions she calmly called the Hospice, went through diagnostic tests and was admitted to the hospital for relief of symptoms. She died peacefully within hours of her second admission in the presence of her husband and two adult children.

Evaluation

Loretta was in charge of the orchestration of her own care. Her wishes were respected. She had decided what she wanted done and the caregivers followed her desires. They made certain that Loretta was kept comfortable and assessed her closely to work toward her death in a setting other than her home. Her personal power was supported and encouraged.

CASE STUDY

George was a 66-year-old male diagnosed with emphysema seven years ago. He was admitted to the home Hospice program in July. The initial assessment of George found him to be alert and oriented but in acute respiratory distress. He was cyanotic and having episodes of acute apnea. His wife, the primary caregiver, panicked at each crisis and called the attending physician, who maintained a busy internal medicine practice nine miles away. Both the client and primary caregiver felt it important to be in a Hospice program, if for no other reason than to have an RN available on a 24 hour emergency basis.

The next month extreme anger was identified by the RN between the client and his wife caregiver. The wife caregiver wanted the client to get out of bed to have his stools and the client expressed inability to do so due to extreme weakness and shortness of breath on slight exertion. He also expressed fear of falling if his wife should attempt to get him out of bed. He exhibited anger at her plan to go on a two day trip even after she arranged to have 24 hour in-home care.

In September, George began talking disrespectfully about his wife caregiver to the RN in the caregiver's absence. His wife set unrealistic goals, stating that George was in remission and should start an exercise program. George's physical condition, having somewhat stabilized by not experiencing apneic episodes, was by no means in remission. George began directing his anger at the R.N.

In October, the caregiver's father died in the home, this increased George's anger and hostility toward his wife. Xanax was started on the client at his request. It was noted by the RN that the caregiver had taken control of the times George received the Xanax, which further added to his irritability. The RN discussed with the caregiver the client's need for the medication and its relationship to the emphysema. The caregiver expressed her fear of George becoming addicted. She felt he was giving up and not fighting anymore.

In December, he called his pastor and talked to him at length about his anger with his former father-in-law and his caregiver. The caregiver and RN felt that this was a positive step. George's anger, however, did not decrease and he became more demanding of his caregiver, expecting her to come to his aid immediately upon calling. The medication "doling out" by the caregiver continued and she was no longer willing to discuss the issue with the RN, instead becoming defensive.

In January, George's hospice benefits expired, but the Hospice continued his care with an RN, HHA, and MSW. The caregiver became financially responsible for his medications. At that time the caregiver became more manipulative with the medications, now citing cost as the reason for withholding it.

*In March, George started weeping during his visits with the RN. He
began grieving his loss of friends and family.*

*In April, his primary RN through the past nine months terminated
with the hospice agency. She did not discuss her termination with the
client. When a new RN saw George at the next visit he was extremely
angry at having a new nurse and not being told the specifics of his
primary RN's termination.*

*Attempts were made by the Hospice to allow George to verbalize
his anger. He refused to talk with the hospice chaplain. He verbally
attacked the next two assigned RN's and asked that they be removed
from his case.*

*In June, he verbally attacked the MSW. George stated that he had
identified his two sources of major stress, his family and Hospice, and
asked to revoke hospice care. The hospice care plan for George follows:*

Nursing Diagnoses

1. Powerlessness related to impending death.
2. Activity intolerance related to COPD.
3. Anxiety related to COPD and perceived threat to self-concept.
4. Ineffective individual coping related to depression in response
   to stressors.
5. Ineffective family coping related to inability to accept terminal
   illness.
6. Grieving related to perceived loss of friends/family.
7. Noncompliance related to unsatisfactory relationship with care
   giving environment or care giver.
8. Self-care deficit related to inability to bathe, dress and toilet
   self.

Desired Outcome

Client will:
   Identify factors that can be controlled by him.
   Make decisions regarding his care, treatment and future.

Plan

1. Identify factors that contribute to a sense of powerlessness.
2. Provide opportunities for George to make decisions.
3. Enhance an internal locus of control.
      Assess client's usual response to problems.
      Explain problem as specifically as possible.
      Explain the relationship of prescribed behavior and outcome.

4. Decrease his external locus of control.
   Encourage participation in care planning.
   Assist in methods to perform own self-care.

Implementation

Physical

1. Assess systems weekly.
2. PRN HHA to assist with personal care.

Emotional

1. All disciplines to encourage client to verbalize.
2. MSW to meet with client/family weekly to facilitate increased sense of control in client and caregiver.

Intellectual

1. Encourage client to exercise his thinking ability at the optimal level.

Cultural

1. Counsel with client/care giver and other family/friends to facilitate grieving process and to choose appropriate behaviors by client and caregiver.

Spiritual

Encourage client and caregiver to seek out familiar spiritual resources.

Evaluation

The client and caregiver were evaluated by three disciplines on a weekly basis.

George and his wife could not identify a workable plan between themselves.

George felt he had lost all control by allowing his wife and the Hospice to participate in his care.

George did not comply with the care plan in a way that satisfied the health care team. He left the hospice program with many characteristics of powerlessness still apparent. However, he did come to his own conclusions about what he needed. His decisions and expression of independence were accepted. The staff kept the lines of communication open between themselves and George to be available to assist him in the future if he changed his mind.

CASE STUDY

Molly was a 59-year-old female who called to inquire about Hospice in January. She had been diagnosed with breast cancer ten years ago. The diagnosis was followed by a right radical mastectomy and chemotherapy. The client had been in remission until October when the disease was found to have metastasized to her bones, resulting in a recent rib fracture and hip pain. The client had taken care of her husband who was diagnosed 23 years ago with M.S. until she divorced him three years ago and placed him in a nursing home. She felt the stress of caring for him and the divorce had contributed to the reactivation of her cancer.

Molly had previously been socially active and cheerful. She had shut herself off from her friends, not feeling good enough to accompany them on social outings and fearing they would not appreciate her presence while she was so depressed. She expressed betrayal by God and stated that she had stopped going to church in the past few years. She said she no longer felt there was any hope for her.

Molly complained of increased weakness and an accumulation of abdominal fluid that required paracentesis for comfort. She disliked the paracentesis procedure and asked her physician for other alternatives.

In February, against the advice of her oncologist, Molly sought the advice of a vascular surgeon for placement of a shunt to decrease fluid accumulation. The shunt was successful in decreasing her ascites.

In March, Molly and the hospice counselor identified her need for more social contact. She resumed some of her previous activities and relationships.

In April, Molly called to cancel Hospice care. She had planned a trip to Mexico with some friends. Her oncologist stated that she was no longer terminally ill. The following was her care plan while in hospice:

Nursing Diagnoses

1. Powerlessness related to perceived lack of personal control in treatment of disease.
2. Social isolation related to withdrawal from support system.
3. Noncompliance related to inconvenience of frequent paracentesis.
4. Ineffective coping related to preoccupation with death and failure of past successful coping measures.

Desired Outcome

Client will:

Increase her sense of personal power.
Establish a strong support group.

Utilize effective coping behaviors.

Demonstrate knowledge of her disease and list the options available for treatment.

Physical

1. Assist client in assessing strengths and disease process twice a week.
2. Assist in getting companion at night when caregiver away.
3. Plan rest periods during each day.

Emotional

1. Actuate listening to verbalization of feelings and concerns by RN/MSW.
2. Assist client in identifying and using coping mechanisms she has successfully used in the past.
3. Assist in making behavior choices that will help her feel more competent in her life situation.

Intellectual

1. Explore and select activities that she has found mentally stimulating in the past.
2. Encourage client to seek information that may be useful in the treatment of her disease.
3. Encourage client to make choices in her treatment after identifying realistic options.

Cultural

1. Assist family members in expressing their feelings about death and dying.
2. Assist in resumption/maintenance of social contacts

Spiritual

1. Facilitate grief process around loss of 20 years of her life in caring for ex-husband and the exacerbation of her disease.
2. Encourage client to verbalize anger and hopelessness.
3. Foster interaction between Molly and her clergy.
4. Expedite her attendance to church activities as desired.

Implementation

Physical

1. Reviewed power assets with client and provided education concerning her disease process and treatment options.
2. Provided caretaker and companion when appropriate.

Emotional

1. Verbalization of feelings encouraged.
2. Past coping styles reviewed and effective choices of behavior were selected by client.

Intellectual

1. Provided information about her disease and treatment options available.
2. Supported her after she decided to seek further treatment against her physician's orders.
3. Provided activities that she found stimulating.

Cultural

1. Urged her to re-establish relationships with past friends.
2. Assisted her in planning her attendance at social activities.
3. During family meetings urged their continued support of Molly and provided them with information concerning her condition.
4. Promoted grief work during family meetings.

Spiritual

1. Provided Molly with safe environment in which to discuss her feelings and work through some of her grief, anger and hopelessness.
2. Assisted her in re-establishing contact with and participation in her faith community.

Evaluation

By urging the client to make her own choices, she was able to delay her disease process and enjoy an improved quality of life. She expressed the desire to choose another alternative than that presented to her by her physician and was noncompliant with his recommendation to not have a shunt inserted. Molly was supported in her decision, with no opinion voiced by the hospice staff about the rightness or wrongness of her choice. She had the willingness to re-establish a positive attitude about her life and, in this way, improved her own immune system and brought about a remission. Both the alteration in attitude and increase in social contacts improved Molly's sense of personal power and reversed the assessed diagnoses of powerlessness and its related concepts, social isolation and ineffective coping.

CASE STUDY

Jerry was a 47-year-old homosexual male diagnosed with AIDS. He had been released from the hospital and required 24 hour professional nursing care in the home. Assessment revealed a cachectic male appearing far older than his stated biological age. His mother was his primary care giver. The client needed continuous oxygen therapy, enteral feeding therapy and a foley catheter. He was extremely weak and bedbound except for active transfer to a bedside commode.

Jerry cried when discussing his disease and expressed powerlessness in altering the pattern his life had taken. He spent several sessions with the mental health nurse practitioner talking about his feelings and possible choices of behavior available to him. He stated that God could never love him and he believed the congregation at his church would not allow him to return.

Jerry refused to see any of his friends from the gay community. He stated that he did not want to get involved in the AIDS support group and knew that nobody really wanted to be troubled with him.

Two weeks after he began counseling sessions, Jerry asked to be up and have a "whole bath." This was facilitated by the HHA.

Jerry expressed concern about his inactive muscles. The physical therapist assisted him in active range of motion and strengthening exercises.

Two months later he was walking with the assistance of a walker. He progressed to riding a stationary bicycle one mile a day. He joined a health club and was able to provide his own care. He attended the AIDS support group. A month later Jerry no longer needed nursing care.

Nursing Diagnoses

1. Powerlessness related to perceived lack of personal control over terminal illness.
2. Ineffective coping (individual) related to life situation and unknown outcome.
3. Social isolation related to refusal to interact with support network.
4. Spiritual distress related to statement that God no longer cared about him and that he was unacceptable to fellow church members.

Desired Outcomes

Client will:

Express control over some aspects of his life.
Select more effective behaviors.
Establish support system that is satisfying to him.
Progress toward a more peaceful understanding of his higher power.

Plan

Physical
1. Twenty-four hour nursing care to assess systems, provide feeding, supervise safety.
2. teach methods for resumption of self-care activities.
3. Support caregiver and instruct in care of client.

Emotional
1. Encourage client to make choices in his care.
2. Explore with client alternative attitudes and coping styles available.

Intellectual
1. Provide favorite reading materials.
2. Encourage playing preferred board games with mother.

Cultural
1. Promote contacts with AIDS support group.
2. Allow client and family to verbalize feelings about AIDS.
3. Encourage him to allow his friends to interact with him.

Spiritual
1. Promote client and family attainment of spiritual support.
2. Contact clergy to talk with Jerry.
3. Arrange opportunities for him to participate in spiritual rituals.

Implementation

Physical
1. 24 hour nursing care provided initially, with caregiver gradually taking over.
2. Instructed in modifications that enabled self-care.

Emotional
1. Client asked for input on care plan and made final decisions.
2. Discussed attitudes and coping skills that might improve situation.

Intellectual
1. Accessed by-mail lending library.
2. Provided new editions of favorite games.

Cultural
1. Provisions made for attendance at AIDS support group.
2. Counseling sessions promoted expression of feelings.
3. Gradually increased contact with his friends.

Spiritual

1. Arranged home visit by Jerry's clergy.
2. Opportunities provided for expression of spiritual needs.
3. Provisions made for transportation to church when desired.

Evaluation

By promotion of the client's choices in his care, he increased his personal power. He moved on to participate in his self-care and eventually experienced a remission of his illness. The establishment of a support system for Jerry gave him hope and built a stronger cultural resource of power for him. By gaining spiritual peace and belonging in his faith setting, Jerry gained a more positive self-esteem and willingness to find more effective ways to cope with his life situations.

Summary

Due to the chronicity of terminal illness and the terminal outcome of some chronic illness, these two divisions were discussed together. The common thread between these two types of illness is powerlessness. Values clarification and the sick role were reviewed in relation to clients with chronic or terminal illnesses.

Encouraging clients to make decisions about their care, to consider all their choices, and come to their own conclusions about what is best for them is threatening to many health care professionals. The fact that the client knows himself best must be remembered. What the health care system would have the client do may not be the choices clients arrive at, and their judgment must be respected. Remissions often happen in spite of the health care professional, rather than as a result of their care.

Several case studies were reviewed with an emphasis on the reversal of powerlessness to a feeling of personal power for the clients. Clients' powerlessness was examined, with appropriate interventions suggested.

References

Anderson, Sandra VanDam and Bauwens, Eleanore. *Chronic Health Problems: Concepts and Application.* St. Louis: C.V.Mosby Company, (1981).

Barry, Patricia. *Psychosocial Nursing Assessment and Intervention.* Philadelphia: J. B. Lippincott, (1984).

Bowlby, J. Processes of mourning. *International Journal of Psychoanalysis.* 42:317, (1961).

Collison, Carol and Miller, Sandra. Using Images of the Future in Grief Work. *Image: Journal of Nursing Scholarship.* Vol.19, Number 1 Spring. 9-11, (1987).

Dimond, Margaret and Jones, Susan Lynn. *Chronic Illness Across The Life Span*. Norwalk, CN: Appleton-Century-Crofts, (1983).

Glasser, William. *Take Effective Control of Your Life*. New York: Harper & Row, (1985).

Hickey, S. Enabling hope. *Cancer Nursing*. 9(3). 133-137, (1986).

Kim, M., McFarland, Gertrude K., and McLane, Audrey M. (eds). *Pocket Guide to Nursing Diagnoses*. St. Louis: C.V.Mosby Company, (1984).

Kneisl, Carol Ren and Ames, Sueann Wooster. *Adult Health Nursing: A Biopsychosocial Approach*. Menlo Park, CA: Addison-Wesley Publishing Company, (1986).

Kubler-Ross, E. *On Death and Dying*. NY: Macmillan, (1969).

Lambert, Vickie and Lambert, Clinton. *Psychosocial Care of the Physically Ill* (2nd Ed.). Englewood Cliffs, NJ: Prentice-Hall, Inc., (1985).

Lewis, Kathleen. *Successful Living With Chronic Illness*. Wayne, NJ: Avery Publishing Group, Inc., (1985).

Miller, Judith. *Coping With Chronic Illness: Overcoming Powerlessness*. Philadelphia: F.A.Davis Company, (1983).

Nichols, Keith. *Psychological Care in Physical Illness*. London: Croom Helm, (1984).

Orem, Dorothea. *Nursing: Concepts of Practice* (3rd Ed.) New York: McGraw-Hill Book Publishing Company, (1985).

Rickel, Linda, Pappas, Malinda, Seidenschnur, Judith, and Williams, Barbara. Therapy with dying clients. In Beck, Cornelia, Rawlins, Ruth and Williams, Sophronia (eds). *Mental Health-Psychiatric Nursing: A Holistic Life-Cycle Approach*. St. Louis: C.V.Mosby Company, (1984).

Simon, Sidney. *Meeting Yourself Halfway*. Niles, IL: Argus Communications, (1974).

Waitley, Denis. *The Psychology of Winning*. Chicago: Nightingale-Conant Corporation, (1987).

15

Power and the Psychiatric Client

N. Rinehart and M. Stallings

Introduction

The psychiatric client is the victim of his own mind. He either battles depression as an outpatient and functions as well as possible in his world or he fights to gain a grasp on reality as an inpatient with schizophrenia. In either situation, the client experiences overwhelming powerlessness (Stuart and Sundeen, 1983).

His self-esteem hits an all-time low as he measures himself against his family's and society's expectations and comes up lacking. He receives many messages from his significant others to "get it together," and, as a result, experiences guilt (Barry, 1984).

Panic is his frequent anxiety level. He is afraid of events, places or persons that are not feared by the people around him. Try as he might, he cannot reach the level of functioning he expects of himself, thereby adding anger to his burdens. He would love to comply with his prescribed treatment, but cannot find it within himself to do so.

However, desires other than compliance become a priority for the client, such as the need to perform obsessive-compulsive rituals. He becomes so involved with fighting his personal demons that self-care may be ignored (Murray and Huelskoetter, 1983). He may not bathe, wash his clothes or shave; there just isn't time when he has to deal with his illness. He may wonder why he should put forth the effort when he believes he is not worth it. His experience with coping has not provided him with the skills to overcome or manage his mental illness. Old behaviors that once worked now fail him.

The inpatient psychiatric unit looms large as a possibility for all psychiatric clients. However, according to Aiken (1987), the majority of all admissions to mental institutions are readmissions of chronic psychiatric clients, such as schizophrenics, resulting in the "revolving door syndrome." Aiken (1987) also states that the "mentally ill are 20 times more likely to be homeless than the rest of the population" (p.122). The census of mental institutions may have dropped significantly in the past decade or so, but the mentally ill population appears to have shifted locations, now swelling the ranks of the homeless and occupying bedspace in nursing homes. As psychiatric institution administrators point to their diminishing population and indicate success in empowering clients, perhaps it would be advisable to inspect the location of those de-institutionalized clients and reassess the self-esteem levels and feelings of control in their lives.

The issue of power versus powerlessness is found in every aspect of psychiatric care. The client involuntarily held in a psychiatric unit experiences the loss or frustration of his power of choice. Providing the safety and security of the locked unit while promoting independent choice-making and assumption of self-responsibility is a delicate juggling act.

If the client is an outpatient, his periods of relief are chopped into fifty minute segments with his therapist. He may live in fear that he will need to be "locked up" or yearn for the security, safety, and balance of the inpatient situation. Collaboration is essential in the therapy team that supervises outpatient care for this client (Lesseig, 1987). Fragmentation of therapeutic goals will increase client feelings of powerlessness rather than promote the pride in self-reliance and productivity hoped for by the providers of outpatient mental health services. Team collaboration, along with an increase in participation by the client in his own health care, usually decreases powerlessness and medication dosage needs and increases compliance with prescribed therapy regimens (Scrak, Zimmerman, Wilson and Greenstein, 1987).

Health Belief Model

The health belief model indicates the client's beliefs about his need for health care, how and when he goes about seeking it and whether or not he values improved mental health. Variables that make up the health care belief of a client might include the following:

1) Opinions of significant others who think going for emotional help indicates weakness.
2) Belief that the client can fix himself without any need for assistance.
3) Experienced panic from terrible stories about asylums.
4) Tolerance for strong and prolonged anxiety.
5) Past experiences with mental health care.
6) Past experiences of significant others and mental health care.
7) Distrust of a dominantly white population of mental health care workers.
8) Articles he has read in magazines about the kind of therapy available.

Any or all of these contribute to the client's feelings about his condition, the importance of therapy and his self-esteem.

The general public has little idea about the realities of mental illness.

With the media spotlighting only sensational cases, it is not probable that a psychiatric client will have many positive feelings about his need for care. This lack of self-esteem is seen in the client admitted for depression who blames himself for failing a daughter who in turn refuses to visit him because she is ashamed that her father needs psychiatric care. The denial of the client's illness by some family members can have devastating results for the client, as in the case of the schizophrenic whose son refused to believe his father could possibly need psychiatric help and withheld the client's medications, leading to the client being jailed and subsequently taken back to the psychiatric unit for certification as a result of his inappropriate behavior in public.

The client in need of psychiatric care is not accorded the same community support as the cancer victim (Beck et al., 1984). He may avoid seeking help to ward off the guilt feelings that he has when considering his need for psychiatric assistance. There are many groups in society that place a stigma or moral judgment on persons seeking to improve their mental health. This harsh disapproval is akin to that placed on persons contracting a venereal disease.

Reality Therapy

Glasser (1965) first wrote about his development of techniques known as Reality Therapy in the 60's, challenging the idea that psychotherapy must last for years and that it must include dwelling on the past. Using these techniques, many professionals certified in Reality Therapy succeed daily in helping clients make more effective behavior choices. Simultaneously, the shorter allowable stays of clients on psychiatric units make long-term therapy styles, such as the psychoanalytic approach, impractical.

As a result of the time constraints placed on the staff, a new body of therapeutic techniques has had to be developed. Reality Therapy techniques are prominent in the eclectic combination of therapy styles that has emerged. Most of the staff members using Reality Therapy don't realize that this style of therapy is the one they have adopted through exposure to the effective styles of others on the therapeutic staff or by reading about it.

Reality Therapy is short-term and works well for the short hospital stays of most clients. In addition to the appeal of short term usability, the brevity of Reality Therapy makes treatment less expensive. It can be used effectively by all staff members, presenting a unified approach to the client in his therapy. Often when using the psychoanalytical approach, staff members other than the doctor or psychologist end up feeling and behaving like custodians rather than part of the therapeutic team. Reality Therapy moves the client to more effectively meet his own needs.

Glasser (1975) identifies the need of all people to share love and to feel worthwhile. The client with low self-esteem neither sees himself as lovable nor worthwhile. This feeling leads to powerlessness. Reality Therapy places an emphasis on the client taking responsibility for his choices of ineffective behavior, getting him to recognize this fact and finding a more effective way to behave (Glasser, 1981).

Since the emphasis of Reality Therapy is that the client choose more effective behavior and have control over his choices, it follows that Reality Therapy is designed to empower clients. Glasser (1985) lists power as one of the basic human needs and he discusses choices of behavior as either effective or ineffective in controlling the client's life.

Aggressive Clients

The aggressive client acts out his powerlessness through verbal and/or physical means (Beck, Rawlins and Williams, 1984). He strikes out against his lack of power. He is "acting out" and is potentially harmful to himself and others. He tries, through words and actions, to handle his high level of anxiety. He expresses his anger and it is increased with a heightened perception of powerlessness.

The aggressive client behaves in a manner resembling the small child who yells at the thunder because it frightens him. The client who behaves aggressively is acting on his feelings of being out of control. He experiences frustration, anxiety, and/or rage and relieves that internal tension by striking out in an attempt to control some factor in his environment (Haber, Hoskins, Leach and Sideleau, 1987). If he acts aggressively and powerfully, he might convince himself and the health care professionals that he has power over the situation. This client has learned to manipulate his environment, and those in it, through threatening behavior. The ultimate goal of care is to move this client to take more control and increase his sense of personal power.

CASE STUDY

Tom's was a familiar name to the charge nurse on the admission unit. He had been hospitalized seven times in the past two years. Prior to this hospital, he had a history of multiple hospitalizations in his home town, before spending his Social Services (S.S.I.) check for a supersaver ticket and flying to this city "to get his life in order." At the time of his first admission to this hospital, Tom had assaulted a stewardess when she refused his request for a second meal; he was brought in by the police for admission.

Tom was a 31-year-old black male who first became ill at age 19 when he was a junior in college. He was a bright, articulate young man who was attending an Ivy League college on a full scholarship in nuclear physics. The oldest of four children, at that time he was the only person in his family to have gone to college. Since that time, two brothers have obtained advanced degrees in education and medicine and a sister is currently a second-year law student.

Tom's presenting symptoms on each admission were paranoid delusions with command hallucinations and thought insertion with occasional thought broadcasting. His affect was flat and his appearance disheveled. He had a collection of notebooks with voluminous formulas that he rarely shared with anyone. He was well known to local and federal law enforcement officers; he claimed to "work" for various government agencies or thought they were following him. Tom had been treated with most of the antipsychotic medications and several times had been on court-ordered long-acting drugs. He continued to be noncompliant. Throughout most hospitalizations, he was admitted out of control and was usually secluded or restrained. Due to his dangerousness to others, Tom received emergency medications and reconstituted quickly. His presentations at hearings to contest his certifications were very impressive and certifications had been dropped on numerous occasions.

On this admission, Tom was admitted after trying to enter the Federal Center and assaulting a guard. He was restrained in the emergency room prior to being moved to the inpatient unit. He had "valuable information" to report to the nuclear regulatory agency and felt that he was being followed by the "CIA and KGB." He declared that he received messages from the television and a device that was implanted in his head that picked up satellite commands. He said his thoughts were read by this device. He had discontinued his community mental health center appointments where he had received court-ordered prolixin injections. He lived alone in a small apartment.

On admission, Tom was disheveled, with disorganized, pressured speech. He acknowledged command hallucinations which he would not discuss. He was delusional, with thought insertion and broadcasting. He was unable to complete a formal mental status and was unsure of the date. He recognized staff members who had worked with him on previous admissions. He was relatively cooperative with the brief admission procedure and questioned the staff's intentions and whether they had received any satellite communications.

Within a few minutes of the initial evaluation, Tom began moving about the unit quickly, refusing to eat lunch saying, "It's poisoned!" When nursing staff attempted low level interventions, Tom threatened to "punch them out." With a show of force, Tom went to the seclusion room and cooperated with the procedures. When Tom refused oral psychoactive medications, emergency medications were begun based on Tom's threats of bodily harm to the staff. An initial dose was administered intramuscularly, with subsequent doses taken orally. Medications and *seclusion were continued throughout the night. Tom slept several hours, but continued to respond to verbal hallucinations.*

By morning, Tom was cooperative with the staff on their entry and exit of the seclusion room. After breakfast Tom was allowed to use the bathroom and shower, and an open seclusion procedure was begun. Medications were taken voluntarily and open seclusion was discontinued before lunch.

Assessment of psychiatric clients continues long after admission and through discharge. During a break in the milieu program, Tom's primary nurse sat down to complete a more extensive admission nursing assessment.

Tom was anxious, and seemed embarrassed to be back again. When asked about his return to the hospital, Tom shrugged and said, "You don't understand." When asked if he would explain so that the nurse could understand, Tom brightened. He had difficulty expressing himself and gave up in frustration. Although he was behaviorally improved, more functional, and had begun recompensating quickly, he had a great deal of difficulty organizing his thoughts and attending to the higher intellectual task of an interview. Using the assessment tool format (Fig. 15-1), the primary nurse gathered data for assessment without a formal extensive interviewing process. Since the client was able to participate, the assessment was expanded as part of the nursing process.

Assessment

Anxiety. Tom expressed his anxiety by agitated and aggressive behavior. He threatened, paced and assaulted, repeating the pattern of his multiple hospitalizations. The most effective interventions in the past had been limits, medications and containment.

Fear. The previously described behaviors and past history could be an expression of fear. Tom expressed fear of his perceptual distortions, stating that they were frightening even though he had experienced them in other exacerbations. Along with limits, medications and containment, reassurance and reality testing were active interventions with Tom.

Grief. The loss of a potentially brilliant future was a major difficulty for Tom. Tom actively grieved for this loss at intervals. His delusional system denied him the status he hoped for with a brilliant career as a nuclear physicist.

Anger. Tom's anger and impulsivity made him potentially dangerous. When he was actively psychotic with command hallucinations he was potentially lethal (Rockwell, 1972). His previous losses of control had included assaults on others, particularly people who had attempted to intervene when he tried to do things based on his delusions.

Noncompliance. Tom's inability to maintain a medication regime had been the major cause for rehospitalization. In spite of court-ordered injectable Prolixin, Tom was noncompliant. Tom stated that he quit taking his medication when he felt better because it made his speech slurred and he had felt better. Tom did not understand his illness and the importance of compliance with his medication regime. When he was reconstituted, his intellect was an important asset.

Self-care deficit. When Tom was psychotic, he did not attend to his personal hygiene. With less than twenty-four hours of psychoactive medications, Tom became interested in his appearance. Tom expressed his first compensatory skills in self-care, stating that he felt better when he shaved and washed up.

Ineffective coping. Tom's lack of ability to more effectively manage his chronic mental illness was a major cause for his repeated admissions to psychiatric hospitals. The chronicity of his disease ruled out active participation in this management.

Low self-esteem. Tom's low self-esteem was enhanced by his perception of being socially unacceptable. He expressed powerlessness to change his self-image.

Assessment Summary

Tom's power assets were his intellect, supportive family, and rapid compensation.

Regardless of the diagnosis, aggressive clients come to the hospital for continuous professional mental health care. They cannot safely receive this care any place other than on an inpatient unit. Public and client safety is a primary purpose of any inpatient psychiatric unit. Treatment cannot occur unless clients and staff feel safe. When an out-of-control client is admitted to the hospital, the focus of treatment is safety. Interventions on admission are directed toward control and safety to allow the most complete client assessment. Power is in the hands of the staff. As the client is able to control his behavior, power is returned to him.

When Tom was admitted, involuntary medications and seclusion were used to control his behavior. With chemical and mechanical restraints, Tom was able to reconstitute quickly, and the continued assessment was possible.

Multidisciplinary treatment planning can be carried out by using a primary care team. This group consists of a physician, various levels of nursing staff, a social worker and various kinds of occupational, recreational and spiritual therapists. Weekly treatment planning sessions should be scheduled. Specific client problems are identified. Problem lists can be generated combining medical and nursing diagnoses and/or descriptive problems (i.e., disposition). Goals, outcomes, and ways to achieve these goals are written to focus on discharge and contribute to the consistency of care (Fig. 15-1).

ASSESSMENT TOOL

SUBJECTIVE	OBJECTIVE
ANXIETY	
How do you know when you are nervous or upset?	Signs and symptoms-describe behaviors.
What things upset you?	
What did you do in the past to reduce your anxiety?	Past History–displays of anxiety–what was effective
What was effective?	
FEAR	
What kinds of things frighten you?	Signs and symptoms–describe behaviors.
What is the worst thing that could happen to you?	Past History-how has client acted when frightened?
How do you feel when you are frightened?	
GRIEF	
What do you think has been happening to you?	History of losses.
What do you think might happen to you?	Responses to loss.
Who could help you through this illness?	Level of functioning after each loss.
ANGER	
What happens when you are angry/frustrated?	Signs and symptoms–describe behaviors.
Have you ever lost control?	
What happened? What is helpful?	Past history–when angry.
Is there a history of violence/-suicide attempts: What did you think would happen when you did this?	History of violence/suicide attempts including precipitants.

SUBJECTIVE	OBJECTIVE
NONCOMPLIANCE	
What has your doctor suggested you do for your condition?	History of noncompliance.
What have you been doing for your condition (details)?	Problems that have occurred with noncompliance.
Why have you chosen not to pursue this course?	
What would help you to comply with treatment?	
SELF-CARE DEFICIT	
Are you able to take care of yourself?	Note appearance and ability of the client to care for himself.
Who will help you through this hospitalization?	What level of care does the client need?
	Past history of incidents demonstrating self-care deficit.
INEFFECTIVE COPING	
How do you handle stress? problems?	History of past stress and coping.
	Observations that indicate ineffective coping.
LOW SELF-ESTEEM	
How do you feel about yourself?	Behaviors that indicate feelings of low self-esteem.
What do you do well?	History of past incidents of low self-esteem.

Fig. 15-1. Assessment Tool

In the first treatment planning session, the following four problems were identified for Tom: 1) schizophrenia, 2) noncompliance, 3) powerlessness, and 4) disposition. Powerlessness was identified as a problem for Tom as reflected by his irritability, resentment, and anger (McFarland and Wasli, 1986). The goal for resolution of this problem was to increase Tom's ability to control his treatment (Figure 15-2).

PROBLEM: Powerlessness related to chronic mental illness
GOAL: To increase Tom's skill in controlling his response to treatment.

Date	Interventions	Outcome	Staff
6/10/88	Encourage Tom's attempts at self-care. Provide structure as necessary.	Tom will take control of self-care activities.	Nursing
	Reality orientation of environment. Reassure and encourage Tom to question distortions. Review treatment plan with Tom as necessary. Provide consistent, predictable milieu.	Tom will have realistic perception of his environment.	Nursing Medicine Social Work O.T., R.T.
	Encourage Tom to attend and participate in all prescribed treatment activities. Provide Tom with the opportunity to talk about treatment. Educate Tom about rationale for treatment program and medication regime. Attend medication groups. Provide medication teaching materials.	Tom will participate in treatment milieu with increasing consistency.	Nursing O.T. R.T.
	Teach Tom problem-solving approach. Encourage looking at multiple options.	Tom will increase problem-solving skills.	Nursing
	Encourage Tom to explore other leisure and stress-reducing activities.	Tom will identify more leisure activities.	Nursing R.T. O.T.

Review Note: Discussed with client. Refused to sign. States "I'll think about it." M. Smith, RN

Fig. 15-2. Tom's Treatment Plan

As much as possible, the empowering activity of client participation in treatment is fostered. In psychiatry, clients are encouraged to participate with the treatment team to the best of their ability. Control is returned to the client as soon as possible. Minimally, the treatment plan is reviewed with the client in order to gain compliance. With higher functioning clients, participation at the planning sessions is encouraged.

Passive Clients. The passive client "gives up" or perceives as futile the expression of loss of personal control. He pulls inward on himself, hiding from or avoiding those situations about which he feels powerless. Powerlessness is the denial of self in the passive person (Robinson, 1983). He acts like an ostrich, denying the presence of painful thoughts, feelings, and memories. He shrugs his shoulders, asking "What's the use?" and believing himself even less worthy of esteem.

Passive clients become experts in the manipulation of others without having to exert the physical energy of the aggressive client. This client has learned strength through fragility, maneuvering significant others in his life through his stance of helplessness and the appeal for sympathy from others. This client wields abusive power over others. This abusive power enhances the client's feelings of powerlessness rather than diminishing them. The client recognizes the resentment and distaste of others for their company. Rather than feeling stronger, the passive individual spirals downward into a well of powerlessness, his self-esteem lowered by the expression of dislike of and bitterness toward him by significant others. He often expresses helplessness to improve his life situations.

As helplessness is often a socialized characteristic of women, more women present with passive methods for dealing with life. Most women are less direct than men in the expression of the need for control of their life situations.

Passive clients are often in despair and express hopelessness and the feeling that "there is no use, existence is a misery" (Robinson, 1983). All motivation for existence is not gone, however, or the client would no longer be alive. Without any such motivation, there would be no eating, attending to where elimination took place, using a bed for sleep or putting on clothing. Therefore, with that spark of motivation still remaining, the health care provider can work to encourage increased strength in those areas and in the improvement of the client's self-image.

With a betterment in these factors, the client no longer needs to use the abusive power of fragility over significant others. These areas of improvement are vital in the pursuit of building the client's personal power.

CASE STUDY

Maria was a 51-year-old Italian Catholic wife and mother of five. During the past eight months, she had become increasingly fearful, depressed and unable to complete her usual activities. She saw a psychiatrist over the past two and a half months and demonstrated little response to two series of tricyclic antidepressants.

Maria was the only daughter of Italian immigrants. She had six brothers. After attending parochial schools, she worked a year as a clerk in her uncle's store. She married and had five children, four sons and a daughter. She never returned to work outside the home. She was active in church and the Italian community. Most of her friends were the women with whom she had attended school or family members. A year ago her best friend's husband died suddenly from a myocardial infarction, Maria's daughter married and moved to California, and her youngest son entered the military. The three older children were out of the home. Following the son's departure, Maria's fastidious housekeeping declined and she stopped cooking. She stopped attending Altar Society meetings and had few contacts with her old friends. She developed a sleep disturbance with early morning awakening, a 20 pound weight loss, and had numerous gastrointestinal disturbances.

At the time of admission, Maria was a tearful, frightened woman who clung to her husbands' arm. Her previously manicured nails were chipped and broken. Her soiled knit dress was obviously two sizes too large. Her pink, fluffy, bedroom slippers were new. When she removed her black matted wig, her previously tinted hair had an outgrowth of approximately three inches. When asked why she came to the hospital she replied, "My family thinks I need to be here."

During the nursing assessment, in addition to the previous information, she reported extreme exhaustion, constipation requiring daily laxatives, and "trouble having thoughts." She reports an inability to complete anything, crying "I was the best cook in my family." She wondered what her husband did when he helped her widowed friend put up her storm windows. When asked about suicidal ideation, she responded "I'm Catholic." When questioned further, she tearfully said, "I just want to die," but denied a plan. She reported her mother "just went to bed" after her father's death.

A conceptual framework that can be used to assess the psychiatric client's power is the list of power sources: physical, intellectual, emotional, cultural and spiritual. These resources provide strength and energy to the client's power and, thus, recuperation abilities. The assessment of these areas helps to identify the client's strengths.

Unlike Tom, Maria was more able to answer formal questions and interview. Her energy level was low and data gathering needed to be done in several sessions. After the usual admission procedures, the primary nurse set up a series of time-limited interviews with Maria to begin a therapeutic relationship and gather assessment data.

Physical. Although Maria had been seen by her gynecologist in the past year, a review of systems was done. Maria had a weight loss of 20 pounds, one of the four vegetative signs of depression (Barry, 1984). Her gastrointestinal symptoms were nausea, dyspepsia and intermittent constipation and diarrhea. Though the gastrointestinal complaints could be a vegetative sign of depression, referral was made to a physician for further assessment. Maria's inability to carry out self-care activities was noted. When asked why this was difficult, Maria replied that she was "too tired" and "I just don't care."

Intellectual. Although Maria has not worked out of the home, she has a number of intellectual talents. Familially, higher education was not valued but Maria had demonstrated the ability to use her intellect in the past. She did not understand her illness and was waiting for it to "run its course" or for the doctor to give her "the right medicine."

Emotional. Maria "clung" to her husband and expressed reliance on her family to meet her emotional needs. When she no longer had her family at home, she deteriorated. She admitted to an inability to utilize her women friends for support.

Cultural. Maria was a middle-aged woman who had spent her life in a culture where the family was all important and pain was intolerable and was to be relieved immediately. She reported that conformity was valued, emotion freely expressed and illness was kept secret (Rozendal, 1987). She had the role-model of her mother taking to her bed when she experienced a loss.

Spiritual. For Maria, the Catholic Church was highly respected and the focus of much of her life. The Church holidays were often the events for extended family gatherings. Strength, resiliency and acceptance of one's life were values that were part of Church beliefs.

Assessment Summary

Maria was a member of a culture that has specific values and beliefs and her care had to include those beliefs in order to be effective. Her care required her participation, which was not necessarily her value. Physical symptoms needed to be further evaluated.

When writing the initial care plan for Maria, her primary nurse identified nursing diagnoses related to each of the resources of power:

Physical. Self-Care Deficit (Level IV)

Intellectual. Knowledge Deficit related to the inability to use information sources

Emotional. Ineffective Coping (individual)

Cultural. Hopelessness
Spiritual. Spiritual Distress

Maria's powerlessness was expressed in all areas. Hopelessness and powerlessness are often difficult to differentiate in the literature. A client who is hopeless is hard to define due to the vagueness and subjectivity of the term. "Hopelessness is defined as a subjective state in which an individual sees limited or no alternatives or personal choices available and is unable to mobilize energy on his own behalf" (Gordon, 1987).

Many defining characteristics of hopelessness and powerlessness are similar to and consistent with depressive disorders. "Powerlessness is defined as perceived lack of control over a situation in which actions will not significantly effect the outcome" (Gordon, 1987). Behaviorally, Maria displayed depressed behaviors. Nursing care plans were developed to address her behaviors.

In using the primary nursing model, Maria's nursing care plan had two purposes:

1. The communication of information regarding care of Maria.
2. To document the nursing process as the foundation of the care plan.

The true value of the care plan is demonstrated by its ability to communicate with other staff members (Manthey, 1980). In order to achieve these purposes, the psychiatric nursing care plan needs to be clear, concise and enforceable.

As with Tom, Maria's participation in her treatment program was important for her empowerment. The more able she was to participate in her treatment, the more likely she was to return to her baseline functioning (Fig. 15-3).

When the care plan was discussed with Maria, she cried, saying "I just want some rest. I can't think about all those things." Maria was assured that meeting every goal was not expected the first day and that the target of keeping herself clean might be all she could work on the first week. Maria seemed to be relieved and then said, "What will you tell my husband?" She was assured that her husband would be told that she was ill and would be in the hospital a while. She expressed appreciation for the staff's understanding.

As Maria began to respond to the structure of the care plan, her response was evaluated. Interventions were altered based on the assessment of the client's current status. Increased control within the care plan empowered Maria to begin again to take charge of her life.

The more Maria was able to participate in the assessment process, the more empowered she became, increasing her self-esteem and decreasing her depression. Daily review of the care plan increased her self-awareness. With depressed clients, this process will have to continue minimally for several weeks and perhaps throughout the period of treatment. Self-evaluation and the ability to see improvement are some of the last elements to return to the depressed client. Maria's baseline lack of ability for self-observation and insight slowed this process. With assistance Maria was returned to baseline functioning within a culturally acceptable framework. Using her culture as a support system while encouraging the self-evaluation and insight begun as an inpatient, was the delicate responsibility of the outpatient therapist.

Goals:
1. Participate in treatment program.
2. Make decisions about treatment and future.

	Problem	Outcome	Interventions
1.	Self-Care Deficit (Level IV)	Will be able to complete her ADLS with little assistance or direction.	Review unit schedule and expectations with client. Encourage her to select time for self-care activities. Help her develop a plan for self-care activities. Review and refine the plan daily with Maria until she is abel to carry out plan with minimal supervision.
2.	Knowledge Deficit related to inability to use information sources	Will understand her illness, predisposing factors and how to avoid relapse.	Will attend education groups concerning depression and anti-depressant medications. Learn to journal: feelings, ideas, likes, dislikes, memories, and any material that is pertinent to her feeling happy and/or sad. Will identify when she knows she is getting more depressed and what, and who, makes her feel better.
3.	Ineffective Coping (individual)	Will be able to identify precipitants and outline a plan of action.	Will have brief one-to-one during each day and evening shift with her primary nurse/designee to discuss: 1. Precipitants of hospitalization 2. Those activities that bring her pride and pleasure 3. Assess her suicide potential

Problem	Outcome	Interventions
4. Hopelessness	Will develop a plan of action	During one-to-ones will develop a progressive plan of action by: 1. Making a list of alternatives to her present homemake/mother role (i.e. volunteer work) 2. Evaluation of support system 3. Activation of support system 4. Setting realistic goals for self in activating plan 5. Integrating those cultural values that support her wellness
5. Spiritual Distress	Will be able to use faith as a support system in her life.	Encouraged to talk about role of faith in helping her through this hospitalization. Encouraged to talk with spiritual advisor regarding lack of support she feels from faith at this time.

Review Note: Discussed with client. States, "Too tired to sign." M. Smith, R.N.

Fig. 15-3. Maria's Nursing Care Plan

Outpatient Clients. The client in this category holds down a job, keeps house, and/or functions within his normal environment. He may see himself as unable to cope with normal stimuli. Medication may make his life more bearable yet reinforces his perception of being incapable of facing the world without a crutch, thus decreasing his self-esteem. Depending on his circle of friends and family, he either brags about being in therapy or lives in dread that someone will find out that he needs some help coping with his world. He feels powerless to change without help.

The trend toward placing or retaining more and more clients in the outpatient environment forces the health care professional to re-evaluate her perception of the disposition needs of these clients (Stuart and Sundeen, 1983). There is a need to change the idea that all psychiatric clients must be hospitalized. As a microcosm of society-at-large, health care professionals must deal with this inaccurate picture of these clients.

CASE STUDY

When Darla came to the outpatient clinic, she wanted to "have a happy life." Darla was a 26-year-old white woman who had had several hospitalizations as an adolescent. She refused to have her previous records released because "they didn't really understand." She did say she had taken two overdoses and that her family "wouldn't come to therapy."

Darla was the youngest of two children. An older brother had died accidentally when Darla was two years old. Her parents divorced soon after her brother's death. Her mother returned to the fundamentalist church she had been raised in, and Darla was raised as part of that community. Darla had very little contact with her natural father after her parents' stormy divorce. Her mother then married a man who was very active in her church community. Darla's upbringing was strict and harsh.

Darla had two brief marriages, both to abusive men. She had a series of clerical and retail jobs. Her friendships and romantic involvements were intense and short-lived. She used alcohol, self-mutilation and prescribed minor tranquilizers to alleviate the anxiety and depression she experienced.

Her only sustained relationship was with a church elder, Clement, who financed her cosmetology training and her very successful beauty salon. The precipitant to Darla's initiating the clinic visit was the elder's wife, Darla's mother, and other church members learning of the twelve year liason.

On presentation, Darla was tearful, with suicidal ideation and a plan for overdosing. She described feelings of depression, beginning with the increasing success of the beauty salon. She reported a sleep disturbance and weight gain of five pounds over the past two weeks.

When asked about her goals for treatment, she responded, "I just want to feel better."

The immediate assessment necessary at Darla's first evaluation appointment was for suicide with a plan for overdosing. Darla had access to numerous prescription medications.

Suicide is a powerful statement. It is powerful tool. In the United States each year about 20,000 people commit suicide, while 100,000 people make the attempt (Amen, 1987). According to Amen, the task of the clinician is to:

1. Identify high-risk people.
2. Attempt to determine the meaning of the behavior.
3. Decide if immediate hospitalization is indicated.
4. Determine if hospitalization would be beneficial.

In identifying high-risk groups, Patterson et al. (1983) use the acronym of SAD PERSONS:

Sex
Age
Depression
Previous Attempts
Ethanol or drug abuse
Rational thinking loss
Social support lacking
Organized plan for suicide
No spouse
Sickness

One point is scored for each factor present. The range is from 0 for little risk to 10 for high risk. Darla scored a 7 and it was determined to admit her for a stay on the psychiatric admission unit.

Client	Assessment
When asked what she thought would happen if she over-dosed—Darla responded with a smile, "Then Clement wouldn't need to make a decision." She went on to explain that the man she had been involved with for many years was considering divorcing his wife. "He needs to make some decisions. I'm not getting any younger. Sure, he knows how bad I feel," smiling.	Darla has a history of two previous overdoses as an adolescent, history of alcohol and substance abuse, an organized plan of suicide and is unmarried. By history, she is a moderate risk.
When asked about previous overdoses—"My mom got real upset"—with a laugh "she got off my back though."	Darla has revealed a hoped-for manipulation—to force Clement to make a decision about his marriage.
When asked about Clement—"He's taking me to dinner tonight."	It appears that Darla has a very powerful plan to maniulate Clement and her mother.
When asked about her mother—"She's real bent out of shape. She always comes around—she feels real guilty."	As it is unclear whether the plan is successful, a brief hospitalization would be indicated to further assess her support systems and the lethality of her plan.

Fig. 15-4. Admission Assessment

After a two day stay on the psychiatric admission unit, several family/significant other meetings were held. It was felt by the adult inpatient unit that Darla was safe to be discharged. A meeting was held with Darla, her mother and stepfather and another meeting with Darla and Clement. His wife had asked him to leave the house. Darla's mother, although embarrassed by the disclosures, planned to "stand by Darla." Darla agreed to continue her outpatient evaluation on a weekly basis for two more sessions. A written contract was drawn up to insure Darla's safety. She would contact the nurse clinician should she have suicidal ideation with or without a plan. If there were any changes with her mother or Clement as support systems, she would call the clinician. Although this might be regressive, safety was the first priority.

Client	Assessment
Darla talked about how difficult it was with her mother and her husband always checking on her.	Unsure of support and trust.
"They want to be sure Clement isn't living with me." She was able to renew her safety contract but was obviously upset by her mother's behavior. "She always expects the worst of me."	Does mother or Darla feel this way? Is Darla dangerous to herself?
When asked about suicidal ideation and plan Darla denied it—"I'm really doing just fine; those two days in the hospital changed my life." She was excited and glad to be back at her beauty parlor. Later she was asked about a prescription for her "nerves." When pushed, she revealed that she hadn't worked all day as prescribed.	The all good/all bad concept described by Kernberg (1976) in his description of splitting. The client needs to see her words as all black or all white. It is important that these clients are evaluated frequently, but not overprotected.

Fig. 15-5. Second Session

When the clinical specialist agreed to see Darla, it was for a three session evaluation. The focus of these evaluation sessions was the client's safety and an assessment regarding long-term therapy.

After the two day hospitalization, Darla carried a diagnosis of Borderline Personality Disorder. She had at least six of the light DSM-III diagnostic criteria. Darla's suicide potential was at least moderate.

A safety contract was outlined with contingencies for out-patient treatment with the clinical specialist. A contract fostered a collaborative process between Darla and the clinical specialist. This relationship empowered the client as a partner in her treatment.

Safety Contract

I, _____ , have negotiated the following agreement with my therapist, _____ . I understand this is a requirement of my continued outpatient treatment. It can be discussed at any session. However, when several sessions are devoted to this, resistance, transference, and countertransference should be discussed.

I agree to contact my therapist or designee if:

1. I have suicidal ideation with or without a plan. I will follow the recommendation. I will have the opportunity to object to the recommendation, but I understand that my failure to comply can result in the termination of my treatment.

2. I have any change in my support system (family and friends). This can be a positive or negative change. I will follow the recommendations. I will have the opportunity to object to the recommendations but I understand that failure to comply can result in the termination of my treatment.

I agree that if I am feeling overwhelmingly like acting on my impulses and other interventions are unsuccessful, I will go to the Emergency Psychiatric Department.

Client's Signature _____ **Date** _____

Therapist's Signature _____ **Date** _____

Fig. 15-6. Darla's Safety Contract

One of the best ways to provide structure and still return control of the care to the client is the behavioral contract. It is a process that nurtures cooperative efforts between the staff and client to meet specific goals (Lippet, 1978). The aim of such contracts is to engage the client in structured participation in the nursing care process, minimize regression, and provide the desired elements of control (McEnany and Tescher, 1985). In negotiating a contract with a psychiatric client, safety is the first priority and the first group of behaviors to be addressed. The behavioral expectations should be written descriptively and in detail. Using the client's words to describe the specific behaviors can give it more meaning, reduce splitting and increase compliance.

Summary

The powerlessness of mental illness is among the most difficult with which to cope. Treatment requires maintenance of client safety while assisting him in appropriate behavior and regaining control of his life. This chapter used case studies exemplifying aggressive, passive and outpatient clients to describe this powerlessness and interventions to empower the clients. Suggested assessment tools for evaluating the degree of perceived powerlessness in the client are included.

References

Aiken, Linda. Unmet needs of the chronically mentally ill: will nursing respond? *Image: Journal of Nursing Scholarship.* Vol.19, Number 3, Fall 1987. pp.121-125, (1987).

Amen, Daniel. Target theory of suicidal behavior. *Resident and House Physician.* Oct. 87 pp.91-101, (1987).

Barry, Patricia. *Psychosocial Nursing Assessment and Intervention.* Philadelphia: J.B.Lippincott Company, (1984).

Beck, Cornelia, Rawlins, Ruth, Williams, Sophronia. *Mental Health-Psychiatric Nursing: A Holistic Life-Cycle Approach.* St. Louis: The C.V.Mosby Company, (1984).

Bruss, C.R. Nursing diagnosis of hopelessness. *Journal of Psychosocial Nursing.* Vol. 26, Number 3, pp. 28-31, (1988).

Campbell, L. Hopelessness: a concept analysis. *Journal of Psychosocial Nursing.* Vol. 25, Number 2, pp. 18-22, (1987).

Carpenito, Linda *Nursing Diagnosis-Application in Clinical Practice.* Philadelphia: J.B.Lippincott Company, (1983).

Glasser, William. *Reality Therapy.* New York: Harper and Row Publishers, (1965).

Glasser, William. *The Identity Society.* New York: Harper and Row Publishers, (1975).

Glasser, William. *Stations of the Mind: New Directions for Reality Therapy.* New York: Harper and Row Publishers, (1981).

Glasser, William. *Take Effective Control of Your Life.* New York: Harper and Row Publishers, (1985).

Gordon, Marjory. *Nursing Diagnosis, Process and Application.* NY: McGraw-Hill Book Company, (1987).

Haber, Judith, Hoskins, Pamela, Leach, Anita and Sideleau, Barbara. *Comprehensive Psychiatric Nursing* (3rd Ed.). New York: McGraw-Hill Book Company, (1987).

Kernberg, O. *Object Relations Theory and Clinical Psychoanalysis.* NY: Jason Aronson, Inc., (1976).

Lesseig, Delores. Home care for psych problems. *American Journal of Nursing.* October 1987. pp. 1317-1320, (1987).

Lippitt, G. and Lippitt, R. *The Consulting Practice in Action.* LaJolla, CA: University Associates, Inc., (1978).

Manthey, Marie. *The Practice of Primary Nursing.* Boston: Blackwell Scientific Publications, Inc., (1980).

McEnany, G.W. and Tescher, Barbara. Contracting for care: one approach to the hospitalized borderline patient. *Journal of Psychosocial Nursing and Mental Health Services.* Vol. 23, Number 4. April. pp. 8-11, (1985).

McFarland, Gertrude and Wasli, Evelyn. *Nursing Diagnosis and Process in Psychiatric Mental Health Nursing.* Philadelphia: J.B.Lippincott, (1986).

Murray, Ruth and Huelskoetter, Marilyn. *Psychiatric/Mental Health Nursing: Giving Emotional Care.* Englewood Cliffs, NJ: Prentice-Hall, Inc., (1983).

Patterson, W. Evaluation of suicidal patients: the SAD PERSONS scale. *Psychosomatics* 24(4): 343-349, (1983).

Robinson, Lisa. *Psychiatric Nursing as a Human Experience* (3rd Ed.). Philadelphia: W.B.Saunders Company, (1983).

Rockwell, Don. Can you spot potential violence in a patient? *Hospital Physician.* October. pp. 52-56, (1972).

Rozendal, H. Understanding Italian American cultural norms. *Journal of Psychosocial Nursing.* Vol. 25. February. pp. 29-33, (1987).

Scrak, Bernice, Zimmerman, Joanne, Wilson, Marie, and Greenstein, Robert. Moving from "the gas station" to a nurse-managed psych clinic. *American Journal of Nursing.* February 1987. pp.188-190, (1987).

Stuart, Gail and Sundeen, Sandra. *Principles and Practice of Psychiatric Nursing* (2nd Ed.). St. Louis: The C.V.Mosby Company, (1983).

16

Power and the Office Visit

B. Long, R. Montemayor, N. Rinehart,

K. Scarbrough, D. VandeWalle, and H. Williams

Introduction

The client in the office setting seeks relief of symptoms or illness prevention from the health professional. This client then returns to his environment and expects to resume his usual level of functioning. It is not expected that the client will perceive himself as powerless to effect this transformation. However, this client is often placed in a powerless position by the health care provider and is expected to welcome the care deemed necessary by the health care professional. If a treatment regimen is prescribed for the client, he is expected to comply with it. How often does the client question the doctor about her credentials, class standing from professional school or philosophic nuances relating to various clients?

Many clients are simply too frightened to question the health professional's opinion or consider it too expensive to shop around and find a caregiver that the client prefers. He does not relish the consequences he imagines would result if he angered the health care provider. Therefore, he either complies out of fear or awe, or goes home in a confused state and does not comply at all with the prescribed treatment.

Obviously, health care professionals need to make partners of their clients. In order to do this, the caregiver must be interested enough in the client to research his client's values and locus of control. It is ludicrous to expect the high-powered businesswoman to meekly accept the usually male-prescribed treatment plan without question.

Rather than expecting the client to quietly submit to the treatments and prescribed regimens of the health care professional, it is more reasonable to gain his cooperation and partnership. The client who perceives himself as still having some personal power will be much more likely to follow a plan of care because he helped create that plan of care. Providing the client with choices instead of mandates takes more time, but this approach insures better recovery and more satisfaction for the client, and more likelihood that he will return and continue to be a client of the considerate and, in this case, empowering health care professional.

There are many professionals in the fields of nursing and medicine who are actively striving for more client participation in health care and less control by the provider. Smith (1987) discusses the desirability of the client keeping a copy of his health records and participating actively in his choice of medical treatment. Gow (1982) lists the characteristics of nurse control as harmful and unpleasant for clients. Encouraging individuals to assume responsibility for their health is a major theme in the writings of Sehnert (1985). Steiger and Lipson (1985) advocate the importance of teaching self-care methods to clients. Authoritarianism in doctoring is criticized by Shapiro (1987). Travis and Ryan (1988) emphasize a growing need for the client to be aware of his health needs and assume responsibility for his health status.

Disciplines outside of nursing and medicine have a wide variety of methods for empowering clients. Some health care professions have yet to address powerlessness, while others such as dentistry have embraced the theory that clients are healthier if they are encouraged to participate in their health care. The following essays on client empowerment are written by health care professionals outside the nursing and medical physician fields:

Denise M. VandeWalle, D.D.S.

Dental health care providers have a great opportunity to help people understand their health choices in a non-life threatening situation. Clients do not die from most dental-related diseases. Dentistry deals with "lifestyle diseases" such as cavities caused by bad eating habits, gum disease caused by tobacco usage and hygiene habits, temporal mandibular joint problems and tooth breakage caused by stress. Although not usually dealing with life-threatening disease, dental training does include oral detection of life-threatening systemic diseases such as diabetes, high blood pressure, and AIDS.

Dental health providers are somewhat different from the general health providers in their opportunity to empower the client. A person can never stop seeing a dental hygienist or stop caring for his mouth in his lifetime if he is interested in long term health.

Wilson Southam of Ontario has developed a new model for health providers which began with dentistry. Wilson's model (1988) states that the health care setting must be one of authentic caring and freedom first, must respect the rights of the individual to choose what is best for their own health future, and that the ultimate objective is to help people help themselves. He believes that most people will choose to strive towards higher levels of self care if provided with the above stated opportunities.

Spending the necessary time with clients at the onset of the doctor-patient relationship develops and enhances trust, and allows people the freedom to have more complete care. This empowerment of the client helps to eliminate some of the typical patient fears of dentistry.

Many people enter a health care provider's office with an urgent problem and are appalled by the lack of sensitivity and communication in the process. This kind of experience leads to questions for the client as well as the health care provider: "What is health? Who is responsible for the health of a person? Can we change? If so, under what circumstances? Will health care providers be dealing with these issues more in the future?"

CARE PLAN

Subjective

49-year-old female presents with a toothache. She would like to have IV medications for any treatment because of fear and bad feelings about her teeth.

Medical History—Complete blindness in left eye for 10 years, unknown cause. Anaphylaxis from cortisone therapy.

Dental History—Last seen by a dentist five years ago and previous to that only episodically.

Objective

Soft tissue: normal

Dental tissues: chronic moderate generalized periodontitis with severe inflammation. Multiple fractured teeth with mobility, decay and posterior crossbite.

Assessment

1. Dental Phobic client with history of poor compliance.
2. Poor oral hygiene with degenerating periodontal condition.

Plan

1. Treat emergency needs to relieve pain and provide antibiotic coverage during treatment.
2. Initial debridement and oral hygiene instructions.
3. Remove 15 teeth (including three impacted molars) in stages and place temporary partial dentures.
4. Referral to periodontist.
5. Permanent replacements and crowns on remaining teeth.

As this client proceeded through treatment and consultations she had multiple episodes of crying, tremors, and syncopy. It became apparent that she had tremendous apprehension and lack of trust in any health care providers. She had an extremely low dental IQ and was not aware of what treatment had been done in the past to her mouth.

After a long educational period of seven visits, with minor treatment each visit and multiple trust-building exercises, she elected to have the complete comprehensive treatment.

The surgical procedures were completed in two appointments utilizing nitrous oxide gas. The surgery was uneventful except for the development of a postoperative inferior alveolar nerve paresthesia.

After one year of maintenance therapy, the client was referred to a periodontist for an evaluation. She was very apprehensive and cried throughout the examination. She was told she needed treatment and would have to take chloral hydrate and nitrous oxide for procedures. The client proceeded to cancel the next several appointments. She was eventually reached by telephone by the general dentist and stated that she did not want to be made to take drugs and that she did fine previously with just nitrous oxide. She wanted to only be treated by the dentist and hygienist she was used to and who understood her.

She then came in episodically for a period of one year. After multiple consultation appointments, a maintenance program was again established, and within one year, she completed permanent replacements and crowns.

This dental case history demonstrates the rewards and advantages of taking the time to educate and develop trust with clients. Helping people to accept health treatment is dependent upon creating an environment of acceptance, congruence and trust.

An example of the barriers a health provider can impose is the specialist (periodontist) this client was referred to. The mistake was to not take the time initially to develop a trusting relationship. The substitute was a sedative which this client had difficulty accepting.

Holly Williams, D.C.

CASE STUDY

A client presents herself to me several weeks after an auto accident in which she was rear-ended. Since that time, she has been experiencing symptoms commonly associated with a whiplash-type injury: neck and shoulder pain, headaches and perhaps paresthesias of the upper extremities. Clinical findings of the postural, chiropractic, orthopedic, and neurologic examinations correlate to the radiographic study. A diagnosis of cervical sprain/strain, myalgia/myositis and headaches brought on by altered biomechanics of the cervical spine is made.

At the second appointment, the client is shown her x-rays; the findings of the films and the examination are thoroughly discussed. In this "report of findings," I explained to my client that there are three phases to the injury process. In the acute phase, there is swelling and congestion in the injured tissues, muscles go into spasm to protect injured ligaments and joints by restricting motion. Spasms and swelling both contribute to pain. But the primary purpose of the muscles is not to hold the joints together but to move the joints around, so even without treatment the acute stage will resolve itself when the swelling subsides and the muscles relax their guard, this in turn relieves the pain. The joints, however, will continue to be weak. In the second phase, the chronic phase, the client will report that she has good and bad days. Activities which used to cause her no problem now cause a return of her symptoms. Each aggravation of the weakened joint leads to recurring inflammation and protective muscle guarding. The body's natural repair process will form adhesions in and around the joint and soft tissue structures: muscles, ligaments, tendons (and bursa if the joint is so supplied). This leads to the common pain syndrome of these structures. The chronic phase will last many years until the body begins to show signs of the degenerative process with permanent loss of mobility. Arthrosis is a complicated process by which injury to a spinal motor segment results in deterioration and compression of the disc, and accumulation of calcium in the retaining ligaments. The resulting spur formation can often be visualized on radiographs years after an accidental injury. Once these changes occur, there is no way to reverse the process. If the client has degenerative changes on films taken immediately after the auto accident, prognosis for her complete recovery is strongly jeopardized.

Empowering Clients

It is explained to the client that there are three stages to the treatment process. The first is the relief stage. We'd like to get the client out of pain as quickly as possible. For that reason we schedule the first few treatments close together. When the client is feeling better, the frequency of treatments is reduced and they move into the rehabilitation stage. Most "healing" takes place in the first six weeks after a traumatic injury, but the replacement tissue is not functionally adequate to meet the need for strength and endurance. A minimum of six months is required to attain functional rehabilitation and some measure of stability. If significant time passed between the injury and the instigation of appropriate treatment, a proportional increase in rehabilitation time and treatment will be necessary. The third stage of the treatment program is the maintenance stage. It is recommended that clients come in occasionally for a "check-up and tune-up." It is explained that it is easier to keep their spine in good functional order than it is to wait until their symptoms return to start the whole process over again. Some clients agree and come in once a month or so; the chronic pain that they've experienced for years never comes back.

Other clients who have no symptoms for long periods of time prefer to call in for an appointment if they feel they need an alignment. Some clients go for years between visits.

In our office, besides chiropractic manipulation, we utilize a wide variety of physiotherapeutic equipment, orthopedic supports and appliances, and stretching/exercise handouts. A treatment regime is developed for each client. However, in order to do this, the client's complete cooperation is necessary. It is vitally important that the client have a clear understanding of their injury and what is necessary to solve the problem. We can only treat a client who comes in for treatment. If the client is unconvinced that the treatment recommendations are necessary for their health and well-being, lack of cooperation may result in permanent impairment, pain, and disability due to lack of complete follow-up care.

Of course, if the client has a condition which is not treatable by means of chiropractic, they are refered to the correct health care provider. We work fairly regularly with dentists regarding TJM dysfunction following a whiplash-type trauma, and with neurologists and orthopedic surgeons when appropriate.

Comment

Because most new patients have very little familiarity with chiropractic and its concepts, each chiropractor finds it necessary to educate the clients who seek his or her help. The chiropractic clients are unique in one respect, they are open-minded enough to be willing to try an alternative type of health care. Some have had previous personal experience with chiropractic, have heard good things from friends or relatives, or just simply do not want to take drugs for pain relief if there is the possibility of an alternative.

As a result of the multiple appointment treatment program to restore normal articular function in the spine and other joints, the chiropractor has the unique opportunity to follow-up on symptoms which may not have brought the clients into the doctor's office initially, and to teach clients how best to take care of their own health.

Each treatment room has a magazine rack filled with handouts. Clients are encouraged to take a copy of anything that looks interesting to them; for themselves, their family or friends. Clients are given specific exercises to strengthen muscles associated with their injuries or postural problems. They are encouraged to become involved in their rehabilitation, schedule time every day to stretch, exercise, and to take the proper nutrition. The client must take the ultimate responsibility for his own health, or lack of it. He makes the decision to live in pain, or make "quality of life" his primary goal.

So much time was spent telling clients to buy and read books on health, nutrition, diet, stretching and exercise that we finally installed a lending library in the office. We send out a bimonthly newsletter and maintain a bulletin board in the reception area full of newsclippings and summary reports from professional journals. We encourage clients to question authority, mine as well as others'. My clients know that I don't always have the answer on the tip of my tongue, but I often have it at the tip of my fingers, and I don't mind taking a little extra time to look it up in my library.

Rosa Montemayor, D.P.M.

Every client that comes into our office is asked routinely about their past medical history, medications, and of course any allergies. Some people resent this, "I am just coming to get my feet worked on." Here is where my quick two minute education session begins. Some clients do not know what medications they are taking. I suggest, strongly, that all the medications they take should be written on the back of their family doctor's business card so the name, amount, and times taken are all easily accessible. Then I explain how the podiatrist may be the first to spot diseases like diabetes, arteriosclerosis, and skin disorders. In those instances we can refer the client to the proper physician for further care.

CASE STUDY

Subjective

The client is a 36-year-old white female who complains of a "burning sensation" to the top of her left foot present for a few months. Her second and third toes are starting to separate. She also has noticed a lump on the top of her left foot where the toes are separated. The pain is worse after walking.

Observation

Vascular and neurological exam was within normal ranges. Hyperkeratosis noted beneath the second, third and fifth left metatarsal heads and beneath the fourth and fifth right metatarsal heads. There is a soft tissue swelling on the dorsum of the second metatarsal head that extends into the web space laterally. Pain occurs with palpation to the dorsal second metatarsal head and the second web space and interspace left foot. There is no pain with palpation to plantar aspects of the metatarsal heads. A tingling sensation was elicited with palpation to the first and second web space. The second and third digits are noticeably separated both in weight bearing and non-weight bearing. AP and MO x-rays show no bony exostosis, stenosis, or fracture to the left foot but there is a noted separation of the second and third digits.

Assessment

Neuroma left foot.

Treatment Plan

Discussed with the client the following options:

1. Nonsteroidal anti-inflammatory drugs for two weeks.
2. Injection therapy to affected area with local anesthetic and a steroid for a total of three injections.
3. Orthotic control.
4. Ultrasound therapy.
5. Surgical excision of neuroma.

The pros and cons of each procedure were discussed. The client was told she needed to make the decision, that I can only recommend. By discussing her options the client had a better perspective on her total health care needs.

Choices and decisions are the operative words here. Not because of my lack of knowledge, but because of my understanding of the client's needs. They need to make their own decision after being given their options. As we all grew up we were told that the doctor's decision was final. We always felt helpless as the decisions were being made. I want to make sure I do not make my clients feel helpless about their health care. When the client is informed he can make a rational decision without feeling helpless.

I find that many clients are still very hesitant about deciding what to do. Clients ask what I would recommend. When they ask I tell them what I feel is their best alternative. I would prefer that clients make up their own mind but I believe there are two different factors working here. One is the fear of the independence they now have in making the final decision. The second is that some clients state that they came to a specialist to get an opinion not choices. What is important here is education of the client.

If the client assists his doctor in the decision process I feel that he will comply more readily with the treatment. Client compliance is important and if the clients made the final decision about their care, they are more likely to follow through on the treatment plan.

Kerri Willis Scarbrough, O.D.

Subjective

A sixty-six-year-old white male presents for "routine examination."
Medical history: hypertension
Medications: hydrochlorothiazide, Pilocarpine 1% O.S.,
Timoptic 0.5% O.S., Propine 0.1% O.S.

Ocular history: vague blindness of undetermined length O.D., glaucoma 0.5 x 4 months

Objective

Visual acuity: 20/60 with eccentric fixation, 20/25
External ocular health: normal
Pupils: 4 brisk round—RAPD
  1 fixed
Intraocular pressures: 24 mmHg O.U. at 10:00 a.m.
Internal ocular health: macular degeneration O.D., Normal O.S.—
  no glaucomatous cupping

Assessment

1. Macular degeneration O.D. causing "blindness."
2. Glaucoma O.S. by history—no glaucomatous cupping.

Plan

1. No treatment O.D.—described how to monitor O.S. for possible changes in the future.
2. Discussed therapy O.S.—suggested alternative to Pilocarpine (Pilopine gel) to stop frontal headaches upon administration.

Over the course of the examination, the client revealed many things not brought up during the history-taking proper. He proceeded to state that what he really wanted was a second opinion. This was difficult due to his lack of understanding of what he had been told before. His "blindness" was explained to him, connecting this with the aging process and the fact that it would not improve. His left-sided "glaucoma" could not be verified by the clinical observations made at this visit, but he was told that it did not mean that he did not have this disease. He was unable to provide his intraocular pressures on previous visits, an important piece of information necessary to form an opinion. Since he had been put on maximum medications in three months' time, it could only be assumed he did indeed have some problem.

The overall problem was three-fold: 1) poor understanding of the underlying conditions, 2) limited time spent in the past attempting to explain his conditions to him (he was well-spoken and intelligent), and 3) multiple healthcare deliverers giving inconsistent or inadequate information.

He was told, by myself, that the decisions concerning his health were his to make, not anyone else's, as this man has only one eye remaining with excellent vision. It is in his own best interest to encourage him to start insisting on adequate and well-explained care. Practitioners must often be pressed by the client for thorough care.

This client was at a crossroads where he could either pick up on his responsibility for his healthcare or retreat into blissful but potentially blinding oblivion. The optometrist took the time to explain his conditions to him and what he could do about them. Prevention of further loss of vision was now his responsibility, as much or more than the health care deliverer's. Noncompliance carries a heavy toll in his case. It is mystifying and appalling how inadequate care—treating the client as a child or a number, using technical terms without checking for comprehension, and understaffing—is passed off as the way medicine should be practiced. For his own protection the client must realize that the ultimate loser from ignorance or omnipotent health care professionals is himself. No one else is going to become blind, have a stroke, or die for him. So the ultimate responsibility is on his shoulders to insist on adequate and thorough care, develop an understanding of the condition, and comply as best he is able.

Partners in health care—partners? Whatever happened to the paternal, grey-haired man saying, "Take these, you'll feel better." That is the way medicine has been practiced for centuries. Now we are partners? Nurses, therapists, and counselors are taught to care for and get to know their clients, whereas doctors, especially those whose clientele are generally healthy, are taught overtly and covertly that the old pattern is still best.

Although clients are pleased to find a doctor-client relationship based on mutual respect, there are those who prefer the "old school," taking comfort in being told what to do. Most of us probably secretly relish that familiar feeling of security in the midst of crises, but it is a dangerous trap for both doctor and client. Not only does being told what to do relieve the client of responsibility, it increases the liability of the doctor regarding such legal issues as informed consent.

The steps one can take to form a partnership with the client are few and deceptively easy: 1) set a good example, 2) educate, educate, educate, and 3) let go.

Consider the three-hundred pound doctor, reeking of tobacco, with a blood pressure of 180/100, telling his client to lose weight, stop smoking, and learn to relax. The old saying is true—one picture is worth a thousand words. Modeling is a prime method for showing clients how to care for their bodies. Displaying wholeness and harmony in the caregiver's life is a strong message.

Another form of modeling is polite gestures such as the handshake. Politeness requires three things: physical contact, eye contact, and verbal exchange. To most societies politeness means coming together in mutual respect, if not equal standing or mutual agreement. Women especially do not expect this courtesy from authority figures and are usually appreciative. Women, after all, are the major purchasers of healthcare and should, therefore, be treated with more respect. One other seemingly minor courtesy is to call clients, especially those over forty or with titles, by their last names. Not doing so can imply disrespect or "coming on."

The second step toward partnership is to educate, educate, educate. Clients deserve to know about their bodies, and more and more are expecting to know what is being prescribed, the side effects, the length of treatment, the treatment options and the expected outcome. These explanations take time and forethought. Even if clients do not want to know or feel they "don't want to bother the doctor," they must be told about their condition. Not only do these explanations keep one out of legal trouble if properly documented, they also enrich the client's understanding of the condition and each partner's role in it. The use of sketches, models, examples, demonstrations, and touching the affected area all help reinforce what is often a technical and overwhelming concept for the client. The routine explanations can be handed over to technicians, but close monitoring is necessary to insure that an adequate knowledge base exists. Clients who arrive stating that they are going blind but do not know why are an indictment against the way optometric healthcare is being delivered by some practitioners.

Clients must be willing to accept responsibility for their bodies in terms of knowing the name of their condition, having a list of their medications and why they were prescribed, and refusing to accept a pat on the hand as an answer for their concerns. They must be willing to listen to what is said and let the care deliverer be a partner, not a god.

This ideal of education over subjugation means repeating everything several times throughout the examination in different ways, then summarizing and asking if there are any questions. To do less is to cheat the client of a chance to be a 50-50 partner and the practitioner of the opportunity to impart some hard-earned knowledge about the condition. Most recipients cannot know the many steps, tests, and deductions it takes to come to a diagnosis and course of treatment unless they are told; then they take on an equal share of the responsibility. If the client then refuses to cut back, stop, start, or modify as prescribed, it is because a choice is made, not because of ignorance. Noncompliance then becomes the client's choice, not the deliverer's shortcoming. Although this is not a guilt "free-for-all," it is sometimes necessary to know where the responsibility lies, even to the extent of saying "See, I am writing in the chart that we discussed...."

The third, and often the most difficult, step is to let go. For most health care practitioners this comes hard. Let go. For the good of the client in front of you, for the client to follow, and for you and your family, one must let go. If the diabetic refuses to lose weight, either adamantly or just through well-rationalized noncompliance, do not take the problem home. Make it clear to the client that the help is there whenever the desire is there. For example, if a glaucoma client is noncompliant the end result is known and the results are irreversible, yet many glaucoma clients are noncompliant. If the first two steps have been followed, then the choice is the client's and must be respected as such. Ignoring further opportunities to restate the condition is foolish, but nagging is counter-productive. This puts the deliverer in the position of "mothering," thus relieving the client of all accountability. It must be stated to the client that the choice is being made by him, not for him. How many smokers are truly ignorant of its link to cancer? How many hypertensives refuse to lose weight? These clients have chosen not to be partners in their health care, they do not want to be. Pump enthusiasm into those searching for direction, be available to those who are not. But, let them all go. These are the steps to being a partner in your clients' health care—not a dictator over it or a victim of it.

Barbara Long, R.P.T.

I specialize in the treatment of cranio-mandibular dysfunction. My particular practice leans towards clients who are experiencing chronic pain of several months, or years duration. Clients are referred to my office by physicians, dentists, oral surgeons, other physical therapists, friends, or relatives. Typically, this individual has suffered with a combination of symptoms including: headaches, neck pains, back pain, facial pain, tinnitus, balance disturbances, and sleep disturbances. Almost without exception, the clients I see have had a long history of medical evaluations and treatments by various specialists. By the time I meet with them for the first time, they are expressing hopelessness and anger at the medical profession that they feel has failed them. It is not uncommon to hear statements such as: "I don't know why I'm here. I was just told to come. Do whatever you want to me." The flip side of this beaten, submissive attitude is anger.

The initial visit is often used as an opportunity to vent feelings of anger and helplessness. Many of these people have undergone a multitude of tests, which usually have shed no light on the etiology of their pain. They have been treated with drugs, splints, manipulations, surgeries, and further referral. At some point they begin to question which referrals are necessary, and which program is worth following. They have been expected to meekly follow whatever plan the attending doctor has prescribed, and they usually have very little understanding of the plan itself, or the relationship of the plan to their pain pattern. They verbalize their feelings of frustration with statements such as: "I've seen every kind of doctor and specialist. None of them know what to do for me. Some of them make me worse. I've spent thousands of dollars and I'm no better. No one will even give me any straight answers. My whole life has changed and no one cares." Clearly, the first obstacle I must overcome if I am to be of any help to these people is to establish some level of trust as early as possible. The second crucial task is to return some sense of control to the client, allowing them to own their own health problem. In this way they can learn to take responsibility for their care and improvement.

Initially, I see varying degrees of attempts to regain some control. Many times the first area for a power struggle is in scheduling. Occasionally, a person may be scheduled two or three times before they finally arrive for their evaluation appointment. Sometimes this remains an important area of control for several weeks, and is demonstrated by inflexibility in scheduling appointments or by canceling or not appearing at scheduled times. Occasionally, clients keep the initial appointment, but are hesitant to commit to treatment. Clients who are having an especially difficult struggle with power issues will dictate to me what they will and will not do on their own. Usually these behaviors change and most clients become more compliant with the program as they begin to gain a sense of control over the course of treatment and the pattern of their pain.

Listening to the history and main areas of complaint at the initial visit and allowing them to vent frustration, fear and anger is a major step towards establishing good communication and a basic level of trust. These individuals need to have their experience validated. They express feelings of inadequacy from having to progressively limit their activities and decrease performance as their pain level has risen over time. They feel guilty that they have failed if they have not been able to live up to their expectations. If we really listen to them, it is not difficult to identify the specific problem areas. We can then take steps to effect a change in the course of their treatment. This may involve referring them to another therapist for treatment closer to home or scheduling therapy less frequently to allow them some relief in a program that is becoming too demanding. Sometimes the client has received fragmented or contradictory care and information. If we hear this message, we can work towards clarifying plans and goals and identify a team coordinator for the client's care. We make an attempt to ease the sense of confusion, failure, and hopelessness. I try always to keep in mind that physical therapy occurs over several weeks or months and truly is taxing on time schedules and normal daily routines.

After hearing the complaints and history, the next step is education. If my clients understand better how their body functions and why they may be feeling the symptoms they complain of, they gain some sense of control over their pain pattern. Constant reassurance that it is important to me that they understand what I am doing, and why, and that their questions are welcomed and necessary for their healing, gives them permission to question and doubt. This helps them feel they are part of the treatment planning, and not just a recipient of treatment. The first treatment does not end without instruction in some kind of home program to begin to control their symptoms on their own. I have noted many times that the improvement verbalized by my clients is almost proportional to the success they find in their home program. As their skill at reading their own bodies improves, and as we add to their tools for self care, their sense of control increases, even though many of the original symptoms may be present to some degree.

Most physical therapists, I feel, are acutely aware of the importance of turning over the responsibility of health care to the client. Our training leans heavily on client education. Without clear understanding of how the body functions, it is difficult for the client to make good choices in their everyday life to protect themselves from further injury and allow successful healing. With this understanding, clients are much more compliant and thus have greater success in a home program. I feel it is very important also to assist clients in understanding and accepting their limits. Wasting emotional and physical energy trying to control or force a body to do what it cannot do will add to the sense of powerlessness and defeat. Working within those limits can bring about feelings of success, new understanding of the body, and healing.

Popular courses of advanced study for physical therapists stress treatment of the whole person rather than treatment of a body part. A "team approach" to treatment is recognized as the most effective way to address all the stages of a client's recovery. For example, it is becoming quite common to progress a client through an acute stage of recovery in the clinic and then refer to a sports therapy center for assistance in developing a long term program. Clients can then take an active part in developing an exercise routine which compliments their life style. It is hoped that this will promote long term benefits of good health.

Many of us are interested in holistic health care. Achieving holistic care, however, may require us to review old ideas of treatment, planning, and goal setting which did not include the client's input. Health care practitioners may need to develop new insights into the psychological position of the client and new skills in management techniques. PT journals and newspapers frequently address these issues. "Clients rights" are discussed in physical therapy departments and PT classes, and lectures on "listening" are given at state meetings.

Therapists are becoming more astute at determining the need to refer to other practitioners for a total team approach. I only caution that we take heed, and remember that the client does have choices in this referral system. I hope we do not get so caught up in determining what is best for the individual client, that we too, forget to listen and allow the client to take part in their health care plan. Their instincts and knowledge of their own pain pattern and past history, along with education, many times are the basis for the best health care plan.

References

Combs, Arthur, Avila, Donald and Puckey, William. *Helping Relationships.* Boston: Allyn and Bacon, Inc., 1985.

Crossly, Larry. *Beyond Illness.* NY: Random House, 1984.

Dossey, Larry. *Beyond Illness.* NY: New Science Library, 1982.

Ferguson, James. The woman with a pain in her neck. *Physical Therapy Forum.* No. 15, April 11, 1988.

Gow, Kathlee. *How Nurses' Emotions Affect Patient Care.* NY: Springer Publishing Company, 1982.

Hadle, Barbara. Chronic pain toward a new perspective. *Physical Therapy Forum.* No. 26, June 27, 1988.

Joy, W. Brugh. *Joy's Way.* Boston: Houghton Mifflin Co., 1979.

Klein, Elanae. When pain is your partner. *Parade Magazine.* July 26, 1987.

Peck, M. Scott. *The Road Less Traveled.* NY: Simon and Schuster, 1978.

Sehnert, Keith W. *Selfcare/Wellcare.* Minneapolis: Augsburg Publishing House, 1985.

Shapiro, Martin. *Getting Doctored.* Philadelphia: New Society Publishers, 1987.

Smith, Stuart L. *Doctor Knows Best:Patient Knows Best.* Wheat Ridge, CO: The Health Professionals, 1987.

Southam, Wilson. *Volitional Practice.* The Group at Cox, Inc. A Center for the Development of Independent Professional Practice. Ontario, Canada, 1988.

Steiger, Nancy J. and Lipson, Juliene G. *Self-Care Nursing: Theory and Practice.* Bowie, MD: Brady Communications Company, Inc., 1985.

Travis, John W. and Ryan, Regina Sara. *The Wellness Workbook* (2nd Ed.). Berkeley, CA: Ten Speed Press, 1988.

17

Power, Women, and the Health Care Professions

N. Rinehart and V. Garner

Introduction

Power is an uncommon term to use in connection with women, particularly those in the health care professions. According to Dowling (1981), many women fear success and avoid those situations that are potentially power building. Therefore, one is led to question whether some women even want to be more powerful or in control of their own lives. Are the women in health care professions comfortable in their powerless positions? Are they uncomfortable when they are encouraged to be more independent? Does their public image suit them?

Women in health care, especially nurses, are seen by much of the public as lackeys or servants and less intelligent than their sisters who work in the man's world of business, engineering and law. However, the public image of women in health care does not have to dictate the reality. The image of women in health care can be altered, but only with the participation of the women involved.

Not all women in health care are powerless and wait for Big Brother to step in and rescue them. Women who have a strong sense of personal control are in the minority, but what they have achieved is possible for the rest of womankind. A sense of personal power is available to all individuals, including women.

The goal of this chapter is the initiation of movement toward personal power for women in health care. This chapter will investigate Power and Women in the Health Care Professions. Relationships with self and others will be explored to depict the evolution of power and the impact history has had on the way women in the health care professions perceive their power orientation. A discussion of the characteristics of women with personal power versus those without power follows.

THE POWERFUL WOMAN HEALTH CARE PROFESSIONAL

As nurses are the largest population of women in health care, a nurse, Julie, is an example of what a personally powerful life can be.

Julie exemplifies personal power and encourages others to reach their potential and take control of their own lives. She is a member of a national nursing association and attends district meetings monthly. Julie writes her congresswoman in support of women's health care legislation. She responds to health issues with letters to the editor of her local paper. She donates one day's salary each year to the lobbyist efforts of her nursing organization. Julie is a member of the board of directors at a local drug rehabilitation center and helped design a program specifically for impaired health care professionals. Julie is a psychiatric emergency nurse. She urges her coworkers to get involved in their interest areas and to get out and vote. She actively explores possible choices for dealing with the issues in nursing and discusses them at work with her peers.

Julie asks her clients' preferences and arranges their care plans to meet their wishes. She discusses her clients' rights with them and encourages them to use assertive communication. She expresses concern for her clients' knowledge deficits and teaches them new methods of self-care. Julie assists her clients to explore their values and motivators. She urges them to reframe their statements to those indicating more personal control and positive thinking. She suggests that her clients remember that they are the employers and allies of the nurses, doctors, and other health care workers, and should expect answers and assistance while fulfilling their part in the partnership.

Julie has two school age children and encourages them to become more responsible in their own lives. When her children blame each other for incidents, she calmly states that no other person can make another angry or sad unless they are allowed to do so. They are encouraged to see school as their work, just as their parents have jobs. Julie does not accept her children's claims that their teachers give them poor grades, but states that they earn grades, and the teacher is not at fault if the grade is less than good. Julie also maintains open communication with her children's teachers and makes sure that her children are not subjected to a teacher who truly does arbitrarily give grades and punishment, rather than fairly assigning what the children earn, as in the teacher who hates little boys and is constantly yelling at and belittling them. Julie assigns her children chores and assists them as necessary, urging them to help out in their home, and be partners in the family.

Julie's husband is supportive and proud of her. She works at their relationship through frequent walks together, talking about what is on her mind with him, and instilling occasional bursts of romance into their days, i.e. love notes in his shirt pocket to be found at work. Julie believes her husband to be romantic and tender, and he lives up to her expectations as she acts toward him in the manner she wants him to act with her.

She belongs to a health club and exercises four days a week after work. Julie quit smoking and has maintained her ideal weight for the past two years, after spending 18 years being 50 pounds overweight. Four years ago she went back to college to earn a bachelor's degree and is now contemplating graduate school. She likes to knit and creates sweaters for her nephews and nieces every year for Christmas. Julie takes spinning lessons to spin her own yarn.

She is an election judge for her precinct's elections and belongs to the League of Women Voters. She volunteers to call others or hand out literature during her political party's campaigns. Julie is an active member of the local chapter of N.O.W. and is openly supportive of the Right to Choice movement in her community. She is active on an advisory board for her church.

When asked how she accomplishes all she does, Julie's response is that she never does anything she does not enjoy so that all work and projects are fun. She states that if work were not fulfilling, she would find some way to make it so, or get another job. Julie looks forward to work each day. She stays involved with, and excited about, the community in which she lives. She believes each individual can make an impact on the world, but only if they participate in life. She lists her two pet peeves as: 1) all the wasted potential power while nurses spend their time fighting within the ranks, and 2) being addressed as a less than intelligent human because of her sex. Julie identifies a strong sense of personal control in her life.

THE POWERLESS WOMAN HEALTH CARE PROFESSIONAL

Nurses and other members of the health team have a tendency to give of themselves beyond their capacity for caring and power (Jacobson and McGrath, 1983). It is as true for health care professionals as anyone else that one can't give away what one doesn't have. Until these professionals build up their own personal power, they will find it difficult to assist their clients in gaining more health care control. Dykema (1985) pleads for the development of power in each professional, and explains that having a sense of personal power determines the individual's ability to lead. The lack of power in the professional promotes lack of power in the health care team, then, powerlessness in the client, as the following example illustrates.

Laura, a staff nurse on an orthopedic surgical unit, is often late to work. She claims to enjoy nursing care but hates the paperwork assigned to her. Every day, coming to work is a chore for Laura with her headaches increasing in strength as she drives closer to the hospital parking lot. Besides chronic headaches, Laura also suffers from irritable bowel syndrome and gastric ulcers. She experiences a great deal of stress in her work position.

Laura is intimidated by the other professionals in her work place. When she identifies a problem on the unit she cannot bring herself to speak with her head nurse about the situation, and thus, is evaluated as unobservant and lacking initiative to improve the unit. Laura has observed many surgeons pass from one client to the next, assessing surgical sites, without washing their hands. Her attempts at getting them to use aseptic technique were brushed aside with brusque irritation by the surgeons involved, so Laura quit trying. She feels guilty because she knows that, as a client advocate, she should do more to protect her clients from nosocomial infections but is afraid of the surgeons.

Laura spends her time off trying to rest up for her next siege at work. She has no hobbies and rarely socializes with anyone other than her immediate family. She complains that she cannot afford the dues when invited to join her nursing organization. She attends church but avoids any involvement with the other members as she is afraid they will ask her to help on some church project that she does not have time for. Laura feels equally negative about the two candidates for the presidency, so does not vote as she believes her vote "will not make any difference anyway."

Laura is unable to manage any of the stress she feels in her daily life. Laura has no close friends to talk to about her problems with work. She rarely exercises. Laura smokes occasionally and often overeats. She takes Valium when her "tension headaches" get severe. She voraciously reads romance novels, particularly when things are more difficult than usual at work.

Laura has a four-year-old daughter. When Laura's child wants to play, Laura sends her outside or into her room to do so. Laura hardly ever plays a board game with her daughter or reads a book to her; she states she is "just too tired." If asked, Laura could not say what her daughter's preschool teacher's name is.

Laura feels out of control, powerless. Observers of Laura's lifestyle and behavior in the health care setting evaluate her as portraying helplessness. Laura's clients are without an advocate to protect them from unhealthy situations, and do not perceive Laura as a nurse that they can trust with their health. Laura's clients' own feelings of powerlessness are therefore heightened by having a nurse who epitomizes the same feelings.

The Problem

This lack of power relates to the overextension and lack of self-replenishing strategies common to many women and, therefore, nursing and other health care professions. Where do these women start? There are so many issues and problems, how does the woman in health care focus on all of them at the same time?

What are the factors that have made health care professions so attractive for women? There continue to be societal expectations that if a girl must grow up and go to work, nursing and teaching are ideal occupations, "until you get married" or "after the children are grown" (O'Reilly, 1980). Is it, then, the expectation that women in health care must continue to follow their socialized role of subservience and sacrifice (Dowling, 1981; Muff, 1982)? Understanding the historical role of women will explain the present situation.

History of Women in Health Care

Women have long searched for their proper place in society. In order to understand the plight of women in health care professions, the role of womankind through history must be mentioned. Stevens (1983) states that the fact that the ranks of health care professionals, other than doctors, are women-dominated, reinforces the continuation of women's traditional role and contributes to the weak power base of women in health care.

Systematic and sanctioned discrimination against women is recorded in Genesis. The *Bible* appears to bestow on these practices of selectivity an undeserved aura of piety. Ensuing centuries seem to have encouraged the persistence of these values. Proponents of female discrimination found it convenient to quote God in support of their position.

Earliest common law suspended the rights of a single female once she married. The unity of flesh between husband and wife, a biblical concept, served as the basis for the doctrine of coverture, or low status of women during marriage, and further supported the 'natural' dominance of the male. Even the woman's legal responsibility was submerged into that of the husband.

Male sexual privileges have similarly been protected throughout recorded history in Europe, America, Egypt, and Greece, to name a few. The social burden and guilt for adultery continues to fall most heavily, if not exclusively, on the female. Furthermore, women have accepted harsher legal penalties for their actions. Ever since Eve exhorted Adam to taste the forbidden fruit, women have been seen as seductresses who tempt guiltless men.

It was in 1860 that a measure of contractual and property rights were given to married women by the Married Women's Property Act (Stephenson, 1981). It was 1920 before women could vote, seventy-two years after it was first proposed at a meeting in Seneca Falls, New York; the 1964 Civil Rights Act banned sexual discrimination; and in 1968 discriminatory sentencing finally became unconstitutional (Stephenson, 1981). In 1923 the Equal Rights Amendment began its uphill battle and the end is not yet in sight. These events have conditioned women to view themselves as powerless and insignificant.

Through their socialization process, males and females have learned that there are well defined roles and places for each of them. This stereotyping has deprived society of the essence of whatever "femaleness" is, and what it has to offer in certain roles. It has also withheld from children and families the economic privileges of being able to provide improved life styles for themselves.

Women and children represent the greatest class of legal non-persons in our country. They have had little access to law except through men. They have little or no voice in the legislature, no standing in court, and little control over the regulations that govern their lives. For years, women contented themselves with their plight. This bleak history is changing dramatically.

The advent of the women's movement in the twentieth century has radically altered the role of women. These changes have impacted behaviors, attitudes, beliefs, and standards. The feminist movement has brought about major changes for all of society. However, women in nursing have not benefited as greatly as those in more nontraditional fields. The feminist movement has directed much of its energy toward moving women into non-traditional fields of study. Unfortunately, nursing has been viewed as one of the female ghettos from which women should escape.

For too long, nurses, because the majority are women, have been caught between their own desires, needs and values, and those prescribed for them by men. Tradition places a heavy burden on women, thus on nurses, because noncompliance creates severe economic and emotional burdens destined to perpetuate compliance.

Nurses must begin to view their roles as having the multiple dimensions of professionalism, independence, and power. Nursing provides an opportunity to participate in an autonomous, independent, extremely specialized, decision-making professional role. Nurses must not allow their contributions and influence upon society to be overlooked.

Florence Howe (1975) urged women to make the most of their dominance in certain roles, and urged that they stop moaning and groaning and use their influence in fields like nursing, education, and social work. Rather than urging the most energetic and talented newcomers to serve as tokens in nontraditional fields of study, Howe supports the maintenance of control over these areas, capitalization on women's strength in numbers and development of "womanpower" to change these three major service professions. Women should focus on their potential for power in these areas.

Nurses are beginning to awaken to the value of their profession as a significant career. They no longer view nursing as preparation for marriage. Nurses are joining other women to work for women's rights.

Women in the health professions can exert their power to influence women's health care. Nurses have joined political groups for example, to fight for reproductive rights.

Relationship with the Public

What is the public image of women in the health care professions? What image do women in the health care professions have in the media, entertainment, and social setting? How do women in the health care professions see themselves reflected in the eyes of the public?

Women in the health care professions have been too passive in allowing non-health care professionals to dictate their public image. Nurses, as the largest group among these professions, are portrayed in unflattering and belittling roles for the public to laugh about and accept as valid. Many women in health care hesitate to tell a social acquaintance what their profession is because of their public image. For example, nursing students often receive unwelcome attention from young men as a result of the loose and easy reputation of nurses that has been promoted by books, television, and movies. The image of the nurse as a woman with loose morals may sell books, but is devastating to the profession itself. Rather than write and protest these false images, many nurses mutter in dissatisfaction, but do nothing constructive to combat this picture of their profession.

The impact of public opinion is clearly reflected in the woman health care professional who echoes the judgment that if she were intelligent, she would have sought a more prestigious job, a profession that paid well and earned respect. When the professional accepts this idea as fact, she is diminishing her self-esteem and forgetting about the effort it took to enter her chosen profession. While other women on campus were taking liberal arts classes, the health professions student took on biochemistry, pathology, microbiology, and the sobering clinical experiences of birth and death. Nursing students are required to complete more clinical hours and accumulate more credits than do most other college baccalaureate program graduates. Women in medical, dental, and optometry schools have to prove themselves qualified far more often than do the men in their classes. With these facts in mind, a woman has the basis for pride in her profession rather than shame for being less than women who work in business or other nonhealth care professions.

Relationship with Self

What is the self-image of women in the health care professions? Some women, according to Shainess (1984), have masochistic tendencies which have their roots in the abuses of power in the parent-child relationship, leaving the woman fearful of others and unable to: set limits, refuse to perform a task, resist the expectations of others, and/or risk offending anyone. In such cases, the abuse against the masochistic woman health care professional is reinforced. These women need the assistance and guidance of the more assertive members of their group.

Health care professionals are, as are individuals in other service professions, prone to experience severe stress that often leads to "burn-out." McGear and Hadley-Meenk (1988) describe the candidate for overstress, or burnout, as an idealist who refuses to compromise her expectations of herself and others and pushes herself too hard and too long. When the hospital administration rewards assessment writing rather than client contact, as described by Jones (1978), the health care professional can hide from the emotional effort of involvement with clients by placing paperwork and a clipboard between themselves and the stress. If the stressors can be identified and dealt with, they do not need to be the enemy (Scully, 1980). Tierney and Strom (1980) describe the nurse as a Type A2 person, or an overly committed worker, always ready to sacrifice her time, family and health for her job, as opposed to the Type A1 individual who works to excess for personal gain.

Very few people are absolutely at ease with themselves; however, many have made a reasonable attempt to establish a self-relationship they feel comfortable enough to live with. Many of these fairly content people are women in the health care professions. They are predominantly women who are bright, articulate, self-directed, organized, and extremely people-oriented. As professionals, many women have been socialized to establish the following:

- High expectations of self
- High expectations of clients
- Orderly work arrangements
- Strong work ethics
- Perfection in professional role

These expectations are demanding and somewhat unrealistic, yet ever-present. They drive many professionals to create unrealistic goals and objectives for themselves. These goals demand that the woman seek to continuously increase personal and professional power, although these characteristics are in direct conflict with her socialization. These aspirations push her to be overly self-critical as an individual and a professional. The end results of unrealistic self and professional expectations are burn-out, abuse of power, illness, addiction, and other stress-related consequences. Women must learn to be more aware of what they do to themselves. They must learn to identify their limitations and live with them.

Limitations

Anne Wilson Schaef, in her book *Women's Reality*, related a startling finding from her intense study of women (1981). She concluded that women normally do not like or trust one another. She further related that women, while intelligent and skillful, suffer from basic feelings of self-doubt. Women often express, by their actions, the notion that they're born "tainted." According to Schaef (1981), women appear to need male validation and approval to feel fulfilled. This theory, if pushed further, implies that since women are socialized to dislike one another they often find it difficult to support one another's efforts.

How does this negative view of themselves impact their personal and professional views of power? Women's individual power orientations are driven by their views of themselves. If women have difficulty accepting power as natural, desirable, or instinctive, it is likely related to their general feelings of low self-esteem. Women must capitalize on the positive end results of their natural tendencies (femaleness). Individually, women must acknowledge that they have special power through their caring, nurturing, professional roles, and expertise. They must accept the fact that they need power. Women have great power through their interdependence and, by acknowledging their own power and the expertise of their peers, they enhance the power of all women.

Singly and as a group, women must acknowledge that they must consistently participate in efforts aimed at: 1) raising the level of awareness regarding their need for power, thus banishing the negative image of power, 2) dispelling the results of their socialization that created stereotyping, and 3) reinforcing the understanding that professionalism and social unity are their strongest sources of power.

Women must tell themselves that change is constant and participation in organized change demands courage, command, or control of their potential, and seek conditioning to be able to deal with individual, interpersonal, and organizational conflict.

Cohen (1980) exclaims, "...in politics, poker, and negotiations, success derives not only from holding a strong hand but from analyzing the total situation so cards can be skillfully played..."(the woman) must realistically analyze the other side's position, as well as (her) own, "in light of three ever-present tightly interrelated variables:"

1. Power
2. Time
3. Information (Cohen, p. 50).

Relationship with Peers

Does the health care team work together? Health care professionals must pool their resources for the collective group so that the group and each of its members can enhance their power and control. The conflicting and divisional ways by which many health care professionals operate indicate that unity is far away. Supposedly, health care professionals are nurturing, caring, and possess a strong sense of human needs, strengths and limitations. Since most are women these special feminine attributes need to be carefully utilized to establish needed unity. However, women do not often use these skills in dealing with each other.

How supportive are women in the health care professions of each other? Chinn, Wheeler, Roy and Wheeler (1987) state, "historically, women's friendships haven't been recognized as significant; and culturally, women's friendships are expected to be less significant than other kinds of relationships" (p. 1456). If this is indeed the societal expectation of friendships and support groups among women, it must be remedied. Far too many women in nursing and the other health care professions are floating loose, with no sense of acceptance by, or support from, their peers.

The esteem in which women hold each other is shakey indeed. A woman optometrist reports having initially received a great deal of respect with the title of "Doctor" from a nurse on a committee they worked on together. The nurse reversed her attitude and totally ignored the optometrist when she discovered the doctor was not an M.D. (perhaps, this nurse did not know that optometrists attend four years of optometric education, similar to four years of medical school and that they serve internships and residencies as well). What does this lack of internal respect and acknowledgment accomplish within the ranks? It weakens everyone and insures that they will not unite, grow strong and accomplish greater things than the perpetuation of personal squabbles amongst themselves.

Nurses, with three levels of educational preparation for the same licensure exams, are prime examples of this wasted energy. In quarreling within the ranks of nursing, they waste the opportunity unity would provide. If nurses united, they could accomplish tremendous reformations toward the improvement of health care. It has been estimated that one in every forty-four women voters in the United States is a nurse, a number not to be lightly dismissed (Ford-Roegner, 1988). Yet George Bush, during his 1988 campaign for the presidency, repeatedly refused to answer the political survey questions of a national nursing organization, the American Nursing Association, and would not appear as a speaker for their candidates' forum (Ford-Roegner, 1988). This is an obvious reflection of the public's impression regarding the insignificance of the nursing profession. In comparison, medical doctors, a male-dominated profession, have strong political lobbyists and are consulted on each governmental decision concerning health care. When the majority of members of the various health care professions are women, this attention to men in health care is blaringly disproportionate.

Nursing, as with women, is struggling with a history of submission and male domination. Even so, it is a time of excitement, change, growth, and opportunity. Women are beginning to openly demonstrate their affiliation and caring priorities. They are also more comfortable with gaining and expressing power.

Women in health care must halt all infighting, as between the nurses of the differing levels of educational preparation. The associate versus the baccalaureate degree battle and others must cease. Women's strength is in their unity.

With a unity of focus, women in the health care professions can determine those skills to be valued. Cohen (1980) exclaims "...whenever you create competition for something you possess...what you have moves up in value" (p. 83).

Cohen lists five characteristics of power that are essential in building personal power:

1) Power of Competition.
2) Power of Risk Taking.
3) Power of Legitimacy.
4) Power of Commitment.
5) Power of Persistence.

To enhance personal power, women need to look favorably upon, and welcome competition. As they are evolving, women must also be willing to practice risk-taking, which is discussed in another section of this chapter. Cohen says risk involves mixing courage with common sense. Women should join their professional organizations, speak out for other women in the health care professions, fight to protect their image as warranted, and be a source of legitimacy for peers.

Powerful women in health care are actively involved in the political process. This reflects the technique of "influencing." To be effective, women must collectively become involved in influencing health care across the continuum of services. Experts in increasing power suggest the use of commitment. Cohen feels the application of power commitment works for women in three ways:

1.) By dispersing the overall risks, the woman can take advantage of propitious situations.
2.) Diminishing her level of stress since her associates share the total anxiety and lend their support.
3.) Transmit awesome power vibrations to the the other side via the shoulder-to-shoulder dedication of your group.

One's ability to be a participant in the commitment of others magnifies the impact of words and gives one power (Cohen, 1980).

Woman to woman, they must presevere in their efforts. They must be tenacious. Persistence is an essential ingredient in their ultimate success. Cohen states, "persistence is to power what carbon is to steel"(p. 83). Collectively, women health care professionals must address ongoing professional and political issues and use persistence. These professionals must develop a solid plan. The importance of timing cannot be underestimated. This strategy demands the use of networking, a concept developed later on in this chapter.

Relationship With the Client

Some health care professionals use abusive power over their clients (Lerner, 1986). Too often, the health care professional participates in a game of trying to keep the upper hand over the client. For instance, when a client comes into the clinic for a sore throat, what purpose does it serve to weigh that client? Many clients complain about the health care professional using such things as their weight as a topic to scold the client, increasing his feelings of powerlessness against the strength of the professional and decreasing the client's willingness to seek out health care. It places the client in the "one down" stance and the health care provider in the "one up" position. This type of power over the client diminishes the power of the professional, as it reinforces the idea that the professional must stay ahead of, or responsible for every client, surely an unrealistic expectation.

If the professional feels more secure within herself, she will not feel the need to rely on having power over her clients. Self-searching determines whether the relationships between the client and caregiver are or are not abusive.

The health care professional has the opportunity to empower the client and gain an increase in personal power as a result. Through giving to others, positive self-esteem and, therefore, the power resources of the health care professional are enhanced.

In emphasizing a partnership between the client and the health care professional, the sensitivity of personal feelings and needs of the professional must be acknowledged and evaluated. The need of the health care professional to be omnipresent, omniscient, and omnipotent for all clients must be dealt with realistically. This extreme expectation by the health care professional of herself sets her up for failure, as clients must eventually go forth on their own, leaving the protection of the caregiver behind. The question must be asked: whose needs are really being met?

In doing everything for the client, the professional diminishes the client's sense of control then perversely expects him to be in control upon discharge from the health care environment. It is vital that self-sufficiency, and self-responsibility be promoted in clients rather than dependence and rationalization. Health care professionals have a need to be needed and often meet that need through handicapping clients. The client already feels helpless or he would not have come to the health care professional. His body is not performing as he wishes, or in ways he lacks the knowledge and ability to control. The assumption is that health care professionals want to do things for others or they would not be in the health care field. **The most important thing that can be done for a client is to enhance his sense of personal power rather than his feelings of helplessness.** Enhancing the client's personal power requires teaching by the professional.

Teaching is a basic skill of all health care professionals. As teachers, the professionals must gain the willingness of the client to learn. Clients are taught a new way to treat their bodies. They are sent forth in improved or maintained health as a result of teaching and application of techniques to enhance that teaching. Doctors teach preventive or curative health improvement measures. Nurses teach methods for implementing improved or maintained health. Respiratory therapists teach improved breathing methods. Physical therapists teach improved muscle and joint movement. Dietitians teach improved nutrition. The recreation therapist teaches methods for having healthy fun. And the list goes on.

Health care professionals are called upon to act as role models for behaviors they wish to promote in their clients. If it is important to encourage an internal locus of control in clients, it is equally important to provide examples of internal control in the health care professional. Does the professional overeat, smoke, lack exercise, use excuses for occurrences rather than own her own behavior, or drink too much? Does the professional demonstrate being "high on life" or promote drugs as a panacea for life's problems? Does the health care giver consider all the possible options for action in a situation and encourage her clients to do so as well?

Health care providers are advocates for the clients in their care. What type of advocacy is it if the client is not encouraged to assert his rights? If the client's cultural or spiritual needs are not being met, does the professional speak out for the necessary time, space, or arrangements to facilitate meeting those needs? Does the caregiver encourage the client to express himself in meeting his needs? Does the caregiver assess the client and respect his concerns or does the professional forge ahead and meet her needs and deadlines, ignoring the client's? Has the health care professional identified the client's intellectual level and made every effort to communicate accordingly, or does the professional go into her routine line of patter in "medicalese?" Does the professional do things with her clients or does she do things for and to them?

Trust is integral in the positive client-professional relationship. Does the health care professional work on developing this trust? Does she follow through with plans or promises shared with the client?

INTERVENTIONS

Although the following topics of concern are by no means comprehensive, they serve as a place from which the health care professional interested in increasing her personal power base can commence on a program of building personal power. The solutions included in this section are not the only possibilities for dealing with each of the selected areas.

Recruitment

Nursing is currently undergoing a severe decline in nursing school enrollment. The image of nursing has long been that of the handmaiden, a career of subjugation: to doctors, administrators, clients, and their families (Paulson, 1988). This public image must be changed. Why, according to the women's liberation movement, should a bright young woman become a nurse and be subservient when she can be an engineer, a lawyer or a doctor? After all, ask those who believe the public image of nursing, it doesn't take any intelligence to be a nurse, does it?

The solution to the nursing shortage, put forth by the AMA, is to train and hire registered care technologists (Selby, 1988). Rather than increase the nurse's time spent in client contact, this measure would further remove them from the nearness to clients that, according to research, they identify as their chief source of satisfaction in the work place. Removing nurses from the bedside will further reduce the number of nurses available as they continue the exodus out of their profession. The tasks of paperwork and supervision of care techs would not gratify nurses who would rather spend their time with the clients, creatively assisting them in recovering or maintaining their health status.

Promoting creativity in the existing health care work force will increase the appeal of health care professions to individuals seeking a profession in which they can express themselves and are credited with a bright mind (Steele and Maraviglia, 1981). Thinking creatively has been found to decrease disease caused by stress (Steele and Maraviglia, 1981). Occasionally, an individual's creativity leads to inventiveness that finds expression. There are many areas in health care that cry for creative improvement.

Tucker (1987) suggests the following steps for developing the inventive individual's ideas in health care: identify the problem, choose a possible solution, research the originality of an idea, assess the marketability of the solution, and gain appropriate approval for its use. Then, the creative professional can proceed with her creative endeavors and locate others with similar interests, founding a support network.

Networking

Networking is a type of support system which advocates becoming known by and meeting others. It is an important means of contacting others who have something to offer or to whom a service can be offered. Connecting with others in the various health care professions and discussing concerns and solutions also strengthen the collaboration among the members of the health care team. Kennedy (1986) lists required elements for the development of a collaborative environment in the hospital setting: the contemporary women's movement, executive modeling, decentralized organizational structure, expanded roles in nursing and primary nursing.

Joining and attending meetings of master mind groups, groups of entrepreneurs, members of society with similar interests and women's support groups all contribute to successful networking (Kennedy, 1986; Stephenson, 1981). Women are finding that the networking system provides them with much needed support that previously eluded them in their efforts to feel more personally powerful. Carrying business cards at all times is helpful and allows you to leave a reminder with people you'd like to meet again; you hope that they too will be passing their cards around. "The process of networking itself can help you boost your career" (Dossey, 1987, p. 161). It is important to maintain contact with other professionals once it is established. Appointments are made to have lunch or coffee in the near future to facilitate a further exchange of ideas, explanation of the needs of each participant and to add to the knowledge about the other professional to more effectively act as a reference for her to others needing her services. Of course, in order to network effectively, the woman must believe herself worthy of the notice of other professionals. She must have a positive self-esteem in order to network efficiently.

Self-Esteem

Many health care professionals consider themselves too unimportant for others to wish to be involved with them. Sinetar (1987) encourages individuals to build a positive self-esteem, suggesting that treating oneself well is a step that leads to this improvement. Our Judeo-

Christian background tends to promote humbleness rather than positive self-esteem.

This placement of others before self is described by Leman (1987) as "pleaser" behavior. He lists the following characteristics of a pleaser: little girls who learned to be pleasers often come from unhappy homes where the father rarely gave them attention or praise, willing to settle for small favors, have low self-esteem, try to keep everyone happy, and need to be "good girls" to gain the approval of men. To move from being the pleaser of others at her own expense, the woman needs to learn to please herself first, to see herself as worthy of pleasure. Leman (1987) advocates the creation of a daily plan of ways to please oneself, diminish the guilt that arises when pleasing oneself, and listing things that "I've always wanted to do..." or "If I ever get the time, I'd like to..." and then doing those things.

Poor self esteem begins in childhood and is not simple to reverse. However, it can be done. Canfield (1976) created a list of over 100 techniques to use with children in improving their self-esteem. His list of possible activities for improving self-esteem includes: keeping a journal of feelings and thoughts, setting aside a time for peers to share accomplishments, making a list of personal assets, listing ways one has encouraged others to feel good about themselves, and practicing positive self-talk (Canfield, 1976).

As a client advocate, it is expected that the health care professional be capable of negotiating changes and policies that will protect and benefit the client. However, without the establishment of a positive self-image, the health care professional will have difficulty asserting herself an in positive way, for instance, in negotiation situations.

Negotiation

Negotiation is the coming together of two or more people to find a palatable solution to a problem. It does not have to indicate a winning situation for one person and a loss for the other. It is possible to arrive at a compromise that pleases all sides at the negotiating table without humiliation or anger for anyone. This is called win-win negotiation.

Glasser (1975) listed 16 tactics that contribute toward win-win negotiation:

1. Make concessions.
2. Find an appropriate place for talking.
3. Select the best time to talk.
4. Back up facts and give good explanations.
5. Have patience.
6. Expect gradualism (small goals, takes time).

7. Remember four partners present during talk (past, present, near future, far future).
8. Anticipate an acceptance time.
9. Stick to an agenda.
10. Write goals down.
11. Keep communications open.
12. Provide clear, written agreements.
13. Make these concessions when the answer can't be yes: listen, treat others with respect, give hope for the future, be consistent, etc.
14. Take notes.
15. Listen actively.
16. State the bottom line ("This is all I've got").

Both individuals can come out of negotiation on the winning side if some simple rules are followed: think of negotiation as collaboration rather than competition, focus on the problem not the people, base discussions on needs not positions, work out several possible solutions, and prepare for the possibility of the worst-case scenario (Hunt, 1988). If these rules are followed, the negotiators can leave the meeting without feeling that they have lost or been verbally attacked.

Verbal Defense

Verbal defense is a necessary skill in the protection of one's self-esteem. The constant verbal barrage of others in the environment is eminently potent and damaging for the health care professional who, all too often, enters interactions with her feelings exposed and seeks to be needed by others (Elgin, 1980; England, 1986).

Elgin (1980) lists four principles of verbal defense: 1) know that one is under attack, 2) identify the type of attack, 3) select the style of defense that fits the attack, and 4) demonstrate the ability to follow through. There are five verbal styles of communication: 1) placater, 2) blamer, 3) computer, 4) distractor, and 5) leveler (Elgin, 1980). A different mode of verbal defense is suggested for dealing with each of these types of communicators (Elgin, 1980).

In her discussion of the verbal abuse tolerated by women in the health care professions, Cox (1987) makes several suggestions for taking the control back into one's own hands. These include: taking a course on assertiveness and dealing with anger, educating coworkers about the effects of the verbal abuse they disburse, and instructing the abused professional about her rights and the appropriate manner for declaring these (Cox, 1987). The skill of verbal defense serves as an effective stress management technique that more women could make use of, decreasing their sensitivity to stress and increasing the hardiness of their emotional defense system.

Development of Hardiness

According to Lambert and Lambert (1987), hardiness is a characteristic of the personality that consists of three components: control, commitment and challenge. Hardiness is a major factor in health promotion. Health care professionals who have not focused on their own hardiness factors have difficulty encouraging client hardiness and, therefore, health promotion. Resistance to stress, or hardiness, is reflected in a commitment to self and job, the retention of control over life situations and the perception of unexpected events as challenges (Lambert and Lambert, 1987).

How, then, can these personality traits be dealt with? Three techniques listed by Fischman (1987) for developing hardiness are: 1) situational reconstruction, 2) focusing, and 3) compensatory self-improvement. Changing the perception of a situation will change the frame of mind from one of negativity to a positive interpretation of life situations. Focusing on the realities of the situation and the areas that can be controlled by the individual will decrease powerlessness and increase the sense of control and hardiness. Compensatory self-improvement is the strengthening of areas of potential to overcome the weak areas of the individual. These techniques assist the individual in withstanding the bombardment of stress in her environment. According to Lambert and Lambert (1987), if women in health care professions "possess or could acquire the personality characteristic, hardiness, they too might be more committed to their work, feel in more control of their lives, and be more challenged by their everyday experiences" (p. 95). This trait is the opposite of the behavior of being overwhelmed by stress and ending up in a "burn-out" situation.

Stress Management

The woman health care professional needs to learn and apply methods whereby she can turn a personally stressful situation into one that is a challenge but no longer stressful to her. Hutchinson (1987) advocates the following methods to combat stress and promote self-care in the health care professional: acting assertively, delegating responsibilities, cultivating goodwill, releasing pent-up emotions, withdrawing from the stress for a time, and using humor. Developing flexibility will assist the professional in dealing with conflict.

Are difficult clients more stressful or do they enhance the perception of stress in the health care professional? Certainly "difficult" clients generate more stress among the health care team, but the team members have a great deal of control of their perception of the situation. Podrasky and Sexton (1988) found that the tone of the unit and the mood of the professional had more of an impact on the interpretation of a client as difficult than the actual behaviors of the client. This supports the statement of Ujhely (1967) that most difficult clients are interpreted as such because of the professional's self-expectations rather than the behaviors of the clients.

In the assessment of health care professionals for their ability to meet their needs, one weakness is obvious. Serious and concerned, giving and overextending herself, the health care professional rarely adequately meets her need for fun. Inappropriate as it may be at times, the laughter in the operating room is an effective stress management behavior. Adams (1984) encourages laughter for lengthening one's life. Glasser (1976) advocates the adoption of activities that are enjoyable and in which the individual's performance can be improved with practice, listing learning as a necessary component of fun.

There are many sources to study that list methods for increasing a personal sense of power and withstanding stress. In an attempt to promote an increase in personal power, Hanson (1986), lists positive choices that enhance stress defense: maintenance of sense of humor, consume proper diet, ability to switch stresses, set realistic goals, comprehension of stress and its effects, relaxation skills and effective sleep, thorough job preparation, establishment of financial security, and development of a stable home. The secret ingredients listed by Amos (1988) for inner strength are: love, positive attitude, self-esteem, commitment, integrity, giving, imagination, enthusiasm, speech patterns, and faith. Hill and Stone (1987) state that "a positive mental attitude and definiteness of purpose is the starting point toward all worthwhile achievement" (p. 33). A positive mental attitude is a prerequisite for one stress management method, creative visualization.

Creative Visualization

Maybe it's time to enhance women's resolution strategies with a more creative catalyst. Many women have used their personal power of creative visualization in an unconscious way. They must tune up their own natural creative imaginations in a more conscious way. Shakti Gawain (1978), in her bestseller *Creative Visualization*, defines imagination as "the ability to create an idea or mental picture in your mind" (p.50). Gawain says imagination is used to create a clear image of something the woman wishes to manifest... then she continues to focus on the idea or picture regularly, giving it positive energy until it becomes objective reality.

In order to understand creative visualization, one must understand certain principles:

1. Physical universe is energy.
2. Energy is magnetic.
3. Form follows idea.
4. Law of radiation and attraction.
5. Using creative visualization.

One must study creative visualization over a period of time, but, to summarize, Gawain (1978) relates that the physical universe is not really composed of any "matter" at all, energy is vibrating at different rates of speed, thus having different qualities from finer to denser. Physically, everything is made up of energy. Energy is also magnetic, explains Gawain, as energy of a certain quality or vibration attracts energy of similar quality and vibration. According to Gawain's theory (1978), when something is created it is first in the form of thought. A thought or idea always precedes manifestation. Gawain's fourth principle is the notion that whatever the individual puts into the universe will be reflected back to her. This means that individuals always attract into their lives whatever they think about the most, believe in very strongly, expect on the deepest level, and/or imagine extra vividly. Gawain's final principle is the process using creative visualization. It urges the exploration, discovery, and change of the deepest, most basic attitudes toward life. It must become a continuous awareness, a state of consciousness in which one knows she is the constant controller of her life.

Effective creative visualization demands four steps:

1. Set your goals. Decide what the desired accomplishment is, work toward it, realize or create it.
2. Create a clear idea or picture mentally of the situation exactly as one wants it to be..
3. Focus on it often.
4. Give it positive energy.

Women must think in a positive, encouraging way. They must make strong statements to themselves, they must visualize themselves achieving their goals. These positive statements are called "affirmations." Use these affirmations to suspend any doubts.

In order to be successful with the aforementioned strategies, one must embrace Gawain's essential elements: 1) desire, 2) belief, and 3) acceptance. These are simple yet difficult. One must truly desire to have the goal realized. The more one believes in their chosen goal and the possibility of attaining it, the more certain one will be able to do so. One must be willing to accept and have that which one is seeking. The sum total of these three elements is what Gawain (1978) calls intention. When one has total intention to create something, she deeply desires it, completely believes she can do it, and that she is totally willing to have it—Gawain believes it simply cannot fail to manifest itself.

Women in the health care professions must individually and collectively have total intention to create these resolution strategies. They must believe, desire, and accept the resolution. They must accept their good offerings. They must set goals and create a clear picture of these goals. They must focus on it often to give it positive energy.

Women have power within themselves to heal their professional and personal ills. They must ask themselves, if they really want to reach these goals, or are they more comfortable with the process of pursuing? Do they truly desire to use their power creatively? The potential for perfection lies in each of them and within every relationship. Creative visualization affords women health care professionals the opportunity to expand their strengths. Positive affirmations are a basic ingredient in creative visualization.

Women health care professionals must create positive affirmations that are individually and professionally acceptable. These affirmations should be used in meditation, they should be used when relating to others and they should be used daily. Affirmation techniques are discussed in depth by Helmstetter (1986), who gives the following checklist for evaluating one's positive self-talk:

1) Is self-talk stated in the present sense?
2) Is it specific?
3) Does it get the job done without creating any unwanted side effects?
4) Is it easy to use?
5) Is it practical?
6) Is it personal and honest?
7) Does self-talk ask enough of the individual?

Positive affirmation, or self-talk, is helpful in building the health care professional's self-confidence.

Self-Confidence

Powerlessness leads to physical, as well as emotional, illness (McLeod, 1986). Lack of self-confidence is not a mentally healthy stance from which to view the world. The individual's belief that she can control her own life events, or at least her perception of them, adds to her feelings of self-confidence. Confidence is "a way of living serenely, independent of the knocks of fortune" (Purves, 1984, p.80). An increase in self-confidence requires the assessment of self as worthy. Bloomfield (1985) says one "has to appreciate (oneself) as she is, including her weak spots and vulnerabilities, as a basis for lasting change" (p. 18).

Methods for gaining self-confidence include: setting daily goals that can be easily achieved and acknowledging that success, promoting risk-taking, nurturing the imagination and diminishing the importance of others' opinions, developing positive thinking, promoting "act as if" behaviors to make the goal become reality, and actively working on changing the perceptions of situations and persons (Glasser, 1976; McLeod, 1986; Purves, 1984).

Self-confidence leads to the willingness to reach one's full potential. Opportunity to reach that potential rarely drops into one's lap. Generally, risk-taking is a necessary skill on the road to success and more personal power.

Risk Taking

Risking is often perceived with fear by individuals (Viscott, 1977). For example, the nurse who has worked in obstetrics for 18 years has many feelings of trepidation when she considers the possibility of transferring to the intensive care workplace. If she stays where she no longer feels challenged, her likelihood of "burning out" is great. The fears connected with a change in location and the necessity of education in many new skills may paralyze her ability to rescue herself. The fear that holds her back is the fear of risking and failing, perhaps even succeeding (Dowling, 1981). "A life lived trying to be secure and free of risks eventually becomes a prison" (Viscott, 1977, p. 28). Propelling oneself to attempt something new and untried is an empowering technique.

Viscott (1977) suggests the following assessment questions when deciding whether or not to take a risk:

> Is this risk necessary?
> Is the potential loss greater than the potential gain?
> What can be done to prevent losses from occurring?
> What information is needed before taking the risk?
> Who wants this effort to succeed? fail?
> How much can change as a result of this risk?
> In what order of priority is this risk?
> Is this risk-taking being done to please someone?
> Has this risk been taken before?
> What is a good time for this risk? Is there one?
> What makes risking necessary now?
> What can be lost by taking this risk?
> Can the goal be reached another way?
> What other information is needed?

Each individual is responsible for her own life, her successes and failures. However, the health care professional does have a responsibility to others, to give them the opportunity to fulfill themselves. The presence of trust between the professional and her client, as well as those between her and her peers, indicates a successful risk-taking situation, since trust is considered a risk by many individuals.

Trust

Trust in each other is vital to the efficiency of the health team. However, one of the stressors in health care is the knowledge that the professional cannot always control who she will be working with and, therefore, does not know whether she will be able to trust her coworkers to come to her aid and place the same emphasis on the care of the client. Outside of having a prearranged schedule for the same team to always work together, there is little that can be done about the permanence of the team in most cases. Promotion of socialization among the members of a staff, outside of the health care environment, helps the members get to know each other and form relationships that enhance feelings of trust in the work setting. Encouraging membership in brain-storming groups, unit committees, and stress management groups creates nonwork situations in which the staff members have the opportunity to get to know each other and develop a rapport with other professionals. Identification of those staff members who are not trustworthy, and encouragement for them to develop that trait, assists the other staff members and provides a criteria for work performance evaluation (England, 1986). If the professionals do not trust each other, they will not develop trust with their clients.

Trust between the professional and her client is essential in providing the best care possible. Lack of trust inhibits learning, decreases compliance, and increases anxiety in the client. Richardson (1987) lists seven ways to win the client's trust: 1) call the client by name, 2) tell the client your name, 3) check your attitude, 4) explain why the health professional is there, 5) talk about procedures first, 6) keep appointments, and 7) be honest. Trust in the other person includes the faith that the other individual will be interested in honest expression of one's feelings and needs, which includes the use of assertive communication.

Assertiveness Training

Many health care professionals resist learning and using assertive communication techniques. Trusches (1985) suggests that the reasons for women blocking assertive behaviors include the fear of rejection and the loss of love. Because of the socialization of women and the pressure applied to the woman from all sides of her society, assertiveness is a difficult, though not an impossible, skill to use in life situations.

Teaching the client to be assertive in attaining his rights can be difficult. However, Palmer and Deck (1987) suggest methods for accomplishing this. "Assertiveness requires two key skills: thought substitution and assertive responses" (Palmer and Deck, 1987, p. 650). The health care professional is prepared to teach assertiveness behaviors if she can: 1) demonstrate ease in conveying assertive thinking and speaking, 2) comprehend response techniques thoroughly enough to give practical examples, 3) assess the clients' communication styles and tutor in appropriate assertive responses that match the clients' communication style, and 4) commit to see the clients through the evaluation phase (Palmer and Deck, 1987).

Chenevert (1978) lists ten basic rights for women in health care professions and suggests using assertive techniques to achieve them. They are:

(1) You have the right to be treated with respect.
(2) You have the right to a reasonable workload.
(3) You have the right to an equitable wage.
(4) You have the right to determine your own priorities.
(5) You have the right to ask for what you want.
(6) You have the right to refuse without making excuses or feeling guilty.
(7) You have the right to make mistakes and be responsible for them.
(8) You have the right to give and receive information as a professional.
(9) You have the right to act in the best interests of the client.
(10) You have the right to be human (p.39).

Assertive, rather than aggressive, interactions aid in conflict resolution because they pose no threat for the other person and indicate that the opinions are those of the speaker, not an accusation or judgment against the other individual.

Conflict Resolution

Resolving conflicts often translates to the woman health care professional backing out of a conflict, and allowing the other individual to meet their needs at the expense of the woman. Beattie (1987) defines this behavior as a characteristic of "codependency." The very traits that make women in health care so good at what they do reflect behaviors that have led researchers to estimate that the majority of nurses, for example, are codependent in their behaviors (Beattie, 1987).

Marriner's (1987) five responses to conflict provide behavior options that promote flexibility: 1) accommodation, 2) avoidance, 3) collaboration, 4) competition, and 5) compromise. These five choices of response to conflict must be alternated, as there are consequences for the user and the receiver if only one style is used. Resolving conflict in a mutually beneficial manner is potentially empowering for all participants in the conflict.

Increasing Power

Del Bueno (1987) has some suggestions for appropriate use of power in health care: reinforce the positive image of health care providers; alter perceptions of work, as it is only the professional who can perceive her work as interesting and challenging; conceal or reveal information; label or praise coworkers and care for them; withhold or confer status according to education and abilities; reward or punish behaviors of each other; and obstruct or assist the group goals. Health care professionals have a duty not to abuse the power others have given them and to build their own personal power so as not to crave power over others.

Betts and Bowling (1984) advocate continual striving toward increasing personal control for the professional as well as the client. They encourage the development of control in three areas: 1) behavioral control, or the management of events that affect the individual; 2) decisional control, or an emphasis on the individual's right to make choices; and 3) cognitive control, or the guidance of perceptions (Betts and Bowling, 1984). Nornhold (1986) discusses the trends that provide nurses with opportunities to increase their personal and professional power: shift the power from providers of care to consumers, remain open for improved relationships within the health care professions, recognize the shift from nursing education to nursing administration as the source of power, form nurse-executive positions in health care institutions, and decentralize power with, for instance, staff nurses assuming more control.

Developing personal power is vital for the health care professional. It is suggested that the health care professional should focus on the two additional areas of referent and expert power (Estabrook, 1986). Expert power depends on a commitment to learning and continual personal improvement. Referent power is similar to personal power with an emphasis on power in health care situations; it is dependent upon consciousness of strengths and weaknesses, behaviors and their effect on others, and working on the development of positive behaviors that attract others (Estabrook, 1986).

Power Assessment

An assessment of power resources and assets will identify areas in the professional's life that need to be strengthened. Then the need to have power over others diminishes. That assessment covers the following areas:

Strength. Is the health care professional's physical strength an example for role modeling? Does she have strength in the spiritual area of her life, expressing hope and faith? Does she derive strength from her cultural group, contributing to the community? Intellectually, does she exercise her creativity, adding to her knowledge base?

Motivation. What motivation for her behaviors does the health care professional exhibit? Not ignoring the importance of financial reimbursement, is she motivated by her concern for her physical well-being, cultural acceptance, intellectual curiosity, spiritual peace and emotional tranquility?

Coping. How does the health care provider cope with her world and herself? Does she do things, physically, to decrease her feelings of stress, like jogging or swimming? Or does she handle her stress through such short-term coping mechanisms as smoking, drinking and sleep? How does she relate within the culture of health care professionals? Does her spirituality guide her in bioethical decisions? Does she compete and work as part of the team in coping with her power needs? How does she cope intellectually? Is she knowledgeably powerful yet ignores her emotional health by intellectualizing and suppressing her feelings?

Support Systems/Networking. What support systems does the health care professional have? Does she network within the ranks of health care professionals, adding to her cultural resource of power? Does she practice her faith and find support in a spiritual setting? Does she have a support system for enhancing her emotional health or does she keep her feelings to herself, afraid to let coworkers or friends know what she is feeling? Does she belong to a master mind group where she can derive mental stimulation and support for new ideas to carry with her to work?

Knowledge. Does the health care professional increase her knowledge to build her own personal power? If she doesn't share the knowledge she has, she may as well not have it. She can increase her knowledge of spirituality, physical abilities, intellectual base, cultural understanding, and emotional responses. In so doing, the health care professional brings more acceptance and understanding to her clients, as well as knowledge from which to individually tailor the plan of care for the client.

Perceptions. Perceptions reflect on the five sources of power. Does the health care professional look at the positive side of every situation? The more she looks for the positive perspective on things, the more in control the health care provider will perceive herself to be. Her perception of different cultures can be helpful if she makes the attempt to look for the positive perspective on them, rather than disapproval or the negative perspective merely on the basis of it being different from hers. Perception of intellectual challenges can affect the basic tenor of the health provider's life. Open and nonjudgmental acceptance of the clients' spiritual beliefs is vital in the enhancement of client power as well as personal power for the professional.

Self-Esteem. Does the health care professional rely on overpowering others to feed her self-esteem? Has she utilized her functioning level as a measurement by which she grades her self-esteem? Her opinions about herself in the intellectual, emotional, cultural, and physical realms combine to establish her self-esteem.

Stamina. The stamina of the health care professional is part of her perception of personal power. Does she have the physical stamina to meet her job expectations? Many health care professionals harbor a feeling of pride for having run the gauntlet of grueling hours in medical or nursing school, for instance. What spiritual reserves does the health care professional have? How much stamina does her cultural base provide her with? Does she believe she can do whatever she sets her mind to, or is she afraid to try anything new after flying in the face of tradition to get as far as she has already? Intellectually, has she flexed and exercised her brain to enable its keener function? What amount of emotional bombardment can she handle before she reaches an overload condition? Does she feel powerless to defend herself when subjected to verbal abuse from other health care professionals?

Consideration of a Brighter Future

Women in health care professions must take control of their own situations which will, in turn, gain control for all women in that field. The following is a list of future possibilities for each woman to consider that would build the strength of women health care professionals:

Professionals who practice under perilous staffing conditions do so only "under protest" and this objection is written, copied, and shared with the director of nursing, board of trustees, and the president of the hospital. Each practicing nurse declines to perform non-nursing tasks, such as secretarial and laundry tasks. Directors of nursing service unite to demand the establishment of formal collaborative practice arrangements between nursing, medicine, and other disciplines in health care.

Every woman health care professional patronizes at least one women's organization.

The various nursing organizations agree to disagree in private and to produce a mechanism for reconciling interassociation controversies that would demonstrate power-sharing and women's potential.

Every woman who sees programs on television or movies that belittle women in health care, protests, in writing, to the producer, network, and station broadcasting this erroneous and sexist material.

Every woman in health care knows the name of her legislator and engages in a letter writing or lobbying drive concerning at least one health problem each year.

Every professional donates her income from at least half a day's work each year on behalf of a favored legislators's election campaign.

The leaders of nursing organizations at all levels form a coalition with women's groups such as NOW and NWPC.

Every nurse affiliates with the apropos professional organization, including ANA, NLN and specialty organizations and honors a obligation to contribute something more than dues to one of them every year.

Every woman in a health care profession gives at least $1 to the national and state political actions committees of their chosen health professional organization, such as N-CAP for nurses.

Professional organizations ensure that one of their members sits on every committee dealing with health issues in the government.

Women health care professionals use their alliances to demand as a portion of their contract negotiation that they be included as members of the boards of trustees of hospitals, nursing homes, home care agencies, and hospice centers in equal numbers as other professionals.

At least one woman health care professional is in Congress and in each state house in the nation.

A nurse is elected President of the United States.

Every professional school and department of health care agencies values and encourages each of these possible situations.

Summary

As the majority of health care professionals are women, women's issues must, of necessity, be addressed in an effort to encourage the empowerment of the health care professional. In order for a client to be empowered, he must have access to empowered health care providers.

References

Adams, Joey. *Live Longer Through Laughter*. NY: Stein and Day, 1984.

Amos, Wally and Gregory Amos. *The Power in You*. NY: Donald I. Fine, Inc., 1988.

Beattie, Melody. *Codependent No More: How To Stop Controlling Others and Start Caring for Yourself*. NY: Harper and Row, 1987.

Betts, Graeme and Ann Bowling. Power. *Nursing Times*. August 18, 1984. 28-30, 1984.

Bloomfield, Harold. *Making Peace With Yourself: Turning Your Weaknesses into Strengths*. NY: Ballantine Books, 1985.

Canfield, Jack and Harold Wells. *100 Ways to Enhance Self-Concept in the Classroom*. Englewood Cliffs, NJ: Prentice-Hall, Inc., 1976.

Chenevert, Melodie. *Special Techniques in Assertiveness Training for Women in the Health Professions*. St. Louis: The C.V.Mosby Company, Inc., 1978.

Chinn, Peggy, Wheeler, Charlene, Roy, Adrienne, and Wheeler, Elizabeth. Just between friends. *American Journal of Nursing*. November, 1987. 1456-1458, 1987.

Cohen, Herb. *You Can Negotiate Anything*. NY: Bantam Books, 1980.

Cox, Helen. Verbal abuse in nursing: a report of a study. *Nursing Management*. Vol 18 No. 11 47-50, 1987.

Del Bueno, Dorothy. How well do you use power? *American Journal of Nursing*. November 1987. 1495-1498, 1987.

Dossey, Barbara. Networking made easy. *Nursing87*. May. 161-162, 1987.

Dowling, Collette. *The Cinderella Complex: Women's Hidden Fear of Independence*. NY: Book Books, 1981.

Dykema, Lynn. Gaventa's theory of power and powerlessness: application to nursing. *Occupational Health Nursing*. September. 443-446, 1985.

Elgin, Suzette. *The Gentle Art of Verbal Self-Defense*. NY: Dorset Press, 1980.

England, Doris. *Collaboration in Nursing*. Rockville, MD: Aspen Publishing, 1986.

Estabrook, Barbara. More power to you. *Nursing86*. April. 89-90, 1986.

Fischman, Joshua. Getting tough. *Psychology Today*. December. 26-28, 1987.

Ford-Roegner, Pat. Dukakis wins ANA support in presidential contest. *The American Nurse*. Oct. 1988. p.1, 1988.

Fuszard, Barbara. *Self-Actualization for Nurses*. Rockville, MD: Aspen Publications, 1984.

Garland, LaRetta and Bush, Carol. *Coping Behaviors and Nursing*. Reston, VA: Reston Publishing Company, 1982.

Gawain, Shakti. *Creative Visualization*. NY: Bantam Books, 1978.

Glasser, William. *Both Win Management*. NY: Harper and Row, 1975.

Glasser, William. *Positive Addiction*. NY: Harper and Row, 1976.

Hanson, Peter. *The Joy of Stress*. Kansas City: Andrews, McMeel and Parker, 1986.

Helmstetter, Shad. *What To Say When You Talk To Your Self: Powerful New Techniques to Program Your Potential for Success*. NY: Pocket Books, 1986.

Hill, Napoleon and W. Clement Stone. *Success Through A Positive Mental Attitude*. NY: Pocket Books, 1987.

Howe, F. *Women and The Power to Change*. NY: McGraw-Hill, 1975.

Hunt, Morton. How to come out ahead. *Parade Magazine*. September 4, 1988. 12-14, 1988.

Hutchinson, Sally. Self-care and job stress. *Image: Journal of Nursing Scholarship*. 19(4). 192-196, 1987.

Jacobson, Sharol and McGrath, Marie. *Nurses Under Stress*. New York: John Wiley and Sons, 1983.

Jones, Carolyn Priester. We used paperwork to hide from our patients. *RN*. April. 50-52, 1978.

Kennedy, Amy. Environment for collaborative practice/professionalism. In England, Doris (Ed.). *Collaboration in Nursing*. Rockville, MD: Aspen Publications, 1986.

Lambert, Clinton and Lambert, Vickie. Hardiness: its development and relevance to nursing. *Image: Journal of Nursing Scholarship*. 19(2). 92-95, 1987.

Lerner, Michael. *Surplus Powerlessness*. Institute of Labor and Mental Health: Oakland, CA, 1986.

Marriner, Ann. How do you spell relief of conflict? Flexibility. *Nursing87*. March. 113-114, 1987.

McLeod, Beverly. Rx for health: a dose of self-confidence. *Psychology Today*. October. 46-50, 1986.

McGear, Reba and Hadley-Meenk, Nora. Burnout. *Update on Human Behavior*. 7(4). 1-4, 1988.

Muff, Janet. *Socialization, Sexism, and Stereotyping: Women's Issues in Nursing*. St. Louis: C.V.Mosby Company, 1982.

Nornhold, Patricia. Power: it's changing hands and moving your way. *Nursing86*. January. 40-42, 1986.

O'Reilly, Jane. *The Girl I Left Behind: The Housewife's Moment of Truth and Other Feminist Ravings*. New York: Collier Books, 1980.

Palmer, Marry Ellen and Deck, Edith S. Teaching your patients to assert their rights. *American Journal of Nursing*. May, 1987. 650-654, 1987.

Paulson, Tom. Nurses are patient people, professionally. *Seattle Post-Intelligencer*. March 13, 1988. F4, 1988.

Podrasky, Debra and Sexton, Dorothy. Nurses' reactions to difficult patients. *Image: Journal of Nursing Scholarship*. 20(1). 16-21, 1988.

Purves, Libby. Confidence. *New Woman*. October. 80-82, 1984.

Richardson, Betty. Seven ways to win your patient's trust. *Nursing87*. March. 44-45, 1987.

Rippere, Vicky and Williams, Ruth. *Wounded Healers: Mental Health Workers' Experiences of Depression*. New York: John Wiley and Sons, 1985.

Schaef, Anne Wilson. *Women's Reality*. Minneapolis: Winston Press, 1981.

Scully, Rosemarie. Stress in the nurse. *American Journal of Nursing*. May, 1980. 912-915, 1980.

Selby, Terry. Nurses find ways to ease shortage; recruit, retain! *The American Nurse*. Oct. 1988. pp. 1, 9-10, 1988.

Shainess, Natalie. How to save yourself from yourself. *New Woman*. October, 1984. 94-98, 1984.

Sinetar, Marsha. *Do What You Love, The Money Will Follow*. NY: Paulist Press, 1987.

Steele, Shirley and Frank Maraviglia. *Creativity in Nursing and Other Professions*. Thorofare, NJ: Charles B. Slack, Inc., 1981.

Stephenson, June. *Women's Roots*. Napa, CA: Diemer, Smith Publishing

Stephenson, June. *Women's Roots*. Napa, CA: Diemer, Smith Publishing Company, 1981.

Stevens, Kathleen. *Power & Influence: A Sourcebook for Nurses*. New York: John Wiley and Sons, 1983.

Tierney, Mary Jo and Strom, Lani. Stress: type A behavior in the nurse. *American Journal of Nursing*. May, 1980. 915-918, 1980.

Trusches, Darlene. *From Fear to Freedom: A Woman's Handbook for High Self-Esteem*. Denver, CO: New Options Publishing, 1985.

Tucker, Annabelle. The inventive nurse. *American Journal of Nursing*. May. 624-625, 1987.

Ujhely, Gertrud. *The Nurse and her "Problem" Patients*. NY: Springer, 1967.

Viscott, David. *Risking*. NY: Pocket Books, 1977.

Index